THE PRACTICE BUILDER
Complete Marketing Library of $1,000,000 Strategies

The 226 Brand-New, Sure-Fire, Ready-to-Use Strategies & Innovations to Propel Your Healthcare Practice to the Prestigious $1,000,000 Mark

Containing the Latest Tried & True Tactics from THE PRACTICE BUILDER—the Health Professionals' Most Renowned and Award-Winning Marketing Newsletter and Advisory

Alan Bernstein, MBA

Donna Freiermuth

Prentice Hall Tax & Professional Practice
Englewood Cliffs, New Jersey 07632

Prentice-Hall International (UK) Limited, *London*
Prentice-Hall of Australia Pty. Limited, *Sydney*
Prentice-Hall of Canada Inc., *Toronto*
Prentice-Hall Hispanoamericana, S.A., *Mexico*
Prentice-Hall of India Private Limited, *New Delhi*
Prentice-Hall of Japan, Inc., *Tokyo*
Simon & Schuster Asia Pte. Ltd., *Singapore*
Editora Prentice-Hall do Brasil, Ltda., *Rio de Janeiro*

Printed in the United States of America
10 9 8 7 6 5 4

Library of Congress Cataloging-in-Publication Data

Bernstein, Allan.
    The practice builder complete marketing library of $1,000,000
  strategies : containing the latest tried & true strategies from the
  practice builder -- the health professional's most renowned and award
  -winning newsletter and advisory / Alan Bernstein, Donna Freiermuth.
      p.   cm.
    Includes index.
    ISBN 0-13-678798-3 :
    1. Medical care--Marketing.   I. Freiermuth, Donna.   II. Title.
  RA410.56.B47 1991   91-34946
  362.1'068'9--dc20   CIP

ISBN 0-13-678798-3

Prentice Hall Tax & Professional Practice
Englewood Cliffs, NJ 07632

Dedicated to the over 40,000
member practices of THE PRACTICE BUILDER

CONTENTS

What Is THE PRACTICE BUILDER? xvii

Chapter 1

SO YOU WANT YOUR PRACTICE TO THROW OFF
MEGA-DOLLARS—GETTING DOWN TO BASICS

The 3 Secrets of Marketing, 1

Prioritize Your Marketing First Things First, 2

How Much Should You Spend on Marketing? 3

Getting Marketing Money, 5

Money Thoughts: How Much Can You Spend to Attract a New Patient or Client? 5

Allocating Promo Budget by Seasonality, 6

What Should Your Promotion Payback? 7

What to Do If Modesty Hinders Your Promoting, 9

Unhappy News from Unhappy People, 9

Your Promotional Checklist, 9

Chapter 2

STRATEGIZING FOR SUCCESS: YOUR SURE-FIRE MARKETING PLAN

Case History: Backward Planning, 13

*Your Quick, Sweet & Profitable Marketing Plan: The Short Form
    a.k.a. The Fine Art of Controlling Your Destiny, 14*

Short Form Marketing Plan, 16

A Sample Completed Short Form, 18

Marketing Strategies & Budget, 19

The Long Form Marketing Game Planner, 22

Marketing Plan—Midyear Evaluation, 29

Marketing Problems & Solutions, 30

How to Track the Results of Your Promotion, 32

Tracking the Right Source, 35

Tracking Sheet, 36

Promotions in Motion, 37

Chapter 3

PUTTING YOURSELF ON TOP BY PROMOTING WHO YOU ARE

The Most Important Things to Promote about Yourself, 38

27 Ways to Differentiate Yourself, 39

Your Credentials: Quantity vs. Quality, 41

Easy Authoring for Hard-to-Get Credibility, 41

Proving Excellent Service by Guaranteeing It, 42

How to Show People You Really Care—And Have Them Believe It, 44

Three Major Reasons You Lose Patients or Clients, 45

Powerful Positions, 47

Putting the Personal Touch in a Group Practice, 47

Tagging Yourself as the Practice of Choice, 49

The Updated Waiting Room Resume, 49

Waiting Room Resume Analysis, 51

Waiting Room Resume Analysis II, 53

Promotions in Motion, 54

Chapter 4

PRICING STRATEGIES THAT SPELL SUCCESS

Why You Shouldn't Cut Your Fees, But Raise Them Now, 57

How to Easily Boost Net Income 14%, 58

Using Guarantees to Boost Your Numbers, 59

How to Price Compete, 60

New Financing Plans Boost Gross, 60

Another Way to Make Services Affordable—Instead of Reducing Prices, 63

Layaways—Prepaid Financing, 64

Marketing Dissection of a High Volume Practice, 64

How to Answer "Your Fee Is Too High," 65

Raising Gross 20% Without Cost, 66

What Beats Giving Away a Free Exam or Consultation? 66

Update: Good/Better/Best Sells the Higher End, 68

Promotions in Motion, 69

Chapter 5

CHARTING THE BEST ROUTE WITHOUT THE
CRIPPLING PITFALLS: YOUR MUST DO'S AND DON'TS

Big, Bad Marketing Debts, 72

Born Losers: Gimmicks to Avoid, 73

Checklist for Explosive Growth, 76

Don't Prioritize Decor or Nonessential Equipment, 77

Promotion by Committee Fails, 77

Promotions in Motion, 78

Chapter 6

THE INSIDE STORY: YOUR PATIENTS OR CLIENTS AS THE OPTIMUM SOURCE OF GROWTH—THE INTERNAL MIX THAT MAXIMIZES RETURN ON INVESTMENT

How to Create a Welcome-to-the-Practice Letter, 80

*How to Protect Your Base, Get Repeat Business, and Generate Referrals—
    All in One Effort, 82*

The One-Minute Message, 87

Why and How You Need to Follow Up on Prospects, Incompletes, and Splitees, 89

Affinity Marketing—Note Writing Generates Record Growth, 92

Internal Signs Sell, 93

The 10 All-Time Best Ways to Convince Someone to Accept Your Recommendations, 96

Objection Handling: "I Have to Talk It Over with My (Spouse/Partner/Dog)," 96

Querying with Waiting Room Survey Boosts Case Size, 96

Promotions in Motion, 97

Chapter 7

KEEP THEM COMIN' BACK IN DROVES: YOUR RECALLS AND REACTIVATIONS

Recall Update: Getting Over 90% Success, 98

Contacting the Right Person in Recalls, 100

Sample: Enhanced Reactivation Effort, 101

Reactivation Strategies: Big Dollars In, Small Dollars Out, 105

What Can Reactivation Pay? 106

Reactivation Analysis: Motivating Immediate Response, 107

When Reactivations Won't Work, 107

Promotions in Motion, 109

Chapter 8

EXPLOSIVE GROWTH FROM SOLID REFERRALS: HOW TO TURN A FIRST-TIME PATIENT INTO A REFERRER

Using Third Party Endorsements for Capturing New Referrers, 111

How to Ask for Referrals the Right Way, 112

The Frequent Referrer Program: Getting Referrers to Refer in Even More, 113

Breaking into the Old Boys' Referral Club, 115

Enlarging Your Referral Area, 118

Controlling Referrals from Nonprofits, 118

New Approach to Cultivating Memberships, 119

Getting Potential Referrers into Your Office, 120

Holiday Gifts for Referring Professionals—Do's & Don'ts, 121

What's What with Who's Who, 121

Getting Known Fast to Gain Professional Referrals, 122

Lunch-a-Week Maintains Referrals, 122

Gaining Mega-Referrals from Professionals for Major Growth, 123

Generating Referrals from Other Professionals—New Approaches, 124

Boosting Referrals from Professionals You Know, 126

How Spouses Can Promote a Practice, 127

Thanking the Right People for Referrals, 128

What to Do If a Referrer Stops Referring, 128

Promotions in Motion, 129

Chapter 9

WHOSE SIDE IS YOUR STAFF ON?   HOW TO MAKE SURE IT'S YOURS

Solving the Conversion Problem, 132

How to Get Your Staff to Support Your Marketing When They Act Like They Don't Care, 133

Newest Program: How to Get Big Payoffs from Your Staff Recruiting New Patients Or Clients—Without Spending Anything Up Front, 135

Getting Employees to Recruit New Patients or Clients, 137

Staff Incentives to Assure Quality, 138

Dumb Move #63: Making Your Office Manager Your Marketing Director, 139

How to Motivate a Marketing Director, 139

How to Motivate Partners and Associates to Ask for Commitments and Referrals, 140

Promoting a Leader Without Having the Leader Do the Work, 142

Promotions in Motion, 143

Chapter 10

LOOKING BEYOND YOUR BASE: THE ABC'S OF SUPERB EXTERNAL PROMOTION

Advertising Vs. Marketing, 144

What to Promote in Your External Promotion? 146

How to Win the Advertising Game, 146

Making Public Relations Pay (Without Work and With Little Cost), 148

Two Kinds of Practice Reps: The Good & the Fired, 149

Promotions in Motion, 151

Chapter 11

THE BEST RETURN ON INVESTMENT: YOUR OFFICE SIGN

Your No. 1 Return-on-Investment in External Promotion, 152

Getting the No. 1 External Promotion to Work for You: Brand New Ideas! 156

Bannering Boosts Walk-In Traffic, 161

THE PRACTICE BUILDER's Office Sign Contest, 164

Promotions in Motion, 169

Chapter 12

SHREWD AND SAVVY PRACTICE BROCHURES AND WHAT TO DO WITH THEM

Stalking the Great Practice Brochure: The Whys & Hows, 170

Anatomy of a Great Practice Brochure, 172

Why 94% of Practice Brochures Don't Work, 182

The 9 Shrewdest Ways to Use Your Practice Brochure, 185

Brochure Analysis: Sales Literature, 186

The Great Practice Brochure: Being Empathetic, 193

The Great Practice Brochure: Selling Feelings, 199

Can You Use Your Practice Brochure as Direct Mail? 199

THE PRACTICE BUILDER's Practice Brochure Contest, 199

Promotions in Motion, 221

Chapter 13

EVERY BIT COUNTS: TURNING YOUR BUSINESS CARDS, LOGO AND STATIONERY INTO PROMOTION

Converting Your Business Cards into Promotion, 222

Business Card Contest Grand Prize Winner, 224

Business Card Contest Runner-Up Winner No. 1, 226

Business Card Contest Runner-Up Winner No. 2, 228

Business Card Analysis: All the Right Ingredients, 230

Business Card Analysis: Unusual Layout Helps, 232

Why You Don't Need a Logo—And When You Do, 234

Logo Analysis: Modern Graphics, 236

Logo Analysis: Positioning as a Specialist, 237

Coordinating & Strategizing for Logo, Stationery, Envelope, & Business Card, 236

Expensive Paper Is Not Worth It, 240

Chapter 14

MAKING A MAJOR IMPACT WITH PR AND PUBLICITY

Getting Charities to Promote You for Free While Looking Like a Hero, 242

Community Involvement Pays Up to 28:1 ROI, 244

Charitable Publicity the Smart Way, 246

Why Hiring a P.R. Firm Is a Bad Move, 247

Patient/Client Appreciation Days Bring 10:1 ROIs, 248

Leveraging Much Appreciated Appreciation Days, 250

Spreading Your "Fame," 250

Sure-Fire Publicity, 251

Easy Way to Get Local Publicity, 252

Promotions in Motion, 253

Chapter 15

THE HIGH-YIELD DYNAMICS OF DIRECT MAIL

*Ultra-Professional, Multi-Page Direct Mail Format Gives Four Big Benefits
     Plus Big Results, 254*

Direct Mail Super Targeting, 256

New Resident Direct Mail—Is It For You? 256

*Why Most New Resident Schemes Fail: How to Attract 8% of All New Residents
     To Your Practice, 257*

Not All New Resident Lists Are Alike, 263

Hot Direct Mail: Tips, Leads, and Ideas, 265

Direct Mail Tips, 268

New Twist to Targeted Direct Mail Scores 22:1 ROI, 269

Cutting Printing Costs, 270

What to Do If You're Closed Out of Co-op Coupon Packs, 270

Test Before You Roll Out a Mailing, 271

Double Checking Your Mailing House, 271

Why You Need Your Own Mailing List, 272

Promotions in Motion, 273

Chapter 16

NO STONE UNTURNED: EXPLORING PROFITABLE
NEW MARKETS

How to Have Easy Pickings And Avoid The Continuous Struggle, 274

Hot Growth Spots, 276

Capturing the Hotel Trade, 278

How to Get Patients or Clients from That Part of Town, 279

Building the Business District Practice (With 100 New Patients/Clients a Month), 279

How to Promote an Urban Practice, 282

An All New Resident Program with Secret Agents, 284

Becoming the Provider of Choice for Small Companies, 285

Promotions in Motion, 288

Chapter 17

THE SECRETS OF TELEMARKETING

Newest Concept in Telemarketing, 290

The Dedicated Phone Recaller, 291

Converting Inquiries into Patients or Clients, 291

"I Now Convert About 50% Of Phone Shoppers," 292

Inbound Telemarketing: How to Convert an Inquiry into an Appointment, 293

Knock-'Em-Dead Scripts for Outbound Telemarketing, 294

Telemarketing Tips for Success, 297

Helplines Expanding Quickly, 298

Promotions in Motion, 299

Chapter 18

WINNING BIG IN TOUGH MEDIA: YOUR *YELLOW PAGES* AND NEWSPAPER ADVERTISING

Scoring Big and Avoiding Failure in the Yellow Pages, 300

How to Construct a Killer Yellow Pages Ad, 301

Advertorials: Effective and Easy, 304

How to Create Winning Newspaper Advertising, 305

How Many Times to Run an Ad Before You Know It's a Winner—Or Loser, 315

Which Yellow Pages to Choose, 316

Promotions in Motion, 317

Chapter 19

A SECOND TAKE AT COUPONS—THEY'RE NOW LEGITIMATE

Coupons Gaining Acceptance, 319

Winning the Coupon Game, 323

Do Co-op Coupons Work in Upscale Markets? 324

Joint Promotion Cuts Costs & Boosts Response, 325

Co-op Coupon Analyses: Making the Professional Likeable, 325

Promotions in Motion, 328

Chapter 20

NOT FOR THE FAINT-HEARTED: RADIO AND TELEVISION ADVERTISING

Where You Can Use TV and/or Radio, 329

Public Service Radio Spots Too Soft for Big Response, 331

How to Get Interviewed on Radio, 332

Radio Spot Analysis: Deciding the Purpose, 333

Radio Tip: Getting What You Paid For, 334

How to Use Cable TV, 334

Ad Tip: Hot TV, 336

When to Use Jingles to Promote a Practice, 336

Promotions in Motion, 338

Chapter 21

PROPELLING GROWTH WITH EXTRA-SPECIAL PROMOTIONAL TOOLS

Free Seminars Generate Up to 250 New Patients or Clients per Year, 340

Seminar Promotion Tips, 341

Converting Seminar Attendees, 343

Restaurant Seminars Attract Big Fish, 344

Internal Marketing with an Electronic Messages Center or Educating and Promoting In the Reception Area, 344

How to Do More Screenings, 346

Launching a New Service or Product for Steep Growth, 346

Making the Most of Mall, Trade, and Health Shows, 348

Starting Clubs to Recruit New Patients or Clients, 349

Do You Need an 800 Number? 350

Running the Record-Breaking Open House, 351

Promotions in Motion, 353

Chapter 22

SPECIAL CIRCUMSTANCES: START-UPS AND OTHER DESPERATE TIMES

How to Promote When You've Got No Money, Honey, 355

How to Market When You Have No Money and Get 50 New Patients Or Clients a Month, 356

Telemarketing for Lead Generation, 358

What to Do About the Slow Start, 359

How to Promote a Price Reduction for Fast Income, 361

How to Fill Your Slow Season, 363

What to Do When a New Competitor Has a Grand Opening, 364

Attracting Those Who Park in Front of Your Office, 365

Special Cases: Expanding Practices, 366

How to Make Real Money from an Associate, 366

Promotions in Motion, 367

Index, 369

WHAT IS THE PRACTICE BUILDER?

Succinctly, it's a think tank. Made up of MBAs from America's top Business Schools and Fortune 500's marketing stars, THE PRACTICE BUILDER is unique to the professions.

Prior to THE PRACTICE BUILDER, professional practices couldn't afford the astronomical salaries and incentives that the best-of-the-best command today in marketing. But now we've joined these Marketing Directors into a group who share their innovative strategies and tactics with PRACTICE BUILDER members in our monthly publication for a fraction of their former cost. This book is a composite of some of their finest thinking and testing.

Besides fashioning new strategies from their business school backgrounds and big business experience, these marketing directors also consult daily—by phone and on site—with professionals throughout the United States and Canada, building practices to ethereal heights.

In addition, they conduct workshops aptly named *THE PRACTICE BUILDER'S Personal Consultation & Workshop to Build the $1,000,000 Practice.* This popular consultation service has been a monthly sellout since its inception in 1987.

Also under THE PRACTICE BUILDER umbrella of marketing services is The Practice Builder Agency, the largest ad agency in North America specializing in the needs of the professions. Begun in 1984, it's not only the largest, but the most praised, having been spotlighted in *ADWEEK, The Los Angeles Times, INC., Insight Magazine,* and *The Washington Post.*

And my name is Alan Bernstein, the 1979 founder of THE PRACTICE BUILDER. With an MBA from UCLA, I was the first-ever Director of Marketing for The American Heart Association (GLAA). And since the beginning of the eighties, we've designed most of the new marketing strategies for the professions (and redesigned all of the old ones).

Our learning curve has been long and steep. We've tested out each one of our concepts across the continent, in all different types of markets—urban, suburban, rural, East Coast, Southern, Western, Central, New England, Mountain, rich, poor, conservative, aggressive, blue collar, white collar, no collar, sophisticated and unsophisticated.

And finally we've been able to document what works where for each type of practice. It's taken a dozen years and millions of dollars. We sincerely hope you enjoy the fruits of this labor and investment.

Alan L. Bernstein
President
THE PRACTICE BUILDER
2755 Bristol, Suite #100
Costa Mesa, CA 92626
(714)545-8900

SO YOU WANT YOUR PRACTICE TO THROW OFF MEGA-DOLLARS—GETTING DOWN TO BASICS

☐ THE 3 SECRETS OF MARKETING

What are they? Commitment. Investment. Consistency.

Commitment means if you don't generate positive results within two weeks, you don't quit. Without commitment your marketing is impotent.

Investment means enough time and/or money to achieve the goal. That it's viewed *not* as a cost of doing business, but as a conservative investment to make money. You invest in marketing the same way you invest in a blue-chip stock, which may retreat before it advances. Done well, marketing will contribute to slow, steady increases for you. And at year end, you'll be able to say you've invested $X and received $X plus $Y in profits. That's just the way conservative investments are supposed to pay off.

Consistency means sticking with your media and messages. And not dropping from the public's eye for long. For the public, your consistency means familiarity. Which means confidence. Which means income for you.

These three secrets are the most valuable you'll learn in THE PRACTICE BUILDER. And the most difficult to follow. Don't leave home without them.

Jay Levinson, *Guerrilla Marketing*, Houghton Mifflin Co., Boston, 1984, $14.95.

☐ PRIORITIZE YOUR MARKETING: FIRST THINGS FIRST

Chiropractor K.J. had so many marketing ideas that he kept a pad with him at all times, even on his nightstand to jot down the 3 A.M. onslaught. The problem was that although he had a mega-mind, his practice had a mini-budget, limited both in time and money.

In exasperation, K.J. finally chose to do only the "sexy" efforts, those high profile strategies that looked exciting. What he ended up with from this emotional decision was plans guaranteed to reduce his overall gain.

The reasons? He didn't choose *by productivity*. Plus he *tried to do too much,* so nothing was done well. For a happier ending, K.J. needed to quell his hormones and opt for a more mathematical approach.

■ **By Productivity.** Every practice (except a brand new one) needs to concentrate internally first. Working with the existing base to generate repeat business and word-of-mouth referrals is cheaper than anything else you could do. Plus the quality of new patient or client is primo. Therefore, the return on investment can't be beat. That means strategies like:

- Asking patients or clients for referrals
- Frequent Referrer Program—recognition activities and gifts to reinforce and further shape patient or client referral behavior
- A recall system with over a 70% effective rate
- Internal Prospecting—quarterly mailings to your patient or client base to create the image of an expert and generate referrals. (This does not mean a newsletter! See from Chapter Six on for details.)
- Reactivation of patients or clients not seen recently
- One-Minute Messages—short messages about a product or service you want to encourage

Then promote externally. In the return on investment lineup you'll find:

- Outdoor office signage for offices not in professional buildings
- *Yellow Pages* with a 10-to-1 return being common
- Targeted direct mail to a specific group (as opposed to cold prospecting direct mail to the general public)

If you live and die by other professionals' referrals, then they take priority. Concentrate on direct mail to pave the way for follow-up phone calls which hopefully lead to a face-to-face get-togethers.

When your marketing is prioritized *by productivity*, you'll find you do the basics first. Only then can you consider an advertising campaign on TV and the Goodyear blimp. So first things first to spend less and make more. Seems like a reasonable approach.

☐ UNWISE FRUGALITY

When the *Yellow Pages* rep came to pitch Ohio chiropractor S.P., she said it cost too much. When S.P. investigated the expense of quarterly mailings to her client base, the postage alone was enough to make her eat an extra fudge brownie with lunch. Essentially the same reaction occurred when she read a PRACTICE BUILDER article on outdoor office signs and solicited price quotes from sign companies.

S.P. was paralyzed. She couldn't bring himself to spend any sizable sum of money when in years past in markets past, she spent nothing. In fact, she just couldn't do anything in marketing, unless it was free. Why?

■ **Cost vs. ROI.** All S.P. thought about was "how much." And when she did this without matching it to the benefits she would receive from the expenditure, of course it didn't seem worth it.

But at the same time, she was always careful to point out the benefits to her patients of the money they were spending with her. S.P. knew they needed to understand the *value* of their expenditure or they wouldn't do it.

Unfortunately, she didn't listen when someone did that for her. For each proposed expenditure, if she had set up an *expected return on investment*, she could see the actual dollars to be generated. Without this ROI figure, S.P. could never hope to take that big leap into a business-like proactive stance. Essentially into the bigger growth she coveted.

■ **Update.** The last we heard, S.P. has still not been able to bring herself to invest in promotion. The practice continues to maintain its ground, but there's been no growth.

☐ HOW MUCH SHOULD YOU SPEND ON MARKETING?

We've been mislead. Since marketing became acceptable, we've been taught to spend a percentage of gross on marketing: 3%, 5%, 7%, depending on how aggressive your advisor is. But these "experts" are *wrong*. And we've been the ones paying the price.

It makes no sense for professionals with different goals, competitive situations and trend lines to spend the same percentage on marketing. One solution can't fit everyone. That is unless you believe every practice should be alike. And believe you should steer your practice solely by where you've been—instead of where you're going.

What's smarter, but perhaps a bit more complex, is deciding what to spend based upon what you want to achieve—given your situation. Want to double this year? No problem. You can achieve any goal *if* you have enough resources to throw against it.

■ **Figuring the Budget.** First, you need a numerical goal. Not "more patients/clients," but a specific *collections* number. (Only collections count because you can't spend promises.)

Then take your last three years collections and plot them on a graph. Now make a judgment call of where you'll be in 12 months if you don't change anything at all. Down? Flat? Up? Figure that number.

Subtract this projected trend line number from your goal. This tells you how much additional collections you must manufacture out of thin air. Call this your *Incremental Growth Goal.* You'll have to set a promotional budget just for this, over and above your existing budget.

Here's where more judgment comes in. If your practice is at least three years old and you've not done a lot of internal promotion and your Incremental Growth Goal is small, figure the incremental budget to be 15% to 20% of the Incremental Growth Goal.

If you've "reactivated" most of your old patients or clients (See Chapter Seven) and you've prospected them for referrals numerous times (See Chapter Eight), or your practice is young, or your goal large, then you'll need to externally promote more. That's more money because media costs more than internal promotion and more repetitions of your message are needed since these people have never heard of you before. In these cases, figure 25% to 30%.

Also, if your collections trend line is heading south, figure on spending more to turn it around. If it's going north, figure less.

Now take your existing promotional budget—which supports your collections—and add it to your budget for your Incremental Growth Goal. This gives you your final *Total Promotional Budget.* Or does it?

■ **Problem #1.** You'll usually spend about 50% of the budget within the first 25% of the time. This is because you need five to seven repetitions of a message to get the body out of the Lazy Boy and dialing. And it's much better to compress these repetitions in time. In other words, front load them.

That means *you can't fund the first 50% out of cash flow.* It's got to come from retained earnings, the bank or your Uncle Harry. Once cash flow catches up, funding the remainder of the budget is no problem. If your cash is too low, then your goal is too high. Put them in synch.

■ **Problem #2.** Sometimes you have the cash, but emotionally you can't make the move. Don't just brush this one off with a macho, "Of course I can spend it." *This is truth time.* Don't plan a budget that you suspect you won't follow. Face the tough question now. Will you *really* spend it? Really?!?

If you won't, figure what you will and work backwards to set your Incremental Growth Goal. Or ...

Acknowledge your feelings of fear, of not wanting to invest in your practice. Examine those feelings. Then place them in a nice, warm, dark place and seal this secret place with a cork. Leave them there. Don't look at them again . . . until you've made the necessary investment and positive cash flow starts. Then you can examine them all you want.

■ **Dotting the "I's."** Now select the specific strategies and tactics you'll use to achieve your goal. Prioritize them by guestimating return-on-investment. Get specific quotes from printers, media and so on to make the budget precise. Massage the numbers a little, making sure you spend enough on each to make each strategy work, dropping those which won't fit the budget.

Voila! That's how the big boys play the game. And that's how *you* become a big boy.

GETTING MARKETING MONEY

When renovating an office, moving into a new one or building from scratch, professionals often take out a loan. Since they also need several months of operating capital, they build it into the loan.

The problem is that new offices often don't produce new patients or clients in and of themselves. Marketing does. So it also makes sense to build a marketing budget into the new loan under operating capital. After all, you need to pay for the new overhead somehow and increased marketing is the answer.

☐ **MONEY THOUGHTS: HOW MUCH CAN YOU SPEND TO ATTRACT A NEW PATIENT OR CLIENT?**

If your average case were $1,000, would you spend $25 to get one? How about $100? $200? $400? $800? Everyone's got a different top number and it's important to know yours so you can determine exactly how much you're willing to spend to attract one new patient or client.

If your average new case generates $1,000 during the first year with you, isn't it worth more than a $25 to attract? Yet, most accountants, for themselves and their professional clients, use $25 as a rule of thumb—no matter if it makes financial sense or not.

So look deep within your psyche and ask the tough question: *How much will you invest to make the amount equivalent to your average case size?*

If you don't know your average case size, figure it out. Otherwise, you'll never know what a new patient or client is worth.

To discover it, have your computer churn it out. Take the total number of dollars that brand new patients or clients brought into the practice during their first 12 months with you. Don't count referrals from them or repeat visits during subsequent years. Even though these are legitimate factors, it makes the equation too complex for most practical applications.

No computer? Choose someone on staff you don't like. Have them pull all the files from the past year and compile the number by hand. Yes, it's that important.

■ **Results.** Dr. D.Y. chose the latter method to find out what an average new patient was worth. His discovery: *$1,263* with an average overhead of 48%, for a net of *$656*. Now to get more patients, D.Y. allows himself the freedom to spend $75 each, whereas before, he would never go beyond the $25 guideline.

"Sometimes I go well beyond $75 because I know it's still profitable right away and in the long run. A lot of that has to do with the fact that I average another referral for every two new patients I get in."

☐ **ALLOCATING PROMO BUDGET BY SEASONALITY**

Veterinarian P.N. knew he had a slow Fall coming up so he pumped up his promotion to fill the void. But the void stayed. The problem was that people only have a propensity to buy at certain times of the year—and not at others—no matter what.

Every practice has a seasonal curve and while there are similarities, everyone's is a little different. To find yours, average the last three Januarys' *production* numbers. Do the same for each month and plot them on a bar chart. Your seasonality is now staring you in the face.

The chart tells you when to go on vacation with the minimum loss in income. And it tells you when you should and shouldn't be promoting.

If you want to fill your slow season, *don't* do it with external promotion. The return on investment is always lower than in higher seasons and most can't afford that with limited resources.

Instead, schedule existing patients or clients in to fill the slow times and keep your busy times open for new business when you've got your promotional machine pumping away. This is easiest in practices which recall people. Then you simply preappoint the recall at the time of the last appointment—and heavily schedule slow months.

Actually, to fill the slow times, promote into your high times. This raises your high times production figures with good ROI. Then cut your promotion as your seasonality curves starts dipping down. Your new repeat business and word-of-mouth will lift your slow time curve. Between this phenomenon and savvy scheduling of existing clientele, you'll fill the valleys.

☐ WHAT SHOULD YOUR PROMOTION PAYBACK?

Dentist J.F. senses his direct mail is working okay. Physical therapist O.M. asks her receptionist how well the *Yellow Pages* is doing. And psychologist U.W. checks her number of new clients. All these methods are bad news when it comes to evaluating how well promotion is working.

There's only one statistic that means anything at all—return on investment (ROI). *That's dollars in from a specific promotion divided by that promotion's cost.* (The importance of tracking by source becomes evident.)

But once you calculate your ROIs, you need to know are the numbers good or not? Use this checklist to compare what your specific promotion should and could be paying you back. (All time frames are one year unless otherwise noted.)

1. Quarterly Internal Prospecting Direct Mail—10:1
2. Reactivation Efforts—10:1
3. Frequent Referrer Program—15:1
4. Asking For Referrals—100+:1
5. Practice Brochure—Incalculable but high
6. Recalls—80% success
7. Outdoor Office Sign—15:1
8. *Yellow Pages*—10:1
9. New Resident Direct Mail—10:1
10. Newspaper and Shopper Ads—5:1
11. Co-op Coupons—4:1 (in 90 days)
12. Cold Prospecting Direct Mail—3:1 (in 90 days)
13. Radio—5:1
14. TV—4:1

Remember: These are ROI numbers, not gross income numbers. Radio, for instance, can produce more profit in gross dollars even though it has a lower ROI than an office sign because of the radio's greater cost. So when you choose strategies, keep the gross dollars in mind also. But always start with the higher ROI ideas.

Caution: These guidelines cover all kinds of markets and suffer from the weaknesses of all statistical means. In other words, every practice in every market can't achieve them nor is every strategy apropos. However, the numbers should tell you if you're in the ballpark. If your numbers aren't close, it's time to experiment. Test new concepts to find out what's keeping your ROI down. Here's what you could be doing wrong:

1. Your execution of the promotion is poor.
2. Your timing is wrong.
3. You've mistargeted your promotion.
4. You've got the wrong message for the right target.
5. Your image is inappropriate for your target.
6. You haven't differentiated yourself significantly.
7. You've got a bad list (direct mail).
8. You've got a bad location (*Yellow Pages*).
9. You don't have enough repetition (newspaper).
10. Your visual is wrong.
11. Your headline is wrong.
12. Your typefaces are wrong.
13. Your tone is wrong.
14. You're promoting the wrong service or product given the target and the competition.
15. Your price of your service or product is wrong.
16. You don't have a direct response offer for people to respond to now.
17. You have no deadline on your offer to stimulate response.
18. Your offer is wrong, contains too much service or is priced too high.

Your task is to discover what isn't working. Test new concepts or new executions of old ones to boost your numbers. You've got to figure that if *other people can get these ROI numbers,* why can't you? The opportunity is there. You just need to discover the right equation of variables for your market and competitive situation. And testing is the *only* way to succeed.

☐ WHAT TO DO IF MODESTY HINDERS YOUR PROMOTING

If blowing your own horn makes you nervous, you've got a dilemma. People need to receive *convincing, sizzling information* about you. And there's no one else to provide it except you. So either you give it ... or they don't get it and you don't get results.

Since we've all been taught to be modest, self-promotion goes against our grain. But only until we've done it *once* and we see positive cash flow. Then it's *never* a problem again.

So do some self-therapy and tell yourself it'll be all right. And if it works, it will be. If not, get help with your promotion so it generates cash flow. That's the best and shortest term therapy.

☐ UNHAPPY NEWS FROM UNHAPPY PEOPLE

Most professionals think perhaps 5 to 10% of their patients or clients are unhappy with them, but not complaining. Wrong!

New research indicates those discontented with you number between 37 and 45%. They're unhappy but not telling you. And it doesn't take much for them to disappear.

■ **Solution.** Send a once-a-year survey to your *past and active* base so you can identify then correct the causes. But send it in the form of a *Report Card*.

This format seems to strike people's imagination and says you're willing to be graded so you must care. Not only are more report cards returned than the normal, boring-looking survey, but some people who previously dropped out start showing up in home room.

☐ YOUR PROMOTIONAL CHECKLIST

There are basic strategies which belong on most professionals' Marketing Game Plan. Use this checklist to discover if you've covered the basics—or you're still acting like a rank beginner.

1. You need a way to protect your existing base from marauding competitors. Also one to generate more word-of-mouth and repeat business from your past patients or clients. Newsletters don't work, but Internal Prospecting does. (See Chapter 6 for details.)

2. Assuming you recall people, you've got to have an effective system. Unfortunately, under 50% success for yearly recalls is the norm.

Even 75% means you've lost a quarter after you worked so hard to get them. If you haven't figured your success percentage, get ready for a real shock! An effective system means over 80%—with 90% possible. (See Chapter 7 for details.)

3. You need a way to bring back all those people who weren't successfully recalled, but have developed a situation which needs your help. Called Reactivation Efforts, they're highly profitable. (See Chapter 8 for details.)

4. In order for people to refer, they must first believe you to be an expert so the referral reflects back positively on them. Your Internal Prospecting helps generate this image. But your Waiting Room Resume carries the main burden. (See Chapter 3 for details.)

5. Then you can engage in the #1 best practice building strategy ever invented, with the highest ROI, generating the best type of patient or client. That's asking for referrals—but not in a way that makes everyone feel uncomfortable. Instead use the ultra-tested wording in Chapter 8.

6. Multiple referrals come from a finite number of personal cheerleaders and you can, in fact, reinforce their behavior so that they'll refer even more. Lots more. Just follow the instructions for the Frequent Referral Program. (See Chapter 8 for details.)

7. And for your outreach promotion, you'll need "sales litera-ture," commonly called a practice brochure. But not all brochures are created equal. Most are dry, unmotivating and aren't worth the paper they're printed on. Follow the instructions in Chapter 12 for details on how to construct the practice brochure that sells, not informs.

These are the basics, but they're usually insufficient. If there's a chance for referrals from other professionals, you'll need strategies to develop those. Plus a *consistent* program of external promotion to gen-erate the new people needed to meet your goal. (Beware of using public relations alone since it lacks consistency.)

■ **Sample Plans.** Then write it all down—in pencil to start until it balances nicely. Figure 1.1 shows a sample plan created at a recent PRACTICE BUILDER Weekend Consultation and Workshop. The next chapter looks at all the elements with which to create your own marketing plan.

THE PRACTICE BUILDER Marketing Calendar & Budgetary Plan - Prepared Exclusively For: JOHN DOE

Date Prepared: 1-2-91   Months *

INTERNAL STRATEGIES	JAN	FEB	MAR	APR	MAY	JUN	JUL	AUG	SEP	OCT	NOV	DEC	Strategy Totals
ASK FOR REFERRALS				←—— ON-GOING ——→									0
FREQUENT REFERRER PROGRAM	1,100 (GIFTS)			←—— ON-GOING ——→									1,100
ONE-MINUTE MESSAGES	CREATE SCRIPTS			←—— ON-GOING ——→									0
QUARTERLY INTERNAL PROSPECTING	2,500 (CREATIVE)			500 (PRINT/MAIL 1,1TPC)			500			500			4,000
REACTIVATION OF INACTIVES	2,200 (CREATIVE)			330 (PRINT/MAIL 1,100 PC)					330				2,860
WAITING ROOM RESUME	CREATE DISPLAY			←—— IN PLACE ——→									0
PROMOTIONAL BROCHURE	4,400 (CREATIVE)	2000 (PRINT 5,000 @)											6,400
EXTERNAL STRATEGIES													
YELLOW PAGES MEDIA COSTS	350	350	350	350	350	350	350	350	350	350	350	350	4,200
" AD DESIGN (1/4 PAGE)	2,500 (CREATIVE)												2,500
RE-DESIGN EXTERNAL SIGN	1,100 (DESIGN)		2,500 (FABRICATION)										3,500
CO-OP COUPONS	1,100 (CREATIVE)			800 (MAIL 2000)	800		800		800		800		5,100
PRINT AD SERIES (3 ADS)	3,500 (CREATIVE)		500	1000	500				500	1000	500		7,500
			8 WKS: 3/15–5/15						8 WKS: 9/15–11/15				
PROFESSIONAL REFERRAL													
CROSS-PROMOTION PROGRAM	RECRUIT PARTICIPANTS	500 CREATE/PRINT CERTIFICATES		←—— ON-GOING ——→									500
Monthly Totals:													

BUDGET: $40,000   GOAL: 750,000   AVE$: 500   #ACTIVE: 575   #IN-ACTIVE: 1,100

FOOTNOTE: CONFIRM PRINT MEDIA COSTS   ACTUAL BUDGET: $37,660

Figure 1.1 Sample Plan

PROMOTIONS IN MOTION

1. Do you know when Campbell's Soup advertises most? It's when cold
    weather hits that the soup giant hastily takes to the airwaves with
    "storm advertising." So chiropractor G.F. does the same. When an ice
    or snow storm hits, G.F. quickly runs sore back, neck and shoulder pain
    commercials on radio. Very timely and very smart.

2. Urgicenters owner L.M. faced a dilemma. Should he position his offices
    against the Emergency Rooms and then develop episodic patients into
    returning patients? If he did that, he wouldn't get referrals from the
    GPs, FPs and pediatricians in the area. If he positioned against the
    Emergency Rooms and turned all patients back to their primary doc
    plus funnel to them all patients not committed to a primary care physi-
    cian, then over time he could get their after-hours referrals. What to do?

    He had two problems. The area docs didn't trust him because in the
    past he'd been straddling the fence and playing both strategies. And
    second, the docs in his facilities were FP physicians who wanted to
    practice on-going family medicine.

    These argued strongly for developing a family practice within the
    centers. The other way would be a longer payback and very unsure.
    One trip-up by an urgicenter doc keeping one patient could doom a
    majority of physician referrals.

3. Dentist G.R. is promoting the whitening of yellow teeth. This smart
    dentist knows that people don't know if they want bleaching, so he
    doesn't lead with that. They just know they want white teeth.

Chapter 2   □

STRATEGIZING FOR SUCCESS: YOUR SURE-FIRE MARKETING PLAN

□ CASE HISTORY: BACKWARD PLANNING

Chiropractor P.E. had never promoted his practice before. But when he decided to take the plunge, he moved quickly. The problem was that he put the wrong foot first.

When P.E. made that decision to be proactive in his marketing, he started to look around for a media vehicle through which to spread his fame. He was eager to move. A local radio station got wind of this and, in a matter of days, had him tied up in a long-term contract.

The media program consisted of a 60-second spot run throughout the day, from early morning to midnight, not just weekdays but weekends, too. This is called an R.O.S. buy—Run of Station—in which the station plays the spot when they can fit you in. No guarantees of time.

But many PRACTICE BUILDER radio tests show that people are more receptive to messages about professional services between *6 A.M. and 10 A.M. on weekdays*. The reason: Weekdays are for taking care of life. Weekends are for fun, relaxing and shopping. (Just look who advertises on weekends.) And during mornings, people have energy. After work, they don't.

When THE PRACTICE BUILDER finally caught up with P.E., it was the night before he was going down to the station to record his commercial. He wanted to know what we would suggest he say.

■ **Backwards Process.** This was not the time for P.E. to ask that question. Weeks ago, he should have asked:

1. What are the demographics of the people I want to reach?
2. What motivates them? (This determines his message.)
3. What media do they respond to? (Maybe radio isn't the right one. Maybe it's not the right station. Only the Arbitron ratings can tell you.)
4. What are my competitors doing? Are they promoting in the media? How do I differentiate myself?

Then he should approach a radio station, if *and only if* it's been selected according to the above analysis. If you go to a radio station first, then radio automatically becomes the answer. The same is true for all media.

The prognosis: Trouble ahead.

The lesson: Keep your rushing hormones in check. Only by following a structured planning process can you stay out of deep trouble. Let's look at the planning needed.

☐ YOUR QUICK, SWEET AND PROFITABLE MARKETING PLAN: THE SHORT FORM A.K.A. THE FINE ART OF CONTROLLING YOUR DESTINY

Pediatrician H.B. stood stark still for two years at $300,000 production. With a target of $450,000 and all the nerve he could muster, he launched a multi-layered promotional effort costing $30,000: *Yellow Pages, Yellow Pages* plastic covers, newspaper ads, refrigerator magnets and The Welcome Wagon.

Results brought production to $312,000 for an immediate loss of $18,000. *But his really big loss was the $138,000 more he had planned on*—his opportunity loss.

And not just for that one year, but for the next few years. Since he then shied away from any promotion at all, he pushed his opportunity loss to over $½ million!

But how could this happen? Perhaps the better question is: How could it not? H.B. would be immediately sued if he treated a patient incorrectly without examining first. Yet that's exactly what he did with his promotional program. The difference is that the unforgiving market-place didn't file a lengthy lawsuit. It crushed him immediately.

What he didn't realize was that the strategies he selected, targeting the people he chose, with the promotion he created, put out at the time he pinpointed—didn't work. It wasn't marketing that didn't work. It was his marketing—at this time.

Also, that without a marketing exam and a plan first, he was easy prey for high-pressure salespeople with gimmicks galore, hot deadlines and the threat they'll give the opportunity to his no-talent colleague down the street.

H.B. isn't alone. Stories like his number in the tens of thousands. They're about professionals who lost money—from a few hundred to a hundred thousand. On newsletters, seminars, direct mail, *Yellow Pages*, TV, coupons and recalls. On referral efforts, ads on maps sent to new residents, Better Business Bureaus directories, *Yellow Pages* plastic covers, refrigerator magnets and public relations firms. On union recruiters, The Welcome Wagon, ads in the free TV listings from the supermarket ... or on the back of supermarket tapes—or on the front of bowling alley pin sweepers! The list is enormous, only limited by the imagination of promoters—and the gullibility of professionals.

■ **A Coordinated Game Plan.** If you fill out the following Marketing Plan Short Form, you can count yourself among the handful of sophisticated professionals who won't lose their minds and shirts from lost opportunities and fast talking salespeople. And at last you'll have a game plan, so you won't feel unsure ... or be unprofitable.

The planner is a quick 15 questions. Your strategies should be taken from the chapters that follow. Estimate your costs as best you can and refine as you go. Following the form itself is a completed exam together with the charted strategies and budget that flow from the plan.

THE PRACTICE BUILDER

Short Form Marketing Plan

1. A. Year before last's gross collections: $_____
    B. Last year's gross collections: $_____

2. A. This year's collection goal: $_____
    B. Next year's collection goal: $_____

3. Given your trend, what will you collect this year *without* changing
    your existing promotional efforts? $_____

4. Subtract #3 from #2A to get the amount of new business to be
    manufactured out of brand new promotional efforts. Call this
    your "Incremental Growth Goal." (This amount will need it's
    own "Incremental Promotional Budget.") $_____

5. Ballpark this year's Incremental Promotional Budget to support
    the Incremental Growth Goal in #4. (Figure 15–30% of that figure.
    See "How Much Should You Spend on Marketing," p. 3 and below
    for exact instructions.) $_____

6. Last year's existing promotional budget: $_____

7. This year's total promotional budget: $_____

8. By computer or hand, figure where 70% of your patients or clients
    are located. (For the best return, you'll target all your promotion to
    this area.) Describe the boundaries:

---

9. Is your market:
    A. ❑ Small town   ❑ Rural   ❑ Suburban   ❑ Urban
        ❑ Business Downtown

    B. ❑ Expanding   ❑ *Declining*
    C. ___% White collar   ___% New collar (low-level white collar)
        ___% Blue collar   ___% No collar

10. What percentage of your practice is:
    A. ___% Female   ___% Male
    B. ___% Under 18;   ___% 18-29;   ___% 30-45;   ___% 46-59;   ___% 60+

C. Business oriented practices: ___% *Big business;* ___% Small business. List % by specific industries: ___% _____ ; ___% _____ ; ___% _____ .

11. What promotion is working for you? (Over 2:1 ROI)

Activity	Return on Investment (ROI)
A. _____	
B. _____	
C. _____	
D. _____	
E. _____	
F. _____	
G. _____	

12. If you do recalls, what is your success rate? ___% (This should be over 75%)

13. List what kind(s) of patients or clients you want—your prime prospects. Specifically state where they are located, income and education levels, age, sex, and other variables, *if* important, such as religion, race, business size and industry, etc.:

_____

_____

_____

_____

14. If prime prospects needed a professional like you, list those colleagues they would find out about *without* a referral. List where and what these colleagues promote. _____

_____

_____

_____

_____

15. For new prime prospects, list *the best way* you can differentiate yourself from your competitors: _____

_____

_____

_____

_____

☐ **A SAMPLE COMPETED SHORT FORM**

Here is a sample plan created at a recent PRACTICE BUILDER Weekend Consultation and Workshop. This is the actual short form for podiatrist T.J. and the plan constructed from his short analysis.

THE PRACTICE BUILDER

Short Form Marketing Plan

1. A. Year before last's gross collections: $338,000
   B. Last year's gross collections: $376,000

2. A. This year's collection goal: $460,000
   B. Next year's collection goal: $535,000

3. Given your trend, what will you collect this year *without* changing your existing promotional efforts? $400,000

4. Subtract #3 from #2A to get the amount of new business to be manufactured out of brand new promotional efforts. Call this your "Incremental Growth Goal." (This amount will need it's own "Incremental Promotional Budget.") $ 60,000

5. Ballpark this year's Incremental Promotional Budget to support the Incremental Growth Goal in #4. (Figure 15–30% of that figure. See "How Much Should You Spend on Marketing," below for exact instructions.) $ 18,000

6. Last year's existing promotional budget: $ 16,000

7. This year's total promotional budget: $ 34,000

8. By computer or hand, figure where 70% of your patients or clients are located. (For the best return, you'll target all your promotion to this area.) Describe the boundaries: **3-mile radius except can't draw from Greenview Estates (richer).**

9. Is your market:
   A. ☐ Small town   ☐ Rural   ✗ Suburban   ☐ Urban
      ☐ Business Downtown

   B. ✗ Expanding   ☐ Declining
   C. <u>20%</u> White collar   <u>25%</u> New collar (low-level white collar)
      <u>50%</u> Blue collar   <u>5%</u> No collar

---

10. What percentage of your practice is:
    A. **65%** Female   **35%** Male
    B. ___% Under 18;   **10%** 18-29;   **20%** 30-45;   **40%** 46-59;   **30%** 60+

11. What promotion is working for you? (Over 2:1 ROI)

Activity	Return on Investment (ROI)
Yellow Pages	**3:1**
Val-Pak Coupons	**2:1**

12. If you do recalls, what is your success rate?   **50%**   (This should be over 75%)

13. List what kind(s) of patients or clients you want—your prime prospects. Specifically state where they are located, income and education levels, age, sex, and other variables, *if* important, such as religion, race, business size and industry, etc.: **(1) 3-mile radius excluding Greenview Estates, female, 40–60 yrs. old, household income $30,000+, bunions, nail problems, heel pain, general foot pain; (2) Seniors, Medicare, 3-mile radius excluding Greenview Estates.**

14. If prime prospects needed a professional like you, list those colleagues they would find out about *without* a referral. List where and what these colleagues promote. **(1) Dr. Templeton: Yellow Pages, weekly Town Crier, free foot exam. (2) Dr. Hill: Yellow Pages, inconsistent co-op coupons, MIS.**

15. For new prime prospects, list *the best way* you can differentiate yourself from your competitors: **experience, laser.**

☐ MARKETING STRATEGIES AND BUDGET

Figure 2.1 shows the plan constructed from the preceding analysis.

■ **Take Note.** Out of a total $32,700, $12,400 is one-time only. This includes the one-time reactivation of past patients/clients, the redesign of the recall system for non-surgical patients, the creative fees for the practice brochure and *Yellow Pages* ad, and redoing the office sign.

The internal budget tallies $12,200 or only 37.3% of the total. This is because it's cheaper to sell something to someone who already knows you than to someone who doesn't know you from Adam.

Also notice the timing. Money is spent during the months when people have a propensity to spend, not during the low periods! People won't spend then, for whatever reasons. Concept: Spending during the high seasons will fill the low seasons eventually by word-of-mouth

Date: December 15, 1991 Podiatrist T.J.'s 1992 Marketing Strategies & Budget

Promotion Type	Jan	Feb	Mar	Apr	May	Jun	Jul	Aug	Sep	Oct	Nov	Dec	Total
INTERNAL STRATEGIES													
Ask all patients for referrals	0	0	0	0	0	0	0	0	0	0	0	0	0
Reactivate old charts	1,700[1]	500											2,200
Qrtly internal prospecting direct mail		500			500			500			500		2,000
Frequent Referrer Program	1,100[2]	0	0	0	0	0	0	0	0	0	0	0	1,100
Redesign Recall System	1,700[1]	200[3]											1,900
Practice Brochure	3,500[1]	1,500[3]											5,000
EXTERNAL STRATEGIES													
Yellow Pages	300	300	300	300	300	300	300	300	300	300	300	300	3,600
Yellow Pages creative	1,500												1,500
Co-op coupons			400	400	400					400	400		2,000
Newspaper ads	2,900[1]		1,000	1,000	1,000	500	500		1,000	1,000	1,000		9,900
Redo External Office Sign	1,000[4]	2,500[5]											3,500
TOTALS	12,200	5,500	3,200	1,700	2,200	800	800	800	1,300	1,700	2,200	300	32,700
PROJECTED BUDGET													34,000
UNDER/OVER BUDGET													(1,300)

1 Creative Costs
2 Premiums for frequent referrers
3 Printing Costs
4 Design
5 Fabrication

Figure 2.1 Marketing Strategies Completed Form for Podiatrist T.J.

Date: _____

19___ Marketing Strategies & Budget

Promotion Type	Jan	Feb	Mar	Apr	May	Jun	Jul	Aug	Sep	Oct	Nov	Dec	Total
INTERNAL STRATEGIES													
EXTERNAL STRATEGIES													
PROFESSIONAL REFERRAL ACTIVITIES													
TOTALS													
PROJECTED BUDGET													
UNDER/OVER BUDGET													

Figure 2.2 Marketing Strategies and Budget Form

referrals and repeat business. Don't spend in the low seasons unless you're desperate for a write-off.

■ **Now It's Your Turn.** This Short Form (Figure 2.2) is a simplified version of the analysis and plan created for each practice at THE PRACTICE BUILDER's intensive weekend workshops. Photocopy it and fill it in. Calendarize and budgetize your strategies. Then work the plan.

Don't do anything outside of the plan! If you do, trouble will gnaw on your profits because you'll make emotional decisions, not well thought out ones like those from your plan. If you construct your plan *right and work it*, you'll avoid 90% of all pitfalls. But if you don't ....

☐ **THE LONG FORM MARKETING GAME PLANNER**

The short form above is an excellent tool when you're first looking at your practice building and inventorying where the practice should be headed. The following long form takes a closer look at several important areas. It gives more attention to the long range direction your practice has taken, how you will finance your growth, what types of promotion have not performed well, what your strengths are, as well as highlighting the need for a combination of different types of promotion to achieve your goal.

An ideal way to use this form is to turn to it as you read about specific strategies and tools in the chapters that follow. Then assess the interplay between them. This long form planner is also straight forward and simple. Estimate costs as best you can and refine as you go.

THE PRACTICE BUILDER

Long Form Marketing Game Planner

Practice Name: _____

Effective date of plan from:_____ **to:**_____

1. How is your practice performing now?
    Gross collections: $_____
    Average number of new patients/clients per month:
    Last year: _____   Three years ago:_____
    Year before: _____   Four years ago: _____
    Current Average Case Size (gross dollars a patient spends within
    first 12 months): $ _____

2. Set specific goals for where you want to be. Consider your personnel,
    physical plant constraints and abilities as a manager.
    Gross collection goal: $ _____
    Targeted average number of new patients/clients per month:
    This coming year:_____   Three years away: _____
    Two years away:_____   Four years away: _____
    Targeted Average Case Size (gross dollars spent within
    first 12 months): $ _____

3. Given the current trend, promotion and promotional budget, what will be
    your projected future billings, *without additional promotional efforts:*
    This coming year:_____   Two years away: _____

4. The amount of increased billings to come from new promotional efforts (#2 – #3):
    This coming year: _____   Two years away: _____

5. The existing promotional expenditure (*Yellow Pages*, newsletters, media,
    everything):
    Last year: _____   The year before:_____

6. The approximate incremental promotional budget needed to attain the desired
    increase in billings (in #4). Range: 15%–30% of increased billings.
    This coming year:_____   Two years away: _____

7. The approximate amount needed on hand to fund the incremental promotional
    budget for the first year. About 50% of budget will be spent in the first 90 days.
    This coming year:_____

Sources of Funds   *Amount*

_____   _____

_____   _____

_____   _____

_____   _____

_____   _____

8. Reconcile any differences between goals and budget. Again make any
    adjustment to overoptimistic goals given your personnel, physical plant
    constraints and abilities as a manager.

9. Your previous promotion that has produced *over* a 2:1 return on investment (ROI):

    Activity   *ROI*
    A. _____   _____
    B. _____   _____
    C. _____   _____
    D. _____   _____
    E. _____   _____
    F. _____   _____
    G. _____   _____
    H. _____   _____
    I. _____   _____
    J. _____   _____

10. Your previous promotional activities that have produced *under* a 2:1 ROI:

    Activity   *ROI*
    A. _____   _____
    B. _____   _____
    C. _____   _____
    D. _____   _____
    E. _____   _____
    F. _____   _____
    G. _____   _____
    H. _____   _____
    I. _____   _____
    J. _____   _____

11. What is your recall success rate of those you attempt to recall: _____%.
    (This should be over 75%.)

12. Market rough cut:
A. Seventy percent of patients/clients are drawn from a ___ mile radius of the practice.
Areas best able to draw from:_____
Areas unable to draw from: _____
B. Approximate drawing population: _____
C. Household Income: ❑ Lower ❑ Middle-lower ❑ Middle-middle
   ❑ Middle-upper ❑ Upper income
D. Mostly: ❑ No collar ❑ Blue collar ❑ New collar (low level white collar)
   ❑ White collar
E. Mostly: ❑ Urban ❑ Suburban ❑ Semi-rural ❑ Rural
F. Mostly: ❑ Residential ❑ Lightly Industrial ❑ Heavily Industrial
   ❑ Agricultural ❑ Downtown Business Area ❑ Other: _____
G. Practice is: ____% Female ____% Male
   Patient's Ages: ____% under 18; ____$ 18-29; ____% 30-45;
   ____%46-59; ____%60+
H. Strong ethnic, religious or language concerns: _____
   _____
I. Business-oriented practices:
   Industries: _____
   _____
   _____
   _____
   _____

   Their average sales: _____
   Average # employees_____

13. Desired market segments and what to promote to each:
   _____
   _____
   _____
   _____
   _____

14. Competition Analysis: List main competitors who promote. What do they promote and where?
   A. _____
   _____

B. _____
_____

C. _____
_____

D. _____
_____

E. _____
_____

15. Main promotable strengths that are desirable to my market segments:
A. _____
_____

B. _____
_____

C. _____
_____

D. _____
_____

16. Area media that target my market segments well:
A. _____
B. _____
C. _____
D. _____
E. _____
F. _____
G. _____
H. _____
I. _____
J. _____

17. *Yellow Pages:*

Book Name & Publisher	Present Size & Section	Recommended Size & Section	Closing Date

18. Promotional activities for coming year (19___):

A. Internal Promotion   Creative $ Media/Mailing/   Total Budget
                                                 Printing $

1. _____ $_____ $_____   (_____)
2. _____ $_____ $_____   (_____)
3. _____ $_____ $_____   (_____)
4. _____ $_____ $_____   (_____)
5. _____ $_____ $_____   (_____)
6. _____ $_____ $_____   (_____)
7. _____ $_____ $_____   (_____)
8. _____ $_____ $_____   (_____)
9. _____ $_____ $_____   (_____)
10. _____ $_____ $_____   (_____)

                              Total 19___ Internal Budget $_____

B. External Promotion   Creative $ Media/Mailing/   Total Budget
                                                 Printing $

1. _____ $_____ $_____   (_____)
2. _____ $_____ $_____   (_____)
3. _____ $_____ $_____   (_____)
4. _____ $_____ $_____   (_____)
5. _____ $_____ $_____   (_____)
6. _____ $_____ $_____   (_____)
7. _____ $_____ $_____   (_____)
8. _____ $_____ $_____   (_____)
9. _____ $_____ $_____   (_____)
10. _____ $_____ $_____   (_____)

                              Total 19___ External Budget $_____

C. Intra & Inter-profession   Creative $ Media/Mailing/   Total Budget
    Referrals   Printing $

1. _____ $_____ $_____   (_____)
2. _____ $_____ $_____   (_____)
3. _____ $_____ $_____   (_____)
4. _____ $_____ $_____   (_____)
5. _____ $_____ $_____   (_____)

6. _____ $_____ $_____   (_____)
7. _____ $_____ $_____   (_____)
8. _____ $_____ $_____   (_____)
9. _____ $_____ $_____   (_____)
10. _____ $_____ $_____   (_____)

Total 19___ Professional Referral Budget $_____

19. Total Coming Year (19___) promotional budget needs:
    Total amount (Sum of 18 A, B & C above): $_____
    By month: Month 1   _____   Month 7   _____
                 Month 2   _____   Month 8   _____
                 Month 3   _____   Month 9   _____
                 Month 4   _____   Month 10   _____
                 Month 5   _____   Month 11   _____
                 Month 6   _____   Month 12   _____

20. Total Following Year (19___) promotional budget needs:
    Total amount: _____
    By month: Month 1   _____   Month 7   _____
                 Month 2   _____   Month 8   _____
                 Month 3   _____   Month 9   _____
                 Month 4   _____   Month 10   _____
                 Month 5   _____   Month 11   _____
                 Month 6   _____   Month 12   _____

21. Suggested Practice Positioning (or the one thing we want people to remember
    about us if they could only remember one thing):

    _____
    _____
    _____
    _____
    _____

22. Important Notes:

    _____
    _____
    _____
    _____
    _____
    _____

☐ MARKETING PLAN—MIDYEAR EVALUATION

At the halfway point through his fiscal year, this Illinois podiatrist evaluated his marketing plan. Here's what it had looked like midyear.

Last year's collections (Actual): $260,554
This year's collections (Goal): $290,000

A. Internal Promotion	Creative $	Media/Mailing/ Printing $	Total Budget
1. Reactivation mailing/ Phone follow-up [Chapter 7]	$1,700	$1,400	$3,100
2. Internal prospecting direct mail, quarterly [Chapter 15]	$4,000	$5,000	$9,000
3. Frequent referrer patient gift program [Chapter 8]		$1,700	$1,700
4. Asking for referrals [Chapter 8]			$ 0
5. One-minute messages [Chapter 6]			$ 0
Total year's internal budget			$13,800

B. External Promotion	Creative $	Media/Mailing/ Printing $	Total Budget
1. *Yellow Pages* [Chapter 18]	$1,750	$6,500	$8,250
2. Seminars to young athletes [Chapter 21]		$ 500	$ 500
Total year's external budget			$8,750

C. Intra/Inter-Professional Referrals	Creative $	Media/Mailing/ Printing $	Total Budget
1. Direct mail "Alerts"/ phone follow-ups to MDs [Chapter 8]	$1,200	$ 200	$1,400
Total year's referral budget			$1,400
Total year's promotional budget			$23,950

■ **Midyear Evaluation.** Collections are projected at about $175,000 for the first six months, but are $30,000 ahead of plan to put the practice on a $350,000 pace. Everything seems to be working. Mailing and phoning MDs started slowly but the program is beginning to show results. It's a long-term strategy to get 10 good referrers, so the practitioner will stick with it and check it again in six months.

■ **Fine Tuning.** In summary, time has come to go for the gold. Add the part-time associate who's been waiting in the wings. Test newspaper promotion. Add $10,000 to the external budget ($2,500 creative/$7,500 media). And good luck.

☐ MARKETING PROBLEMS AND SOLUTIONS

■ **1. Problem.** Optometrist P.Y. is the first O.D. in her town. The problem is that people still go to her competitors in the small city 15 miles away. They perceive that the care is better in a city—that anyone who practices in the boonies can't be any good or very modern. They're also used to going to the city for shopping and work. How do you break the cycle and change perceptions—quickly?

■ **Solution.** For a quick solution, a little fire in the belly is what's needed. There are two roads in and out of town. Rent a mini-billboard (called a junior bulletin) on each road for six months. Since everyone in town will pass them numerous times, your message is guaranteed to get out.

And what's the message? One of quality.

Question: Where can you get great eyecare?
Answer: <u>Dr. Paula Young</u>, Thompson's first optometrist,   At 4th & Pear

■ **2. Problem** California chiropractor W.K. called the Advisory Hotline with a problem on how to spend his limited promotional budget—send a newsletter to his patient base or stick with his newspaper ads?

Background: $100,000 gross/year; 17 new patients/month; stagnant production; 10 years in practice; town pop. 600, draws from three towns up to 25 miles away; no other DCs; running "Chiropractic Outlook" public service newspaper column (1 col. × 8") in local paper for seven months, not well tracked but number of new patients remains constant; many existing patients comment they've read it.

■ **Solution.** Generic newspaper columns don't work. They only work to attract new patients or clients when written specifically about how *the practitioner* solves a problem. (The fact that patients or clients comment is a sucker play because only new patients or clients and return on investment counts. In this case we have neither.)

W.K. should reposition the entire practice into a back and neck pain relief center to appeal to the medically oriented patient. They're used to going to a "specialist," but not to a D.C. Repackage the practitioner as a back-and-neck-pain specialist with a new practice name, sign, stationary and logo. Then he'd appeal to nine times more people.

Then run newspaper ads to announce the opening of the center and its benefits. (If you don't tell the world, the world doesn't know.) Plus make sure you use direct mail to your patient base every 90 days to farm them for referrals and repeat business.

Next, open a satellite office in one of the towns 20 miles away. W.K. gets 20% of his patients from there now, but he could get a lot more if he was convenient. Rent space from another professional on a part-time basis; staff it only when he's there; use call forwarding to answer the phone in the main office when he's absent. That keeps overhead down.

■ **3. Problem.** Ophthalmologist C.J. wanted out as an associate of a two-man, West Coast practice. Not only out, but up and running in his own, directly competitive shop. With a local hospital providing external promotion, the question became internal promotion—and more basically, how to get 4,500 past patients to follow. You know the old practice isn't going to refer them!

■ **Solution.** C.J.had been diligently and legally copying names and addresses for months, but by long hand. First he needs to put them up on a data base on a computer. Any computer will do since the file isn't that big and he's just going to create a mailing list file to be printed out on pressure-sensitive labels. If he has no computer, the easy way is to have a computer service bureau input the names on their computer.

Then don't send a simple announcement. It's not enough. Yes, it's true that some patients will follow C.J. anywhere, even to the grungiest of third world countries. But he doesn't want just some. He wants them all.

Well, he won't get them all, but he can increase the percentage who'll follow by a factor of five to ten. The problem is that announcements don't motivate. They don't tell why they should follow. Nor what it will do for them if they do. Nor the improvements in care they'll receive by following.

But well-written, interesting, multi-page letters can. So send one on your new stationery by third-class mail two days before you move. Then send a follow-up letter with the same message and perhaps more new benefits three weeks later. One-two. That's good punching.

Ninety days later begin your program of quarterly, internal prospecting direct mail to foster repeat business and referrals. (See Chapter 8 on Referrals for strategy details.) That's how you don't lose them, whereas a "professional," whimpy announcement will.

☐ HOW TO TRACK THE RESULTS OF YOUR PROMOTION

Unless you like to make *expensive* decisions off the cuff—and pour megadollars down a bottomless pit—you'll learn to track your promotional results. In fact, you'll learn to love it. Because without accurate feedback on each effort, you'll never make *big* money and you'll easily lose BIG money. Without it, you'll throw away opportunities to capitalize on winners. Plus you're easy prey for quick-witted salespeople who are out to take you to the cleaners.

Tracking is the *only* way to stop them. And to achieve your goals.

At THE PRACTICE BUILDER, we live by numbers. Since we hate to say "We think...," tracking let's say "We know...." It will do the same for you.

■ **How to Track.** In much of your promotion, you can build in a "key." Then just look for the key to track each promotion. Here are the various types of keys:

Extension Numbers: After the phone number in each promotion, place a nonexistent extension number. Each extension number keys a different ad. These can also be changed to key a specific ad in a specific medium. *Example:* Ext. 4 keys the contact lens ad running in the

Socket City Sentinel. When the caller asks for ext. 4, your front office simply marks the code in the appointment book next to the person's name. Also include it in the file and on your tracking sheet.

Dedicated Phone Lines: If you have several infrequently used lines, you may key your promotion with the number from a specific line. Therefore, when someone calls on that line, you know exactly how they heard of you. But ask anyway. The problem is that if they're rotary lines and the person calls when other lines are busy, the system spills over onto your dedicated lines.

Coupon/Certificate Code: Oftentimes, you can place a small letter and/or number code at the bottom of a coupon or certificate. Different coupons and media should have different codes. Val-Pak needs a different code from ADVO. Therefore, when they call in because of a coupon, your receptionist should ask *then and there* what the code is. If you wait to have them bring it in before finding out, you lose because many will forget it.

Mailing Label Key Code: In stand-alone direct mail, it's possible to place a code above the name of the mailing label. Just tell the list broker to key code your labels when you order them. Then ask the caller for the key code on the label and you'll know the source. It's also possible to key different lists differently. Suppose you're mailing to seniors and to females 40 to 55 years old with a household income over $25,000. By keying the labels differently, you'll know which group pulls better right away.

■ **If There's No Code Built In.** But such of the time it's impossible to build in a distinctive key. In that case you still track because it's imperative.

First, the front desk *must* ask each new inquiry on the phone how they heard about you.

■ If they're looking at an ad, ask them what paper it's in.

■ If it's *Yellow Pages*, ask what page they're looking at.

■ If it's direct mail, ask them to describe the envelope.

■ If it's radio, ask which station or, if they don't know, ask them to describe the format.

■ If it's TV, ask the station or the program.

But above all, *ask!* If you wait until they come in, many will have forgotten. How many? Perhaps 30% or more. And another 30% unintentionally will give you inaccurate information. Now you're really in a fix trying to make $10,000, $50,000, even $100,000 decisions based on insanity.

What happens if your staff misses getting a caller's source? *They call them back!* What should you do if you still can't get it? Have the front desk ask when they first come in. Keep samples of your ads behind the front desk as well as covers to all *Yellow Pages* your ad is in.

- Ask: "Did you see this ad or this ad?"
- Or while showing the covers of *Yellow Pages*, ask: "Did you find us in this *Yellow Pages* or this one?"

What should you do if your front desk won't ask callers? First of all, it should never get to that point. The front desk really does want to help. They just need to understand the absolute importance of tracking. Explain it fully. Explain the serious consequences of not tracking. Explain the upside of tracking. And explain how they'll benefit by it at bonus time.

Then if you receive a file without a source code or key, refuse to see the patient until the front desk gets it. This staunch, behavior-shaping rule will do the trick *fast*.

■ **Testing the Right Way.** No one knows the optimal placement or timing of a specific promotion beforehand. You can make fairly good guesses, but there are so many unknown variables in every market that the only way to be RIGHT is to test. And tracking allows you to know the test results.

If you're running newspaper ads, move the ads around in different sections of the paper. Test different days. Test different papers. Some sections will get good results; some bad. Some papers will get great results; some will not. Only testing and tracking will give you the answers.

And don't test just once. Because of the possibilities of bad placement, busy news days and a thousand other things, you'll need to test four to six insertions of the ad to know if it's working. If it's not pulling by then, pull the ad out of that section and test elsewhere.

If you're using a co-op coupon, you'll need to test at least two insertions, sometimes three, before evaluating a specific coupon deck and coupon. Results are often uneven from time to time so multiple insertions are required for your numbers to be meaningful.

■ **THE PRACTICE BUILDER Tracking Sheet.** Following is a tracking sheet which your front desk should fill out as the calls come in. Please reproduce it and use a different sheet for *each medium and ad*. Then tally monthly. It's self-explanatory.

■ **How to Evaluate Your Numbers.** As explained above, in promotion there's only one number that means anything at all—return on investment (ROI). Period. That's the number of dollars a specific effort generates divided by the cost of that effort.

If your ROI is greater than one, you're over break-even. Actually you're a little under since you haven't factored in the costs to provide your services and products. But still it's showing promise, so tinkering is in order.

At an ROI of three or four to one, you're starting to look pretty healthy. Over five to one and you've got *a real winner*.

Don't forget the repeat business and word-of-mouth that's also coming. These make anything over a one-and-a-half to one worthwhile.

■ **A Final Thought.** Remember, you can't take "I think the ad should do well in this paper" to the bank. You can only take "I know. . . ."

☐ TRACKING THE RIGHT SOURCE

Scenario: Someone calls in, the front desk asks how he or she heard of the practice, and the caller lists three sources like a friend, *Yellow Pages* and the newspaper.

Your Dilemma: For the purpose of tracking and figuring return on investment (ROI) by source, which one gets the credit?

The answer: The *last* source that actually got the caller to finally pick up the phone. Several sources may have influenced a person, but the analysis of factor interplay is far too complex. You never know how much of each played a role.

And if you do play that game, you start spending scarce resources on virtually *untrackable* sources. And that's a sure fire way to throw your marketing budget out the window—quickly—and drive down your ROI.

So even if giving the credit to the *last* source isn't a perfect system, it's *by far* the safest.

THE PRACTICE BUILDER
TRACKING SHEET

Media Source: _____Key or Source

Code: _____

Appeared in Which Section of

Media: _____

Headline: _____

Date	Name	Date of 1st Appt.	Appt. Kept?	Total $ Generated Through End of Service	Comments

A. Total $ Generated:	$
B. Cost of this Promotion during this period:	$
C. Return on Investment (A/B=C):	$

PROMOTIONS IN MOTION

1. Surveys are critical to finding out what's wrong in a practice so you can fix it—and what's right so you can keep doing it. But mailed surveys get awfully low response rates and the information is therefore incomplete and suspect.

   But veterinarian V.L. uses a surefire way to get this valuable information. He prints the questionnaire on the back of a $1 check.

   In a short cover letter he asks for their cooperation and tells them the check is not to reimburse them for their time, since he knows their time is more valuable than that. It's a token of his appreciation.

   His response rate is 92%.

2. Optometrist G.F. thought he should analyze exactly where his referrals were coming from. What he discovered was many came from local learning and study centers. With the concept in mind of pushing his winners, G.F. developed a direct mail campaign targeted just to centers to pave the way for phone follow-ups and personal visits. He emphasized his results with kids who have had "learning problems." Now he's expanding the concept into his quarterly letters to his patient base by encouraging parents to bring in kids in need for testing. Now he's developing special letters for psychologists, pediatricians, GPs and FPs.

3. A Northeastern psychotherapy group has done the same referral analysis and found their number one referral source was internists. So off they went to their typewriters to bang out a special direct mail letter to all the area internists. Plus they had a special brochure created just for them. Their comments: "It was very satisfying," psychologically speaking, of course. (Cash flow wasn't bad either.)

4. A Miami doctor recently began attracting Cuban patients to his practice. He didn't know why, so to find out he held a focus group, a consumer research group led by an experienced leader who asks open-ended questions to discover the unknown.

   He invited those Cuban patients who were already referring, figuring them to be concerned enough to come. What he discovered was the usual: *What they liked about him and what they didn't.* Plus he learned a variety of *cultural tips to make Cubans more comfortable* in the practice.

   "This was an eye-opening experience. If you want to know how you're perceived and what problems you have and don't even know about, a focus group is the way to go. And if you're the type who knows something is wrong but just hasn't gotten around to fixing it, you will as soon as you hear how they blow you out of the water about it. This sure beats patient surveys."

Chapter 3 ☐

PUTTING YOURSELF ON TOP BY PROMOTING WHO YOU ARE

☐ THE MOST IMPORTANT THINGS TO PROMOTE ABOUT YOURSELF

What you communicate about yourself makes the most difference in the response to any promotion. In fact, it's the essence of the message. The message's form, or the *how,* is also important, but form with the wrong essence just doesn't produce. However, you can get a fair response if you have the right essence with little form.

What then are these essential messages that people find irresistible? Recent research into how new area residents look and decide on a dentist sheds light for all professionals. What's interesting in the findings is that much of the information wanted by people is *not* what they get from professionals' promotion.

■ **Essential Messages.** Here are the percentages of those surveyed who rated these subjective and objective factors as:

Very Important or Important:

Quality	99.3%
Concern for Patients or Clients	97.2%
Friendliness	78.6%
Time Spent Waiting in Office	75.7%
Office Hours	73.8%
Waiting Time to Get Appointment	72.6%

Whether Office Prepares Insurance Forms	65.5%
Personal Appearance of Professional	64.9%
Price	58.5%
Physical Location	58.3%

Now study the less important factors:

Number of Years Experience	44.3%
Office Atmosphere	44.0%
Whether Office Provides Credit	41.5%
Professional Association Memberships	32.1%
Professional School Attended	16.9%
Whether Office Accepts Credit Cards	15.9%

Wow!!! The implications are enormous. For instance, in your *Yellow Pages* ad simply address the top list and ignore the bottom. In fact, in any promotion, this becomes a strong guideline since it puts your best foot forward—as defined by the only people who really matter.

Also interesting is people's desire to see the professional beforehand. This argues strongly for a photo in all promotion.

Caution! When you make a claim, you better prove it or else it won't be believed and you'll blow your credibility.

For instance, you can't just say that you do quality work; you must support it. You can use years of experience, memberships, school attended, amount of continuing ed and so forth to *help prove* this claim. But you can't put these out there alone and expect someone to make the connection with quality. Lead the reader by the hand.

More research needs to be done, but this study not only points you in the right direction, it puts you 20 paces ahead of your colleagues.

JADA, Vol. 112, p. 840-843, 6/86, ADA, Chicago, IL and THE PRACTICE BUILDER

☐ 27 WAYS TO DIFFERENTIATE YOURSELF

It used to be that all physicians, all dentists, all podiatrists, all whatever were all alike. Or so the professional associations would have everyone think. And with public information restricted, they were able to pull it off. But not so today. The public's wised up fast.

Now the public wants to know—demands to know—*why they should choose you* and not one of your competitors. They look for the answer in the *Yellow Pages*, in fact in any external promotion. And the professional who best answers the question is the one who wins this game in a big way.

Why so big? Because few professionals even know this game exists and even fewer know how to play well. But you can because here's 27 ways to differentiate yourself *meaningfully.* Your not-so-impossible mission—if you choose to accept it—is to pick those that best *excite your market.* (Notice it's not the ones that best fit you or excite you the most.) So get out your pencil and start checking and prioritizing.

- ☐ Quick relief
- ☐ Quick service
- ☐ Great experience
- ☐ Specialization
- ☐ Great expertise in a certain area
- ☐ Caring (Remember, you must *prove* each claim with specifics for it to be believable!)
- ☐ Affordable
- ☐ Save people money
- ☐ Convenient hours
- ☐ Convenient location
- ☐ You come to them for their convenience
- ☐ You cater to a particular type of person, income level or size or type of business
- ☐ High technology
- ☐ Aggressive
- ☐ Conservative
- ☐ Beauty- or fashion-oriented
- ☐ Colleagues or other respected people use you
- ☐ Highly credentialled
- ☐ You're an author ("Now You Can Go to the Professional Who Wrote the Book")
- ☐ You teach ("Why Go to One of His Students When Now You Can Go to the Professor?")
- ☐ Gentle
- ☐ Famous
- ☐ You're one of the "guys"
- ☐ Individualized service (Again remember, you must prove this claim with specifics.)
- ☐ Specialize in fearful people
- ☐ Modern
- ☐ You have a family tradition of service in your profession

■ **Making Your Claims Stick.** If you just say it and don't back it up in your copy, forget it. People aren't stupid and they don't buy empty claims. So prove them all. Support them. Missourians have the right idea—"Show me!"

   Example: On a caring claim, never say *"I care."* Instead, talk about how you're the MD who'll get to know them. That you know that in medicine many symptoms come from emotional situations and lifestyle. So the more thoroughly the doctor knows you, often the better the diagnosis.

That's the reason you take so much time getting to know a new patient. So don't expect a quick in and out. In fact, your average new patient's first visit takes over an hour. It's an investment you make in their health. So when someone chooses a doctor, doesn't it make sense to choose the one who gets to know you? That's good medicine.

Plus, you bill their insurance for them because your staff cares. You have Tuesday night hours because you're concerned about those who work all day. (Lots and lots and lots of support!)

Use facts, figures and personal quotes of philosophy. Specifics, specifics, specifics. If you do that, you'll be the next big winner.

☐ YOUR CREDENTIALS: QUANTITY VS. QUALITY

You know how professionals are always using credentials to impress prospects? But are they doing it optimally? You judge:

Arthur Sims, MD
Board Certified

or

Melvin Gluckstein, MD,
FACOG, ABLS, CRT, ABDS, MRA, NOGC,
NBA, NRA, BSA, AMA, CMA, OCMA.

The first guy may be better qualified, but the public would never know it. After all, they can't appreciate the quality of credentials, only the quantity. The second guy loves to pay dues, but the public thinks he's a winner.

☐ EASY AUTHORING FOR HARD-TO-GET CREDIBILITY

Of course she was good, but most people didn't take their troubled teens to psychologist M.R. The problem—she looked like every other psychologist. But she did become THE name in her town for treating acting out adolescents. And what made the difference was that in their eyes, she became an expert.

How? M.R. wrote a 36-page pamphlet on why teens can run into trouble and how she treats them. Entitled *How to Make Your Teen a Member of Your Family Again*, it's liberally sprinkled with case histories to prove her contentions and which display her effectiveness.

Then she offered parents a free copy in her Yellow Pages and newspaper ads. Her headline: "Now You Can See the Therapist Who Wrote the Book on Troubled Teens." The *Yellow Pages* ROI jumped to 26:1 and her newspaper promotion to 17:1.

■ **How to Become an Instant Author.** It's simple. Pick a problem of which you want to see more. Write a 24+ page whatever. Use your own experience plus info from journals and texts. (See Figure 3.1.)

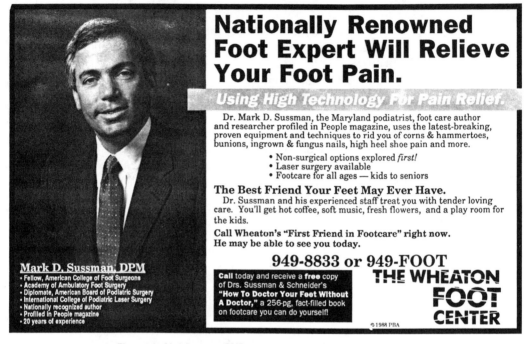

Figure 3.1—Mark Sussman, DMP

Then edit, edit, edit. Proof, proof, proof. And have an editor or writer edit and proof it again. Get a local desktop publishing shop to lay it out for you and send it to a competitively-bid printer. Now you're an author! And you're credible.

Then offer a free copy of your pearls of wisdom in all your external and internal promotion. More prospects will choose you because of your expertise. And existing patients or clients will revere you more and refer more.

☐ **PROVING EXCELLENT SERVICE BY GUARANTEEING IT**

These days every professional says they care and everyone says they provide great service. And let's not forget the claim of personalized service. Well here's a flash bulletin—*no one believes any of these!*

The reason is that no professional proves them—until now. Veterinarian H.T. thought of the idea when he went to his local bank which had just started *guaranteeing* great service. Then he got serious about it when the next day, he went to his dentist and waited 45 minutes. And then felt he was charged too much.

It made H.T. reflect on what was going on in his practice. So he took the bank's program and modified it to fit his clientele. After all, the bank's in the service business and so is he.

Historically, whenever a guarantee's been tested in controlled-variable studies to find the best ways to promote, it's usually won hands down. So over time, sophisticated marketing pros have come to include a guarantee as standard fare wherever possible. People trust those who offer a guarantee and trust is *the* name of the game in professional services.

■ **Guaranteeing Great Service.** In order to guarantee service, you've first got to *define service*. Then you've got to figure out what the *consequence* will be if you don't perform. Then *train your staff* to provide the services to the degree guaranteed. And finally promote the guarantees both *inside* the practice to retain your present patients or clients and *outside* to attract new ones. Here's what H.T. designed:

Courteous, Personal Service. Guaranteed. You'll always be treated with respect, thanked for your patronage and called by your name. If you feel we've failed in any way or you've been treated unfairly, just talk to the doctor. You'll receive an apology and a $5 credit to compensate you for your inconvenience.

Prompt Service. Guaranteed. Whenever you call the office, we'll answer your call in four rings or less. If not, you'll receive an apology and a $5 credit to compensate you for the inconvenience.

Convenient Service. Guaranteed. We'll give you an appointment within 24 hours so you'll never be concerned about getting in to see us. If not, you'll receive an apology and a $5 credit to compensate you for the inconvenience.

Quick Service. Guaranteed. If you wait more than 10 minutes, we'll buy you coffee and give you one of our special mugs for the inconvenience.

Credits can be used for professional services and products. The limit on credits is $25 per year per client. (The limit is imposed to control any abusers of the program.)

■ **Promotion.** Promoting your guarantees in-house binds your existing patients or clients more tightly to you and slows the erosion of your base. The reason it's so critical to emphasize retention is the incredible cost to recruit new patients or clients. So use tabletop promotions (table tents) and an 8½" × 11", two-fold flyer about your guarantees for your waiting room. Also promote them in your quarterly Internal Prospecting Direct Mail program.

Plus, promote the program on the phone. When your front desk answers a call, have them announce the name of the office and add: "... where we guarantee excellent service." The word will get out fast.

To reach beyond your existing clientele, your guarantee program should become part of your *Yellow Pages* ad and any newspaper, magazine or direct mail promotion you do. You needn't talk about all the details in external promotion. Just that the program exists and that the reason is to prove how confident you are that the reader will be satisfied.

Of course, don't mention a cure or results which you aren't guaranteeing and is illegal in most states and provinces.

■ **Results.** H.T. quickly noticed several effects of his guarantee program. The staff worked harder to provide what he promoted. With all the noise in the practice about excellent service—especially on the phone—it was on their minds all the time. Also, every time the practice gave out a coffee mug or a $5 credit, it went on a sheet in the employee lounge area. The constant feedback helped employees monitor their own behavior.

Fewer patients *left the practice* because fewer mishandlings occurred so the gross went up. Plus, they *converted many more phone shoppers* who asked about the guarantee. And *Yellow Pages response climbed* when the guarantee was added to the practice's ad.

Last, when H.T. *raised his fees*, he felt there was less resistance. In fact, he's now realigned his pricing to become among the highest in his area without suffering shrinkage in the overall number of patients or clients. It seems people will pay for quality and they define *service as quality*, not technical ability.

Guarantees work because they're the mark of confidence. And they prove the usually unsupported and unbelievable claims of excellent service. Since real service is such a strong draw, it makes sense to find a way to promote it convincingly. Bingo!

☐ **HOW TO SHOW PEOPLE YOU REALLY CARE—AND HAVE THEM BELIEVE IT**

Another study, this one by the Rockefeller Foundation, also surveyed why people leave their professionals discovered:

■   14% left because complaints weren't taken care of;

■   9% because of competition;

■   9% moved;

■   and 68% left because of ... no special reason!

Three Major Reasons You Lose Patients or Clients

A riveting study recently revealed that people won't leave you because of your proficiency—but instead will split because of your failure as a *manager*. So if you've been counting on "quality work" to keep 'em from fleeing, better redirect.

The three most common answers given as to why people leave professionals are:

1. *Overbearing staff:* the front desk or an assistant, but not you.

2. *Improper explanation of fees:* not the fees themselves. But if they understood what they're being charged for, why, and the value of the services, then no problem.

3. *Waiting too long:* if you don't treat them and their time as important, they're gone.

A phone call to those who don't return will quickly point out your people's reasons. Just tell them you're trying to improve your practice and ask.

That means almost seven out of ten abandoned you because: (1) You didn't tell them you cared; (2) You didn't make them feel special; (3) You didn't keep in touch; and (4) You took them for granted.

But if you were to ask 1,000 professionals why people should choose them rather than a competitor, 1,000 would answer "Because I care more." (In fact, *your* competitors answer in exactly the same way.)

The real problem is that while professionals might feel that way, they *don't show it*. And the bigger problem is that patients or clients *never perceive it*. So they don't know it ... and wouldn't believe it even if you said it. They've got to have proof!

■ **Showing Them.** Here's how family practitioner I.M. shows his concern so they actually notice it.

1. Patients fret about sitting in waiting rooms for an inordinate amount of time. So I.M. lets his patients know that he values their time as much as they do. His office calls if they're running late to let people know by how much. If they don't reach them or if they wait more than 20 minutes, he apologizes and gives you a VIP pass to General Cinema. It's the thought that counts. It's a nice thought and it works.

2. He guarantees their satisfaction.

3. He provides a courtesy phone for local calls while people wait.

4. His refreshment list includes chilled bottled water, coffee and several soft drinks.

5. He's creatively affordable with four ways to pay: 10% courtesy for advanced payment; interest-free monthly payments for nearly a year on approved credit; layaway plan with no credit check needed; or pay as you go with cash, MasterCard, Visa, check or most insurance plans.

6. He's responsive by always seeing emergencies the same day.

7. He always answers phone inquiries regarding insurance, treatment planning, or anything else by the next business day or sooner.

Isn't this the way Mercedes Benz, Infiniti, and Lexus treat people to get repeat buyers? Here are more ways:

1. Follow-up by phone later in the day if the patient or client has received uncomfortable service earlier. The call is not only to uncover problems, but *to reassure them* that everything's going to be all right. They'll be astonished you called.

2. Touch your patient or client in some way. Men and women. On the shoulder, on the forearm. Your touch is worth several hundred words.

3. Look them directly and intently in the eye. This lets the person *know* you understand. Then nod your head up and down. This tells them you not only know, but you're on their side. It makes people like you.

4. Optometrist L.C. has his front desk ask each patient for two things at the end of each visit: (1) Is there one more thing we can do for you? (2) Please rate us on a scale of 1 to 10. He gets lots of compliments and some good information. But above all, it keeps everyone on their toes.

5. Convenient hours work in today's working world. Take a day, start it early (and end early). Take another, end late (and start late). Take another, work through lunchtime (and take a late lunch). Add a Saturday morning once or twice a month (and take an additional half-day off during the week). Then make sure you put a sign in the waiting room not only telling people of your new hours, but also that you're doing it for their convenience.

All of this is *in addition to* a smiling and courteous staff which isn't nearly enough in these sizzlingly competitive times. People simply expect more.

Remember: Caring is not just being available. Caring is taking the initiative *with tangible services.*

☐ POWERFUL POSITIONS

How you position yourself is the one thing you want people to remember about you if they can only remember one thing. And the reason this is so important? Because, if you're really lucky, people who don't use you will remember *one* thing about you. If you're not lucky, you're relegated to oblivion.

There are all sorts of positions: experienced; specialist; affordable; convenient; etc. But of them, a few rise above the weeds in most markets.

For instance, *family tradition*. If your father or uncle was there before you, your family's longevity in the area makes people feel comfortable with you. They'll reason, "Your family must be good to have prospered in the area for so long. And besides that they're our kind of people."

Or if you've been in the media like radio, TV, or the newspapers, then you're famous. Or if famous people use you, then you're truly good.

Or if you've won an award. Of course people want to use an award-winning professional.

■ Spreading the Word.

And how do you let everyone know? By putting your positioning everywhere. As a tagline after your name. On your business card and stationary. In your logo. On your office sign. In the headline of your *Yellow Pages* ad. Everywhere.

And if you're really lucky, people who don't use you will remember this *one* thing about you. And when they need your services, you'll be at the top of the list.

☐ PUTTING THE PERSONAL TOUCH IN A GROUP PRACTICE

Yes. Groups, institutes, clinics, and centers often convey an impersonal feeling, yet people overwhelmingly like to believe in a specific person. So it makes sense to have a lead practitioner out front as *the* personality of the group.

This is the person who people can like and respect. The person who'll make sure everything will turn out all right for them.

This doesn't mean that this is the person they'll see. If the promotion is done correctly, it'll convey that the way this person practices is the way everyone here practices. Or that this person is responsible for setting and maintaining quality standards, so the prospect can rest assured. (See Figure 3.2.)

New in Davenport

Lives Dedicated to Pain Relief & Wellness

New Chiropractic Specialists in Davenport

Dr. John Whitney is well-known in the chiropractic profession both as a dedicated proctitioner and as a professional trainer of chiropractic doctors. Since beginning practice in 1958, he has helped many thousands of patients and trained hundreds of chiropractic professionals.

Now he has opened his doors in Davenport with a staff of top palmer chiropractic graduates dedicated to chiropractic and total wellness.

A Team of Skilled Palmer Graduate Professionals

With your health in the hands of The Whitney Chiropractic Group, you can be assured that the most effective methods are being used to end your pain.

Each member of the team is a handpicked professional who has met the following qualifications:

☑ Graduated in top of postgraduate class
☑ Keeps up with current state-of-the-art
☑ Socially concerned
☑ Caring personality
☑ Enjoys treating infants to seniors
☑ Dedicated to total health

Our Services Include

- **Applied Kinesiology**
- **Expert Accident & Worker's Comp. Treatment**
- **Activator Technique**
- **Nutritional Counseling**
- **Motion Palpation**

Over and Above Your Treatment: The Extra Touch of Concern

Relief of your pain and discomfort is our first priority. But frankly, that is not quite enough. Robust health is more than being pain-free.

More vigor, reduced stress, improved energy, less fatigue, more flexibility, better sleep. That is what "wellness" is all about.

After your symptoms are gone, we will help you feel like your old self again.

We now know that at age 60 you can have the vigor, body, and vitality of a 30 year old. Studies at the University of California confirm this.

Sincerely,

Whitney, S.C.

We Don't Want You to Worry About Cost

☑ We take most insurance plans, and Worker's Comp. Plus, we'll fill out the insurance forms and file them for you.
☑ If you do not have insurance, we can arrange for one of several types of payment plans.
☑ Please do not hesitate to call just because you do not know if you can afford treatment. We can usually work it out.

Whitney Chiropractic Group
at Davenport
Dedicated to Your Good Health
2310 Jersey Ridge Road

For an immediate no-cost exam and consultation (not including X-rays) call today:

355-2324
Appointments
7 days a week
©1988 PBA

Figure 3.2— Ad Demonstrating "The Extra Touch of Concern"

Even so, some people will come in and expect to see the lead. (Not everyone reads or listens as carefully as you want.) In these cases, just explain that the lead is unavailable, but his or her associate, who is just as skilled and competent, will take care of them. Yes, some will still be miffed—but they'll see the associate and then they'll rarely be miffed anymore.

So don't let this "problem" stop you from using a spokesperson, because there is no problem.

Also, don't select a spokesperson democratically. Egalitarianism has no place in promotion. Instead choose the person the market will most like and respect from a photo. Remember: The marketplace is cruel to people who don't please it.

☐ TAGGING YOURSELF AS THE PRACTICE OF CHOICE

If most professionals have a common blind spot in marketing, it's the failure to differentiate themselves from the competition. How you differentiate has been discussed above, but once you decide on what differentiates you, how do you communicate it?

For one thing, your major differentiation (also called your positioning) must appear everywhere you promote: logo; business cards; stationary; office sign; *Yellow Pages* ad; practice brochure; direct mail; co-op coupons; newspaper, magazine and shopper ads; billboards—whatever.

Some practices put their positioning in their name: The Pain Relief Center of Masonville. But oftentimes, you don't want to use a fictitious name because people like to buy specific people. It makes more sense to promote yourself, or both partners, or a single lead professional in a group as the group representative. You then practice under your own name, but you also add the positioning in a tagline.

The tagline then follows your name everywhere and tags you as the practice of choice. Remember: Your tagline says the one thing you want people to remember about you. Examples:

Caring is what we do best

We treat your whole family...gently

All babies handled special delivery

For all a woman's health needs

The art and science of beautiful skin

☐ THE UPDATED WAITING ROOM RESUME

What do your patients or clients know about you? (1) How long you've kept them waiting. (2) Your deskside, chairside, or bedside manner. (3) If you hurt them. (4) How much you charged. And that's about it.

You could be the best trained, most respected professional in your field ... and they wouldn't have the foggiest idea. (Actually, you needn't be the best to be respected since most patients or clients don't know enough to make qualitative comparisons.)

But to receive referrals, you need to be perceived as an expert *and* that impression needs to be repeated umpteen times. But how can you achieve that without bragging to their face?

■ **The Waiting Room Resume.** In a past issue, THE PRACTICE BUILDER recommended a waiting room resume displayed in a Plexiglass stand. After all, while they wait, people are a bored, captive audience.

But in addition to a waiting room display, many PRACTICE BUILDER members now report they *also hand a resume directly* to the patient or client when they first walk in. So when they get to the professional, they're already impressed. *Very savvy.*

Remember: Write your resume for RPs—Real People. And write as if you were talking to Martians; otherwise they won't understand. Short words. Short phrases. And no $25 technical words. Here's a fictitious sample. (See Figure 3.3.)

Figure 3.3—A Sample Resume

Arthur Sherwin, PhD
Licensed Psychologist, Certified School Psychologist, Registered Psychologist, APA, MPA, HFS, AAP, MA, BA

Former Asst. and Assoc. Professor of Psychology

Colby College
University of Connecticut

Honored Numerous Times

Past President and Ethics Chairman, Maine Psychological Association
Elected to Psi Chi, National Honorary Society in Psychology
Certificate of Recognition, Federal Aviation Administration

Award of Appreciation, Maine Dept. of Mental Health
Appointed, Maine State Board of Examiners of Psychologists
Appointed, Governor's Mental Health Advisory Council

A Sought After Consultant

Federal Aviation Administration, Eastern Region
Children's Development Project, Mid-Maine Medical Center
Industrial Medicine Program, Redington-Fairview General
Hospital
Office of Biological & Behavioral Sciences, FAA
Five major grants and contracts

Involved

"Everyday Parenting" Newsletter, Reviewer
Kennebec Valley Voc. Tech. Nursing Program, Advisor
State Task Force on Rights of Recipients of Mental Health
Services
Ken-a-Set Association, Bd. of Directors
Help, Inc., Bd. of Directors
Waterville Drug Abuse Council

Author & Media Personality

17 authored articles in respected professional journals
Numerous film, TV, and radio appearances including WCBB,
WMEB, WTOS, and Maine Public Broadcasting

☐ WAITING ROOM RESUME ANALYSIS

Here's an excellent waiting room resume designed to teach people how brilliant this professional is and to generate word-of-mouth referrals. First notice the use of descriptive words in the subheads:

A WELL-ROUNDED EDUCATION

CONTINUING THE SEARCH FOR NEW AND BETTER THERAPY TECHNIQUES

IMPRESSIVE WORK EXPERIENCE, ACTIVE IN HER PROFESSION.

No dry, stand-alone, academic terms here.

Second, see how the writer uses quotes below each head, not only to reinforce the headline's idea, but also to make the professional real and likeable.

A nice photo, good layout, professional typefaces and clean graphics complete this terrific piece. (See Figure 3.4.)

Vanessa L. Reed, P.T.

A WELL-ROUNDED EDUCATION

"I attained a degree in Health Science as well as Physical Therapy, so I could utilize a comprehensive approach with my physical therapy patients."

B.S. in Health Science, Boise State University, Boise, ID, 1979
M.S. in Physical Therapy, Texas Women's University, Houston, TX, 1982

CONTINUING THE SEARCH FOR NEW AND BETTER THERAPY TECHNIQUES

"In an ideal situation, the therapist should use a combination of tried-and-true manual techniques with the latest in precision therapeutic equipment. I've attended classes and workshops that not only enhance my technical skills, but my evaluative skills as well."

"Manual Therapy Techniques for the Neck," Dale Hoistad, P.T., 1986
"Muscle Energy Techniques for the Lubosacral Spine," Allyn Woerman, Ph.D., Steven Stratton, P.T., 1987
Cybex Training Program, LaCrosse, WI, 1987

IMPRESSIVE WORK EXPERIENCE

"My professional experiences up to this point have allowed me to work with all sorts of patients, from arthritis conditions to knee and chronic back conditions. But the one thing that I learned was that no two patients are alike."

Staff Physical Therapist/Development Coordinator, Idaho Elks Rehabilitation Hospital, Boise, ID, 1984-1988
Staff Physical Therapist, Acute Care, Mercy Medical Center, Nampa, ID, 1984
Staff Physical Therapist, Acute Care, Idaho Falls Consolidated Hospital, Idaho Falls, ID, 1982-83

ACTIVE IN HER PROFESSION

"As with all my associates, I like to stay in touch with the profession through regular meetings and activities. Peers are an invaluable source of new information."

Member, American Physical Therapy Association
Member, Idaho Physical Therapy Association

Figure 3.4—A Waiting Room Resume

☐ WAITING ROOM RESUME ANALYSIS II

Your resume is for display in an upright Plexiglass holder in your waiting room and for giving to new patients or clients.

This is another fine execution of the waiting room resume strategy to position you as an expert so people will feel comfortable referring more. The subheads either make you respect or like him. The quotes beneath the subheads personalize each. And there's proof to support

DR. LAWRENCE H. COPPOCK, JR., OD

Respected teacher, writer and lecturer
"I want to use my knowledge and experience to help others do a better job."

<u>Faculty Member</u>, University of Houston, College of Optometry, 1981-1984
<u>Assistant Professor</u>, Pennsylvania College of Optometry 1985 - present
<u>Lecturer</u>, Newman College, Delaware County Community College
<u>Professional Scientific Articles on Contact Lenses</u>, Review of Optometry, 1988

Meeting the high standards of his peers
"Membership in these organizations lets me gain insight into events which are shaping the future of optometry."

<u>Member</u>, American Optometric Association
<u>Member</u>, Pennsylvania Optometric Association
<u>Member</u>, Chester/Delaware County Optometric Society
<u>Member</u>, International Contact Lens Conference

Serving his country
"It's a privilege to contribute to my country's well-being and at the same time continue to care for people who depend on me to see."

<u>Head of Optometry Section</u>, U.S. Navy, Regional Medical Clinic, 1981-1984
<u>Member</u>, Armed Forces Optometric Society, 1981-1984.
<u>Optometrist</u>, Naval Reserve Fleet Hospital, Philadelphia, 1985 - Present

Involved in better care
"To me, a challenge is an opportunity to do something better, and my work is filled with challenges."

<u>Graduate,</u> Bachelor of Arts, Gettysburg College, 1976
<u>Winner</u>, Armed Forces Health Professions Scholarship, 1979
<u>Internship</u>, Naval Medical Center, Orlando, FL, 1980
<u>OD</u>, Pennsylvania College of Optometry, 1981
<u>Licensed Optometrist</u>, State of New Jeresy, 1981 - present
<u>Licensed Optometrist</u>, State of Pennsylvania, 1981 - present

A nationally recognized expert in the field of contact lenses, Dr. Coppock has performed clinical studies in the development of new contact lens plastics for the U.S. Food and Drug Administration. In addition to his demonstrated expertise in contact lens fitting, Dr. Coppock's contributions to his community make him a valued resident of Cheyney, Thornbury Township

Figure 3.5—A Sample Waiting Room Resume

each claim. Note how he didn't throw in every conceivable credential. Only the most powerful *from the point of view of real people, not colleagues.*

The professionally taken photo makes him look as if he's worthy of respect. That's the right kind.

Promotions In Motion

1. Physical therapist T.K. didn't know how to differentiate herself from her competitors in a believable way. Everyone was claiming quality work, individual attention, etc. All of which were tough to prove so no one paid attention to them.

   Then she had a brainstorm. She positioned her clinic as "The Doctors' Choice." With so many physicians already referring to her, it was an easy claim to prove. She was then perceived as endorsed by an entire profession.

   In the absence of conflicting information, the professional who makes the claim, owns the claim.

   "The Doctors' Choice" became her *Yellow Pages* headline and was the lead idea in her brochure, stationery, and business cards.

2. Veterinarian V.S. did a Waiting Room Resume to inform all comers about how good he is and to raise their referrals. But V.S. blew up his resume to 20" × 26", matted it on foamcore and hung it on his waiting room wall. You just can't miss it, nor be impressed by his training, credentials, special services, etc. And as the size of the resume jumped, so did referrals.

3. Psychologist T.H. is successfully targeting a new niche—people's un-controlled spending. And the way she's going about it is interesting. Yes, there's the expected PR stints: radio and TV talk shows and a free seminar promoted by newspaper called "How to $top $pending $o Much Money and Regain Control of Yourself." But she's also mailing heavily to CPAs asking for a face-to-face meeting to educate them that help for their clients is available—and she's that help.

4. In his newspaper ads, ophthalmologist F.S. is heavily promoting the relief of dry eye using his reimbursable argon laser procedure and collagen implants. Another key is his work with optometrists to get them to refer their dry eye cases to him. He positions himself as an expert in the condition and points out how ODs can get reimbursed for testing before referring out a contact-lens-caused case. Gross is up over 30% in just three months.

5. Optometrist P.L. promoted contact lenses like most other ODs. But he never really hit pay dirt until he rented a Department of Motor Vehicles list of near- and far-sighted people. Now he could clearly target his market with direct mail and avoid buying the wasted coverage of newspapers, co-op coupons, or broadcast media.

   Another case: To diversify from the shrinking reimbursements of the cataract market, ophthalmologist R.S. has been promoting radial keratotomy (RK). Now he also uses this same direct mail strategy. (Note: The availability of this glasses and contacts list varies by state.)

6. Along the same lines chiropractic physician T.M. reads the daily local newspaper to find out who's been injured in an auto accident. Then he mails them a letter talking about how he has special expertise in this area. His return on investment is 40:1.

   Quirk: His state law says you cannot solicit individuals for treatment but you can solicit a class of people. This is a very strange edict, yet common in many states. But his letter's salutation of "Dear Injured Neighbor," rather than using the prospect's name meets the criteria of the law.

7. Ophthalmologist L.M. understands that people don't always comprehend everything the first time they hear it. Especially when surgery is involved and emotions fly high. So for those who don't commit even though they need cataract surgery, L.M. holds a monthly, follow-up pancake breakfast. Here L.M.'s staff goes over everything in reassuring tones, uncovering and answering all sorts of misconceptions and concerns. And the practice's *Cataract Support Group* of past patients talk of their own pleasant experiences. Out of 11 attendees at the last breakfast, two have committed with more on the way. Return on investment—19:1.

8. Optometrist P.W. has parking meters galore near her office. So whenever she passes an expired meter on the way to lunch, she plops in a quarter. Then P.W. places a promotional piece printed to look like a parking ticket beneath a windshield wiper. It reads:

   This is not a parking ticket. I happened to walk by your car and noticed your meter was running out or had done so. To help you avoid the expense of a $15 parking ticket, I've taken the liberty of putting a little money in the meter for you. Compliments of (name, address, and phone.)

   Imagine how you would feel if someone did that for you. Astonished! And grateful!! You should see the thank you cards and calls...and patients. What a productive $300 to $400 per year promotion.

9. Dentist T.O. is providing that extra added bit of service for his upwardly mobile clientele. He's installed a phone in a quiet area of the

waiting room and invites his patients to use it for local calls. (Long distance calls are blocked.)

This way they don't object to waiting if they can accomplish something in the meantime. And it says that T.O. values and respects his patients' time.

10. Psychologist L.R. knows that people don't like to make decisions. They're risk aversive. So she's made it as easy and low risk as you can get. L.R. offers a full refund of a patient's first three visits if they're not satisfied.

    Yes, she has given one refund, but she's also attracted about twice as many people as she formerly did. "If I can just get them in, I know they're mine."

11. Veterinarian H.T. is a hot-shot marketer. Here's some of his tips: Always mention in your promotions aviary services if you provide them because few small animal doctors do. Also say you take difficult cases to attract that kind of business and build the aura of an expert.

    H.T.'s got a convenient (and busy) drive-through window for buying pet supplies. Plus a drop-off reception cage in the back where people can leave their pets early in the morning.

    Then he distributes without cost gift certificates (dollars-off coupons) for boarding through local travel agencies. Also through real estate agents to new move-ins.

    H.T. is also successful selling large animal feed through ads in the classifieds.

Chapter 4   □

PRICING STRATEGIES THAT SPELL SUCCESS

□ WHY YOU SHOULDN'T CUT YOUR FEES, BUT RAISE THEM NOW

Thinking about cutting your fees to attract more business? Think again. Here's some interesting data from the research department at Eastman Kodak on how hard you have to work just to stay even.

Assuming an anticipated profit of 25% on a fee:

- A 10% cut means you must increase your volume by 67% to make the same profit.
- A 15% cut means you must increase your volume by 150% to make the same profit.
- A 20% cut means you must increase your volume by 400% to make the same profit.

On the other hand:

- A 10% fee increase means the same profit on only 71.5% of previous volume.
- A 15% increase means the same profit on only 62.5% of previous volume.
- A 20% increase means the same profit on only 55.5% of previous volume.

Therefore, if a professional wanted an anticipated profit of 50% and he cut his fees 20%, he'd have to increase his gross by 200%! If he's working eight hours a day, he could work 16 more—or all 24 hours, just to stay even. Harder is not smarter.

But ... if he'd increase his fees 20%, he'd only need work about half as much. That's smarter, not harder.

■ **Fee Raising Guidelines.**

1. Shop competitors' fees twice yearly on common services and products, in the same way callers shop you. Keep these common services and products competitive. Then raise all nonshopped fees aggressively.

2. Raise fees in small increments so that they're hardly noticed. Large steps set off alarms.

3. Raise fees often, such as twice a year. Since they're not noticed, you have the freedom to do it. With this approach, your fee rises will be greater than any single, yearly jump.

4. Don't back off if you get a complaint. In fact, from experience we know that *unless you get a few complaints, you haven't raised your fees enough!* (Enough is defined as maximum volume.) Remember: It's okay to lose a few to raised fees.

5. If you have a broad range of fees for a service or product, make the fee on the bottom level low and quite competitive. Then upgrade to better quality when they come in.

HOW TO EASILY BOOST NET INCOME 14%

Of course it pays to raise fees, but do you know the exact effect on your bottom line? It varies with your overhead percentage. So checkout this eye-opening chart and you'll discover how much even a small price increase skyrockets your net income:

INCREASE IN NET INCOME

% FEE INCREASE

Current Overhead	5%	10%	15%	20%
80%	25%	50%	75%	100%
75%	20%	40%	60%	80%
70%	17%	33%	50%	67%
65%	14%	29%	43%	57%
60%	13%	25%	38%	50%
55%	11%	22%	33%	44%
50%	10%	20%	30%	40%

At 65% overhead a modest 5% fee increase shoots your net up 14%! Look at what happens at 10%!!! The numbers make it abundantly clear what you should do—now.

The other question is, of course, does cutting fees increase profitability? Hardly. See for yourself how much increase in sales you'll need to maintain your current profitability for a specific fee cut:

PROFIT MARGIN	FEE CUT	SALES INCREASE REQ'D
25%	5%	25%
25%	10%	67%
25%	20%	500%
30%	5%	20%
30%	10%	50%
30%	20%	300%
35%	5%	16%
35%	10%	40%
35%	20%	233%
40%	5%	14%
40%	10%	33%
40%	20%	200%

The only way to make a total discount operation work is to ride roughshod over overhead, slashing mercilessly and monitoring daily. If that's not you, then overall discounting isn't you.

The Blair/McGill Advisory, April 1990, 4601 Charlotte Park Dr. #230, Charlotte, NC 28217, monthly, $99/yr, and THE PRACTICE BUILDER.

☐ USING GUARANTEES TO BOOST YOUR NUMBERS

Optometrist C.C. guarantees everything he does. Either the patient is satisfied or C.C. keeps working at it until he or she is—without additional fees. If his eyewear is unsatisfactory, he'll upgrade or downgrade with a price adjustment, but won't charge more for his time. That's just the way he is.

Then, since he already gave guarantees, C.C. decided to promote the idea outside of the practice. As recommended in Chapter Three, he did it *to communicate that this was a high quality practice* and the guarantee was a mark of that. It worked.

C.C. ran a newspaper ad aimed at disenchanted contact lens wearers. In it, he guaranteed he could fit them with contacts or he wouldn't charge. C.C. knew he couldn't fit everyone and would have to handle a few patients for free. But he counted on big numbers who would pay big bucks.

That's exactly what happened because this wasn't a price sensitive crowd. It was *risk sensitive* and the guarantee calmed their fears.

■ **Ways to Promote.** Do it externally through newspapers, magazines, direct mail, co-op coupons, or an outdoor office sign. Internally to generate referrals through quarterly Internal Prospecting direct mail to the patient base, One-Minute Messages, and waiting room placards (see appropriate chapters).

But first: Check your state regulations regarding guarantees. Note that "satisfaction guaranteed or your money back" is different from guaranteeing or promising a cure.

☐ HOW TO PRICE COMPETE

This strategy is *not* about using a loss-leader to generate foot traffic into the practice. Instead, it's how to truly be the low price leader in your middle- to lower-income area and grab market share galore.

If you want to play this tough game, there are tough rules. Violate them and make two or three big mistakes, then don't pass GO. Go straight to the "Poorhouse" because you're dealing with thin margins.

1. *Price governs everything.* Selling at the lowest fee controls every decision. From supplies to advertising to the kind of people you employ.
2. *Know every cost.* If it's cheaper to do something in house, then do it there. Most of the time, it's cheaper to subcontract and keep your fixed costs bare boned. If you've tried it inhouse, then you know the costs of doing it and you can bargain hard with your suppliers and independent contractors.
3. Manage and train your staff on incessant cost-control.
4. Heavily promote your low fees with co-op coupons, shoppers, and local newspapers.

Most professionals don't enjoy this kind of hard-nosed environment where you need to be *ruthless* about the rules. The pressure's always on because one mistake can eat the slim profits from a dozen good cases.

Can it be done? Absolutely, especially since there's so little competition for this large segment of the market. Just be prepared.

☐ NEW FINANCING PLANS BOOST GROSS

Dentist L.K. states it's his best promotion. So does surgeon P.B., optometrist E.G. and scads of other professionals. They're all talking about *financing.*

What financing does is make their services more affordable without having to lower their fees. And because it's easier for people to fit into their monthly budgets, more people buy.

More *existing* patients or clients buy. And you can use financing to attract *new* prospects who will buy. It's that powerful. The reason is simple. When you quote a price, people think whether they can write you a check for that amount *now*. And if the amount is $70 instead of $1,500, a lot more people say yes—even though the $70 goes on for many months.

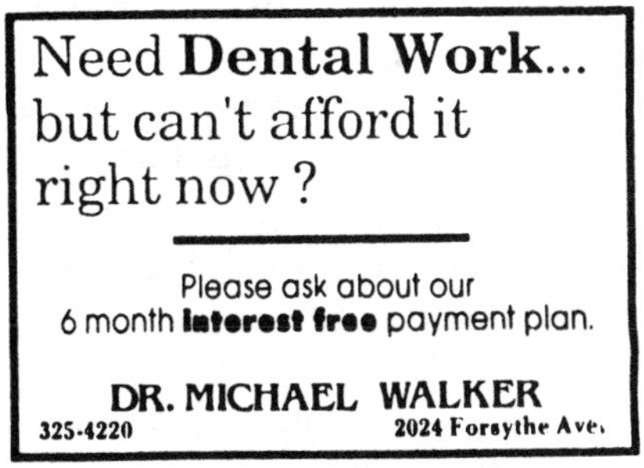

Figure 4.1 Michael Walker "Need Dental Work But Can't Afford It?"

But the problem with financing has always been convenience. In the past, banks and finance companies have made it difficult for professionals to give credit. These companies could relate to refrigerators and other hard goods, but not to services. Consequently, they wanted the prospect to make a special trip to their office. Then a lengthy application. And a long approval time.

■ **New Plans.** Well, things have changed. The world's become competitive and professionals are the beneficiaries. Health Line, a subsidiary of Blue Cross and Blue Shield of Maryland, is now test marketing Medcash. This is a credit card for all types of professional services and allows the card holder to take up to three years to pay off a balance.

Louisiana has it's own state-sponsored financing plan called PICO. This allows the professional to get quick approvals and about 90% of the bill right away in cash. It also permits the professional to offer no interest for six months, a big pull.

Finance companies are also getting on board. Many have fashioned programs for nonrecourse loans (the professional's not responsible in case the loan isn't repaid) that can be arranged and approved in less than one hour while the patient or client is still in the office.

And they're good for many professional services like elective services not covered by insurance, even insurance deductibles and copayments. The only restriction is that the patient or client cannot be out of work for an extended period which would make repayment difficult.

The minimum loan amounts start about $200 but can go much higher, up to the person's ability to repay. And as far as loan term goes, some will loan up to 24 months. Some even to 36 months.

■ **How They Work.** The plans are amazingly simple. When you have a patient or client who needs financing, all they do is fill out a half-page application which takes about five minutes. Your front desk calls in the information and within the hour you have your authorization. If it's after hours or a weekend, there's usually an 800 number which gives approvals. The patient or client then signs the contract which you've filled in.

After the work is done, you simply present the contract and the company cuts you a check quickly for a certain percentage, depending on the plan. The patient or client then pays about 16 to 20% interest (interest varies by state) on the loan.

Oftentimes you can make the financing even more attractive. You can reduce the amount of interest the prospect pays by paying any part of it. If the company charges 18%, you can offer 8% financing and the company will reduce your check by 10% of the financing charge.

■ **Some Ideas.** This financing plan is better than taking credit cards. Banks and American Express charge 2 to 5% service fees. Look at the plan that pay you 100% of your bill without deductions. The downside is the amount of extra time (although short) it takes to fill out the application and get approval.

These plans are not particularly good for long term, on-going services like orthodontics because the work must be completed before payment is made. This is true even though the amount has been pre-approved and the prospect has signed the contract. For these cases, companies have now developed a revolving line of credit like a credit card.

It helps to promote the plan inhouse. Use table tents for your reception area to inform your patient or client or clients. Remember to highlight your new financing options in your quarterly Internal Prospecting Direct Mail letters to your existing base. This will motivate more to come in to have work done now and they'll tell more friends and family about you.

■ **For More Information.** Finance companies will find you. Their direct mail campaigns are far reaching. But if you've alluded them, just ask your colleagues for the companies soliciting them. There are so many new ones that a list here would be out of date before this book went to print.

And make sure you get several plans inhouse. Some approve prospects easily ... and others don't.

☐ ANOTHER WAY TO MAKE SERVICES AFFORDABLE—INSTEAD OF REDUCING PRICES

"It's not the price. That's not the stumbling block. It's whether they can fit it into their monthly budget. That's the key." This is optometrist O.M.'s advice after using a new technique to accommodate more patients—without reducing his fees.

"What I did was to give them the benefits, then the fee. If they balked by saying they couldn't afford it, I'd tell them that I'd like to help them finance it interest-free. Then I'd ask them if they had a MasterCard, VISA or Discover Card. Then I'd ask if they could afford $40 a week until the total was paid off.

"Most of my patients can say yes to these, so I explain that what we'll do is put $40 on their credit card every week until it's paid off. When they get their statement, they can then pay it off at no charge over the next couple of months ... or let it ride.

"So it's not the fee the patient is then concerned about. It's $40 a week. That's what they focus on. That's the question. Also, I don't charge them $160 a month, which would be easier for me, because $40 a week 'feels' more affordable."

■ **Guidelines.** Fill out as many $40 credit card slips as you need. Date the first one that same day, the second the next week, the third the week after, etc. Make sure the patient or client signs *all* the $40 charge slips right then. Since it's under $50 for VISA and $75 for MasterCard, you won't need to call in for authorization, so you're *guaranteed* payment. (Double check on this with your bank since one in 100 says you must call in everything.) Also make sure you don't write a slip dated beyond the expiration date of the card.

This financing is perfect for any kind of elective service, especially if it's expensive and not covered by insurance. Examples: orthodontics, cosmetic dentistry, eyewear and eyecare, certain orthotics, vision therapy, psychotherapy, veterinary services. Also for insurance-covered services which take a year and a day for reimbursement. This system not only ensures full payment, it sometimes speeds up cash flow.

But cash flow isn't the purpose here. (Any bank would be willing to fund a credit line assured by signed credit card slips.) The real purpose is to vastly increase acceptance of your recommendations. That's the bottom line.

Now you've got to promote the availability of your affordability. In your direct mail to your patients or clients, on your outside reader board sign, in flyers in the waiting room, in newspapers and other external promotion, and by talking it up in the office. Without spreading the word, the word doesn't spread.

■ **Results.** "I don't know how many more patients we've had because of this new 'financing,' but I do know people like the option. Our gross is also up 9% over last year at this time and we really haven't done anything else differently."

☐ LAYAWAYS—PREPAID FINANCING

If people want to have expensive work done which isn't covered by insurance, they don't have the bucks in the bank...and you don't want to extend credit, then have them save up for it. And you be the bank.

It's like a Christmas Club savings program. Or in other vernacular, a Layaway Plan. Whatever you call it, the concept's the same. They pay weekly or monthly into the plan and when they have enough, you do the work or provide the goods.

You can even combine this with any existing financing program. In this case, they can layaway a certain amount (like 75%) and then you can finance or arrange financing for the balance.

The more ways you can make services affordable with easy monthly payments, the more people will buy. This is especially true when the economy heads south.

☐ MARKETING DISSECTION OF A HIGH VOLUME PRACTICE

We recently visited a highly successful, 14-treatment room, chiropractic practice to study its marketing dynamics. Here's what we discovered.

■ **External Promotion Abounds.** They use newspaper ads, radio spots, and local billboards on busy streets. Plus the practice itself has an enormous outdoor office sign to capture many prospects from the heavy traffic flow.

When someone calls in responding to the offer of a free exam, the receptionist performs beautifully. Obviously well trained, she closely queries how the caller heard about the practice. She'll ask the day the ad appeared as well as which paper. And she'll even find out what in the ad made the prospect call them versus someone else. Very sharp tracking and market research.

The practice also promotes through a booth at the local county fair. They provide a free screening at the fair and a free, "no-obligation" exam afterwards at their office.

At the screening, one of the doctors delivers a well-rehearsed speech about the history and benefits of the practice and why it's special. (This is a smart step needed to establish credibility.)

He then gives you a quick screening and if he discovers a problem, he asks if you'd like to set up the free exam at the office. The receptionist schedules your appointment right then and gives you some paperwork to fill out beforehand (an involvement technique). To cut down on no-shows, a representative calls to confirm two or three days prior to the visit.

■ **In-office Presentation.** Once you're in the office, you see the insurance coordinator first. She explains what you need to do if you choose to pursue treatment. In this way, you have all the information you need so when the doctor recommends treatment, you have no reason not to decide right then—not later which would decrease the acceptance rate.

The waiting room contains an overkill of promotional literature. All the exam rooms are similarly packed: testimonials; brochures; before-and-after x-rays; etc. So there's no way to avoid knowing how good this office is.

Another interesting fact—all the doctors are good looking. One suspects it's a requirement to work there as an associate. The suspected reasoning: This market contains a majority of 25- to 45-year-olds and good-looking professionals of the opposite sex can easily sway decisions.

During the free exam, the doctor assumes the prospect wants to start treatment and starts talking about it as a foregone conclusion. (In sales, this is called *The Assumptive Close.*) If the prospect balks, the doctor answers objections and asks for the okay to start. If he doesn't receive it, the prospect gets a call a day later from another doctor (the closer) to gain the commitment.

■ **Analysis.** This blue collar-oriented practice is obviously busy and successful. The external promotional efforts are continuously monitored to assure no wasted budget dollars. The patient handling procedures are, on paper, optimal for maximum production. But, but ...

... But the flavor of the practice is "business before caring." That's a possibly fatal flaw for any practice because it's sure to set up poor word-of-mouth which is hard to overcome. In high turnover areas, you can get away with it more easily than in stable communities, but it hurts tremendously in either case.

This practice should keep the mechanisms it has but embellish them with caring. It's not the mechanisms themselves that create the bad feelings; it's the way they're carried out. And it's easy to turn around.

□ **HOW TO ANSWER "YOUR FEE IS TOO HIGH"**

Everyone gets fee objections, but rarely are they valid. What prospects are really saying is that they don't think the fee is worth the service. So simply answer them by establishing your value.

If you price a service at $500 and a competitor prices it at $450, answer the price objection like this:

"$450 is the fee for the work. Plus $35 is the premium for superior durability due to superior materials. Plus $25 is the premium for superior reliability from the extra training I took in this area. Plus $20 is the premium for superior service. Plus $20 is the premium for your satisfaction guarantee.

"That's a total of $550. Then we give you a $50 discount, so the final fee is $500."

Bingo! Value ... and acceptance.

☐ RAISING GROSS 20% WITHOUT COST

Chiropractor L.R. raised his gross 20% recently without cost and without losing patients. How? At a PRACTICE BUILDER workshop, his market planner inspected his pricing structure and discovered an easy opportunity.

L.R. had kept his office visit fee at a level he thought was competitive for shoppers in his blue collar area. And using this as his benchmark fee, he adjusted all other fees by it. What he didn't know was that he was way behind what others in the area charged. When he had his front desk shop competitors' fees, he discovered the difference.

These are easy fees to raise for two reasons. First, the insurance companies won't bark if you raise fees to stay in line with the market. And patients or clients won't croak because they concentrate on the price of an office visit, not on ancillary services. They pay willingly, so these types of services are referred to as "inelastic." They pay what you ask. Whereas with "elastic" demand, such as the office visit, volume inversely varies with price.

So L.R. raised his inelastic fees and kept his elastic ones steady. The result: a 20% increase in gross without cost. Pure profit.

■ Once-a-Year-Fee-Survey. You have no idea what the profession is charging in your area unless you survey your competitors' fees once a year. Have your front desk call and act as a prospect. Query lots of fees. This is okay to do. It's actually a fundamental of the free market system. In fact, it's exactly what your colleagues are doing to you all the time. Ask your front desk. They suspect it, but don't know who's calling.

Then you can adjust your own fees. But when you do, keep the elastic ones competitive and raise the inelastic ones to the top of the scale.

☐ WHAT BEATS GIVING AWAY A FREE EXAM OR CONSULTATION?

One would think it's the most frequently asked question by professionals who promote. Actually, it's most frequently asked by those who don't advertise, but want to.

Those who advertise know from their own experience and from controlled-variable advertising tests that nothing beats "FREE" for generating volume—*in the following environment:*

1. Where there's already a great amount of advertising.

2. And where the market is mainly blue collar or those highly-educated, short-on-cash new-collar workers like administrative assistants, technicians, teachers, nurses, etc. This is your basic, big numbers, middle to middle-lower income market. They respond because free means a deal.

3. Or where the market is middle-upper because these are sophisticated patients or clients who buy value—that balanced combination of price and quality. These skeptics respond to free because it's a low-risk way of trying you out before they fully commit.

Where there's no promotion, usually *anything* works. People are so starved for information that the first professional to break the promotional barrier can have a punky, "heavy metal" image and still soar to record income.

But where the environment is hot and steamy with promotion, nothing beats a free something to bulk up the numbers.

■ **Expanding the Market.** Free also works well with getting people to try something new. (Think of how Procter & Gamble sends out free samples of a new detergent?)

Free also works with high cost, elective services.

■ **But Beware.** Free creates volume. Therefore, you must have a quick screening method to find the cases you want so you can devote more time to them.

Also, the staff must be aware and supportive of the strategy. If not, don't do it ... or get yourself a new staff. Resistance will sabotage your effort, not to mention frustrate you.

■ **Sometimes Free Brings in the Wrong Types of Prospects.** In this case, free is the wrong tactic. Just raise the height of the gateway to the practice. Don't give anything for free; instead, charge a modest amount for the introductory session or service. This *increases quality,* but decreases quantity.

The only way to discover the optimal balance is to test. If it's not perfect, change the height of the gateway.

■ **Doesn't Giving Services Away for Free Demean Your Practice?** This is an attitude normally fostered by older practitioners with full practices. The more productive question is, "What will my market respond to so they can come in and find out how good I really am?"

Choose the question you prefer to answer.

■ **Results.** Two California specialists in pain management and rehabilitation uncovered the fact that a free screening works well to introduce blue and new collar people to their practice. So they promoted it heavily. The more heavily they promoted, the better it worked.

But then instead of promoting it even more heavily, they built a small, permanent screening facility in a heavily trafficked area. Where? Right at a bus stop where 40,000 people a day take the bus. Then with outside signage and active recruitment at the bus stop, they've brought in thousands for a free screening just feet away.

An associate does the screening. If a problem is found, the aide makes a referral to the nearby office. He also tells them that the first visit costs $110, but if they prepay now, it's only $60. That's how they gain commitment on the spot and cut down dramatically on no-shows.

How well does it work? Over $2,000,000 a year. For them, nothing beats free.

☐ UPDATE: GOOD/BETTER/BEST SELLS THE HIGHER END

Sears is smart. Long ago they figured out that if you give people a choice of different quality levels in the same product, most will buy the middle quality. Some will buy the best. And a few will buy low. Even today, Sears still markets their products as Good/Better/Best and captures the bigger margins on the more expensive alternatives.

Then a few years ago, when THE PRACTICE BUILDER wrote an article on Sears' idea, a smart dentist applied the Good/Better/Best strategy to dentures. Because he was losing business to cheap denture shops, he created low-, middle-, and upper-end dentures and promoted each with their prices.

What he discovered was astonishing. Very few bought the low end. *Most bought the best,* unlike the Sears experience. So he added a fourth level—Ultimate. Then they bought that. It seems that people were attracted to the concept of a new product, idea, package or presentation. "New" attracted attention. And quality sold well.

Also, most bought additional services like crowns and bridgework. Plus they became continuing patients and referred.

He differentiated each denture by the quality of materials. But with only minor differences there, he further differentiated each by the amount of time he spent with the patient and the guarantee he gave.

■ **Update.** Recently another smart dentist applied the concept to a commonly shopped item—*crowns.* He created three levels of crowns, again differentiated by quality and appearance of materials, lab used, time spent and guarantee. He then promoted their availability in the newspaper with their prices.

Bingo! Most people bought *the upper end.* No cheap business here. It appears that people responded, not to the inexpensive low end, but to the high-end alternative. Again, "new" attracted attention and quality sold. The existence of the middle and low alternatives just helped to sell the high end since people rarely buy them anymore.

PROMOTIONS IN MOTION

1. Hearing aid dispenser A.D. differentiates himself from his competitors by promoting affordability as well as miniaturization. Seniors on fixed budgets figure they can afford the monthlies a lot easier than writing a lump-sum check. Consequently, more say yes. A lot more.

2. Credit cards just for professional services are here and more are coming. They exist in health care, dentistry, even plastic surgery. And for the most part, they're a great idea.

   This is especially true for high ticket, elective services where radically increasing the number of patients or clients requires that you promote a *low monthly payment.* That's what most middle class people care about—can they afford it on a monthly basis? These cards give you that vehicle without carrying the paper inhouse.

3. Chiropractor L.H. is located in an economically depressed area. Many of his good patients have stopped coming because of lapsed insurance, loss of job, or static wages. And his new patients don't take all the treatments they need for the same reasons.

   So L.H. abolished his fee structure.

   He keeps one for insurance purposes, but the going policy is to pay what you can afford. The results have been surprising.

   First, most people still pay full price. Second, they're more conscientious about paying now. Third, he's stopped losing patients while every other professional in town continues to downtrend. Yes, he does treat a number of people for free, but his *bottom line is up!*

   Gross was $346,000 last year, up 17% since going to the new format. It's up so much that he's opened another office.

   "I did it originally because I wanted to be busy helping people. If people couldn't afford care, they should still get it ... and I'm the kind who hates to sit around. I had no idea it would actually make me money."

4. Veterinarian P.W. knows how to build foot traffic from his solid middle class market. In his newspaper and Pennysaver ads, P.W. not only tells people why to choose his practice, but also offers a free flea dip. He tells them to bring a towel and the leash and his office will do the rest. The staff sets aside a special day to accommodate the flood of respondents.

   Why does he give something for free? Because the follow-up business generates a tracked 15:1 return on investment.

5. How do you build a crown and bridge practice? Dentist S.H. advises by promoting dentures. First, he created a selection of dentures to promote, but not two kinds, or even three, or five. But six, the sixth being an implant alternative. Each had different materials and a different price. Literally he had something for everyone. And even though he sold lots of dentures through his unique newspaper promotion, he sold truckfuls of crowns and towers of bridges. That's where his big money is.

   The implication for dentists wanting to emphasize implants: Test the promotion of an array of dentures instead of the tougher straight implant promo. Then upgrade the patient to implants if appropriate. During your presentation, de-emphasize the price and emphasize an affordable $X per month. Since the price scares them to death, financing is a must.

6. Orthodontist E.H. is over 70. Even though his practice has slowed, he hasn't. Located in a middle-lower metro market and being short on cash, he's formed a group of four colleagues to price promote in the TV Guide section of the city's major paper.

   His reasoning: "No one's doing ortho for $1,800 like I am, even though it's profitable. All I've got to do is let people know and I'll have a flood. This middle-lower market is perfect for price promotion and the Sunday TV listings is perfect to deliver the message. By forming a group of noncompeting practitioners, I'll cut my media costs by 75% and won't give up a thing."

   Warning: Promote the $60 per month payment option in the headline, not the $1,800 price tag. Why? Affordability is more important than price.

7. Hearing aid dispenser L.J. adapted a bright idea from a contact lens outlet. He knew that most hearing aids sold were replacements. So to

sell his higher end line, the one with the biggest markup, why not take trade-ins.

Instead of giving a discount to move the line, he now gave a credit for used hearing aids. He didn't care whether or not they worked since he just sold them to a large repair facility for parts anyway.

The perceived value of the trade-in was great enough to boost the volume substantially without giving up much of the profit.

8. Optometrist N.B. is in an extraordinarily tough market. He's got super-stores to the left; superstores to the right; and all volley and thunder. One's even selling contact lenses for $1!

But he's fighting back with a combination of offers in this now *product-driven* marketplace: 2 for 1 on glasses or contacts (second pair from a budget selection); discounted exam to build traffic with no discounts on product; a free pair of disposable contacts; a straight-out price comparison chart between him and the more expensive chains while playing up his personal attention as an added value; a guarantee to beat any price; and 50% off frames with the purchase of lenses.

Chapter 5 ☐

CHARTING THE BEST ROUTE WITHOUT THE CRIPPLING PITFALLS: YOUR MUST DO'S AND DON'TS

☐ **BIG, BAD MARKETING DEBTS**

What are some of the worst marketing expenditures around?

1. Buying in too many *Yellow Pages* directories and not tracking their results by section and book.
2. Poor and erratic time slots for commercials on radio and TV.
3. Expensive, over-produced, poorly conceived practice brochures.
4. Professional announcements.
5. Advertising specialties like pens, magnets, match book covers, or T-shirts.
6. Public service announcements and publicity from PR firms because of the inconsistency and cost.
7. Most for-profit referral services, not because of the efficacy of the concept, but because they're so poorly run and your territory isn't guaranteed or large enough.
8. Straight *Name Awareness* advertising (without any direct response) which requires deep pockets to work.
9. Advertising in poorly read (and cheap) publications.

And the dumbest of all? Not tracking the results of your promotional efforts so you end up dumping more good dollars down a black hole.

☐ BORN LOSERS: GIMMICKS TO AVOID

Some things just never seem to pay. They usually run in the $300 to $600 price range so almost any professional can afford them. That's one of the things their hustling salespersons count on. The other is your impulse buying spurred on by the threat of giving the opportunity to your competitor instead. But remember, since these gimmicks hardly ever work, you *want* your competitor to do them!

Instead, go out and spend the money on a wonderful dinner. You'll have several hundred dollars left over to spend on productive strategies. Plus, you'll have had a great time.

1. *Supermarket register tape ads:* They'll print your ad on the back of supermarket tapes. Large distribution numbers, few responses. And those who do respond are usually a pain in the derriere. We've heard of only one recorded "success" story at THE PRACTICE BUILDER in six years. That was a vet offering a DEEP discount which generated 40 new clients a month—but the wrong kind of client for his higher fee, lower volume practice. That's success?

2. *New neighbor welcoming services.* The Welcome Wagon was the granddaddy of these with hit or miss home visits to new move-ins. It's not proven to be the big winner it claims to be because The Welcome Wagon lady won't aggressively sell you. Plus the visit occurs too soon after the move when people aren't yet ready to select new professionals. Hairdressers, yes. Professionals, no.

Getting To Know You is a take-off. Their program delivers a telephone and address book along with community info by UPS. Sponsors names are listed in the appropriate category and you have the opportunity to offer a gift certificate. It's another bad investment because of lack of repetition at the time people are ready to enter the professional market.

Only repetitive, stand-alone direct mail sent quarterly over the first year to credit-checked move-ins seems to work well. Pass on all the welcoming services.

3. *Free magazines distributed in stores:* Whether from the convenience store, supermarket, health food store or anywhere else, these are true born losers. They claim they distribute 9,999,999 copies. Unfortu-

nately, no one reads them, so all those paper pulp trees died in vain. And so will your promotional budget if you bite at this one. (This is not necessarily the case if the free magazine is mailed or delivered to a residence which ensures greater readability.)

4. *Supermarket shopping cart ads:* Bad news! Not only won't you get any business, but the cost can run up to a couple of thousand a year—and you're usually stuck for an entire year. But if you are, a call to your attorney may open an exit.

5. *Talking or on-line Yellow Pages:* These are actually very large scale media pools of professionals and businesses which, managed by an entrepreneur, can afford to buy big time media. Then when someone calls the toll-free number, the "operator" suggests one or two professionals and tells a little something about each. You can also have the "operator" announce a special offer.

Unfortunately, this concept of people calling in for a *Yellow Pages* referral has failed to capture the public's imagination. And it's failed to produce because these organizations simply don't buy enough external media to raise awareness and convince people to call. And people just find it easier to use the regular *Yellow Pages.*

The concept's sexy at first glance, but you don't want to marry this one. The best strategy is to wait until you can call a bunch of happy campers who'll give the Talking *Yellow Pages* a great report. Don't worry about getting shut out. These kinds of things always have high turnover because of the humongous thousands in cost.

6. *Co-operative mailings to new homes:* These "exclusive" mailings to new homeowners contain a short letter recommending about 10 professionals. The envelopes are handwritten for greater attention. But there are two problems. Once you get the envelope opened, the contents are unconvincing. There's no lengthy copy to extol the virtues of each individual. It simply banks on the concept of an official "recommendation," but there's no credibility for the recommender—or the 10 professionals who forked over $800 each.

And even though the letter is mailed three times to a household, only 50 houses a quarter are targeted! Talk about not understanding that this is a numbers game! These are bucks dropped on a mail drop loser.

7. *Bus benches:* These don't keep your name in front of anyone, but they do put bucks in the promoters' pockets. Use bus benches only if you're looking for a sure write-off.

8. *High school and college yearbooks:* It's fine to advertise in these, but make sure the cost comes out of your charity budget, not promotion.

9. *College newspapers:* If your target is truly college-aged kids, perhaps for sports medicine, this might be worth a trial. But for the vast majority of cases, pass. College students don't buy enough professional services to make it worth your while.

10. *Church bulletins:* Once in a blue moon we discover a church bulletin that's an advertising winner. But most advertising in these should come out of your charity budget. So don't expect any rewards in this life.

11. *Theater programs:* Don't even be tempted.

12. *Sponsoring local school or charity events:* The exposure will be low, people's memory of you even lower, and response rock bottom.

13. There's a number of companies soliciting professionals who advertise in the *Yellow Pages to "professionally" redo their ads* for $200 to $300. Their direct mail packages are personalized and slick, but their products fail to follow the proven precepts of THE PRACTICE BUILDER. The result is like buying a fancy computer with software written by a high school student. It's better than a third-grader's (the *Yellow Pages* themselves), but so what?

The *Yellow Pages* cost too much to use less than optimal strategies. It's not the $200 to $300 in production or $1,000+ in space costs you'll lose, it's the *$50,000 you could have made with the right ad.* Play it safe and profitable.

14. *Ads on magazine covers in professional offices:* Here's a new one. Salespeople—with hot deadlines and threats of selling the opportunity to a competitor—place your logo and vitals on covers that go on magazines in waiting rooms in all kinds of doctors' offices. For two whole years. For only $600. What exposure! (Actually, this should read, "What exposure???") When was the last time you chose a professional from a plastic magazine cover? Neither does anyone else.

15. *Ads on sampling postcards:* One of the ways companies promote consumer goods is to mail free samples. Since packaging often makes label adherence difficult, they need an accompanying card to carry the address label. To recoup mailing costs, these companies are now selling the other side of the address-carrying postcards. At first glance, they're cheap and attractive. But your promotion falls on blind eyes because the free sample steals all the attention.

16. *Relying on your professional society* to promote your field and to build your practice is tantamount to marketing suicide. These organiza-

tions are too political to produce effective promotion. They're run by people who know absolutely nothing about marketing. Even if your association or society is one of the miniscule few with a killer promoter on staff, forget it anyway. The marketing committee will emote over everything and kill your killer's creations.

Even the well-funded biggies have tried and failed. You just can't do effective promotion by committee. And absolutely never in a political environment composed of the marketing-unwise and conservative.

17. How about marketing *messages on postage meter imprints?* (This is really starting to get far-fetched!) Suffice it to say that few people would be imprinted by a postage meter message about your practice enough to act. On second thought, you might get a couple of philatelists.

So now you're forewarned and forearmed.

Don't let swift-talking salespeople fleece you out of your dear promotional dollars. Remember that gimmicks like these won't work at any price.

CHECKLIST FOR EXPLOSIVE GROWTH

Some practices do everything right and here's a checklist of those elements they have in common. Carefully check your own practice against these standards of excellence.

❑ *Compete on value, not price.* Winners deliver services that provide consistently superior value. Often, these services cost more, not less. That doesn't mean you can't use direct response offers to generate traffic. It does mean extra value once they're in the door.

❑ *Think like patients or clients.* Winners put themselves in their clientele's shoes and see through their eyes. Their clientele's concerns are truly their concerns.

❑ *Motivate with money.* Incentive pay tied to performance is more common at winning practices. A vested interest by employees proves itself again.

❑ *Set a clear, countable goal.* Winners know if they've won because they set clear goals: production, collections, appointments kept, recalls, etc. No goals mean a lackadaisical attitude.

Donald Clifford, Jr., McKinsey and Company, "The Winning Performance of Midsized Growth Companies", American Business Conference, 1025 Connecticut Ave., NW, Washington, DC 20036 and THE PRACTICE BUILDER.

☐ DON'T PRIORITIZE DECOR OR NONESSENTIAL EQUIPMENT

Dentist D.A. was moving from a traditional office building into a shopping mall. Luckily, it had both a high-volume grocery store and busy health club as anchors, but what she didn't have was a lot of money.

The build-out was a costly $50,000, plus moving expenses and sundries. When speaking with her PRACTICE BUILDER Hotline Advisor, D.A. said she didn't have any budget left for external promotion to announce her new move, especially after decorating anew and buying two pieces of equipment she'd always wanted.

■ How Not to Prioritize Expenses. Her advisor candidly pointed out that decor and the equipment she chose rarely produce income. And that with increased overhead, what D.A. needed now was cash flow. She could always add the finishing touches later, but it makes no sense to have a beautiful office and no traffic.

The smarter play is to invest in heavy internal promotion to assure that your base follows you. And then to spend on external promotion to start drawing from the new area. Serious exterior office and window signage to attract foot and drive-by traffic is paramount, followed by a high profile in the health club (perhaps direct mail to the membership) and media promotion to the surrounding three miles.

Keep the old chairs another six months. And no, you won't lose patients or clients over old furniture.

☐ PROMOTION BY COMMITTEE FAILS

Chiropractor P.N. has two partners, two offices, and one big headache. Each partner wants to approve all practice promotion before it's launched. Unfortunately, each shows it to his spouse and staff. All of them give their opinions and, in the spirit of compromise, P.N. tries to accommodate them.

That headache becomes a migraine when P.N. realizes that before the two partners and extra office, his office promotion did fairly well. Now it doesn't do at all.

■ Multiple Opinions from Non-experts.

A sage once noted that the greatest drive in mankind isn't greed. Nor sex. Nor power. Instead, it's the need to alter someone else's copy.

No one can resist. And it seems that the less someone knows about the subject, the greater the need to alter. *Beware:* Asking a non-expert in promotion what they think about a brochure, letter, ad or logo and inviting changes invites disaster.

What is valuable is to ask people *familiar with p·omotion* whether the effort will accomplish a very specific goal with a very specific audience. If you simply ask, "What do you think?" your headache's on the way. If you're politic enough to include most suggestions, it's going to be Excedrin #666.

The worst feedback comes from people within the practice or family who are not intimately involved with the practice's bottom line. These people feel free to emote without regard to financial reality.

Instead, concentrate the promotional authority in one or two people. *And these people must be involved with the bottom line and have a strong propensity for promotion.* If they don't, take it away from them! It will save you from an addiction to Ibuprofen.

PROMOTIONS IN MOTION

1. At THE PRACTICE BUILDER we keep hearing horror stories about The Talking *Yellow Pages.* These are call-in referral services promoted only on radio or TV. The only problem is that as soon as the advertising stops, people stop calling. It seems there are no legs to this program. So only participate if the media schedule is *constant* and *pervasive;* if your exclusive territory is large enough to support you; and if you're not contractually tied up past three months at a time.

Chapter 6 ☐

THE INSIDE STORY: YOUR PATIENTS OR CLIENTS AS THE OPTIMUM SOURCE OF GROWTH—THE INTERNAL MIX THAT MAXIMIZES RETURN ON INVESTMENT

If your practice is a healthy organism, most of the business it sees—its nutrition—comes from internal promotion. In fact, the healthiest goal is an all referral practice.

Most practices have the same internal "core" requirements. There are certainly differences among practices, but these tend to be reflected in the way a strategy is executed—not in the choice of the strategy.

The following is a list of big payoff strategies that target your existing clientele. There are plenty of other ideas, but few produce the punch to equal these. Add more internal strategies only after you have these basics in place.

1. Internal prospecting: Since the biggest asset of any practice is your existing and past base, farming it for repeat business and referrals is a must. To do so, send a multi-page letter on your stationary mailed third-class bulk rate, metered or with a precancelled stamp for that first-class feel. Its purpose is to position you as an expert. So share ideas for better living that you pull out of your experience or the literature. Now you're a respected fountain of information.

Then mention improvements in the practice. And any speeches or interviews you've given or articles you've written so they know *other people* consider you to be an expert.

At the end tell them to call if they need any assistance. Also instruct them to share this information with friends and loved ones who may need it. You'll do your share in helping them by enclosing a "pass" they can present at your office for a bite-sized bit of service.

Then mail a different internal prospecting letter quarterly because *repetition works! Repetition works!*

And forget newsletters. Surveys have shown a newsletter doesn't do nearly as well as a personal-looking letter from you.

Yes, you need a mailing list of past and current patients or clients. The potential increase in revenue is so large that the cost of creating it is immaterial.

2. Reactivation efforts: A gold mine lies among those patients or clients you have not seen for some time. Many now need you but have put off returning. Write them a letter telling them why it's important to come in—now—and what *specifically* can happen to them if they don't. Call those who don't respond during the evening with the same message. This effort alone will make your year.

3. Frequent referrer program: Learn how to shape referring behavior because the goal of all these efforts is to have a practice based solely on word-of-mouth.

4. One-minute messages: These are actually 15- to 30-second talks that let you educate your patients or clients about a single topic so they can spread the word or take advantage of the idea themselves. Examples: Patient Appreciation Day; when a child should first see the chiropractor; a breakthrough in contacts; a new IRS ruling.

5. Recalls—the right way: Most recall systems lack the right message. It shouldn't be "Come back; it's time." Instead tell them why it's important to come in now—and what specifically can happen to them if they don't. Since most don't understand the ramifications of missing a recall, many won't come in. And guilt will only go so far.

6. Asking for referrals: Most professionals hate this one, yet it's the most effective way to get to an all-referral practice. Simply say, "If you've liked what I've done, would you please recommend me to someone you think I can help as well? I would appreciate it." It's so simple. . .and after you've done it a few times, it's so easy.

☐ HOW TO CREATE A WELCOME-TO-THE-PRACTICE LETTER

Bonding, that's the name of the game for any practice; also called Affinity Marketing. Basically, it's getting people to like you and your practice—and one of the cornerstones is to start the relationship right.

■ **Step 1: Greet them right.** Perle Mesta, the Washington hostess with the mostess, used to say it's all in the greetings and good-byes. When they first come in, act like they're your long lost friend. And when they leave, ask if they must leave so soon.

In a practice the execution is a little different but the strategy is the same. When they come in, the receptionist acts extraordinarily glad to see them. (Now you know why you need a hostess up front.)

Then she introduces them to everyone in the office. Isn't that what you do with a close friend of the family? Treat them that way and they become that.

And when they leave, reiterate how happy you are to have them choose you and be part of the family.

■ **Step 2: Send them a Welcome Letter.** But not the traditional type. That's the kind you save for when you're having difficulty sleeping since it's better than Sominex. Instead, send them a prewritten warm and fuzzy which you can generate by computer—but throw in one paragraph which you can easily personalize. Therefore, they'll fee-ee-eel special and it wasn't time intensive to write.

Remember: The best direct mail is the most personal and written from one specific human to another specific human. The personalized paragraph does that for you. Here's a sample:

Dear   :

I just wanted to take a few minutes to drop you a short note and let you know something.

No, unfortunately you haven't won the office sweepstakes and a lifetime's worth of free services from our practice. Truly, it's not quite as good as that, but I think still it's important.

I simply wanted to let you know how happy I am that you've become part of our practice and part of our family. And just like in any close-knit family, you can count on your new family members when you need us. I was brought up to believe that blood is thicker than water, and even though we have quite an extended family here, we still live by that precept.

This means that if you have an emergency, we're always available. Just call 677-5358 anytime and I or one of my most trusted people will get back to you post haste. Because an emergency's an emergency.

It means that if you work, we have extended hours on Tuesday and Saturday mornings and on Wednesday evenings, in addition to our regular daytime hours. Because I'd want that from my practitioner.

And it means that if you have any problems or concerns at all, I'll work with you in any way I can. Because that's what family does.

[To personalize, insert a two- to three-line paragraph here about them in particular: their condition or needs, hobby, etc.]

Again, just let me say how glad I am—and how appreciative the whole staff is—that you've chosen us over everyone else. Thanks and welcome to the family.

Sincerely,

☐ HOW TO PROTECT YOUR BASE, GET REPEAT BUSINESS, AND GENERATE REFERRALS—ALL IN ONE EFFORT

Ten or 20 years ago, there weren't any super aggressive, advertising, go-get-'em colleagues. All you needed to *retain a patient* was to do a good job and have a pleasant bedside manner.

But today, everything's different. There are a ton of marauding practitioners. And if you don't cultivate your base, the promotional repetition of your no-longer-colleagues-but-now-dire-competitors will start eroding it. And the insidious thing about it is that you won't even know it's happening until the damage is done and hurts—badly.

But the nice thing is that if you actively protect your base, you also produce lots of repeat business you wouldn't otherwise see. The reason is that your communication creates business by addressing needs that would have simply been ignored.

And at the same time, if you execute this strategy well, you can produce beaucoup referrals because you'll actually influence referral behavior.

Because we know that newsletters don't work ("work" means increased production, more referrals and business really up), THE PRACTICE BUILDER invented and tested a new format that accomplishes these three objectives. It's a *direct mail* format with a specific construction.

■ **Internal Prospecting.** The strategy is named Internal Prospecting because you'll be prospecting for business within your existing base.

When you *prospect for repeat business*, you need to describe *the benefits* of new developments or new services or products you provide. Or you can remind your patients or clients of existing services or products that they may not have taken advantage of, but with repetition of this message, they'll now consider. After all, people change and timing is important.

Then, when you go *prospecting for referrals*, you'll need to convince people of your expertise—because people will only refer after they consider you to be an expert. No convincing means fewer referrals. Also give them specific reasons *why* they should refer people in and specific directions *how to do it*. We're not sure why people respond to directions. But all we need to know is that tests show over and over they do.

By establishing your expertise to generate referrals, you also *protect your base* against the marauding hordes of advertising competitors. The reason is simple—no one leaves an expert. You can even have a witch at the front desk and hatchetmen for assistants, and still they'll stay—because no one leaves an expert.

■ **The Direct Mail Formula.** Send your Internal Prospecting direct mail package to your active patient base. Also to the people you saw up to three years ago. You can also safely send it to those seen up to five years ago if you have the kind of profession that is not often used. After all, even if they don't return periodically, they can still refer.

Remember: (1) Use inexpensive paper for your packages since costly paper doesn't buy you results; (2) Print "Address Correction Requested" on the envelope so you can update your mailing list (the 25¢ for each correction is worth it); (3) Use a mailing service (lettershop) to affix labels, stuff envelopes and mail so they'll affordably get it out in one day; (4) Mail third class to save money; and (5) Use the lettershop's bulk mailing permit so you don't have to get one.

Layout both the envelope and letterhead like your stationery. You want this to look as much like an important letter from you as possible. This means you also use a bulk rate postage meter mark (which your lettershop will affix) instead of a preprinted indicia which makes the package look like junk mail.

■ **Letter Construction.** When you write a letter, the first sentence must give people a really strong reason to read on. Otherwise, many will roundfile it. One of the best ways to start is the Problem/Solution format. In it, you tell people they have a problem and that you have the solution. Develop the problem in your opening paragraph and make it sound important.

One good problem to use is their lack of knowledge. There are new developments in your field all the time and this information can be crucial to the reader. But the problem is that the media they read, see, and hear don't study the same journals you do. But because you're their professional, you'll keep them informed. Then you describe the *benefits* of one or two new developments in the following paragraphs. If the information is mundane, forget it. *Boring* copy won't be read. Spice, please.

By acting as a source of information and putting it in print, people will begin to think of you as an expert. That's one of the purposes of this section as well as the entire letter.

Next have a subhead entitled *What Else Is New?* Here's where we prospect for repeat business. Describe what's new in the practice: services; products; hours; financing options; computers; equipment; and personnel *only if* they bring new expertise. If your newness is slim, create something new. (It'll be good for the practice.) If it's still slim, describe oldness—those services we want people to come back for.

Then have a section headed *Make Sure You Watch* or words to that effect. Describe here your *third party endorsements* so that readers know that other people consider you to be an expert. You just can't create the impression of an expert once. It flits away. You've got to repeat it—over and over—to make it stick.

If you're going to be on TV, radio, or in a magazine or paper, then tell them to look out for it. Also list any talks you give, *future and past,* at a professional meeting, to the garden club or public, or even to Mrs. Cromwell's first grade class. Who cares if they watch or listen? You just want them to know you're respected. The endorsement is everything. Of course offer to mail them a summary sheet of important points if they call in. People rarely do unless it's a very hot topic.

Now close. Tell them to call if they have questions about anything you've described. Or to set an appointment if they have needs.

■ **P.S.** Always include a P.S. In this effort, use it to tell people they should refer in people who need help, but for some reason have not sought it. Everyone knows people like that and the reader can really help loved ones and friends. Not only can they, but they should.

People with a problem needn't suffer if they only knew that help was available. And to that end, you'll do your part by providing a free or low-cost consultation or exam so they can learn firsthand without risk. Readers should do their part for their friend or loved-one's sake and give them the enclosed certificates. (Yes, put the offer on a separate 3½" × 8" "buck slip" and enclose two.)

The referral strategy works terrifically. It should since it's based on a time-tested concept in business called the "Friend-Help-a-Friend" program.

■ **Follow-up.** One mailing will work, but once isn't enough. Repetition enhances your response rate. So mail quarterly. Put it on your calendar and you'll do it.

Keep the construction of the direct mail package exactly the same each time. Change the opening paragraph slightly: *Remember when I wrote to you a few months ago about the problem of not being kept informed about crucial developments? And how I sent you three revolutionary ideas which were important to you and your family? Well, this time the ideas are bigger and their importance even greater.*

Now you're off and running with the rest of the construction. Just update the information and close with the "Friend-Help-a-Friend" program.

How long should your letter be? Two to three pages. Not one page. Short copy is an old wives' tale propagated by people who don't write direct mail often and certainly don't study the volumes of test literature. Long copy works. Period.

But you must use short words, short sentences and short paragraphs. Plus plenty of subheads to break up the copy and make it inviting to read.

You know what else is nice? Handwritten notes in the column. Or circling words or ideas. Or indenting entire paragraphs to highlight them. Or *underlining* things. Try them.

■ **Sample.** There are many ways to write these and yet follow the construction. Sometimes you can substitute one section for another. Sometimes, you can include a case to illustrate a point. But be careful when you do. Remember, the package must generate repeat business, foster your image as an expert, and boost referrals. These are the acid tests.

Here's a slightly different execution that still accomplishes these tasks. It was created by The Practice Builder Agency.

Dear Friend,

As your eye doctor, I am always on the lookout for ways to protect your vision.

This is an important part of my follow-up care. If you're not seeing your best, and if your eyes are not kept healthy, I'm not doing my job.

And with so many potential dangers to your eyes, it's important to keep you informed. So do yourself a favor: Take just a few minutes to read this information. Some of it's crucial. I'm sure you'll find it well worth your time.

Why women should "date" their mascara

Mascara is a great breeding place for germs and bacteria. You may not see them, but they're there. And many women with itchy, burning or red eyes just don't think to try a different mascara, or to follow some simple health guidelines. Instead of using the same mascara till the tube runs dry, throw it away after three months. The few cents you'll lose just may save you a major eye infection!

How to fix contact lens fitting problems

As one new patient, Jane, settled into the chair she commented, "I've been everywhere trying to get contacts that fit right, but they all tell me I'll never be able to wear contacts well."

I hear this often, and my answer is always the same: "Not true." Hard-to-fit contacts are a specialty of mine. I enjoy my work, and I'm always willing to invest the extra effort, patience and imagination to fit you. Many companies make contacts, so I find the company that makes just the right contact for hard-to-fit challenges like Jane.

I have access to the latest and best products because I conduct a great deal of clinical research for major contact lens and lens care manufacturers such as Bausch & Lomb, Allergan, and Ciba Vision Care. My patients benefit from this research as much as the companies do.

After a complete exam to get her exact eye measurements and prescription needs, I fitted Jane with trial lenses from several manufacturers. And, as I'd promised, I found "the perfect lens." Jane was thrilled, and so was I.

So, if you know anyone who wants to wear contacts, tell them that instead of taking "no" for an answer, come see me. I love hard-to-fit challenges!

Good news for children's vision problem

Many times we can prevent a child's nearsightedness from becoming worse. It has been proven scientifically that hard or rigid contact lenses will help prevent advancement in nearsightedness in children. Although they can sometimes be uncomfortable at first, they gradually become just as easy to wear as other lenses.

And remember, children are generally more adaptable than most adults. So, look into a lens that will help prevent a condition from worsening. Especially with children who still have the advantage of preventative help.

Call me. I'm happy to give advice

Of course, I always want you to have the newest and best eye care. In fact, as your eye doctor, I usually learn about new techniques in professional meetings, in my journal, and through my relationships with major eye care products firms.

But before trying something new that could damage your contacts—or even your eyes—give me a call or come by and get all the details. I'm always available to give a few minutes to patients who have concerns about their eye care.

Help save a friend's sight

Chances are you've got friends who don't know they need regular eye exams to make sure their eyes are healthy. Friends who don't know that some of the most serious eye problems, like glaucoma, have absolutely no symptoms before they cause permanent damage. Friends who may actually be going blind without realizing it!

So why not share the enclosed gift certificate with a friend who's been putting off that eye exam.

You know ... the friend who can't read menus or street signs. Or maybe the one who's always complaining about headaches and "tired eyes." Or even a friend who's new in town and doesn't have an eye doctor yet.

And especially that friend who's sure "nothing is wrong." If they're over 40, they definitely need to see me because of the glaucoma threat.

Believe me. Your friend will thank you forever. And we'll do our part to protect eye health by offering a great discount on an initial exam for them. Won't you do your part by passing along the enclosed certificate to someone you care about?

Sincerely,

P.S. Remember to keep current with your eye exam. Once a year is recommended because changes in your eyesight are often unnoticeable.

■ **Certificate Sample.** The certificate for the "Friend-Help-a-Friend" program, shown below, encourages the reader to pass it on. The certificate first tells the friend what the doctor treats and then enhances the value of the offer by telling the reader other reasons why he or she should choose this practitioner.

☐ THE ONE-MINUTE MESSAGE

What's the least costly and second most potent (asking for referrals ranks first) promotional effort in your arsenal? It's the one that launched cosmetic dentistry as part of a Massachusetts dental practice. This practitioner, without any other promotion, placed $225 porcelain laminates on 63 teeth for a total of $14,175 in just two months. It's also what California psychiatrist L.L. used in promoting her weekend seminars for women, generating full house after full house.

What these professionals used was a one-minute message to her existing patients or clients. Thoughtfully designed and *pre-scripted*, the message described an additional service that was available. And not only for the patient, but for *friends and family*. It's how you turn your present base into recruiters.

In the case of L.L., she described a weekend seminar of 12 to 15 women who would explore issues together and get to know each other in a way one rarely finds today. There'd be group dynamics, exhilaration, emotional sharing and personal growth. And what did L.L. receive? More income, more new patients and more committed ones.

But you don't always need to promote a new service. Old services work just as well. This example is in family practice, but you can use this construction, too.

> Something happened the other day that I wanted to share with you. A patient of five years came in and finally told me she'd had migraine headaches for all that time. She'd gone to three doctors without results and had become convinced she was incurable. Well, I told her one of my fortes was curing migraines and, in fact, within about three weeks I'd done so.
>
> So I want to tell all my patients that if they know someone who suffers from headaches, tell them they don't have to because there is a cure. Headaches are terrible things and these people can be helped. Would you tell people you know that?

■ **How To's.** Make a list of services or products you'd like to promote. Write a 30- to 60-second script for each. Practice into a tape recorder until it flows easily. After each one, mark it in the file so you don't repeat it. Then reap the results: increased sales now and up to two years later; increased new patients or clients and no cost.

■ **Results.** Optometrist K.R. sold 31 pairs of sports eyewear in one month, including ones for skiing, golf and scuba diving. Veterinarian S.C. increased his kennel's occupancy rate by over 40%. Chiropractor M.P. successfully introduced a line of nutritional supplements into the office with monthly sales hitting the $1,000 mark after 90 days. Attorney N.O. states he substantially increased his billable hours by regularly repeating the need for him to review all contracts and potentially damaging situations to prevent future problems.

☐ WHY AND HOW YOU NEED TO FOLLOW-UP ON PROSPECTS, INCOMPLETES, AND SPLITEES

Dentist W.R. figures it this way. Each new patient generates about $700 in production during his or her first 12 months in the practice. And each stays an average nine years, the time it takes for his patient base to turnover once. Then during these subsequent years, they pay about $150 a year, taking into account maintenance and major work. That means they actually spend roughly $1,900 in toto.

In addition, each will refer an average of 2.1 new patients. Who will then spend a total of $3,990. So what one new person produces for the practice makes a grand total of $5,890.

A little farsightedness opens the eyes widely.

Having stared at the calculator tape for a long time, W.R. felt tremendously motivated. His vow—not to lose a single patient and, if he does, to get them back.

■ **Working the Phones.** This new bigger picture helped motivate him and the staff to provide exquisite service, but there will always be people who'll become fringe patients, those easily lured away ... or driven away. So W.R. adopted a technique he ritualized into the practice.

Before he leaves for home each night, he makes five phone calls. He'll call those who started work but never finished. And those who called but never made an appointment. And those who haven't responded to a recall notice. He'll call them in that order—from greatest to least return-on-investment.

His office manager also makes five calls.

During each call, they try to solve any problems, from motivation to money to poor service. And they always ask for an appointment. About 45% agree. Most do so just because someone called and asked.

Results. With no other changes in the practice, production is up $52,500 over last year and accelerating. "Everyone's working a little harder, now that they know what each patient represents. They see it in their checks through our incentive program. But also the calling is just tremendous. The people we call are surprised to hear from us. Most appreciate our follow-up because they don't have the self-discipline to motivate themselves and stick with the program.

"Since we're so busy here, we were very careful not to add more work to our loads when we started to call. So we had to drop some less productive tasks to make time and that produced a net gain with no additional work."

☐ **AFFINITY MARKETING—NOTE WRITING GENERATES RECORD GROWTH**

It's all the rage these days among big corporations. It's called Affinity Marketing, a fancy term for the really old concept of simply being friendly and, therefore, likeable. And their medium of choice—the mail because of efficiency and low cost.

But chiropractic physician M.P. never heard of big corporations' Affinity Marketing programs. He just wrote letters to his patients in every spare minute he had—after hours and weekends included. The reason? Because he cared about them. Plain and simple.

He's lucky he did. In a hotly competitive market and from a cold start with hardly any external marketing, he rose to over $650,000 in collections last year. Without his compulsive note-writing campaign, his good looks and gentle touch would perhaps have taken him to only $425K.

His 10 to 20 notes a day is truly the mark of someone who cares. And even though *all professionals say* they care, they *rarely display it overtly*. Therefore, patients or clients don't perceive the caring. And if they don't perceive it, it doesn't exist, no matter what the professional feels.

■ **Success.** M.P. has among the highest patient loyalty and best word-of-mouth of all practices in the country. True, he would never enjoy these chevrons if he didn't provide quality care and had the right table-side manner. But his note-writing campaign leveraged these personal attributes and gave him a forum to display them in a meaningful way.

M.P. used to write all his notes by hand—talk about long and arduous. But then he bought an Apple Macintosh computer to generate them more easily and quickly.

Also he was able to format many of the letters so all he had to do was edit each slightly on the screen rather than write a new one each time. This cut the time necessary by more than half. Now it takes less than five minutes for him to conceive of a letter and print it out.

His next improvement will be to get a small tape recorder. He'll then dictate to his front desk that such-and-such patient should get Standard Note #14 and to add his best regards to her Aunt Emily. In this way he can personalize each note, get it in the mail and take only five to ten *seconds* of his time for each. After all, his time is more valuable now, but he certainly doesn't want to abandon the strategy that made him a humongous success.

Also with only five to ten seconds to dash off a note, he can now write a lot more than 10 to 20. Conceptually if he increases that number, the gross should jump correspondingly. It's worked in the past and should do so again in the future.

■ **Types of Notes.** Patient notes can cover a lot of different territory. Here's a list of possible subjects:

  1. A new service, product, drug, modality, etc. to help a particular person.

  2. A bit of new information you've discovered about a patient's interests:

- hobbies (gardening, sewing, collecting, photography, cooking, antiques, decorating, writing, etc.)
- vacationing & travel
- investments
- business (management, personnel, marketing, finance, purchasing, taxes, accounting, computers)
- people
- mutual friends
- charities
- civic activities
- sports (spectator and active)
- restaurants
- children
- education
- entertainment (movies, theater, dance, music, art)
- shopping (where to buy something, local sales, catalogs)
- reading (books, magazines)

  3. A thank-you for information a patient gave to you that you've now used in your life.

  4. A congratulatory note on their new house/job/marriage or their/spouse's/kid's performance at school/sports/whatever. Local small newspapers are a bible of this information.

  5. And of course, a thank you for a referral, but this letter is only part of a series of thank you actions. For complete steps see The Frequent Referrer Program in Chapter 8.

■ **How to Start.** You can do it by hand but that takes time. If you're going to do this efficiently, then overcome your phobia and get the easiest computer to use. You'll be able to generate lots of notes much faster.

Today the easiest computer to use is the Apple Macintosh. It's a tad more expensive than the cheap IBM clones, but you can literally be up and running with no prior computer experience in a couple of hours.

If you don't know how to type, no problem. Just get a typing tutorial program for your Mac and it'll teach you.

You'll need a computer, a hard disk of at least 20 Megabytes of memory and a printer. The printer doesn't have to be a super letter quality one or a laser printer. An inexpensive printer will do for this task.

The IBM clone packages will cost $500 to $700 less but are more difficult to learn. However, most office management programs are written for this type of machine so if you'll expand your usage later, the IBM environment might be a better buy. But not if you're computer resistant. Then the Mac's for you.

■ **Index Carding.** How do you know what to write to someone about? You can try to remember what all your patients or clients are interested in or you can write them down. A simple 3" × 5" index card on each patient in an alphabetical file easily does the trick.

Put the information on the card you wouldn't put on the chart. This is the meat for your letters. You needn't input all of these. Instead use the list as a smorgasbord:

- Problem(s) you're helping them with
- Hometown
- High school or college
- High school or college activities
- Military service
- Marital status (spouse's and kids' names)
- Spouse's and kids' interests
- Previous and present employment
- Future plans
- Professional or trade association memberships
- Clubs or service organizations
- Politically active?
- Religiously active?
- Favorite restaurants
- Hobbies and recreational interests
- Vacation habits
- Spectator sports interest
- Money interests

- Mutual friends
- Other topics they like to talk about.

An ancillary benefit is that as you ferret out this information, your patients or clients will sense your interest in them. More good feelings.

And if you received one or two personal notes a year from your professional, what would you think of him or her? Wouldn't you like to be thought of like that? And get those inevitable mega-referrals that follow? Then remember: Doing at least five notes a day keeps the competition away.

☐ INTERNAL SIGNS SELL

ENT physician M.E. was astounded. Why did one of his patients go to a hearing aid retailer and not to him when she had a hearing problem? Actually a better question was why M.E. should expect any patient to come to him for hearing problems—when he's *never* told them he treats hearing loss!

All professionals have experienced this in different forms. Patients or clients don't know all you do and go someplace else, even though they like and respect you. The antidote is *education and repetition*. And since we often forget to do it verbally, use interior office signage which never forgets.

Choose those services you want to promote (or other benefits like hours or financing) and place multiple signs around the entire office. No, one wimpy sign doesn't do it. You need beaucoup.

■ **Types of Signs.** Wall frames for posters; table tents; staff badges; counter cards; danglers; banners; balloons; "take one" displays; and electronic message bars. Place them in lots of rooms. Mix and match types of signs. And periodically change the services you promote.

Calendar example: In January, promote headache relief; February—leg pain; March—Patient Appreciation Day; April—sports injuries; May—work injuries; June—shoulder pain; July—back pain; August—children's checkups; September—financing; October—neck pain; November—convenient hours; December—nutrition.

The good part—these cost very little. And you never forego the chance to provide services to existing patients or clients again for failing to educate them.

Jeff Slutsky, *Street Smart Marketing*, John Wiley & Sons, New York, 1989, $14.95 and THE PRACTICE BUILDER.

☐ THE 10 ALL-TIME BEST WAYS TO CONVINCE SOMEONE TO ACCEPT
YOUR RECOMMENDATIONS

Sometimes you know in your heart a patient should accept your recommendation, but he hems and haws to his own detriment. How can you close your presentation and get him to "Yes" in spite of himself?

Just use one of the all-time best closes for presentations. Not all of these tested ways are appropriate for every practice or every situation. So study them carefully. Choose those apropos for you. And practice, practice, practice. Then watch your ability to convince impress even you.

1. *The Ben Franklin Close:* For rational thinkers, tell them how Ben Franklin made decisions. "He'd put all the positives on one side of a sheet and all the negatives on the other. Like in this case, Ben would write down [you list the benefits again]. These are the benefits. Now, besides costing a few dollars, can you think of any negatives?" [Allows you to answer any hidden objections.] "Well, I think you'll agree it's a good idea. Can we get started?" If the objection is still money, pull out your list of financing options.

2. *The Assumptive Close:* This is for people who get too nervous to say "Yes." Don't ask if they want to accept your recommendation. Just assume they do and go straight into planning the details. This way they don't have to say "Yes," which is what paralyzes them. "So unless you have an objection, I'll schedule you in again for next Tuesday."

3. *The Dual Alternative Close:* This time you give two alternatives to the nervous and hesitant person, both of which assume agreement. If they say "Yes" to either one, they've said "Yes" to your recommendation. "Would you want to start next week or wait until after the holiday?"

4. *The Double Positive Close:* In this effort, you give two options— one to say "yes" and one to continue your presentation so they can say "yes" later on. Repeat the benefits, then add: "Have I given you enough information to start or do you want me to continue with more information?"

5. *The Puppy Dog Close:* This is what pet stores do when they encourage you to take home a puppy for the weekend. They know you'll never return it. Give the patient a free sample of the service so they can feel the benefits. If a product is involved, encourage them to use it for a few days. If they like it, then they pay. For security take a credit card imprint as a hotel does.

6. *The Probability Close:* This is for the patient who's thinking and thinking, but not committing. "Let me ask you a question. You understand the benefits. What's the probability you'll accept my recommendation?" Then be quiet, no matter what. If they answer "80% yes/20% no," say, "May I ask what's the 20% against?" This forces the prospect to focus on the real objection and gives you a chance to answer it. Oftentimes, it's a misconception.

7. *The Second Appointment Close:* Some people won't commit the first time no matter what. Some want to shop, others want to think. When you're convinced they won't say "Yes" today, keep the door open. "Good. Let me suggest you (compare/think) for a few days. Then I also suggest we schedule another appointment at no charge. At that time I'll have some more information I can gather for you so you can truly have the complete picture and then make your decision. Isn't that a good idea?"

8. *The Impending Event Close:* If something will happen soon that will affect the prospect's decision, make sure you tell them. It may be a price hike or even that you're going on vacation. If a product is in short supply, it might be that it won't be available. Or that your time is filling up.

9. *The Negative Option Close:* Again, for the nervous types, make the decision for them. "Listen, we're awfully busy so let me suggest that we schedule this up just to save the spot in case you want to go ahead. If you decide against it, just give me a call and cancel. It's no problem." This is a weak close. You will lose one out of three, or even four, although you know it's in their best interest. But that sure beats a "maybe" from them.

10. *The Price Drop Close:* Some people won't move off the dime, even if you finance it forever. They need a deal. First, try to throw in extra services or products, without lowering the price. If that doesn't work, tell them you have a category of fees you reserve for other professionals called Professional Courtesy Fees. Offer to treat them as you would a colleague. Or offer one of your Professional Grants which can be credited toward their bill. Either way, don't lower the price and therefore cheapen your services.

Steven West, *Advanced Closing Strategies*, American Sales & Marketing Institute, 61-47 188th St., Fresh Meadows, NY 11365 and THE PRACTICE BUILDER.

OBJECTION HANDLING: "I HAVE TO TALK IT OVER WITH MY SPOUSE/PARTNER/DOG"

In 99% of cases, no one has to talk anything over with anyone. It's simply an excuse to postpone a decision. So to deal with this objection, follow four steps:

1. Soften the objection.

2. Isolate it.

3. Get a positive opinion.

4. Suggest your solution.

When someone says they need to talk it over with _____, to soften the objection just say, "I understand." Don't argue!

Then, to isolate the objection, say, "Let me ask you this. Other than talking it over with _____, is there any other reason why you wouldn't be able to give the go-ahead right now?" Usually not.

Next, to get a positive opinion, ask: "Then, in your opinion, is there any reason why you think your _____ wouldn't want you to do this?" "*No, but I think it's a good idea to get (or I need) his/her permission/opinion.*"

Finally, suggest this: "Great. Then let me make a suggestion. Why don't we get the ball rolling now, and in the meantime, you talk it over with your _____. If there's any problem, give me a call. Fair enough?"

This will help about 50% of the time. Many will not even talk it over with anyone. Others will present it as something they're going to do. And fewer still will seek counsel and/or permission—instead of most.

Now the odds are in your favor.

Jeff Slutsky, *Street Smart Marketing*, John Wiley & Sons, New York, 1989, $14.95 and THE PRACTICE BUILDER.

☐ **QUERYING WITH WAITING ROOM SURVEY BOOSTS CASE SIZE**

Optometrist S.M. never had time. He was always rushed and as a result, usually missed something. Not in pathology, but in patient needs.

You see, S.M. didn't have time to ask the right questions such as: What sports do you play? Do you watch TV lying down or sitting up? Do you work with a CRT?

Each answer could well point to an unmet visual need. For instance, S.M. practices right in the backyard of the largest scuba diving market in the U.S.—Southern California. But he never asks if his patients scuba, even though he provides the needed and expensive eyewear.

To fill that void today there's an interactive computer with a touch screen on the market which does the querying of needs for you in the waiting room. Called Niche 1 (1-800-NICHNET), its beauty is that the practitioner can hold up the printout and say that "The Computer" recommends the following for you. And if "The Computer" says so, well it must be true. Bam! The case size goes up.

But being low on investment cash, S.M. did it the cheaper way. He put together a *checklist* survey to be filled out by hand each time a patient comes in. It takes three minutes and covers all those areas S.M. either has no time for or forgets to ask about. Now he never forgets. The survey's done it for him. And bam! His case size went up.

This same strategy can work for any practice with elective services or products or with patient or client needs which take time to ferret out.

PROMOTIONS IN MOTION

1. Veterinarian H.F. prebooks all vaccinations and care for puppies and kittens for the first year. Appointments further out than 30 days are reconfirmed by postcard and phone. There's been no client resistance and follow through is almost 100%, rather than the more usual 75%.

   H.F. also runs seasonal promotions: Lyme disease; Heartworm; spay and neuter; geriatric animal care and feline leukemia. To promote each he uses: Internal Prospecting quarterly mailings to his client base; dressing the waiting room with information; PSAs (public service announcements) to newspapers and electronic media; and 40,000 co-op coupons in Val-Pak and ADVO. Results: Production up 37% over last year.

2. Optometrist S.B. now suggests a pair of eyeglasses just for evening wear. He argues that a woman would think nothing of spending $300 on a gown, but would wear the same old everyday eyewear with the outfit. And that doesn't make sense. Obviously women agree with him. Second pair sales are up 31% since he started asking and convincing.

Chapter 7 □

KEEP THEM COMIN' BACK IN DROVES: YOUR RECALLS AND REACTIVATIONS

□ RECALL UPDATE: GETTING OVER 90% SUCCESS

Repeat business is the cornerstone to any practice. But if you look at individual recall ratios, most are abysmal. Physician K.T. runs at 28% recall for those he deems need a bi-yearly physical. Optometrist W.E. is lower at 22%. Chiropractor T.C. still lower at 16%. Even pediatrician F.L. isn't happy retaining only 81% every year—and he shouldn't be.

But dentist J.G. recalls at a humongously beautiful 91%!!! What's he doing right which the others aren't? It's not because of his field since many dentists recall well under 50% each year. It's just two concepts that fill his book a year in advance—*specificity and repetition*. The approach is worth borrowing and adapting.

■ **Specificity.** Most people have no idea what the ramifications are for ignoring a recall. They simply have never had the bottom line clearly explained before. Therefore, many are happy *not* to think about coming back. They'd rather be concerned with NFL football, why their child wasn't picked to star in the class play, or how to afford Club Med. With these weighty matters to contemplate, why think about your service— when they don't have an apparent problem?

Good question. Can you answer it? If you can't, many patients or clients aren't going to come back. Like up to 80% of them.

First, let's assume you're ethical and recalling only those who need it. So you do have a good reason to see them. Well, what is it? Just to see them again? To check out their situation is not the reason. That's the modality. The real reason is to make sure *something bad doesn't happen.*

In ophthalmology, it's to check for signs of glaucoma. If undetected, glaucoma leads to blindness. Yet most people haven't a clue as to what this danger is. They have even less of an idea what it's like to be blind. If they don't know, it's easy to ignore.

And those professionals who don't explain the risks in ultra-detail are adding to the problem. Most people will ignore a recall if it doesn't seem important. And the only way to make it important is to be specific about the risks.

What would life be like being blind? Or with advanced, degenerative, spinal disease? Tell them ... and tell them over and over again.

■ **Repetition.** Today, peoples' minds are cluttered. Information has exploded. And competition for mind space is keen. So if you want your patients or clients to return, you best repeat your reasons frequently. Here's how.

First, precondition the recall. At the first or second visit, tell them you're going to recall him or her and explain why. Lots of specifics, please.

Second, at the time of the last appointment, remind the person again of the recall need and reasons why. Then look each one in the eyes and ask if he or she'll promise to come back so you can help prevent these things from happening. Everyone says yes.

Third, walk the patient or client to the front desk and instruct your scheduler to pencil in the recall appointment, even if it's a year away. Then explain to the person how the practice has become busy and you need to reserve your most convenient times for your existing patients or clients. You'll send a reminder a few weeks in advance and if he or she needs to reschedule, it can be done at that time. But at least the time is reserved.

You want them to commit right then! They're enthusiastic, at least more so than when your glow has faded from their heart in a year's time.

You also want them in the books now because it *psychologically takes them out of the market.* If they already have an appointment with you, why pay attention to the gilded words of your promoting colleagues?

If they don't commit now, far fewer will do so in the future. Period.

Fourth, have the patient or client hand address a recall postcard right there. File it in a tickler file to be mailed three weeks prior to the appointment. The card reminds them of the appointment. Their own handwriting reminds them they've already agreed to it, so there's no need to think about whether to come back.

The card also repeats the magic words—*why it's important to come back now and what specifically can happen to you if you don't* just in case they have second doubts.

Fifth, reconfirm by phone two days before. This is crucial to reduce no-shows. Hard-to-gets can be called from someone's home between five and nine at night. If someone balks, repeat the magic words and ask for the appointment. Script this out for your caller.

Sixth, if they don't show, call within 15 minutes. You don't want to reinforce unacceptable behavior. Polite but firm, please. If they balk, again repeat the magic words and ask for the appointment.

Seventh, if you can't get hold of them to reschedule, send a letter with the magic words and tell them to call for an appointment.

Eighth, if they don't respond, mail them another letter with the same message in a month. Things may have cleared up for them by then and they'll be ready to come in. Tests show the more times you contact them, the more people will respond.

Is all this repetition a bother to people? It depends. If you sound self-serving, it's all a bother. If you sound like the guardian of their well being, then you're watching out for them and it's no bother at all. To be safe, keep your message to why it's important to come back now and what specifically can happen to them if they don't.

Caution. The most common screw-up is with the message. The professional "thinks" he or she is being specific about risks, but, in fact, is still too general. If you're going to err, err on the side of too many specifics.

Therefore, *generic and general recall cards* purchased from a catalog are *universally useless*. Write your own.

■ **Results.** The system works in every situation where a patient or client needs to be recalled in the future. In every profession, THE PRACTICE BUILDER has numerous examples of practitioners with over 90% recall success. If you follow the steps exactly, you'll count yourself among them.

☐ CONTACTING THE RIGHT PERSON IN RECALLS

Optometrist R.L. is a student of human behavior. He saw a recall notice on his own family's notice board for his 25-year-old son even though the son hadn't lived there in years. His wife explained the obvious, "If I leave it up to him, he'll never respond to this notice and go for his dental checkup. So I have his dentist send me his recall notice and then I make the appointment and tell him when to go."

R.L. stood shaking his head. Not because a 25-year-old needed to have an appointment made for him. But because he wondered how many people he had missed recalling successfully by not contacting the right person. All the sons, daughters, and husbands who delegate their professional services to Super Mom. Is that hundreds? Over the years probably thousands.

■ **The Right Person.** R.L. then started asking all the moms on his intake form about which family members they wanted recall notices for. The specific figure has not been tabulated, but R.L. is impressed by how many more it is than even he thought. Now he contacts both the patient and the family "gatekeeper."

Compliance is bound to go up ... along with production and referrals.

□ SAMPLE: ENHANCED REACTIVATION EFFORT

Tests repeatedly show reactivations of past clients or patients work well. Those who you think have fallen off the face of the earth or who even dislike you can miraculously reappear after the appropriate nudge.

However, reactivation only works with a large base that hasn't been vigorously recalled, including tele-recalling. So you need minimally three to four years in practice to build sufficient numbers because only a fraction will come back—but a highly profitable fraction.

The appropriate nudge then is a letter talking about why they should come back *now* and what can happen if they don't. *Specifics* are required. And an offer always increases the numbers. Run-of-the-mill reactivations are short one-pagers. But you can *enhance* the effort and your response by lengthening the copy and the arguments why they need to come in now.

■ **Sample Of Enhanced Reactivation Effort.**

Dear Friend,

We haven't seen you for quite some time. This could mean serious consequences for your teeth and gums, such as eventual tooth loss or worse, major gum surgery.

Many types of dental problems require continuing care; the kind of care you can only get from your professional dentist. Without this continuing care, the problems can progress and worsen. And this can have dangerous effects on your dental health.

Gum disease ... no one is immune.

For example, did you know that gum disease is blamed for approximately 50% of all missing teeth? Did you also know that some form of gum disease affects 87% of the population? And, did you know that gum disease can be *prevented* with proper care?

Know the warning signs of gum disease.

Healthy gums are firm and resilient. And, even though gum disease sometimes progresses without symptoms, there are some symptoms that almost always mean a problem with gum disease.

Warning sign checklist:

❑ Gums that bleed when you brush or floss
❑ Swollen, red and tender gums
❑ Gums that have separated from the tooth
❑ Loose teeth or teeth that look long because of receding gums
❑ Changes in the way teeth or partial dentures fit together
❑ Persistent bad taste or bad breath

If you're experiencing any of these symptoms, it's important that you come in right away. When we catch it in its early stages, gum disease can often be treated non-surgically. Remember, too, that gum disease doesn't always display symptoms. Since you haven't been checked in awhile, it's important that you come in so we can find any problems in their early stages.

Don't wait until you have problems to call.

Tartar that forms on the base of your teeth and under your gums can, and will, actually pull your gums away from your teeth. This process causes pockets in the gums where diseases flourish—and become harder to get to. Your teeth will become loose, and you may eventually lose them.

We use the best gum care available. It's called soft tissue management, and it's a non-surgical approach that is less costly and far less painful than having gum surgery. Gum disease doesn't have to be a fact of life.

And that's the message we want to get across to you. When we're able to detect gum disease early, you won't have to suffer painful surgery or the expense of replacing lost teeth.

Remember, only the trained eye of your dentist can spot problems like these in their earliest stages, and prevent pain and discomfort later.

Why you should replace those missing teeth.

If you're missing one or more permanent teeth, those empty spaces can lead to serious problems affecting your entire mouth.

A lot of people think, "If it doesn't show, it doesn't matter." This is not true, however, because teeth are designed to support each other. When a tooth is missing, adjoining teeth tend to move toward the open space to fill it in. In addition to serious bite problems, this tooth movement can contribute to cavities and gum diseases, and often results in even more teeth being lost.

While our main goal is to prevent the loss of teeth, there are things we can do to replace them and prevent further problems. But, we can't help if you don't come in.

Now you can see what I see.

Thanks to revolutionary advances in dentistry, new technology has made it possible for you to see the same things I see when you come in for a check up. We're one of the first offices in the area to offer Dentacam video screening.

It looks like a wand with a light at the tip. That light is a TV camera that magnifies the inside of your mouth and projects the image on a screen. But what does all this mean to you? It means that when I talk about plaque and gum disease, you'll be able to see it. That may sound a little gruesome, but it will help you understand how important good dental hygiene and regular cleanings are to your teeth and gums.

Please call us for an all-important exam.

Don't rely on your own eyes to spot problems. Or on your own judgment to diagnose conditions. Again, it takes training to spot most tooth and gum problems in their earliest stages. Remember: Only a dental professional can see many problems and know how to treat them.

Before you have a problem that needs extensive care, come and see me. Preventive care is your best defense against tooth and gum decay, not to mention possible surgery.

Because we have not seen or heard from you in some time, we would like to give you a complete exam and see how you're doing. It's so important to us that we've enclosed a gift certificate for you to receive your exam, plus a consultation and Dentacam video screening for free.

Remember: The time to stop dental problems is while they are still minor.

Give us a call at 775-3003, and set up your appointment today! Remember, our efficient office always runs on time, so you rarely have to wait. Please don't put off this important checkup.

Sincerely,

P.S. Don't ignore your dental health call us today. And use the enclosed gift certificate!

Then for those who don't respond within 30 days of your mailing, call with a scripted phone call reiterating your main message: Why it's important to come back now and what specifically can happen to them if they don't. Your caller should be paid an incentive for every appointment booked and kept.

■ Sample Telemarketing Script

Hello, (patient or client's name), my name is (caller), and I'm calling from Dr. ____ office. The doctor asked me to call you because you haven't been in for your regular checkup. He's concerned because you may be in the 87% bracket of adults that have some form of gum disease and, if left untreated, can lead to the need for gum surgery. Dr. ____ wants to make sure that if you have a problem, we catch it in its early stages—before any of this happens. And you'll be glad to know that Dr. ____ feels so strongly about it that he's authorized me to set up a free examination and consultation for you. How about (day, date & time)? Or (day, date & time)?

Also be prepared for the following common objections with scripted rebuttals:

1. "No, that's not a good time for me ..."
2. "It's inconvenient to make the trip to your office ..."
3. "I'll think about it and let you know ..."
4. "Your office staff is very uncooperative ..."
5. "I'm not happy with the doctor's attitude ..."
6. "I'm going to go to someone else where I can get ..."
7. "I really can't afford to come in right now ..."
8. "I'm going to another doctor who's less expensive ..."

■ Results.
In practice eight years, podiatrist W.R. had never contacted any past patients for any reason—until he reactivated his base. Then just his direct mail alone turned up 21 surgeries in three months time. ROI: 26 to 1.

"Of course I knew that people with one foot problem tend to have others. But I was always under the impression that people would be motivated to take care of them, especially if they'd been to me before ... . That was a gross misunderstanding on my part."

☐ REACTIVATION STRATEGIES: BIG DOLLARS IN, SMALL DOLLARS OUT

Podiatrist T.D. had accumulated over 20,000 charts during 16 years of practice. He had halfheartedly recalled his patients for continuing care, more or less unsuccessfully. But one slow day he decided to crank up his computer and generate labels so he could mail to 7,500 patients from the last five years, reminding them to come in.

What did he get? *204 calls and $61,740 in income in 90 days*, including a host of surgeries. Cost: a mere $1,500. Return on investment: *$41.16 in for every $1 out.*

■ **Reactivation Strategies.** "Reactivation" is for someone who has been recalled, not responded, and whom you haven't seen in a few years. It may seem that you're never going to see them again, but overall that's not true. Plenty of these people need additional services—even if they've gone elsewhere in the meantime. Some will be disenchanted with their new professional. Some will now realize they should come in for a recall, but have put it off. How do we know? Actually, we're only guessing the reasons. But the numbers of responses to reactivation efforts *tell us they respond,* whatever the reasons.

Here's how to do it. First, compose a one- to two-page letter. *Be very specific as to why it's important to come in now and what can happen to them if they don't.* The more specific you are, the more response you get. Spell out what can happen from glaucoma, degenerative spinal disease or not having a mammogram. Since this is the most important part of the strategy, tell them. Pull few punches. (Ethics: One assumes here that you don't contact anyone whom you don't truly believe may need to come in.)

Usually when professionals reactivate by mail, they merely offer a deal ... and that works. But if you tell them *why* they need to come, the response rate is exponentially greater. Then if you add a "deal" on a separate enclosure, it pumps up response even more. Is a deal necessary? No, but in middle to lower markets, it helps. However, put most of your effort into the "why."

If your software can sort by diagnosis or type of case, you can write specific letters to each type of patient or client, rather than a more generic—and less responsive—one. If you can't sort, mail the generic one anyway. The results are too big not to.

If you don't have a computer, put your past files, sorted by condition, up on a mailing list at a computer service bureau. You should have file labels anyway to "farm" your base quarterly for referrals and repeat business.

Now mail to all those patients or clients who should be seen but haven't been in three years. You'll do well with them. Also take a random sample from the four- to seven-year range and mail to them. If they respond well, mail the whole group. Also test the eight-year and beyond group with a randomly selected sample and rollout if warranted. You need to test these other groups because some practices will do well with them and some won't.

Mark on the envelope for this bulk rate mailing "Address Correction Requested." This cleans your list of the dead and gone to reduce your costs for future mailings.

■ **Extending a Good Thing.** T.D. remembered two key PRACTICE BUILDER concepts: Repetition works. And phone communication is more powerful than mail. So he hired college students to work between five and nine at night phoning those who needed to come in but hadn't responded to the mail. Reading from a script, the caller told the patient that the professional had asked the caller to phone. Also why the patient needed to come in and what could happen if they didn't. The caller then asked for the appointment. The callers were also prepared with scripted rebuttals for the most common objections.

That effort brought in *421 more patients and $103,977* within six months.

■ **Rollout Strategy.** Mail first because it's cheaper that phoning. Then phone those who don't respond to the mail.

■ **Results.** In practice eight years, orthopedic surgeon W.R. had never contacted any past patients for any reason—until he reactivated his base. Then just his direct mail alone turned up 21 surgeries in three months time. ROI: 26 to 1.

"Of course I knew that people with one problem tend to have others. But I was always under the impression that people would be motivated to take care of them, especially if they'd been to me before ... . That was a gross misunderstanding on my part."

Conclusion: Any professional with a sizeable base of past business is sitting on a humongous opportunity.

☐ **WHAT CAN REACTIVATION PAY?**

Northwest veterinarian V.T. had never done much to cultivate his past client base, those he assumed didn't like him and went elsewhere. Then he tried reactivating them.

■ **Results.** V.T. followed the classic PRACTICE BUILDER Reactivation format and mailed the direct mail package to 3,000 of the long gone. Over 500 quickly came back. Return-on-investment: 17.75:1. Key: The base was largely unworked and the previous recall system was weak with only a single postcard effort.

☐ REACTIVATION ANALYSIS: MOTIVATION IMMEDIATE RESPONSE

When you reactivate past patients or clients, you can increase your ROI if you include an incentive—especially by printing it on a separate enclosure. This is true even if you've already mentioned it in your letter. The repetition works and the separate enclosure highlights it.

The foldover piece in Figure 7.1 covers all the bases to get your past clients back into the fold. Also notice how the copy just doesn't mention an exam. It also explains what's in one to help motivate the reader even more.

Nice graphics and copy for a nice response.

☐ WHEN REACTIVATIONS WON'T WORK

Patients or clients unseen and unheard from for some time (for many practices a two-year period) means that they've stopped coming because they don't understand the need to return. So THE PRACTICE BUILDER recommends two reactivation efforts every few years to bring the forgotten back to the fold.

As described above, you first send a direct mail package—a letter plus direct response insert in an office envelope with no teaser copy. The essential message: Why it's important to come in now and what specifically can happen if you don't.•

The second step is a telephone follow-up within 20 to 30 days to those who don't respond to the mail. The essential message and direct response offer is the same. At the same time, the caller asks to schedule an appointment. Mailing first rather than calling is less costly.

■ **But Reactivation Won't Always Work.** Gastroenterologist T.O. reactivated his long gone file to disappointing results. Upon close inspection, here's what we discovered.

T.O. is a true student of THE PRACTICE BUILDER. He can quote it chapter and verse. So it's not surprising that he's had a complete and successful recall system for many years, one that basically cleaned out his long gone file. There wasn't any gold left in those hills.

If you've implemented a recall system with multiple contacts including a telephone call, then your reactivation file is going to be pretty clean. Those left in it don't want to come back, at least not in sufficient enough numbers to make it profitable. So pass.

But if you've only had a one- or two-step recall system even with a phone recall, then your forgotten base is prime for plucking. Pluck away.

Figure 7.1 A Foldover Piece

PROMOTIONS IN MOTION

1. Chiropractor R.G. recently bought a sleepy little practice in a sleepy little town. When he took over, both things stayed that way. So he decided to reactivate past patients by mailing a letter. Only two responses out of 700 letters. (Bad news, but probably due to what he said rather than the usually successful concept of mailing.)

Then he called. Obviously he said something different (like *why* it's important to come in now and *specifically what* can happen to you if you don't. That's *the* motivating message.)

His response rate: 50% of those he called came into the office right away.

Chapter 8   □

EXPLOSIVE GROWTH FROM SOLID REFERRALS: HOW TO TURN A FIRST-TIME PATIENT INTO A REFERRER

You can actually turn a *first-time* patient into an enthusiastic babbler about you—if you pay attention to a few basic rules of human behavior. Then, when you finally ask for referrals at the end of your first set of servicing appointments, you'll discover many already are referring. So study these carefully.

■ **Rule #1.** Most new people have post-purchase dissonance. This psych term refers to the uneasy feeling that the person may not have made a wise choice in seeing you. If their first visit is unpleasant or even neutral, the feeling persists. It's a certainty you won't get referrals and some may not return. Bad news, but common.

■ **Rule #2.** People must consider you to be an expert since people only refer to "experts."

■ **Rule #3.** If you exceed people's expectations, they'll be extraordinarily happy. To do so, you must do the unexpected.

Based on these rules, here are the referral-producing tactics to use:

1. On their first visit, make a *big deal* of their coming. Give them a short tour. Introduce them around so they feel comfortable. Everyone

should give them an *overly big* hello and smile. In order to do this well, you must think of it as *theater* because, in fact, it is. And it will make people like you much more.

2. To position you as an expert, you'll need to educate people about you. So before you see them, have the front desk hand out your Waiting Room Resume. You'll find details in Chapter Three. Also, for repetition, have one displayed in a Plexiglass stand in your waiting room.

3. In order to exceed people's expectations, you'll need to give them something they didn't expect. Think about this in the context of your practice. Is it a free cholesterol test? Tell them you're giving them this gift as a welcome to the practice. And so they appreciate the value, tell them what you usually charge for it. The gift will make them pleasantly surprised.

4. And if one gift makes them very happy, two will make them ecstatic. So give them another. Choose your gifts so they cost you little but have *high perceived value*. And since the outlay is low, don't worry about the money. The payback of an enthusiastic referrer is enormous.

■ **Implementation.** Don't these all make sense? Wouldn't you feel good if someone treated you this way? Of course. But even though all professionals may want to treat their patients or clients this way, many won't. The reasons are twofold.

First, you won't insist on the program to your staff. You'll mention it once and when they stop doing it tomorrow, you won't mention it again. Training takes lots of repetition. You must keep at it.

And second, some on your staff will tell you why they can't do it. These are the people who make excuses for everything. They've done this before, many times. And you know it, but it's easier to let them go on as before rather than fight to do it right or to replace them.

These are your mediocre people. They cannot be retrained. *They need to be fired.* The only reason to retain them is because you've decided you want a mediocre practice.

To turn a first-time patient into an immediate referrer takes effort. But if you want the *all-referral practice,* this is how you spend your effort.

☐ **USING THIRD PARTY ENDORSEMENTS FOR CAPTURING NEW REFERRERS**

Psychologist N.R. had a satellite within a respected internist's office in a busy Washington, DC hospital complex. She hadn't networked yet within this fertile complex and had little flow except the small but steady stream from the internist. No question she needed more.

However, before doing anything she smartly went to the internist (who thought she was terrific) and asked him to first speak to his colleagues about her before she did. N.R. would give him a list of those she wanted to target and he'd lay the groundwork for her follow-up call to get a face-to-face.

With the respect colleagues had for the internist, the scene was now set for a much easier cultivation of referrals. Cold calling would have proven productive, but much, much harder.

Concept: Always use a mutual friend or respected professional to talk you up before contacting a potential referrer.

Result. A successful satellite launch.

☐ HOW TO ASK FOR REFERRALS THE RIGHT WAY

Everyone knows it works. Everyone's sick of hearing it. So why doesn't everyone do it? Ask for referrals, that is.

Asking every patient for a referral is *by far the most effective, least costly way to build an all-referral practice!* Then why must it feel so uncomfortable?

■ **The Answer.** Who knows? But the way to become comfortable is to do it two or three times—the right way. You'll quickly see how people want to help—as long as you tell them how.

After all, you're the authority figure. And since you've done a good job for them, they're eager to be in your good graces.

So ask during their last appointment. Look them in the eye—because you're sincerely going to ask them for a personal favor. The eye contact indicates the importance of the request. By positioning the request as a favor, it indicates they'll please you by acting on it. That's their reward. In this case, it's what makes Johnny run.

Then say:

> I'd like to ask you for a favor. If you've liked what I've done for you here, I'd like you to send me someone I can help the same way I've helped you. I'm sure they'll be pleased. And I'd appreciate it, too. Will you do that for me?

Everyone says yes! What positive feedback. So it won't hurt at all.

Does this mean you need business? That's a thought that crosses *only your mind.* The people you're asking are thinking they now have a way to please an authority figure in their lives. That's all they're concerned about.

One more bit of interesting info. Volumes and volumes of tests show that *if you ask, you get.* If you don't ask, you don't get. In fact, the tests are so unanimous, that this tactic is a rare slam dunk.

With Space Mountain providing a dramatic backdrop, Disney's Contemporary Resort welcomes visitors to a new dimension in hospitality, comfort and recreation. Relax and enjoy the many amenities our resort has to offer or let the monorail transport you to the Magic Kingdom Park, EPCOT Center and much more. For the business traveller, our state-of-the-art Convention Center provides the perfect setting for meetings and conventions.

Disney's Contemporary Resort

☐ THE FREQUENT REFERRER PROGRAM: GETTING REFERRERS TO REFER IN EVEN MORE

This isn't tough at all. Just make people feel good about referring in and they'll do it even more. That means you don't wait until the third or fifth referral to make a big deal out of it. You do it on the *first.*

And making a big deal means a big deal. Make three responses to each referral. Three! One is a phone call from the professional. Two is a gushy letter restating the phone call. And three is a small gift imprinted with a thank-you message. But when professionals start on this "slam-dunk-to-double-word-of-mouth-referrals" program, they usually start poorly. The problem is they convey a weak message during the phone call.

Instead of writing or vamping your own phone call script, use this time-tested PRACTICE BUILDER script:

> Hello, _____. This is _____. I wanted to call you today because I understand you referred in _____ and I wanted to personally thank you. You see, our practice is based on word-of-mouth referrals and, quite frankly, not everybody takes the time to refer someone in. So when someone does, we're very appreciative and we consider that person to be very special. So I just wanted to say thank you—and that we think you're a very special person.
> By the way, we'll take extra care of _____. I hope everything is fine with you. [If appropriate:] And also my best regards to your family.

The program is known as the Frequent Referrer Program. It's based on the fact that what's true in beer drinking is also true in referrals. Twenty percent of the people are responsible for 80% of the action. What's also interesting is that of those 20% there's a handful of patients or clients responsible for a great portion of the 80%. But what's even more interesting is that there's a proven way to quadruple this referral activity—with little cost.

■ **Shaping Behavior.** For those who took Psych 101, you'll recall how researchers taught a pigeon to turn in a complete circle. While moving randomly, the pigeon would eventually turn 10 degrees to the left. When it did, the researchers would drop a food pellet into the cage. They would reinforce the pigeon again when it turned further to the left. Eventually they had a pigeon spinning on his heels—all for a pellet.

At least in this realm, people are like pigeons. For a certain amount of recognition, they'll refer and refer and refer.

But until now, the physician's problem has been that conventional wisdom told them to reinforce referrals with a thank-you note. Unfortunately, a short note pales by comparison to a yummy pellet. The problem is that written communication is far less potent than phone or face-to-face. Also, that it's read and gone in 15 seconds, so shelf-life is short.

Therefore, if you're truly looking to shape referring behavior, make the reinforcement stronger ... and make it stay around.

■ **Stronger Communication.** For the first referral, you'll want to make a big deal about it using strong recognition activities. And because phone is more powerful that a note, it's the vehicle of choice.

Since the professional is the respected figure, he or she should do the calling. Not the office manager. Does it take time? Yes, but if you're trying to build a practice based on word-of-mouth, *you* work the referrals.

Tell the referrer how much you appreciate their confidence and how you'll make sure the friend they referred will feel as pleased as they. Also say that you now consider them to be a special friend of the practice. Don't ask for more referrals at this point; this program is far more subtle than that.

Then send them a note with the same message. And enclose a gift.

■ **The Right Gifts.** Gifts should not be expensive, but not look flimsy. Think in the $5 and under range for the first referral for a middle-lower all the way to a middle-upper market. For business referrals or in upper-income markets gifts should be more expensive since the referrer is more sophisticated and used to pricier things. But the average person isn't, no matter what's the size of the referred case.

Also select your gifts so they'll be displayed in the home or used frequently. Visibility or use gives the gift longevity, so they'll be reminded of your thoughtfulness for years to come.

Also make sure your gifts are *inscribed.* Your imprinted message is what constantly reminds them of you. Sample inscription: With sincere thanks, Dr. Tim Mahoney, Obstetrician.

■ **Sample Gifts.** A number of gifts that fit the guidelines c f visibility or use and yet don't look flimsy are in the $5 range. A digital clock set in a Plexiglass stand fits the bill. Now available is a high tech flashlight for emergencies with inscribed stand that adheres to the wall. Also the ever-popular first aid kit for car or home.

Use any of these for the first and second referrals. No phone call is needed with the second referral, but a *strong* note singing their praises is a must. Whimpy, lackluster copy kaboshes the effort.

Beware of sending flowers. Yes, women appreciate them, but husbands oftentimes don't. A woman may even stop referring for fear of offending her spouse again. Besides, you can accomplish the same for less without the potential downside.

On the third referral, bump the gift. In the $5 to $15 range you can buy a handsome 5 × 7" calculator built into the cover of a useful note pad box. Also extremely useful is a handy car care kit. Plus a hot & cold thermos for school, work, picnics or sporting events. All inscribed.

For every fifth referral, give an expensive gift based upon your knowledge of them. Examples: dinner at their favorite restaurant or an opportunity for a portrait photo. Fifty bucks is a small investment for the mega-money they bring in.

Where can you find *inscribed* gifts like these? Either look in the *Yellow Pages* for companies which call themselves premium, incentive or ad specialty firms. Or you can now order them through THE PRACTICE BUILDER, complete with five free accompanying letters written by the Creative Director of The Practice Builder Agency.To order a catalog, simply call or write THE PRACTICE BUILDER, 2755 Bristol, Suite 100, Costa Mesa, CA 92626; (714) 545-8900.

■ **Guideline.** Don't promote the program. The reinforcement is given *after the fact* to shape referring behavior nicely. If you promote the gifts, it can come off as paying for a referral. That violates the spirit of the program.

Not promoting the gifts doesn't mean you shouldn't ask for referrals. That's a given. "He who doesn't ask for sterling silver gets one wooden chopstick."

Since you won't promote the program, it will naturally start slowly. But six months down the line, it will *take off like gangbusters.* Keep that in mind.

■ **Results.** Drs. C.Y. and M.S. send out a vinyl address book with pen for the first referral. (Cost—$4.) For the second referral, they give a quartz clock set in Lucite. (Cost—$8.) For the third, a large pad calculator. (Cost—$10.) All come with a powerful letter.

"Since we wanted to build a practice based on word-of-mouth, this is the best thing we ever did. It began slowly, but now it's spreading like wildfire ... Also it didn't cost us anything unless a referral came in. Now we buy in quantity to keep our costs down."

☐ **BREAKING INTO THE OLD BOYS' REFERRAL CLUB**

After moving his practice 45 miles to a new town, psychologist H.L. was shut out. As the new boy on the block, not only couldn't he get referrals from physicians and surgeons, but he couldn't even get a face-to-face to dazzle them with his abilities and credentials. The referral patterns were already set. He didn't think he'd ever break in. What to do?

H.L. called his Hotline Advisor who told him that above all, this was a numbers game. He's got to make lots of contacts, target on prime prospects, and then maintain the referral stream. Here's what he instructed him to do.

First, talk to all the physicians and other professionals he already knew who could give him names of other physicians in the new town who might refer. At this point, H.L.'s looking for *names he can use to get through the front door*. And a name will almost always pave the way.

Then write a personal letter. His computer was marvelous for this because he took a standard letter and just modified it slightly. He started by mentioning the person who gave him the reader's name and then why he was writing.

Of course he talked about his credentials and training and noted the names of other physicians who referred to him in the past. (This is tapping into the bandwagon effect.) He even got permission to use a quote from a physician referrer in his old location.

And then he added *an information tidbit*. It was a tip that H.L. picked up from the literature which was useful in the reader's practice. He positioned it as something he came across that he believed the reader would find useful.

He closed the letter by saying that he'll follow up in a few days with a call to introduce himself. Now the call's been preconditioned. No cold call with a *Who are you?* answer. No, the name's got you in, your background's wowed him and the tidbit's endeared you. The stage is set.

In the follow-up call, again mention the name of the person who referred you to get past the receptionist. Mention it again to the potential referrer. Tell him you're calling to further introduce yourself since so-and-so thought that you and H.L. should work well together. But since this is so difficult over the phone, might you suggest a face-to-face that week, perhaps lunch? The whole purpose of the call is *to get the meeting*.

At the meeting—and at every meeting—*always bring another tidbit to share*. In this way the person will always go away with the feeling that meeting you has been immediately useful. What a wonderful image.

■ **Just the Beginning.** Most professionals may go this far, but most then drop the ball and don't finish. They forget that others are continually vying for these referrals and if they don't nurture their sources, they'll lose them over time. Some competitor will succeed in doing this, especially since a competitor may be reading this same strategy, too.

You've got to think *continual repetition* because you've got to continually court your referral sources. They're fickle lovers who need never-ending attention. If you condition yourself to think of it this way, you'll succeed. Because the biggest cause of failure is thinking referral sources are safe.

Courting is necessary after referrers begin to refer to keep them doing so and to increase their rate. But it's as important when you're just trying to break in. Here's how.

■ **How to Court.** Make a list of five things the potential or actual referrer likes or has an interest in. It may be an outside interest, like traveling to Asia or bass fishing. If you don't know, ask the person who gave you his or her name. If you know their friends, ask them about his or her hobbies. Always include areas of professional interest that you've discovered during your meeting.

Then whenever you find an article on those topics, cut it and send it with a note. Or if you come across a tidbit, jot it down and send it. Don't friends send notes every once in a while when something of interest comes up? It's like giving a gift ... one that says you're watching out for them. A gift like this *once a month* is your target. That's nice long term repetition.

Then add to your calendar a *"lunch-a-week."* Once a week invite someone out. Force yourself. After awhile, you'll actually like it because your anxiety goes away after about two or three of them. Remember: Always bring a tidbit to share.

Also ask potential and actual referrers to do an *in-service talk* for you and your staff. This is to improve the knowledge of your staff and it's an honor few will decline.

What it also does is to get them into your office where you and your staff can impress them even more. This is a strong *visceral impression.* Plus they'll see how committed you are to improving your practice through in-service talks. All the while they're feeling honored that you turned to them.

But what if they're not referring? *Keep at it.* This is a long-term strategy since you must create enough repetition of impression to overcome the existing referral pattern. Even if you're not making headway, *keep at it.* Sooner or later the person now getting the referrals will screw up. They'll be an unhappy camper who'll complain and you'll have your shot. So you've got to think in a *one-year time frame.* If you haven't scored by then, go play in someone else's court.

■ **To Summarize.** (1) Find a name to use to get you through the front door. (2) Send an intro letter to precondition the call. (3) Follow-up with a call to get a meeting. (4) Bring a tidbit to share and wow the person at the meeting. (5) Make a list of their interests. (6) Court them once a month by sending a clipping of interest. (7) Do one lunch a week for your actual and prospective referrers. (8) Ask each to do an in-service talk. (9) Keep it up with prospective referrers for at least one year. Stop then if they haven't referred.

■ **Results.** H.L. followed the program and found it wasn't that difficult to break into the Old Boys' Club. True, he'll never be a "Good Old Boy," but he's still getting his share given this restriction. After six months, H.L.'s got nine professionals referring to him—not totally, but enough so that he's cooking. The long-term repetition will then increase the rate.

☐ ENLARGING YOUR REFERRAL AREA

Pediatric ophthalmologist S.R. thought his referral area had about a 10-mile radius. Beyond that, he figured eyecare doctors wouldn't refer to him. But his first direct mailer to potential referrers changed that assumption quickly.

S.R. discovered that many professionals aren't heavily courted for their referrals. And this is especially true in less populated areas. Also that with a professional's referral, mental and physical market barriers just melt away, so people are willing to travel huge distances.

The final tally from his direct mail included referrals from as far away as 70 miles. S.R. has decided to keep up the direct mail since he can't court distant professionals in person and that he'll even start mailing further out than 70 miles. After all, his original assumption was wrong. Maybe the 70-mile limit isn't really his limit either.

☐ CONTROLLING REFERRALS FROM NONPROFITS

Podiatrist A.D. was looking for more diabetic patients, so he joined the Diabetes Association. But on top of that, he invited the two people who give referrals to inquirers to come to his office for a private seminar on diabetic foot care. In this way, they would be better trained to advise callers. At the meeting A.D. examined their feet as well. Plus he offered to be their foot doctor at a reduced fee.

Guess who gets the lion's share of referrals now.

Then A.D. joined The Arthritis Foundation.

■ **At the Local Society Too.** Dentist R.P. always makes sure he chats with his local society's receptionist. This is the person who makes all the referrals for the society's *Yellow Pages* referral line. Then every time R.P. gets a referral, he sends her a thoughtful gift. After every five or so he gives her a slightly more expensive gift, in the $50 range.

The receptionist is a relatively low paid worker whom members tend to ignore. So when a professional pays attention—lots of attention—she feels special.

So does R.P. He gets six referrals a month.

Ever wonder why some society members get the lion's share of referrals ... and you get none? Now you know.

☐ NEW APPROACH TO CULTIVATING MEMBERSHIPS

Having been gone from practice for a year, chiropractor L.B. needed to rebuild her once robust base. Besides copious amounts of direct mail to recapture her past patients, she also needed to attract new blood. So her PRACTICE BUILDER marketing advisor targeted another arena where she was already well known.

Dr. L.B. was president and a founder of The Women's International Network, a 1,500-strong group dedicated to supporting female businesses. She'd received a few patients from the group already, simply by networking. But what she needed now was a concerted effort at recruitment.

◼ Cultivating the Club.

Part of the reason people join anything is for a sense of belonging. And the reason for much of their club activity is to enhance that identity. Bottom line is that most members will support most things affiliated with the club—including its other members—because of what it does for their own psyches.

But one-on-one cultivation of club members has limitations. It's uncomfortable to "sell" to them directly; plus you can't reach many of the members repetitively. So direct mail makes a lot of sense in club situations. Actually, direct mail is perfect in any situation with a defined group built around some commonality, and where a mailing list is available. If you can't rent the mailing list, it's usually easy (and profitable) to compile it just from the membership roster.

With those criteria met, it's time to go into the mail. The package: a multi-page letter on practice stationery, plus a special club offer of preferred service or pricing on a separate insert.

◼ Sample Letter

Dear Network Member,

In late 1984, together with some of the most talented women in our city, I helped found The Women's International Network to support female-owned businesses. Since that time, our efforts have helped countless women achieve goals that they would not have been able to accomplish on their own. Our network works and I feel good to be a part of it.

For this year, I am also fortunate to have been selected president of the organization. It is my way of continuing to support our efforts.

I also support the members of the network by patronizing their businesses whenever possible, assuming the person and business is of a high caliber. But I find it difficult to personally meet our many members to find out just how qualified they really are. And since I'm not one for choosing businesses or doctors on blind faith alone, I'm in somewhat of a quandary in finding out about members before I try their services or products.

It is to this end that I'm writing to you today. So that if you ever find yourself in need of a Doctor of Chiropractic, you will have all the necessary information to consider me in your list of candidates. I believe when it comes to health care, every woman should make informed choices.

[The letter goes on to describe L.B.'s professional credentials, what she treats and other benefits of coming to her office.]

Also as a member of The Women's International Network, I believe you should be entitled to special consideration in my office. Therefore, I'm pleased to waive my fee for your initial exam. (Treatment or X-rays are charged for.) Instead of a bill for $55, there will be no charge. Just bring in the special Women's International Network Certificate I've enclosed.

I'd be honored to be your doctor and I truly thank you for your consideration.

Sincerely,

Dr. L.B.

■ **Another Case.** Pediatrician V.F. is an active member of a local synagogue. "I send letters four times a year to the congregation, making sure I've deleted those whom have become my patients. These are very low key affairs. I simply tell them how important the synagogue is in our family and that if they would like to have a pediatrician who's a member of the congregation, I would like to present my qualifications. Then they can make a knowledgeable decision. I also offer them an initial discount.

"I figure about 12% of the members have become my patients. And when I go to the synagogue, I now have a lot more friends."

☐ GETTING POTENTIAL REFERRERS INTO YOUR OFFICE

It's always a problem getting potential referrers down to your office to show it and you off, but not so for podiatrist L.R. "It's fairly simple. All I do is figure out a topic I want my staff to learn about that the referrer could teach. Then I write him or her a note asking if they would mind coming to the office to put on a short, in-service training session. Every one I've asked has agreed. Then when they come, they get to see and experience what we could do for their patients."

This is also an excellent strategy for maintaining and protecting existing referrers from upstart competitors.

☐ HOLIDAY GIFTS FOR REFERRING PROFESSIONALS—DO'S & DON'TS

Some professionals like to give holiday gifts. Others loathe the idea. But reinforcement for referring works with professionals, just as it does with your clientele. The rules, however, are a little different.

First, each holiday gift of recognition should be tailor-made. It's truly the thought that counts, so put lots of thought into it. After all, aren't they responsible for your future?

What does the referrer like? Some like fine wines, certain foods or gadgets from the Brookstone catalog. Don't know their personal likes and dislikes? Call their office manager for confidential suggestions. Or if you know their spouse, then tap that source of input, too.

■ **Be Careful!** Some professionals get upset if you send anything. So call and ask your undercover sources. If the professional bridles at gifts, consider a donation to his or her favorite charity in their honor. Pass that idea past your sources. If it doesn't pass, send nothing.

In any case, write a *handwritten* letter. Make it personal. Tell the practitioner how you feel about the fact that he or she refers. Not too bland, please.

Then, because repetition works, call. Basically reiterate your letter and thank them again.

Positive reinforcement with recognition. Repetition. And full reports. These are the key elements for protecting and encouraging referrals.

☐ WHAT'S WHAT WITH *WHO'S WHO*

Dr. C.T. noticed that his Waiting Room Resume (See Chapter 3) got an awful lot of attention. It was constantly moved around the waiting room and he was happy to see new fingerprints over its Plexiglass cover each day.

During the same time C.T. saw his referrals rise. True, he was asking for them and had two other referral strategies in operation. But he also knew that he wouldn't get any referrals unless people considered him to be an expert. His Waiting Room Resume laid the groundwork for his referral strategies to work.

■ **More Positioning as an Expert.** C.T. figured that if one vehicle worked, why not use two. After all, repetition does work. So when a solicitation came in the mail to submit information to be included in one of the *Who's Who* editions, he jumped at the chance.

Now he leaves the impressive looking, coffee-table book in his waiting room with his page permanently marked. If you pick up the book, you can't miss his citing. And you've got to be impressed since most people have never seen one before. Voila, more referrals.

The public has no idea this series of publications sells most of their copies to the people included in the books so they can place it on their coffee table. *Who's Who* literally has built-in sales.

After seeing the frayed pages of the *Who's Who* and hearing patients' comments, C.T. is convinced, "This stuff really works!"

☐ GETTING KNOWN FAST TO GAIN PROFESSIONAL REFERRALS

Internist P.K. was waiting to open practice in two weeks when his office would be completed. He decided to put the two weeks to good use.

P.K. spent the entire time meeting with every potential referrer he could find. Attending surgeries. Doing lunches. Meeting in their offices. With so much time and because he knew that repetition works, he saw many of them more than once.

The result was an awareness rating that would otherwise have taken him six months.

Fast food for thought for referral-based practitioners.

☐ LUNCH-A-WEEK MAINTAINS REFERRALS

Reconstructive surgeon K.H. noticed that a referring pediatrician wasn't referring anymore and he wondered what happened. When he checked his books, K.H. discovered to his surprise that this colleague hadn't referred in six months. He was never very friendly with this referrer and he felt uncomfortable trying to build a personal relationship, especially now that the referrer had professionally rejected him.

At this time, it was tougher to fix what went wrong. A lot tougher.

A myriad of things go wrong with referring relationships: New competition moves in; you make a patient unhappy; or your front or billing desk does; you're not as available as "they" want you to be; and dozens more.

The smart thing is to *nurture the relationship* so when little things do come up, you can immediately take care of them. It's called maintenance, but few professionals *methodically* do it. The consequence is erosion of the referring base—after you worked so hard to get them.

■ **Lunch-A-Week.** Eating is such a social thing. It's actually a way of bonding in our society. So it makes sense to lunch or breakfast with referring colleagues once in awhile to maintain your relationship—and your referrals. It needn't be often. Once every three months is usually enough.

Programming it to make sure it gets done is critical. Otherwise, it doesn't happen because socializing for business sake often makes us feel uncomfortable. So schedule yourself for a lunch or breakfast once each week. It'll keep your relationships smooth.

Keep the meetings productive for your referrers or else they won't want to come for subsequent munches. *Therefore, bring a tidbit of professional information to the meal that your colleague would personally find interesting and useful.* Two are even better. Then they'll always feel meeting with you was worth it.

Remember: Schmooze 'em or lose 'em.

☐ **GAINING MEGA-REFERRALS FROM PROFESSIONALS FOR MAJOR GROWTH**

Physician L.R. runs a pain relief center. He's successful but feels his concept and operation have lots of unrealized potential. When you look at his situation, you can easily see the reason why growth isn't soaring the way L.R. wants. The way it could.

L.R. is well known. He has written extensively in the professional literature as well authoring a popular book. Plus he's so personable and credible that he's been on *Oprah Winfrey* and several other talk shows.

The problem is that in the office, L.R. does all the intake work with new patients and "closes" each deal since the ticket price is high and commitment long. He's good, but if he ever wants to grow, he's got to release himself for more productive work.

■ **Leveraging Yourself.** His practice works off referrals and L.R. is the only one who can get them from the other MDs. So the more time he spends calling on potential referrers, the more successful he'll be.

To introduce his concept of a multi-professional, multi-modality center and to gain direct referrals, L.R. needs to do copious direct mail. Not just any, but very targeted direct mail.

L.R. should load all the names and addresses of *potential referrers* into a database by specialty. Then he should write a monthly letter to each specialty and have the computer spit out personalized copies.

Each letter should talk of ways to treat the pain that specialty normally sees. This approach not only exhibits L.R.'s expertise, but also trains the referrer when to refer. The letters should go out *monthly* for lots of quick, compressed repetition to generate high visibility and response.

The letters also precondition the referrers so when L.R. calls and asks to come and explain his program, his reception is warm.

The concept of frequent direct mail and follow-ups to gain face-to-face meetings can be used by any professional with any referring group. It's a way to play the numbers game to make your referral numbers look good.

In this case, the strategy can only succeed if L.R. hires a "closer" to take his place and free him from working the "intake" and "closing" of patients. If he's properly leveraged, he can devote his time to potential referrers. Otherwise, he'll never grow at the rate he seeks.

☐ GENERATING REFERRALS FROM OTHER PROFESSIONALS— NEW APPROACHES

Psychologist C.F. was stymied. When she called all the potentially referring MDs in her area to introduce herself, the effort produced little. But others had been successful. So why not her?

The problem was that C.F. didn't realize that with referrers getting calls all the time, hers didn't stand out. She didn't know that with so much competition, her key need was to *precondition the potential referrer to the call.* Instead of the referrer coming to the phone thinking this is *just another practitioner* looking for referrals, with some prior groundwork, the referrer would have had a positive impression of her *before* they talked. Her reception would then be much warmer.

Remember: In order to receive referrals, the referrer must consider you to be an expert, so the referral will reflect positively upon him or her. Therefore, you need to establish the *image of an expert.* And then, you need to *repeat it* over and over. And over. No repetition means a fleeting impression.

Three Methods to Precondition. All involve direct mail to establish a favorable mind set. Choose the strategy most apropos to you.

1. *The Straight Introduction:* This personalized letter generated on your word processor does what the title indicates. Include credentials. Publications. Schooling. Special expertise. Experience. All the good stuff. If you've got the right stuff to make you look *special,* this should do the trick.

2. *The Alert:* But let's face it, we all don't look like Einstein on paper. If not, consider sending an alert to all your potential referrers.

Chiropractor S.I. sends a one-page alert. In it, S.I. writes how a patient recently came in exhibiting certain symptoms that had been diagnosed by someone else. He, too, might have diagnosed the situation in the same way, but he decided to look a bit further and discovered that the true diagnosis was altogether different. The patient was then treated successfully.

S.I. continues that the doctor might want to be on the lookout for the condition to avoid the same problem, especially considering the *overwhelming malpractice problem* today. S.I. also added that if the practitioner had questions about this or another case to feel free to call. No other pitches.

What this letter does is: (1) Stand out from all the other mail the practitioner receives. (2) Positions the sender as an expert. (3) And as caring. Then when the sender follows up with a call, it's not out of the blue.

The strategy should be repeated every 90 days for the sake of repetition. Of course, with a different problem each time.

3. *Professional Service Letters:* These personalized, word-processed letters also establish the aura of an expert for those who weren't in the top 5% of their class. In this quarterly effort, you tell the recipient that you understand there's a need in their type of practice for information from your specialty and that you don't believe it's adequately covered in their professional journals. So you've taken it upon yourself to send them the necessary information whenever you come across it.

The letter then describes information from your field that the referrers can use in theirs.

Here's what this effort does: (1) Stands out from all the other mail the practitioner receives. (2) Puts you in print so you're more credible. (3) Makes you a fountain of information so you're now automatically an expert. (4) And it also positions you as caring.

■ **The Next Steps.** Phone calls are next because voice-to-voice is far more convincing than a piece of paper. But the call has only one purpose—to get a face-to-face meeting, the most convincing of all communication.

With the Professional Service Letter and the Straight Introduction, the call is also straight forward. Your reception should be greatly improved over a cold call.

With the Alert approach, call and ask if they've ever seen a situation like you described. Reiterate that you think it's wise to be on the lookout for this because of malpractice risks. Then, if the call progresses well, suggest a meeting to get to know one another better.

Think *medium-term* for all these approaches. They will take six to nine months to flower. They may take less, but if you think short-term, you may quit too early in disgust.

Repetition works. So repeat the letters every 90 days. With follow-up calls also every 90 days.

Things change. Since your last letter and call, one of the regular referrees will have upset one of your potential referrers. Now you're in the right place at the right time.

Repetition works. So talks at professional meetings or hospitals help. Study clubs, too. Or invite a potential referrer to watch you work.

■ **A Numbers Game, Pure and Simple.** Probably all you really need is 10 more good referrers. Not more. And in order to get 10, the numbers game tells us that you'll need to mail to *200 or more!*

Rejection can become an overwhelming problem since to be successful, you'll need *190 rejections! So you must think that you want 190 rejections. You have to have them.* Because if you get them, you'll have achieved your goal of 10 good referrers who will thrust your practice to ethereal heights.

Welcome the rejections. They're good for you.

■ **Good Luck.** Now you're set to become an expert in the eyes of your colleagues. It's not at all an uncontrollable situation. It's simply up to you.

□ **BOOSTING REFERRALS FROM PROFESSIONALS YOU KNOW**

After receiving his share of referrals for many years, surgeon S.R. watched his market share dwindle bit by bit, finally plunging during the last two years. The docs who had always referred seemed to stop. The reasons were identifiable: new, aggressive and younger competitors; referring docs retiring; and hospital politics. But probably the main reason was that as the situation changed, S.R. shrank from being proactive.

If *you* don't do anything in the face of others doing a lot, guess what happens? S.R. found out. But it doesn't have to be that way.

■ **Getting Referrals from Professionals You Know.** Actually getting more referrals from professionals you already know is easier than getting them from people you don't. The reason is that they already feel somewhat comfortable with you, even if they're not referring. The idea, then, is to get them to trust you more.

But not all of them. Just a few. If you could *add just five* good referrers, chances are you'd be in referree heaven. So cultivate those five in an intense way. Actually, cultivate is the wrong word. *Court* is much better. It's as if you were looking for a girlfriend or boyfriend. That kind of courting. With that kind of intensity.

■ **Individual Marketing Plans.** To start, keep these points in mind: The first key to any referral is that the referrer must consider you to be *an expert.* The second is that you must do things to create that impression *repeatedly.* If not, it simply won't be made. And the third is that *not all referrers are alike.* In fact, the more you think of them as individuals, the more referrals you'll get.

So it makes sense to create a specific marketing plan *for each of the five most likely referrers* you're going to court. After all, you're marketing yourself to a specific market. In this case, however, the market is just one other person. That makes your marketing easier because it makes your marketing more specific and, therefore, effective.

To begin, do a *needs analysis by individual.* What is this individual interested in? What to they like to see professionally? What turns them on? Write the answers to these for each person on a separate page. If you don't know, ask around.

Next to each answer, write down *two to five things you can do* to make that person like you. After all, you're *courting* them. (Isn't that what you're competitors are doing?) So be nice to each in ways that create your *image of an expert, repeatedly, in ways most likeable to them.*

Ideas can include often sending reprints of articles on professional topics they're interested in; sending reprints of appropriate articles from THE PRACTICE BUILDER; or articles on management or personal finance; or on hobbies or travel; or inviting them to assist or observe you providing service to a type of patients or clients they might be interested in; or to give talks on topics they specifically like. And your plan should always include seeing and talking with them as much as possible: in the halls, at professional meetings, at lunch.

Repetition works. Repetition works. Repetition works. That's why just wining and dining referrers and doing little else is too puny to change referring behavior in a major way.

■ **Results.** Child psychiatrist V.F. targeted five pediatricians for more referrals, creating an individual marketing plan for each. Within 60 days, she saw a 20% jump in her practice hours. Within six months, her practice doubled, filling all available time.

"It's just a matter of focusing your efforts on highly likely referrers and treating them like you like them. Most importantly, I had to write it all down because then I could add lots of detail to my approach and I knew exactly what I was going to do ... It worked."

☐ **HOW SPOUSES CAN PROMOTE A PRACTICE**

Audiologist L.T. doesn't excel at marketing. In fact, laid back would be an understated description. But his spouse isn't shy at all. She loves to talk about how good her husband is and because she's socially active and community oriented, she talks a lot.

But she never had any "sales" tools to help. So couch potato L.T. finally got off his couch long enough to get new more powerful *promotional* business cards designed along with a zinger of a practice brochure. Then he climbed back on the couch and let his wife do her thing.

Because professionals have difficulty talking about themselves, spouses can often speak with greater enthusiasm about the practice. So encourage your spouse to tell everyone he or she meets about you. But first provide the tools needed: hot business cards and an even hotter brochure.

☐ THANKING THE RIGHT PEOPLE FOR REFERRALS

Often it's not another professional who directly makes a referral to you. Instead, they have an approved list at the front desk and it's the front desk who directly refers the patients or clients.

So when you get a referral from another professional, also thank the appropriate front desk person, nurse, or whatever. No one ever pays attention to them and a little niceness goes a long way. A small bouquet of flowers or an inexpensive gift like two tickets to the local movies makes a humongous impression. And rockets the referral rate.

☐ WHAT TO DO IF A REFERRER STOPS REFERRING

Endocrinologist D.A. wondered what happened. A GP who had been a long time, heavy referrer turned off the tap. What should she do?

First, ask him why. You've got absolutely nothing to lose. Nada, zilch. You might actually hear the truth. And you might be able to turn on the spigot again pronto.

Second, think about how you're going to *court* this referrer again—like you should have been doing all along to maintain the referring relationship. Follow the techniques described above for courting prospective referrers. Make a list of all the things the referrer likes and is interested in. Ask his or her colleagues and office manager. Then next to each interest, write down two or three things you can do to ingratiate yourself. Clip good articles from journals and magazines and send them with a note that you thought they might be of interest.

Meeting for lunch or dinner also keeps you on their minds. Choose the best place in town. Personally call the maitre d' beforehand to have him give you his best table. And give him your credit card number, telling him to add 20% for the waiter—and *not* to bring the check to the table. At the end of the meal, notice the expression on the referrer's face when you suggest they go. You see you've just turned the best restaurant in town into your private club. And everyone wants to be associated with a winner. Talk about the aura of success.

Asking the other professional to do an in-service talk for your staff brings them in to see your office and the quality of your staff. And it helps reestablish your relationship.

Plus a six- to twelve-times-a-year letter summarizing information from your field that would be helpful in theirs positions you as an expert, that crucial perception absolutely necessary for referrals.

It's okay if the other professional perceives that you're interested in them and that you want their referrals. That's fine because you are. That's what you want from courting. Just keep it professional and they'll perceive the attention as flattering. If you can't emotionally get over this hurdle, chances are you'll continue to lose referrers and gain few new ones.

PROMOTIONS IN MOTION

1. A Massachusetts counseling center has attacked the problem of getting clients to refer in their friends and loved ones. Most people are hesitant to refer others for various reasons. But this center produced a pamphlet to convince clients it's good to help others. Then it instructs them exactly when and how to refer.

   By telling them to refer, making them feel good about it and giving them instructions so they can do it with few trepidations, guess what happens!

2. Dentist M.B. has done a lot of promoting, but for him, even this one is new. He's running a Patient Recruitment Contest for his mostly middle-lower income clientele. He's announced it in a mailing to his entire patient base and here are the prizes everyone can win:

People Referred Who Actually Become Patients	Expected income during first 12 months	Prize (His cost)
1	$700	High-tech acrylic table Clock ($6)
2	$1,400	Dinner for two ($50)
3	$2,100	Family/individual photographic portrait ($75)
4	$2,800	An airline ticket anywhere in U.S. ($300 or less)
5	$3,500	Two airline tickets anywhere in U.S. ($600 or less)

There was a two-month time limit, so M.B. sent a letter every two weeks about the contest to spur people on. Within 60 days, M.B. saw 63 referrals *more* than normal ... for an *increase* in production of $47,300. His cost: $2,800 for prizes and $3,000 for mailings. Return on investment: 8.1 to 1.

3. What's the most opportune time to ask for a referral? Chiropractor N.M. didn't think it was when he finished helping a patient. Instead he figured that people were highest on him after their second visit so that's when he asked. The timing for him was perfect and referrals climbed an additional 7% more than if he waited until the end of treatment.

4. Veterinarian L.O. now does cryosurgery, especially for older pets which can't tolerate more traumatic procedures. As the only vet in the area capable of this new technology, he'd like to get referrals from other vets, but can't because of their fear they'll never see the client again. But there is a solution.

   Have the client deliver the pet to the primary veterinarian. Then L.O. will transport the animal to his facility and return it afterwards. (L.O. gets paid by the primary doctor who collects from the client and marks up the bill for his trouble.) Now there's no risk for the referring vet.

5. Optometrist J.M. knows how to shape referral behavior. For every patient referred in by a contact lens wearer, he thanks the referrer with an extra pair of contacts. Meaningful and inexpensive. Not only that, but it really motivates because of the large perceived value and ongoing need.

6. Audiologist K.C. knows cross promotion. She got nearby professionals who target her same audience to give out her coupon for a free hearing test to their patients and clients when they come in and she does the same for them. However, she took it a step further by getting everyone to include them in their quarterly mailings to their existing base. Now their past patients or clients who need hearing help also know about K.C.

7. Here's a unique referral source. A psychologist and vet have teamed up to provide grief counseling because of a pet's death. The vet arranges it and the therapist does it. The vet also offers a pet adoption service to help owners who have lost a pet to get a new one easily. Both of these add great value to the practice and bind clients emotionally.

8. Chiropractic physician M.L. promises a free massage to any patient who refers three new patients. Lots and lots and lots of response.

9. Ophthalmologist P.S. knows that people do things in their own best interest. As a young practitioner in a rough market, P.S. began conducting cataract screenings in optometrists' offices, doing the promotion himself and thereby creating traffic for the ODs.

Also, when P.S. discovered a patient in need of cataract surgery at a screening in an OD's office, he or she was given back to the OD for follow-up care. This co-management approach also boosted regular referrals from the ODs to P.S. It's a Win-Win-Win situation.

10. Midwest physical therapist P.K. learned an invaluable lesson. Since he can only treat with a doctor's referral, of course, he cultivated those nearby docs. But he soon came to realize that they often do not do the referring. Instead, it's the rehab nurse.

So now he cultivates both. The MDs with direct mail and follow-up phone calls. The rehab nurses also with direct mail, follow-up calls, plus luncheons and even a special open house.

Chapter 9

WHOSE SIDE IS YOUR STAFF ON?
HOW TO MAKE SURE IT'S YOURS

☐ SOLVING THE CONVERSION PROBLEM

On average, podiatrist H.G. had 16 new prospects call his office each week from the *Yellow Pages*. Of the 16, only 9 made appointments. Of the 9, only 4 became patients. Of the 4, only 2 completed treatment. That meant a 16% conversion rate. Poor by any standards. But H.G.'s problem is actually a number of problems.

■ **Problem #1.** *The front desk was not handling the incoming calls correctly.* There was no prepared script and anyone who answered dealt with the call in any way they felt. On top of that, asking the caller for the appointment was a hit and miss proposition. Plus, there was no set answers to address objections if they did say no. (No one even probed for objections.)

■ **Answer #1.** Have only *one or two hostesses* responsible for the phones. Then *script everything* including asking for the appointment and probing for and answering objections. Role play with them until they've got it down pat. Practice is a must before doing.

When someone asks for pricing information, make sure they're first given all the nonmonetary reasons to choose you for the service before hearing the price. In this way you're much more valuable than the price alone would indicate.

■ **Problem #2.** H.G. was a fine doctor but *a lousy presenter.* With the personality of a wilted flower, he couldn't convince people to turn on the lights when it was dark. No wonder they didn't respect his recommendations.

■ **Answer #2.** Hire a *"closer."* H.G.'s inability to gain commitment is an extreme case, but most professionals aren't tops in convincing. (It wasn't one of the requirements for professional school.)

So hire a person who can convince Eskimos to buy the proverbial icebox. The professional then presents the findings, makes the recommendations, and answers any questions. Right after, the closer meets with the prospect to ask for the commitment, answer objections and money/financing questions and ... close.

If you choose the right person, the closer should pay for his/her salary (and incentive) in the first week.

■ **Results.** H.G. got smart. He did organize his front desk to put the cheeriest of the crew up front and armed them with a poignant script that would convince the most reluctant troops to follow commands. Then he hired a sharp lieutenant to do his convincing for him.

The numbers improved almost immediately. And after six months, the 16% conversion rate climbed to 57%. "It was a case of doing things a little smarter and realizing that someone else could do the convincing better than I could. I admit there was some ego involvement that was the biggest impediment to my own success."

■ **Another Application.** Ophthalmologist M.E. conducted cataract screenings galore. His promotional materials were professionally produced and the media got 'em in the door. But prospects galore didn't convert into patients galore in spite of need.

■ **Answer.** Hire a *"closer."* And upon doing so, M.E.'s numbers became glorious.

☐ HOW TO GET YOUR STAFF TO SUPPORT YOUR MARKETING WHEN THEY ACT LIKE THEY DON'T CARE

Ophthalmologist E.M. just couldn't seem to get her front desk to track the sources of her new patients—no matter how high she flailed her arms. Her office was conducting free cataract screenings galore, but the staff wasn't converting prospects into regular appointments in spite of the opportunities. What to do?

The best laid marketing plans often go to pot, not because of poor planning ... and not because of your poor execution ... but because your staff acts like they don't care. They're not owners, so one can't expect them to act like you. But they can act like they care and they can support your marketing efforts ... *but* you need to show them why and how.

■ **Why and How.** Staff members basically have a good heart and want to do the right things, but for the most part we haven't taken the time to really teach what we want. In marketing, this requires that you explain all the parts of the marketing plan in great detail.

First, explain why you do your marketing in such a manner: the analysis of the market and the competition; what your goals are; why you've chosen the strategies you have; your budgets. Yes, everything. Your staff must understand the underlying theory behind your marketing strategies because it makes it meaningful to them. A simple command to do something doesn't.

Everyone needs to know everyone's part. Explain the inter-dependencies of everyone's actions so they can appreciate their role in the entire process—and how if they don't perform, they'll let down the entire team. This is the *how* of the process.

Then they need a numerical feedback mechanism. Everyone wants to measure their efforts, so give them a yardstick. That may be total income or production for the month, or total number of missing source codes, etc. If they have numerical feedback, they can fine tune their behavior. If they just have an inconsistent you blowing hot and cold—who may or may not remember to tell them whether you subjectively like their work—they're sunk.

■ **Role Playing.** If you want them to ask a patient for something, then they need to role play it. You can't ask and expect it to happen the way you want. Pros know that the bottom line grows enormously when the staff has role played.

And role play not just once, but until they're sick of it. And then you do it one more time. Then they'll be able to do it in their sleep—or more importantly, when they're on the front lines in the heat of battle.

■ **Results.** Dr. S.R. finally sat down with his front desk and explained everything: whom they were targeting with direct mail, why he chose them, how the direct mail packages were crafted, using which tactics ... and how he evaluated the success of each effort through tracking. With no numbers or incomplete numbers everything would go down the drain. He'd have to start all over since he couldn't make any decisions.

Bingo! The front desk remembered.

☐ NEWEST PROGRAM: HOW TO GET BIG PAYOFFS FROM
YOUR STAFF RECRUITING NEW PATIENTS OR CLIENTS—
WITHOUT SPENDING ANYTHING UP FRONT

Chiropractor W.T. is not only smart; he's rich. In the last two years, W.T. has *added $312,800 in gross.* And a major part of his success has been his *Frequent Recruiter Program,* which cost him *nothing up front!* That's the kind of cash flow he likes.

W.T. has always wanted to motivate his staff to recruit new patients for him, but lacked the key. Then he read a book on behavior modification theory and another on motivating a sales force. Here's what he learned and how he applied it:

1. The staff needed to be shown *specifically* how to sell the practice to others. How to bring up the practice when they met new people. How to mention it to old friends. What to say about their services.

2. After the instruction, they needed to practice what they learned with W.T. He gave them immediate feedback about what they were doing wrong—and right. Lots of critiquing. Lots of praising. Each staff member got to role play repeatedly.

3. Then he gave them a practice brochure to hand to everyone they met. This was professionally created *sales literature* about the practice, not a home-grown, patient information piece that looked out of date and boring. (That's not to mention that they normally contain demotivating messages and actually discourage people from calling.) The brochure addresses concerns the staff member neglected, reinforces the positive impression made, and creates the right image for the practice.

4. He also gave them each a business card with their name on the front and lots of nonmonetary reasons to try the practice. On the back was an offer of a bite-sized piece of service so the bearer could try the practice with little risk. In W.T.'s case it was a free exam.

5. Then they needed to go out and try recruiting prospects from the real world.

6. In every weekly staff meeting, they discussed the feedback they got while recruiting. When someone brought up a point, they role played it. If nobody brought up a point, W.T. did and then they role played it.

7. Above the coffee pot, W.T. posted how many people each staff member recruited. The list was updated every two days.

8. W.T. also posted the bonus a staff member would receive, depending upon how many new clients or patients he/she recruited.

They could claim a bonus anytime they had enough new patients or clients recruited for that level of bonus. So they could receive a quick bonus or work towards a larger one.

9. To figure the bonuses, W.T. first determined what a new patient generates in collections and net profit. In W.T.'s case, a referred patient brought in an average of $963. Overhead was 56%, leaving a net profit of $424.

10. W.T. then decided to pay $35 per patient (3.6% of gross revenue or 8.25% of net profit) as a bonus to his staff—*if* the patient came for at least two treatments. He correctly figured that the staff needed to receive immediate reinforcement for their efforts and that it couldn't *seem too hard* to get a bonus. After all, he would make plenty of profit and it wouldn't cost him anything unless they produced. It was all found money.

11. He also decided against paying most of the bonuses in money. He learned that he could buy certain items or create experiences with *greater perceived value* than their actual cost. So if these things felt like they were worth more, they would be more motivating.

When he put the whole program together, the bonus schedule looked like this:

THE FREQUENT RECRUITER PROGRAM

# Recruited	Bonus
1	$10
2	Dinner for two at Juliano's, Koto's The Beef House, or Shanghai Palace. Cost:$40-$70.
5	Choice of a Seiko desk clock, food processor or trip for two in a hot air balloon. Cost: $125-$175.
10	Choice of portable color TV, stereo receiver, disc player or home or car tape deck. Cost: $250-$350.
15	Choice of $500 in cash or a weekend for two at a local resort. Cost: $400-$500.
20	An extra week of paid vacation. Cost: $300-$600.
25	Two airline tickets anywhere in the continental U.S. Cost: $400-$900.
30	Two airline tickets to Hawaii or Jamaica. Cost: $700-$1,100
40	Two airline tickets to Europe. Cost: $900-1,500.

■ **Putting It to Work for You.** It's simple to modify the program to fit your practice. First, figure the value of a single new patient. Then determine the bonus amount. W.T.'s figures in step #10 are good guidelines. Then put together a list of bonuses. Even ask your staff for ideas, but you set the number of recruitments needed to earn each item or experience.

Then simply follow the steps that W.T. took. The closer you stay in his footsteps, the more success you'll have. And success he had.

■ **Results.** W.T. had some real go-getters. Everyone on the staff got to go out to dinner at least once. (Before this, many staff members had never recruited any new patients or clients.)

Other rewards claimed: two color TVs, $500 in cash, a week's vacation and two tickets to Hawaii—all without laying out money ahead of time.

☐ **GETTING EMPLOYEES TO RECRUIT NEW PATIENTS OR CLIENTS**

Called the "Employee Referral Contest," this generates a big bubble of business and it's simple and fun to do.

Give full- and part-time employees 50 special cards to start. When they run out, they can get more. The card entitles your employees' friends and family to an extra special saving or value on your services.

Print a signature line on the card for your employee to authorize the value. This strokes your employees and makes the program feel extra special for the recruit. The signature also tells you which employee is responsible for the referral.

Because you have a friend at Glenbrook Veterinary Hospital

Free Flea Dip & Pet Exam

Because your friend is a valued employee at Glenbrook Veterinary Hospital, you can now have a free flea dip and pet exam. Isn't it nice to have friends in important places!

Not valid with any other offer. Only one special employee value per person. Please call ahead for a preferred appointment.

Glenbrook Veterinary Hospital

702 South Main Street

Cedar Grove   891-0466

Authorized by _____

Certificate expires: July 31, 19XX

To get employees thinking profit, figure the results based on *total dollars generated*, not total referrals. The most dollars wins first prize and so forth, but everyone who brings in someone wins something.

■ **Rules and Prizes.** The contest is voluntary. It's done on employees' own time and cards cannot be distributed within the perimeter of the parking lot. Also, the cards are valid for new patients or clients only, but sometimes that's difficult to enforce. However, the problem is small so don't worry about it.

The grand prize can be a color TV, a free trip for two or a day off with pay. (The latter carries a high perceived value.) Also designate second and third-place prizes. Remember, everyone wins something if they participate, even if it's a free car wash.

In addition, have weekly winners to keep up interest. (Make a rule that an employee can't win two weeks in a row, but can still accumulate total dollars towards the grand prize.) Prizes can include: movie passes; gift certificates for CDs; gift certificates at clothing stores; small electronics; free dinners; and tee shirts. Ask your employees for ideas and then try to barter services for prizes.

Award the grand prize at the end of four weeks. The short term assures everyone pushes hard. And make a hoopla out of the weekly and final winners. This helps sustain interest for this and future contests. And run the contest two to three times per year.

What's also nice: This is a self-funding program with zero financial risk. Plus it gives your employees a vested interest in growth.

Jeff Slutsky, *Street Smart Marketing*, John Wiley & Sons, New York, 1989, $14.95 and THE PRACTICE BUILDER.

STAFF INCENTIVES TO ASSURE QUALITY

Incentive programs have been around a long time as a means to get the staff to act like owners, but they've been getting a bum rap lately. *But it's not staff incentive programs that don't work. It's their bad design or rotten implementation.*

Programs like those described above need to be custom-made for a practice. Just follow the key concepts:
1. Only pay incentives on profit, not collections. Figure your salary as an expense when determining profit.
2. Only permit those who perform well according to preset and trackable criteria to participate in the incentive pool.
3. Pay often, monthly or biweekly.
4. Have a weekly chart of collections, expenses, and profit by the coffee pot to provide constant feedback.
5. Talk it up in staff meetings.

Example: Monthly plan. For up to $40,000 in collections, 15% of profits over break-even (including professional's salary as an expense) goes into pool for staff to split; a 17.5% pool up to $60,000; 20% over $60,000. Each staff member has numerical goals to meet in order to partake in the pool. For instance, receptionist is tracked on percentage of appointments kept and dollars per appointment produced since she affects that number by the way she schedules.

Analyze your practice. How can you track each staffer's performance to take the subjectivity out of it? Remember to keep at the implementation to work out the bugs. Then see what owner-like attitudes can do for your quality.

☐ DUMB MOVE #63: MAKING YOUR OFFICE MANAGER YOUR MARKETING DIRECTOR

By dumping your promotional decision-making on your office manager, you've abdicated control of your marketing program. True, office managers can help *execute* marketing plans, but they should never be empowered alone to *create* them.

Here's the reason. Nothing is more important than bringing in new business. Not even what you do afterwards. After all, if your practice doesn't survive, you won't be around to do your patients or clients any good. And everything else is predicated upon front-loading the practice: cash flow, profits, repeat business—your viability. So it doesn't make any sense to abdicate responsibility for your survival. In fact, it's downright dumb.

So you have to be the person responsible—and active. If you don't have time, dump something else and take this on. Otherwise your priorities are screwed up.

Remember: Use your staff to help you, not to relieve you of being active and responsible. In fact, it makes sense for you as the professional to also carry the title of *Director of Marketing*, and your assisting staffer becomes the *Marketing Assistant, the Assistant Manager of Patient Relations, or the Assistant whatever.*

☐ HOW TO MOTIVATE A MARKETING DIRECTOR

Marketing people are success driven ... or else they don't last long in the field. Therefore, they respond extremely well to incentives. If you interview candidates who don't want a big incentive program but rather a secure, high base, *don't hire them.* And if you have a marketing director who won't work on that basis, fire them. Otherwise, they'll never produce big numbers.

So pay yours with a low base and high monthly incentives. Set the base on the low end for your area for comparable slots in similar sized companies.

Then set a minimum goal of new patients or clients per month. The goal should reflect the trend line that you would have achieved if the marketing director didn't work there. Make sure you adjust the goal for seasonality by figuring the average new patients or clients by month for the last three years.

Then pay $X for each new patient over that monthly goal. The incentive can run $10 to $25 or more depending on your average case size. As an added incentive, throw in a high kick bonus. If the goal is 40 new patients or clients and the incentive is $20 for each over 40, then add an *extra* incentive of $10 or more for each over 60. Works like a charm.

Remember: (1) Pay incentives monthly to keep your director motivated. (2) And there are two types of marketing directors—the good and the fired. Don't accept excuses, only numbers.

☐ HOW TO MOTIVATE PARTNERS AND ASSOCIATES TO ASK FOR COMMITMENTS AND REFERRALS

Dentist L.B. was at wits end. He spent a small fortune on external marketing to promote the practice's specialization in sexual dysfunctions which luckily worked beyond his expectations. L.B. actually thought this was the hard part, which it usually is. But what he hadn't anticipated was that his older partner wouldn't convert these expensive prospects into patients. Nor did he follow a program of asking everyone for a referral. What to do?

■ **Working with Partners and Associates.** Other professionals, especially older ones, may resist marketing for a number of reasons—all of them emotional.

■ **Objection #1.** Older professionals were brought up in the old school and often fear what their colleagues think. *Answer:* Tell them you can't serve two masters at one time. That colleagues are actually competitors. And that colleagues don't pay your bills.

■ **Objection #2.** "All marketing projects an image unacceptable to our colleagues." *Answer:* This is false. Much of the garbage that masqueraded as marketing in the past was offensive, but not necessarily anymore. Good external and internal promotion now projects an image that *enhances* the credibility and respectability of a practice. That's what attracts people. It's the kind of image that colleagues admire—and causes envy. (It's also the kind of image you need to pay to have created for you. It takes too much expertise to do it yourself.)

■ **Objection #3.** "Marketing is unprofessional" translates into "It's uncomfortable because it means I have to compete and I dislike competition in business—which is one of the reasons I entered the professions." *Answer:* Local and state associations, the Supreme Court, and the FTC all say it is professional. But beyond that you have an obligation to inform people who don't know you about your practice and the benefits you can bring to them. Without your direct efforts, they'll never find out.

■ **Objection #4.** "If you market, it means you need business." (That's ego talking, isn't it?) *Answer:* Recognize it as nothing more than an ego issue which needs to be dealt with and overcome. But if you can't, then fool yourself with this: That it actually means you want more business, not need it, and there's nothing wrong with wanting.

■ **Objection #5.** "We really don't need this business." *Answer:* This means your partner doesn't need additional business because he's already made it and is satisfied with what he has. He's working as hard as he wants. (But you want it and you're not ready to retire yet.) So tell him you're going to increase the entire value of the practice so when he's ready to retire, it'll be worth two to three times more than it is today. And that would be a nice bonus for his kids.

■ **Objection #6.** "I don't really understand what's going on." *Answer:* Explain the entire system. All of your research, all of your plans, the *why's* of all the minutia. He needs to have a thorough understanding and, therefore, an appreciation of the efforts in order to support them. Otherwise, he'll just feel like a cog in the machinery without an overview of the importance of his role.

■ **But Not Enough.** These intellectual arguments are fine, but we're dealing with emotional issues. So use these in addition:

1. Show how others promote their practices. How it can be done tastefully and effectively. Give your colleagues copies of THE PRACTICE BUILDER to see samples and help educate them.

2. Tell them to trust you for a little while—but only until results start coming in. Then you'll watch the numbers. With an accurate tracking system and good marketing, the numbers will calm *all fears and objections*. Remember: Success without numbers can't be proven.

3. Start small. Take one program like "Asking for Referrals" and implement that successfully. This is a good one to start with because everyone agrees to give referrals when asked properly. (See Chapter 8 for the how-to's.)

But don't just give your colleague the issue or instructions. Show him how to do it. Then ask him to role play with you until he's got it right. Tell him he'll feel uncomfortable the first time, but not the second. Tell him everyone will say yes.

4. When your colleague does something to support the program, make a big deal out of it. This is reinforcing his behavior through recognition and it encourages him to do more.

5. Keep mentioning it. Don't let it off your agenda. This highlights the importance and doesn't let him forget. Besides, *repetition works wonders.*

Of all the above, always do #2. If someone believes in the scientific method, nothing motivates like numbers.

■ **Results.** L.B.'s partner did come around, but it took several weeks of applied pressure and convincing. And once he did, they took a long hard look at their new associate who did good quality work, but didn't produce enough ... and emotionally didn't support the marketing program. After many attempts to get him on the bandwagon, they decided the associate should work elsewhere, like for a competitor.

☐ **PROMOTING A LEADER WITHOUT HAVING THE LEADER DO THE WORK**

Psychologist R.T.'s practice is full. Yet he has several associates who aren't completely booked so he promotes externally to fill those slots. But understanding that people like to buy people, R.T. uses himself as the practice's frontman. And when people respond, he passes them off to his associates. How does he do this?

First, the *Yellow Pages* ad and so forth all talk of R.T. as the leader. He hand selects each therapist. He oversees their efforts. And sets the philosophy for the practice. None of it says he'll actually treat you.

Then he does all the screening of prospects to assure they fit the practice and they're convinced to choose the practice. At this 45-minute meeting, he doesn't allow them to talk too much in-depth about their problem, because that would bond them too tightly to him. Rather he asks some simple questions and tactfully cuts them off at an early point. His purpose is simply to find out enough about their problem to then sound authoritative.

R.T. then tells them that he has someone with very special expertise in their specific problem right in the practice. *And* that this person is better than he is for their situation. R.T. then goes on to describe the colleague in depth, list his or her credentials, and heap praises on him or her.

If R.T. doesn't set his colleague up as a *greater* expert, he has trouble passing them on. (Some professionals have trouble doing this because of ego reasons, but if the regimen is followed, it invariably works.)

One other thing has worked well. R.T. raised his own prices far above those of his associates. This helps pass on new prospects as well as adding to the bottom line.

PROMOTIONS IN MOTION

1. General dentist C.K. has been thinking about how to capitalize on his big, marketing-built practice even more. A line extension to add orthodontics was obvious, but he and his associates didn't want to do the work. So he lured an orthodontist from just outside his immediate area to come in for a half-day a week. (None of the local orthodontists were interested.)

   The deal was a 50%/50% fee split. C.K. would market, bill, collect and administer. The orthodontist would bring the necessary staff and do the actual work. And the patient would experience convenient, one-stop shopping.

   Now on all C.K.'s external promotion for the general practice, he simply adds a line or two on orthodontics and doesn't spend one single dime more doing it.

Chapter 10

LOOKING BEYOND YOUR BASE:
THE ABC'S OF SUPERB EXTERNAL PROMOTION

□ ADVERTISING VS. MARKETING

The terms are often confused and the best way to understand the difference is to list what each covers. But the lesson is even more valuable than merely understanding. It provides you with a checklist of promotional thought you need for dollar maximizing.

■ **Advertising.** Paid space must be involved.

- ■ Newspapers
- ■ Magazines
- ■ Shoppers
- ■ New resident direct mail
- ■ Cold prospecting direct mail
- ■ Postcard mailings
- ■ Radio
- ■ TV
- ■ Billboards

- Bus stops
- *Yellow Pages*
- Co-op coupons

■ Marketing:

- Demographic analyses
- Psychographic analyses
- Competition analysis
- Market prioritizing & planning
- Location selection
- Public relations
- Professional relations
- Stationery and business cards
- Logo
- Practice name
- Practice brochure
- Outdoor office signage
- Interior design
- Interior office signage
- Waiting room resume
- In-office (point-of-purchase) promotions
- Advertising specialties (gifts)
- Case presentations (sales)
- Sales incentive programs for staff
- Patient/client direct mail
- Recall system
- Reactivation system
- Telemarketing
- Pricing
- Affordability options
- Service offerings
- Product offerings
- Quality of services and products
- Quality of staff

■ **Advertising Lessons.** (1) Most professionals fail in their marketing because they don't think of all the variables when they plan. (2) Advertising is one small part of marketing.

☐ WHAT TO PROMOTE IN YOUR EXTERNAL PROMOTION?

The answer is "gateways" and it's quite logical when you focus on an underlying principle of human behavior. Namely that people have specific needs, so they buy specific solutions to specific problems.

Seen in this light, it makes sense to figure out the gateways into your practice, those main problems that bring people in the front door in either big numbers ... or in little numbers with big case sizes.

This means that the old idea of a newspaper ad or co-op coupon that promises everything to everyone—or worse, simply announces you exist without promising a thing—won't work. So save your money.

To plan your external promotion, first list all the logical entry points or gateways into the practice. Do not put down any service or product that is normally sold only after the patient is part of the practice. Be very careful about this.

Then choose only those that are high volume or high ticket.

Now that you know what they're coming to see you for, tell them why they should choose you rather than a competitor. And provide them with convincing proof of your claim(s). Throw in a direct response offer to test a slice of "gateway" service with little risk on their part as long as they respond by the expiration date and you've got a winner.

In the *Yellow Pages* the game's a little different. Here you can place a general ad covering all the problems you solve. But you must list all the "gateway" problems so people know you can help them. Then on top of that, add the parts about why to choose you and supporting proof. That's your award-winning recipe.

☐ HOW TO WIN THE ADVERTISING GAME

Dentist H.Y. was a game player. He saw advertising as a game, with the risks inherent in losing—and the spoils going to the victor.

With a yearly advertising budget of $28,000 designed to generate $100,000 on top of last year's base of $371,000, H.Y. thought everything was realistic. He "borrowed" some "good" ads he saw in a neighboring city newspaper and began spending.

The results were slow in coming—very slow ... very, very slow. After three weeks his tally was: six phone calls, two patients (one of which had a big case but hadn't committed), plus one now empty Maalox bottle. So H.Y. picked up what was left of his bankroll and hit the showers. What went wrong?

Well, actually not much. H.Y. simply didn't understand the game. Not only that, he didn't even know the name of the game.

■ **Two Games.** Advertising is really two different games. One is Name Recognition; the other Direct Response. In H.Y.'s case, he played Name Recognition is which the ad's message was, "When you need a pediatrician to accomplish *X*, remember my name."

Direct Response ads, on the other hand, say, "Here's an offer with a deadline which is a good reason to call now."

If you play the Name Recognition game, you must remember that the average body needs five to seven repetitions of a message *before* it responds. That means front loading your promotion to get over this initial hump quickly.

It also means little response in the beginning. At the same time cash is pouring out. That's the usual time for a Maalox break. (See Figure 10.1.)

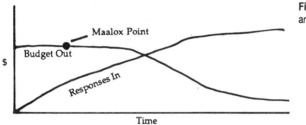

Figure 10.1 Name Recognition Graph: Response and Outflow

In Name Recognition, if the ad's good and you've chosen the right newspaper or other media, response will build, but slowly. In time it will level off. Then you can cut the budget back and not see a decline. If you cut it altogether, new business will fall off, but again it'll happen slowly.

You can't play the Name Recognition game with the idea of a quick payoff. H.Y. did and failed. But if he knew the rules and hung in there, the concept would eventually have worked. Whether he had the money or stomach lining to play is another question. He needed both.

■ **Quick Cash, But ...** In the Direct Response game, the response and cash flow are fast, as you can see from the graph. And when it's over, it's over. There's no carryover. (See Figure 10.2.)

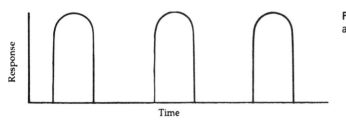

Figure 10.2 Direct Response Graph: Response and Outflow

However, there is a long-term problem. Since most offers that professionals use involve a price reduction, you create the image of a price-cutter if you repeat the promotion too often. Every time you run a similar effort, you reinforce the image. Now that's not bad if that's the market you want. It's not bad at all. But if your practice is more upscale, then heed the caution flag.

■ **The Preferred Hybrid.** Since most professionals can't afford to play Name Recognition (even though they prefer it) and pure Direct Response has its hazards, a hybrid makes sense. But follow the construction closely, since this is a tricky execution.

The Hybrid game is basically Direct Response modified to include lots of nonmonetary reasons to come to you: your experience, credentials, special expertise; that you're famous, respected, etc. *Sometimes,* the offers don't have to be discounts. Free information can be a strong enough pull. So can a free book. Or an extra service.

The Hybrid game solves all the pitfalls. Cash flow is quick so you can sleep at night. And with high repetition, prospects will now view you as highly qualified and offering value.

Remember: You can play any game you want. Just understand its rules.

■ **Results.** Psychologist N.R. stated in her newspaper ad that she often had the answer to "Why isn't my marriage working?" The ad pointed out she certainly had the credentials. But it wasn't until she worked the idea of her 30-minute free consultation into the ad's headline that response took off.

"I practice in an upper-middle income neighborhood where I thought they wouldn't respond to that. But the amount of response tells me I was wrong."

The numbers: six ad insertions over four weeks, 23 calls, 11 serious prospects, six new patients. Good game playing.

☐ MAKING PUBLIC RELATIONS PAY (WITHOUT WORK AND WITH LITTLE COST)

Canadian professionals operate under the strictest of guidelines. You can't do this, you can't do that, and you can't even think about that. So northern brothers and sisters are eager to explore every nonadvertising opportunity available. From that experience, optometrist B.F. reports her all-time winner.

A group of local professionals and even merchants gets together to sponsor a free gift to commemorate a significant event in a family's life. A birth or silver anniversary, for instance.

B.F.'s group celebrates all the new births in her small town with a plaque stating the baby's name and date of birth and the names of the sponsors. The plaque is perfect for displaying on the wall. It's even more perfect for showing to the baby's visitors.

The sponsors always get thank you letters. Isn't that nice? And even nicer, they always get referrals. (Talk about word of mouth—people who have their babies out of town get angry because the system doesn't pick up their name and they don't get a plaque! The group obliges, of course, when they find out.)

B.F.'s cost? About $500 Canadian a year. "I've had enormous success with this approach." This could be an understatement.

☐ TWO KINDS OF PRACTICE REPS: THE GOOD AND THE FIRED

There should be only two kinds of practice representatives—the good and the fired. Physician D.E. found that out the hard way.

To represent his multidisciplinary clinic to businesses, D.E. hired a smiling, engaging rep who looked great on paper. With a high, guaranteed salary plus a percentage of the action, this addition was expensive, but certainly worth it—*if the rep performed.* Then D.E.'s waiting began.

Three to four months is a normal lead time for a rep to produce. D.E.'s problem was that four became five, then six, eight, and finally ten. Excuses abounded and D.E. bought them.

■ Good or Fired. The real problem, though, was D.E.'s lack of understanding that he actually hired the rep as a "salesman"—but he treated him as a public relations person who wasn't responsible for hard numbers.

The best way to manage a practice rep is to make them responsible for trackable cash in. Then if there's no numbers, there's no job. Give the rep three to four months lead time, five if the numbers are showing promise. Yes, producers are hard to find, but you've got to find a rep who gets the business. If you're hiring a marketing director, he or she should have hard number goals for overall production. The lead time should be a bit longer, even up to nine months. Then, the same thing: no numbers, no job.

If you don't treat these slots this way, you'll have money going out with only excuses coming in.

P.S.: D.E. fired the rep and hired another who within 12 months produced over $1,000,000 in new corporate business. Nice awakening.

PROMOTIONS IN MOTION

1. Chiropractor A.S. knows the power of synergistic media. He drops a mass mailing direct mail package to a different zone each week. Then hired college students call within 72 hours to follow-up. The mail sets up a more responsive reception for the caller. So more get through and get results than a stand-alone telemarketing effort would.

   The students screen to find a prospect with back or neck problems. Either a doctor or a "closer" on staff calls to convert the prospect into a patient and schedule an appointment if the students can't.

■ **Results.** Over the first year of the program, return-on-investment has been a solid 10:1. Recently, ROI has dropped to 5:1. Suspicions are that a few of the current college students are failing.

2. Dentist K.R. is two blocks from an apartment complex boasting over 700 units. And as in any complex without an extraordinary number of seniors, the population turns over frequently. So to reach newcomers as soon as they move in, K.R. has his high school son deliver a door hanger to each apartment once a month. Not only does he attract newcomers, he gets oldtimers who are ready for a dentist change or haven't been to a dentist in years.

   "They can't miss my door hanger because it's not buried in with all the mail they get everyday."

■ **Results.** 8 to 1 return-on-investment.

3. Podiatrist M.D. does what? He takes two bags full of business cards to Dallas Cowboy games. Then on big plays when everyone stands and cheers, he throws them into the air. No kidding!

   When the cards fall into laps, people see the offer of a free exam. (Could it be a message from heaven?) No, just from M.D. who claims revenues in excess of $10,000 per game. Now there's a reason to route for the Cowboys.

4. Optometrist E.J. continues to take advantage of a time-proven strategy. In his contact lens ads, he specifically addresses people who have stopped wearing their lenses, but still want to see without glasses. That message starts in the headline. Then the ads push new developments in contacts. Since the vast majority of contacts sold are refits, E.J. is speaking directly to the personal concerns of the *big* part of the market.

Chapter 11   □

THE BEST RETURN ON INVESTMENT: YOUR OFFICE SIGN

□ YOUR NO. 1 RETURN-ON-INVESTMENT IN EXTERNAL PROMOTION

Is it TV? Newspaper? Must be *Yellow Pages*? Nope, none of the above. The #1 return on investment (ROI) for an external promotional dollar spent is *outside office signage.* Yup, your sign.

If you think of the ROI equation, you realize why: ROI = Revenue/Cost. Your sign costs you only once, but the revenue keeps coming forever. So the ROI number shows a big kill.

How potent are signs? In April, 1989, the city of Lynwood, California eliminated all pole signs—and total business volume dropped 10%. Imagine, pole signs alone accounted for 10% of all business!

Many of the entries in THE PRACTICE BUILDER's First-Ever Office Sign Contest sent accompanying notes testifying to their sign's power. J.S. wrote, "My signs, visible for two blocks in any direction, especially at night when they're illuminated, account for 25-30% of my new patients." And R.B. said, "(They) cost $300 and account for an average one-fourth to one-third of our new patients each month." Not bad numbers.

But this is true only if you can have the right outdoor sign. Freestanding buildings, strip mall, and storefront locations can. Professional building locations usually can't unless you can have your own stand-alone sign. The normal tombstone listing doesn't cut any mustard.

■ **But, But, But—You've Got to Think Smart for the Sign to Work.** Not   every sign works. When they fail, it's almost always because the practitioner messed up one or more of the variables in this promotional equation. So be careful. But if you are, you'll have a big kill, too. In fact, it's easy because so few practitioners know how to execute signage properly that if you just come close, it'll work.

One of the main reasons practitioners fail is because they listen to *sign companies* for advice. It's natural, but deadly.

Sign companies know how to construct signs. They know a lot about wires and durability—but they know absolutely zippo about what should go on a sign. Why should they? They probably can't even spell your profession, yet you're going to trust them to design your promotional message and execution? Not smart.

One of the keys to a great sign is to treat it not like an announcement, but more like an ad. Unfortunately, sign companies don't think that way because if they did, they'd never be able to design a sign. You see, they don't know a thing about advertising or promotion, only about announcements.

So here's your checklist of variables to consider. Remember: Ignore one and you'll learn an ugly lesson from an unsympathetic marketplace:

1. Location
2. Colors
3. Size
4. Illumination
5. Shape
6. Headline
7. List of symptoms
8. Phone number
9. Point of differentiation
10. Layout and typography

■ **Location, Location, Location.** Just as in real estate, it's crucial, but for a different reason. In this case, the sign must be seen or it won't work.

Take Southeast physician G.M. She's been located at the end of a strip mall for the past ten years. Since she was operating on a shoestring, the first thing her PRACTICE BUILDER Advisor told her was to shred her feeble outdoor sign and do it right.

After the new one was installed, it began showing up as a source on her tracking sheets. Again and again. By the second month, the sign produced 11 new patients, up from an average 0.7 from the old one. Over and over people asked if she'd just moved in!

How much business had G.M. lost over the last 10 years? Let's see, 10 new patients per month times 12 months times an average case size of $326 for each during the first 12 months with the practice. That's $39,120—and doesn't include twice that much from word-of-mouth referrals plus more from repeat business. The actual total is closer to $125,000 to $150,000. That's a lot of grits and mint juleps.

■ **Exposure Should Be Primary.** If 5,000 cars a day pass your office and your sign is recessed or difficult to see, you've literally cut your viewing population down to 2,500 ... or 1,000 ... or less.

So to discover the place for the greatest exposure, get out and look for yourself. Carry a Polaroid or 35mm camera with color prints so you can take photos to study later. Revelations often don't come until you've studied the snapshots some evening over a fine French Cabernet Sauvignon.

Ready to start? Walk out the front of your office to the sidewalk, turn right and walk 50 feet. Stop, turn around and take a photo. Now think. If you were driving or walking by there, where would a sign need to be for you to see it *clearly and quickly*?

Play these "what if" games. What if it were on the ground? At eye level? Ten feet high? On a 20-foot pole?

What if it were curbside? Recessed?

What if it were attached to the building? Perpendicular? Or flush? On the front and sides of the building? What if you had two signs touching tips and each at a 45-degree angle to the front?

Now walk another 100 feet further from the office. Stop and repeat the process. Then walk another 100 feet and repeat. You're now 250 feet away on the same side of the street.

Cross the street and study the viewing angle from there. Take a photo and walk 100 feet back toward the office. Stop, shoot and study. Continue another 100 feet. Stop, shoot and study. Walk another 100 feet and repeat. (Now you're 50 feet past the office on the other side of the street.) Go another 100 feet. Shoot and study. Then another 100 feet and repeat.

Cross back to the same side of the street as your office. Shoot and study. Walk toward the office and repeat. And then 100 feet more for your final shoot and study. If there's a cross street within the area you've covered, also walk down it to shoot and study the viewing lanes. Within 15 minutes you'll know the *optimal* location—certainly by the time you've finished your Cabernet.

Now check any landlord or city sign restrictions. You'll want to check these *after* your brainstorming so as not to restrict your thinking. Place your sign for people first, for your landlord or the city second. If there are restrictions, try to negotiate or ask for a variance. (Your sign company often has the political clout to get a variance.) The potential revenue is always worth the attempt.

■ **How Big?** Size only has to do with noticeability, not with image. Image is determined by color, typestyle and layout. If these look retail, then that's what people think of you.

Since exposure is paramount, make your sign as large as you can. The bigger the better. More people will respond. Then make sure you project the right image on it. A bigger pallet actually means you can convey your image more powerfully.

■ **What Color and Shape?** The answer's whatever pops. If everything in the area is brown, make the sign yellow. If everything's grey, make it red. If all the signs are square, make yours round. If they're round, make it freeform.

The idea is to break the visual plane and make sure your sign doesn't melt into the surroundings. It shouldn't blend, but stand out. So color and shape depend on context.

■ **Convincing Copy.** To turn your sign into a recruiter, it must deliver the following information:

1. What do you do? A list of symptoms helps.
2. Why should I choose you rather than someone else? Put your most potent reason here.
3. How do I get in touch with you? List your phone number.

Then, of course, list your practice name which many times is your name. If it's different, you needn't list your name in addition to the practice name unless you're well known. You certainly needn't list partners' and associates' names. There's no marketing reason for it.

■ **Logos.** If you have a logo, put it on your sign. Also make sure it's in your *Yellow Pages* ad so people can make the connection. This is one of the key ways that a logo fosters promotional synergy.

■ **Sign Construction.** Shop heavily. For the same specs, you'll get wildly different bids.

■ **Inquiring Minds Want to Know.** When colleagues ask you about your big, new sign, tell them you're having second thoughts. Tell them you're doubting your wisdom. Tell them anything that'll discourage them from considering a new sign, too! Above all, don't tell them how well it's working!

☐ GETTING THE #1 EXTERNAL PROMOTION TO WORK FOR YOU: BRAND NEW IDEAS!

When building his practice, podiatrist H.G. was shortsighted. He came from the old school where you put out a shingle with one-inch lettering and delivered quality work. That's all.

What he failed to think about were all his practice's assets which he could have developed to produce more patients. For instance, the *staff*. And the *patient base*. And especially the 50,000 cars that passed his office each day. *50,000!* Virtually none knew he existed. How could they with only his one-inch effort?

■ **Harvesting Traffic.** Outdoor office signage is the only way to reap financial rewards from that traffic flow. Remember, you're actually paying increased rent for that potential. Don't offices on busy streets cost more than ones tucked away in unpopulated nooks of town or on rears of fifth floors in hard-to-reach professional buildings?

Remember, signage is the #1 return on an externally spent promotional dollar. The reason is simple. With a sign, you pay only once, yet it recruits year after year. After year after year.

But not all signs are created equal. A sign is an equation of variables, all of which must be considered.

For instance, if H.G. merely put up a sign that said "PODIATRIST," the improvement would be puny. A sign shouldn't just *announce*. To justify the $1,000 to $10,000 investment, it must *recruit.*

■ **Three Questions.** To convince someone to come to you, *any* promotion— signs included—must answer three questions:

1. *What do you offer, so I can figure out if you're for me?* Don't assume people know. And modalities don't answer the question since people don't know if they need a type of service. Better to list symptoms or problems.

2. *Why should I choose you RATHER than someone else?* Experience, expertise, high tech, friendly, affordable ... Make your case. Remember: He who makes the claim, owns the claim!

3. *Can I trust you?* This is answered graphically. Is the image the sign portrays professional—or retail? Your graphic artist provides the answer.

Your answers to these big three can be either words or visuals. If you have a logo—especially a marketing-based one which instantaneously communicates your major selling point—include it. That answers the second question.

For creative brainstorming, here are examples of strong answers to put on your wooden, metal, concrete, plastic, monolithic or pole sign. (See also Figures 11.1 and 11.2.)

Figure 11.1 Terrence Clark Sign

Back and Neck Pain Relief

- Quick, Proven Relief
- Auto, Work and Sports Injuries
- Special Treatments for Chronic Pain

Thomas McNabb, MD
990-PAIN

San Antonio

Center For Hypnotherapy

Over 20 Years Experience

Fast, Effective Treatments
Lose Weight
Quit Smoking
Build Confidence
Cure Fears

Call 333-HELP

The Gentle Dentist

For Adults & Kids

- Beautiful and Handsome Smiles
- Cleanings and Checkups
- Emergencies Welcomed

Dr. James Grayson

Gentle Dentist
999-9993

Augusta Hearing Aid Center

You Can't Get The Right Aid Unless You Have A Choice

Huge Selection
New *Invisible* Hearing Aids
Free Hearing Test, Here or At Home
Small, Monthly Payments Available

888-2222

Bayside Animal Hospital

Treating Your Pet Like A Member Of Our Family

- Checkups, Shots, Spaying & Neutering
- Complete Hospital Facilities
- Doctor-Supervised Boarding

All With A Caring Touch
Call 667-PETS

Foot & Ankle Specialist

Non-surgical Treatments Emphasized

Foot Pain, Nail Problems
Bunions, Broken Bones
Diabetic and Arthritic Foot Care
Sports Injuries
Laser Technology

Dr. Paul Carston, Podiatrist

DPM, APMA, CPMA, AAFS, AAPA

559-5900

Therapy Need Not Take Years

Confidential, Effective Counseling For:

- Anxiety, Panic • Marital Problems • Feeling Unloved
- Sexual Problems • Overcoming Fears • Career Worries
- Grief • Difficulty Getting Close • Worrying Too Much
- Child or Adolescent Problems • Substance Abuse
- Children of Alcoholics • Sexually Abused • Depression
- Eating Problems • Fears • Forgetfulness
- Losing Control • Couples • Individuals

Hundreds Helped
Fully Certified Psychiatrist

John Greenstein, M.D.

858-5858

The Family Optical

Work, Play, Sports, Reading, Computer & TV Eyewear
For Kids and Adults

One Hour For Most Glasses
Huge Selection—Budget & Fashion
Bring Your Rx

Call 474-EYES

Mountain Rd. Physical Therapy

No Referral Needed For:

• Back or Neck Pain • Jaw Pain or Popping
• Headaches • Whiplash
• Leg, Hand or Arm Rehabilitation

Fully Certified
Over 15 Years Experience

Call for Appointment

444-PAIN

The Women's Health Center

Checkups, Pap Smears, Mammograms
Obstetrics, Infertility Problems
Complete Gynecology

Dr. Patricia Garner

Board-Certified Obstetrician & Gynecologist

497-5555

Figure 11.2 Types of Signs

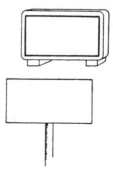 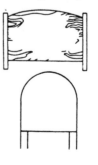 

■ **More Sign Rules.**

1. *The Law of Change:* Plexiglass is the best material for your sign face because things change and changing a plexi face costs only $200-$300 instead of $2,000-$3,000 for an entire sign.

2. *The Law of Light:* Signs should work 20 hours a day since traffic goes by at least that many hours. That means lighting it. And interior lighting is superior to spotlights for getting attention.

3. *The Law of Location:* Place the sign on your property to maximize its exposure. Walk your street stopping every 100 feet to study the optimal location from that point. High, low, curbside, perpendicular to the street ... where? If the city won't let you put it where you want, go for a variance. The stakes are that big.

4. *The Law of Size:* How big should you make your sign? As big as the law and landlord allow. Size has nothing to do with image. Graphics are the sole determinant of that. Size has to do with getting noticed.

5. *The Law of Money:* Shop your sign construction. Costs vary tremendously for the exact same sign.

6. *The Law of Limitations:* Sign companies know about construction, nothing about marketing strategies. Don't let them tell you what to put on your sign.

☐ **BANNERING BOOSTS WALK-IN TRAFFIC**

The stories catch your attention. The figures rivet you.

1. Convenience sells. Physician W.P. knows that. He was savvy enough not to position his general practice against the emergency rooms as an UrgiCenter. He suspected if he did, he wouldn't get enough repeat business to fully utilize his expensive square footage.

Instead, he positioned his practice as a general practice with expanded services (minor emergencies) and expanded hours (evenings and weekends). In this way he could attract patients and hold onto them instead of having them revert back to their "regular" MD. Smart.

But how was he to get the word out? Located in a strip mall, he had the traffic. But the area was *conservative. Very conservative.* This wasn't California where they give a free car wash and ear piercing with every checkup. How could he do it tastefully?

W.P. felt he could do it with a banner. (See Figure 11.3.) Was he filled with trepidation? Greatly. But only until he saw the books fill up on the weekends ... and then begin to fill more during the week from repeat business and word-of-mouth. Trepidation was then replaced with elation.

Figure 11.3 A Storefront

2. Ophthalmologist K.U. began stocking disposable contacts. He smartly promoted them in the logical manners: by targeting direct mail to his existing contact lens patients; talking up the new lenses in the office; and using interior office placards. All of these made sense because internal efforts are the easiest and fastest ways to produce numbers on the income column.

But K.U. was never one to advertise, so he lacked a viable way to inform nonpatients of this breakthrough. In keeping with his definition of advertising, he decided to hang a banner across his office fascia. He felt that since he would not be paying for media, it wasn't advertising.

The banner read:

> **NO MORE CONTACT LENS PROBLEMS!**
> **NO MORE CLEANINGS!**
> **NEW—DISPOSABLE LENSES.**
> **VERY AFFORDABLE.**
> **ASK INSIDE.**

Advertising or not, it sure boosted income. Twelve walk-ins during the first week alone with four conversions. The next week, he was six for 20, then eight for 22, and 10 for 28 in the fourth week. Then his city banner permit expired. Down came the banner ... and his numbers.

3. General practitioner P.L. had heard it often before, but

couldn't understand how people would simply assume he wasn't accepting new patients. Not only that, he didn't know what to do about it.

After talking with his mentor on THE PRACTICE BUILDER Advisory Hotline, he began rectifying the situation internally by directly asking patients for referrals, instituting a formal "Friend-Help-A-Friend" program in his quarterly patient-base mailings, and by shaping referring behavior with a gift-giving Frequent Referrer Program.

They all worked, but only internally. There was still nothing to communicate to the public that he was available. Until his advisor suggested a seemingly brazen move: a banner on his free-standing building announcing the unobvious.

The 3′ × 20′ banner with its red letters on a white background read: "NOW WELCOMING NEW PATIENTS." Yes, the sign was big but not gaudy. The layout and typeface had a clean, nonretail professionalism about it that communicated the right image.

P.L.'s market is a quickly growing area so what he needed most was to squash the no-new-patient misconception. The banner did it—not only with those new to the area, but also with his existing patients who now referred even more.

Results: *a doubling of new patients by the end of the second month*. With no city banner ordinance to restrict him, he's leaving the banner up.

4. Located in a strip mall two doors away from a 25,000 customer-a-week supermarket, Dr. H.F. had a gold mine on his hands. Even in his ultra-competitive, blue-collar market, his practice was more than healthy, just from the strip mall traffic alone.

But H.F. was a smart miner. In an effort to screen as many people as possible for his three-doctor group, he hung an eye-catching banner across the overhang in front. Now 100,000 people a month saw his offer instead of the handful that actually read his ad in the local throwaway.

New patients swung up from an average 68 per month to over 100. Cost for the banner was $112 plus $25 for the 30-day city license.

Then when the banner license expired, H.F. lowered the banner but put up a new one inside his office window. Was it still effective? Yes, but not as much due to lower visibility.

H.F. explained, "For me, the offer of a free exam works and when I put it on that outside sign, many more people became aware of it. So when I had to pull it down because the city only allows one banner for 30 days a year, you bet I was going to figure a way to keep it."

■ **Banner Guidelines.** Foot and drive-by traffic are among the top assets of a practice, along with the existing patient base and the staff. Unfortunately, it's only a profitable asset *if developed*. Otherwise, color it a void.

Temporary banners, along with permanent signage and reader boards, are usually the main keys to filling in the color. Banners in particular are perfect for the following situations:

1. Announcing a new service or product
2. Announcing that you're accepting new patients or clients
3. Reminding people of a seasonal service or product they need
4. Educating people why they need a service
5. Promoting a special offer
6. Announcing a special event
7. Announcing a change in the practice
8. Promoting convenient hours
9. Promoting an old service for a new purpose

On the banner remember to promote only one concept at a time. More than one dilutes the issue and drives down response. Also include a phone number as an additional way to respond. (The more ways you give to respond, the greater the response.)

Keep the copy somewhat short but strong. The slower the traffic, the longer the copy can be. And if you use a visual of some kind to grab attention, response will go up further.

Also make it *big!* How big? As big as the landlord, county, city and whoever else needs to approve it will let you. *Big!* The bigger the banner, the bigger the response because more people will notice it.

But watch your image. Use a professional typeface and a clean layout. No junky, retail hype, please. If you avoid that, you'll look professional. Remember, size doesn't dictate whether the image's professional or not—graphics do.

That's it. Follow the rules and then see if your figures go as high as the banner. Chances are they will.

☐ THE PRACTICE BUILDER'S OFFICE SIGN CONTEST

■ Grand Prize Winner

The terrific outdoor office sign shown in Figure 11.4 does it all. First, it immediately tells you whom the practice is for and its basic positioning as a specialty center.

Then it describes the practice's services and gives two additional benefits for coming there. The logo is for recognition and continuity from the newspaper campaign which also displays it. The tagline reinforces the positioning. And the phone number gives you a way to get in touch with the office. These are all the elements a great sign needs if it's to become a recruiter instead of the normal "Obstetrics-Gynecology" announcement.

But then it goes one step further. It creates a beautiful feeling with the graphics of flowers and warm colors. So color this one a super sign.

Figure 11.4 A Prize-Winning Ob/Gyn Sign

■ **Honorable Mentions**   Figure 11.5 presents a number of professional service signs.

OHANA HEALING INSTITUTE

Harmony · Balance · Fulfillment

Alternative Therapies
for health & healing

❦ A healthier body
❦ A more loving heart
❦ Accelerated personal growth

Pauline W. Farina, Ph. D., Director

589-4555

PROMOTIONS IN MOTION

1. A small town hearing aid dispenser is putting up a new banner every month on the office front. Things he promotes: special events, new products, free hearing test. Average response: 10 to 12 new patients per month totalling about $6,000 income at a cost of $100. Sixty to one return on investment is okay with him.

2. A Midwest podiatrist increased response to his outdoor office signage with the use of a reader board he recently put up. He changes the message every three days so drivers and walkers keep looking up—and remembering him. Recent messages:

   "Painful nail problems quickly fixed. 223-9900"

   "Bunions now treated with new technology. 223-9900"

   "For foot pain, come to a specialist. 223-9900"

   "Free foot exam. Expires Friday. Call 223-9900"

   "We're praying for rain!"

3. Most people didn't notice podiatrist G.K.'s office since it was located in a weakly anchored strip mall. However, it did have plenty of drive-by traffic. But since his signage opportunities were limited, he used balloons to grab attention. When his office manager first suggested them, G.K. thought the idea too brash. But his troops did it anyway—and proved the balloons' value with almost a 20% increase in walk-in traffic. Now they balloon the outside of the office everyday. And the patients like them.

4. Family doctor T.H. was getting into the lucrative allergy business. To launch his new endeavor, she talked it up to her patients, sent out an announcement to her patient base and placed an ad in the *Yellow Pages*. And then she added one more effort. T.H. knew that repetition was important so she placed a poster in every office room—including the restroom. Now with a captive audience, everyone knew she treated allergies. Not only was it inexpensive, it was a must read.

Chapter 12 □

SHREWD AND SAVVY PRACTICE BROCHURES: AND WHAT TO DO WITH THEM

□ STALKING THE GREAT PRACTICE BROCHURE: THE WHYS AND HOWS

Every *big* practice has one. In fact, every sophisticated business in the U.S. does, too. In business, it's called sales literature. In the professions, it's called a practice brochure. No matter what the environment, it fulfills the same purpose. It sells.

Or at least it should. At the very least, it should. Which brings up a curious point. If the purpose of the brochure is to convince prospects to come to the practice, then why do most contain information that make readers cringe ... or go to sleep?

The cringing part comes when the brochure tells patients or clients what's going to happen if they don't show up for an appointment. Or menacingly warns about ultimate responsibility for payment.

The sleeping part comes from everything else. Generic prose that doesn't differentiate you from every other look-alike in town. A layout that is copy-intensive with no subheads or short paragraphs to make it feel inviting to read. And that graphic look that dates from somewhere between Attila The Hun and Woodstock.

Unfortunately, recipes like this don't sell.

■ **Why You Need One.** When you meet someone and make an impression, you've completed only part of the selling process. A good start to be sure, but don't blow it now by only handing out your business card. Most cards don't convince anyone to do anything.

Instead, hand over your practice brochure. The brochure will reinforce the impression you made—or might even clean-up and improve a botched job. (You may get the patient in spite of yourself!) In any case, *a single impression by a practitioner is often insufficient* to bring in a new prospect. The reason is that people need repetition *before* they feel comfortable, before they act. The right brochure does the trick. The chiding and snoring kind doesn't.

The same thing goes when your staff recruit prospects. Not only do they need a "leave-behind" to repeat the message, but since they're not trained as salespeople, the brochure can say things in ways they never dreamed of.

When you give talks, your brochure again provides the needed back-up. Not only that, but it can say things about you that you can't— because they would sound like bragging. Plus it never forgets to say those convincing things that tantalize prospects, whereas professionals forget all the time.

And next to last, you need to mail it (when possible) to prospects before they come in. In this way, its convincing power keeps down the no-shows. If you don't send it before they come in, hand it out when they come in. People aren't always convinced you're the greatest thing since sliced bread, even though they've committed to the first appointment. Your practice brochure keeps the "sale from unraveling."

And last is the 1,001 other ways you'll use your sales literature: for mall shows, health fairs, phone inquiries and so forth. No practice that wants to be *big* can afford to be without one—but only the right one.

■ **The Right Brochure.** Here's your main guideline: *If a point doesn't convince or sell, it doesn't go in your brochure!* That's the acid test. Chances are if you have a brochure and it's like most, you should toss 96.8% of the material in it.

Your brochure is not a place to inform—only to sell. So figure out those salient points that convince prospects to choose you ... and choose you over competitors. Then *only* use information to support these points.

This means not listing your hours, unless you're trying to prove they're convenient. And no maps, unless you're supporting a convenient location. But if you feel the need to inform, then do it on your intake sheet or explain it in person—and only when they've become a patient, *not before!*

■ *Tricks of the Trade.* The following rules make sure your brochure is read. Ignore any one and you lose this game.

1. *Use subheads.* Big blocks of type are intimidating. Tests show they cut readership. Use subheads to break up the type for easier reading.

2. *Use short words, short paragraphs, and short sentences.* These also make for easy reading. Since brochures are normally four to eight pages, short everything is needed to get the reader through the length. Short everything also provides a certain crispness or energy to the writing which is fun to read, not a chore.

   And lastly, because most of your clientele doesn't have PhDs, short also lowers the copy's reading level. Notice the writing in this article—the length of its words, its sentences, its paragraphs. And look to whom we're writing!

3. *Use modern, non-retail typefaces and photos.* Study the examples in this chapter. Notice the typefaces, how non-retail they feel. And how modern or timeless they are to avoid a dated look. Show them to whomever does your artwork.

   Also look at how photos are used. They break up the copy for easier reading. Plus they support points made in the writing. That's a nice marriage of copy and graphics.

4. *Use a benefit or teaser in your headline.* The front cover needs to give the reader a reason to open the brochure and read on. No reason, no reading. Using the practice name alone on the cover impresses only your family, friends, and YOU. So don't fall into this ego-trap. Write for the people who don't know you.

   Now you're ready. Is it easy? Probably not, since anything you do for the first time isn't easy. (Of course, it seems easy if you don't know the right way. Because anything you produce is right.)

   But don't worry. Just make a list of your selling points and what you do, order them for presentation, and then write, rewrite, rewrite, rewrite, and rewrite. Allow four to six weeks creative time plus two weeks in the artist's hands. Then you're ready for the printer.

   But is it worth it? YES, because you need sales literature.

☐ ANATOMY OF A GREAT PRACTICE BROCHURE

   What makes a great practice brochure? (See Figure 12.1.) We're not talking about a good one, or an average one, but a work of art. You'll discover exactly what does in the next few minutes from the analysis of the following brochure, but first some ...

Figure 12.1a Mielcarek Brochure, Front Panel

Older Eyes - The Best Is Yet To Be

> Grow old along with me!
> The best is yet to be,
> The last of life for which the
> first was made.
> **ROBERT BROWNING**

Even if you've had 20/20 vision all your life, cataracts and glaucoma can sneak up on you with no warning at all.

With regular checkups, we can discover these problems early on, when they're easier to treat. Left to progress unchecked, cataracts and glaucoma could eventually rob you of your sight forever. The best is yet to be, and we'll help you see it in all its glory.

CATARACTS

Cataract surgery is safe and effective when a qualified surgeon is in charge, and when the most advanced methods are used. At Mielcarek Eye Associates you will be in the hands of surgeons who are on the leading edge of medical eye care, even teaching our future ophthalmologists at major universities.

You'll be happy to know that we use the latest phacoemulsification and foldable implants. Your affected lens will be removed and replaced with a permanent, trouble-free artificial lens, and you will be back to normal or near-normal vision in no time.

GLAUCOMA

As a board member of the Delaware County branch of the Pennsylvania Association for the Blind, Dr. Mielcarek is dedicated to early and correct treatment of this number one blinder.

Glaucoma is an eye disease that usually affects people over age 40. It begins with virtually no symptoms. As it progresses, it causes a loss of side vision, severe pain and, eventually, permanent damage to the optic nerve.

That's why it's critical to have your eyes checked regularly. At Mielcarek Eye Associates, the glaucoma screening is a standard part of your regular exam. And should we find glaucoma, there are a variety of modern treatment options available.

You Can Call On Us 24 Hours A Day

> The eyes are the windows of the soul.
> **PROVERB**

If you experience a sudden loss of vision, or accidentally injure one of your eyes, please call us at any time of the day or night, weekday or weekend. Within our own surgical suite we can competently handle most emergencies. And, for more serious injuries, we can treat you at Crozer-Chester Medical Center, Riddle Memorial Hospital, Taylor Hospital, Scheie Eye Institute, or Delaware County Memorial Hospital.

Younger-Looking Eyes Mean A Younger-Looking You

> Take a pair of sparkling eyes,
> Hidden, ever and anon,
> In a merciful eclipse.
> **W. S. GILBERT**

Eyes show age sooner than any other part of your body. And now many people are discovering that the ease of cosmetic eye surgery means there's no reason to live with eyes that age you before your time.

If you'd like to have younger-looking eyes, there are a number of simple procedures we can perform right in the privacy of our own office, including:

Smooth away wrinkles with collagen injections and Retin A
Perk up droopy eyelids with simple eyelid surgery.
Define your eyes with our permanent lash liner

Figure 12.1b Mielcarek Brochure, First Half of Inside Spread

A Full Spectrum Of
Choices In Eye Wear

My heart leaps up when I behold
A rainbow in the sky.
WILLIAM WORDSWORTH

Because convenience is so important, our optometrist is available to help you make your eye wear selection.

And because there are so many new contacts that offer better correction and better comfort than ever before, we'll let you "test drive" the contacts that interest you.

Don't Worry About The Details

I am a man, and nothing human can
be of indifference to me.
TERENCE

In many cases, your insurance covers eye care. Our staff will be happy to review your insurance coverage with you, and help you with any necessary forms. We can even provide you with an itemized

service report to help you get the highest possible insurance reimbursements.

If there is ever a problem with your ability to pay, please don't let it keep you from the quality of eye care you deserve. Call us, and let's discuss some payment alternatives.

Eye Care Professionals
With A Vision

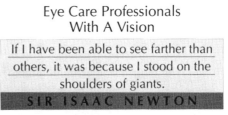

If I have been able to see farther than
others, it was because I stood on the
shoulders of giants.
SIR ISAAC NEWTON

The people at Mielcarek Eye Associates are dedicated to providing the highest quality eye care to our community, and we prove it every day. All of us attend courses in our own areas of specialty to continually expand the variety and quality of services we offer you. Many of us teach courses as well, and write articles for publication in medical journals. And we're always available to answer questions and solve problems for you.

Figure 12.1c Mielcarek Brochure, Second Half of Inside Spread

Dr. Nancy Crawford

An international ophthalmologic consultant and surgeon, Dr. Crawford earned her M.D. from the Albert Einstein College of Medicine. She studied with world-renowned ophthalmology specialist, Paul Henkind, and with retina specialist, Alan Bird. She has worked for the United States Public Health Service, and as an investigator of intraocular implants for the FDA.

Her expertise has been recognized by the staffs of four Delaware County hospitals where she is a staff member. She also lectures frequently to hospital staffs and community groups.

- *Preceptorship, Moorfield's Eye Hospital in London, England*
- *Preceptorship, Behrhorst Clinic in Guatemala, Central America*
- *Member, Phi Beta Kappa*
- *Board certified by the American Board of Ophthalmology*

Dr. Leon Mielcarek

Dr. Mielcarek has lived in Delaware County all his life, but his work has reached the far horizons. He earned his M.D. from Thomas Jefferson University, and completed specialized training in ophthalmology at the Hospital of the University of Pennsylvania and its world-renowned Scheie Eye Institute.

Today, he instructs aspiring ophthalmologists at six different schools. He is on staff at six prominent hospitals. He has made frequent media appearances and is a renowned guest speaker.

His contributions to the advancement of ophthalmology are well-known in business and industry. As a member of the Professional Standards Review Organization, he has monitored and helped to maintain the quality of eye care in our community. And the medical industry has called on his expertise in evaluating advanced, new products.

Dr. Leon Mielcarek's concern for the betterment of eye care has been recognized and appreciated in Media and beyond.

- *Board certified by the American Board of Ophthalmology*
- *Fellow of the American College of Surgeons*
- *Board member of the Delaware County branch of the Association for the Blind*
- *Recipient of the American Medical Association's Physician's Recognition Award*
- *Professional speaker on many local radio and television programs*

Dr. Lawrence Coppock

Dr. Coppock joined us as an optometrist in 1984. Licensed and Board certified, he is a graduate of Gettysburg College and the Pennsylvania College of Optometry.

In addition to his responsibilities here at Mielcarek Eye Associates, Dr. Coppock instructs aspiring optometrists at the Pennsylvania College of Optometry in the latest techniques and equipment.

- *Served as head of the Eye Section of the Naval Regional Medical Clinic in New Orleans*
- *Clinical preceptor at the University of Houston College of Optometry*
- *Member of the extended faculty at the Pennsylvania College of Optometry*

Mielcarek
EYE ASSOCIATES
Our reward is your healthy eyes

319 West State St., Media, PA
(215) 566-1227

Figure 12.1d Mielcarek Brochure, First Half of Outside (Back) Spread

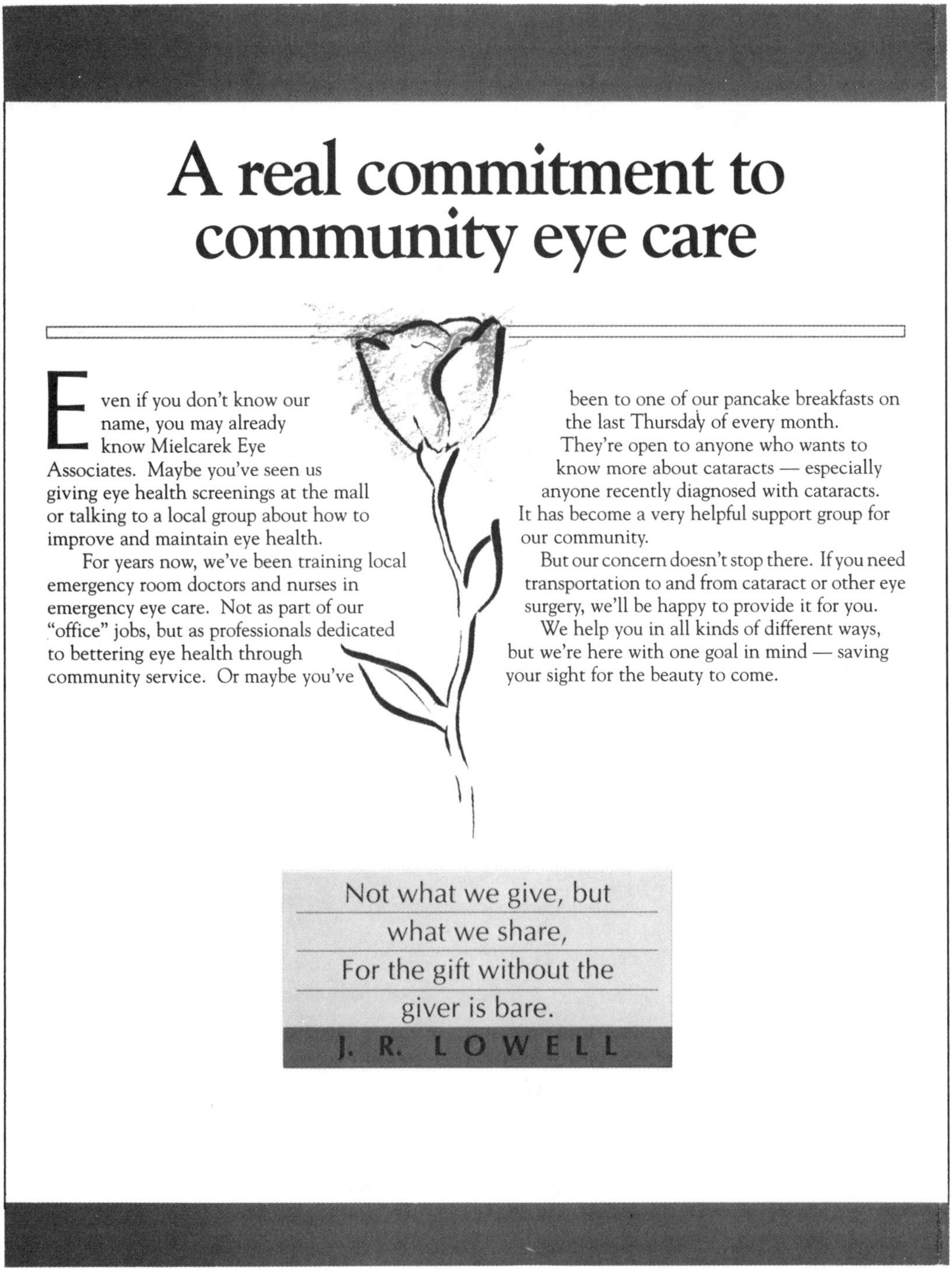

A real commitment to community eye care

Even if you don't know our name, you may already know Mielcarek Eye Associates. Maybe you've seen us giving eye health screenings at the mall or talking to a local group about how to improve and maintain eye health.

For years now, we've been training local emergency room doctors and nurses in emergency eye care. Not as part of our "office" jobs, but as professionals dedicated to bettering eye health through community service. Or maybe you've been to one of our pancake breakfasts on the last Thursday of every month.

They're open to anyone who wants to know more about cataracts — especially anyone recently diagnosed with cataracts. It has become a very helpful support group for our community.

But our concern doesn't stop there. If you need transportation to and from cataract or other eye surgery, we'll be happy to provide it for you.

We help you in all kinds of different ways, but we're here with one goal in mind — saving your sight for the beauty to come.

> Not what we give, but
> what we share,
> For the gift without the
> giver is bare.
>
> J. R. LOWELL

Figure 12.1e Mielcarek Brochure, Second Half of Outside (Back) Spread

IMPORTANT INFORMATION

Please keep this handy - it contains information on how to contact our
doctors at Mielcarek Eye Associates in case of emergency.

Appointments and Hours

Hours are as follows:

Monday	8 am - 8 pm
Tuesday	8 am - 8 pm
Wednesday	8 am - 4 pm
Thursday	8 am - 8 pm
Friday	8 am - 4 pm
Saturday	9 am -12noon
	(Except July and August)

Patients are seen by appointment only, except in the case of an
emergency. If you need to cancel an appointment for any reason, please
notify the office 24 hours in advance so that we can use that time to schedule
another patient.

Emergencies

In the event of an emergency, you can reach our doctors through their
24-hour service or call the office during above hours. Emergency cases will, of
course, be seen immediately. The number of the answering service for
emergencies is: 566-1228.

Fees

At the end of your visit, you will receive a statement which explains
services performed and the fees for each. Unless otherwise specified, we ask
that all charges be paid at the time services are rendered. We accept personal
checks, MasterCard and Visa for payment. Please call the office if you have
any questions about billing.

Insurance

Our staff is prepared to review your insurance qualifications with you and
assist you with any insurance forms if necessary. Services rendered by our
office will be charged directly to you, and payment is expected in full at the
time those services are rendered. All reimbursements of expenses will be
made directly to you. You will receive an itemized service report to assist you
in filing any insurance claims. We do accept Medicare and several other
insurances. Please ask for a complimentary insurance consultation.

Mielcarek
EYE ASSOCIATES
Our reward is your healthy eyes

319 West State Street, Media, PA (215) 566-1227

Figure 12.1f Mielcarek Brochure, Front of Black and White Loose Insert

IMPORTANT INFORMATION

Your first visit

On your first visit, we will initiate a permanent medical file for you, so kindly bring insurance information, any past medical records that may help our doctors, a list of current medications, and your old eye prescription.

Surgery

Some surgical procedures are performed in-office. As with any outpatient surgery, you should make transportation arrangements so someone can take you home. Eye operations are performed in the hospital. Cataract and laser surgery are outpatient hospital procedures. You will generally be admitted to Crozer-Chester Medical Center, Riddle Memorial Hospital, Taylor Hospital, Scheie Eye Institute, or Delaware County Memorial Hospital.

The doctors at Mielcarek Eye Associates are always available to answer questions about surgery.

Call us anytime you have questions.

Though we are a busy office, we'll always take time out to talk to our patients. The staff is well trained to assist you. If you need to speak directly to the doctor, a message will be relayed to him as soon as he is out of his appointment. He will then either have a qualified staff member return your call if it is appropriate or schedule a time when you can talk to the doctor personally.

Brochures

Ask for your personal copy.

Mielcarek
EYE ASSOCIATES
Our reward is your healthy eyes

319 West State Street, Media, PA **(215) 566-1227**

Figure 12.1g Mielcarek Brochure, Back of Black and White Loose Insert

■ **Underlying Principles.** As mentioned earlier, your practice brochure should communicate those important things that *convince* people to come to you—*convince, not inform!* This is the biggest mistake most practices make with their promo literature. They want to tell everything, plus all those things they think people will need to know *after* they become patients or clients. There's a technical term for this approach—dumb.

Also, in order to convince, the information must dazzle them—*not you.* Get your head into the mindset of your most likely buyers and evaluate all the information from their perspective. Whatever pushes their hot buttons is what goes in. *Nothing else.*

If you already have a practice brochure, now's a good time to test it against this standard. Most fail because they fail to convince. In fact, most don't do a thing. And yes, they need to be redone.

■ **Other Concepts.** Yes, people buy facts and figures. But they also buy emotion, perhaps even more so than the "rational" approach. The copy should be emotional. And especially the graphics. What kind of emotion? That depends on your market and what moves them. Seniors are different from parents. Just make sure there's fire in the piece's belly, not sleeping pills.

The brochure also needs to answer the following questions:

1. What do you do? (Symptoms, please; not modalities.)
2. Why should I choose you rather than a competitor? (Answer with a point of differentiation important to them, not you.)
3. How do I know I can trust you? (Good graphics create your good image; poor ones put you in the junker.)

■ **The Great Practice Brochure.** Now look closely at the brochure on the preceding pages (Figure 12.1). The creators took the tack that *if they cloaked the practice in beautiful ideas and images, the reader would feel warm and wonderful about the practice.* They wanted to differentiate this practice emotionally—by associating it with beauty. Here's how they went about it.

First, the colors in the piece are extraordinary. If you could see them, you'd see bright orange where you now see dark grey, light orange for light grey, even lighter orange for white, black for black, and mauve for the headlines and flowers. Together, they're luscious and truly high design.

No maroon and grey of the '70s. Or brown-on-brown of the '60s. Colors like these are common ways to make a practice appear out-of-date.

Now note the line drawings of the flowers. They, too, are beautiful and add to the feeling. Also study how the designer used the drawings as a graphic theme throughout the piece, not only to reinforce the feeling of beauty, but to tie the piece together. That's very sophisticated, very powerful graphic design.

The copy then reinforces the cloak of beauty. First the headline does it: *"Saving your sight for the beauty to come."* See how it establishes the theme while also communicating a benefit to the reader? (And notice how the practice name is *not* the headline because the name doesn't give people a reason to read the piece.)

Next comes the imaginative use of quotes by Browning, Wordsworth, Newton, and others to create mental images of beauty. This is the power of lofty prose which just makes you feel good.

Stop here for a moment and reflect upon what the creators have done. They've made the reader feel really good about the practice—and they haven't even said a single word about what the practitioners do or who they are! These are wonderfully sophisticated ways of using emotions to sell a practice.

■ **Other Notes.** The subheads tell the entire story of what the professionals do and the benefits they provide. And the copy has none of the typical "riot act" information found in most patient information pamphlets.

Notice the one large photo of the target market. It clearly shows to whom this practice is meant. Also that they're good looking seniors implies that you could look like them if you use this practice. This is the "after" picture.

The photos of the professionals are perfect. Everyone's smiling brightly (well almost) to show you that everything's going to come out all right. And each is shot against a light background to give them more depth and contrast. Good photography. (You can bet the doctor's night school nephew didn't shoot these.)

The logo is also outstanding. Its visual displays *the* benefit of coming to this practice—and does it in a very powerful way. What more intense benefit could you conjure up for an ophthalmologist to provide a senior than the ability to read to his or her grandchild? Awesome, isn't it? The typeface is also very clean and quite professional, not at all retail. And the tagline adds to the caring feeling created everywhere else.

One last touch: On the final panel where the copy describes the community involvement of the practice and some additional benefits, it ends where it began—*saving your sight for the beauty to come.* A touch like this ties the piece together and gives it a very smooth and professional feel. As if there's not a hair out of place. This is what creates the feeling of perfection and communicates that people can trust you.

■ **Facts and Figures.** The piece unfolded is 11 × 25", then folded twice down to a finished size of 8⅓ × 11". It has six panels and three colors, but appears to have six because three screens give the impression of additional colors without the additional expense in printing. The large photo has a drop shadow bottom and right to make it pop off the page. The paper is 80-pound to stop bleed through and coated (shiny) to help the photos pop.

The total design cost for research, copywriting, art direction, and all photography was $3,995. Printing bids ranged 40¢ to 55¢ apiece, depending on quantity.

This is an extraordinary practice brochure which will last five to ten years and create $$millions$$ in business.

☐ **WHY 94% OF PRACTICE BROCHURES DON'T WORK**

During the PRACTICE BUILDER's Brochure Contest, our members sent hundreds of entries from every U.S. state and Canada. And of these, 94% don't work.

First, let's define not working. The *only* purpose of a practice brochure is to get people *to call and come to you. Nothing else.* So if it motivates and moves large numbers of people to action, it works. If it doesn't, it fails. It's that simple.

There is another type of brochure—a patient information brochure. This piece is designed to *inform*, not sell. In it, you can put your payment policies, hours, etc.

But that handout isn't marketing. So don't put money into it—a one-color handout is fine. And don't ever give it out *before* someone's a confirmed, they'll-never-leave-you patient. It contains too many negatives. And don't ever combine the two types of brochures for the same reason.

■ **15 Royal Screw-ups.** Now get your brochure and compare it to these royal bloopers. If you come out unscathed, you've got a winner.

1. *It's boring!* Do you like to read boring material? Then why would you produce any? Yet, in your desire to look "professional," you make things dry and unappealing. Well, you'll look "professional," but no one will read it. Now what?

A great way to bore people is to have no visuals. An all-type brochure looks uninteresting and low energy.

Another way is boring copy from untrained writers. They don't know how to grab interest and *make sure* the piece gets read. That takes a pro who knows the tricks—action verbs, colorful adjectives, vivid images, hormone-inducing adverbs, and striking layouts. This takes years of training and critiquing. And that's why 99% of practitioners are *boring* writers.

Even public relations people are *boring* writers since they write press releases which inform but don't sell. Only advertising copywriters have been taught how to produce interest-piquing *sales literature.*

2. *Overuse of "We".* Nobody cares about you, so to interest them, you've got to write about them while describing you. It's confusing but simple. Just before you write about yourself, put "you'll" and a verb like: find, discover, uncover, get, love, have, like, enjoy, receive, etc. Then add as many more "you's" as you can fit in.

"We have free van service." becomes *"**You'll discover** our free van service makes **your** visit so convenient, **you'll** also enjoy **your** coming and going."* Look at all the *"you's."* It makes everything more interesting for the reader.

3. *Name as the headline.* Over half the contest entries had the practice name as the cover headline. But why do that when the purpose of the headline is to get the piece *opened and read*? A practice name rarely does that. And if you don't get them inside, it doesn't matter what you've got there.

To do that, either put your *big* benefit(s) right in the head or use teaser copy to stimulate interest.

4. *Stodgy subheads.* Subheads break up copy to make reading easy, but most kill interest, like *Practice Philosophy.* People don't read philosophy, so why should they start with yours? (Even in Greece, philosophy doesn't pull anymore.)

You forgot the crucial question—"What's in it for the reader?" If you have a benefit for the reader, put it in the subhead! Benefits, benefits, benefits! And more benefits. Then you'll write subheads like: "With 7 Different Ways to Pay, Of Course You Can Afford Beautiful Teeth" and "Caring Is Not Only Remembering Your Name, It's Remembering How Important Your Time Is!"

5. *No differentiation.* Readers ask "Why should I choose this professional rather than someone else?" Better have a good answer (or lots of them) and better put them in your sales literature. If you don't convince people to choose you over the competition, you lose.

6. *You don't come across as likeable.* People buy people. And on top of that, they buy people they like. Are you smiling in your photos? Do you look caring and empathetic? Do you share something personal about yourself so they think you're real, not just a statue on a pedestal? Here's a nice example:

> Away from his practice, Dr. Gallegos is an avid sports enthusiast, enjoying skydiving, scuba diving and basketball. He referees for the local Basketball Officials Association and is counted among the Century Members of the YMCA. And he still finds time to enjoy cooking.

Get the idea?

7. *No proof for generic claims.* Everyone writes that they provide excellent care, personalized service, and that they're caring. But rarely does anyone support their claims. So no one believes them.

Instead list those things which show you care, that you're terrific or whatever. Proof, proof, proof! With photos that support your claims.

8. *Reading people the riot act.* These are actual samples we received: "Visiting: Any visits should be made with the understanding that this is a working institution." (Thanks for the warning.) "Please understand that because of our heavy patient load, it is sometimes difficult for new or even old patients to be seen immediately." (Why are you telling me your problems?) "Please cooperate to the fullest with our staff." (Is it my job to make your life easier?) And the favorite—"Payment is expected at the time of your appointment. You are ultimately responsible for all charges incurred." (Why not rub my nose in it a little more?)

You don't convince someone to come to you by telling them all the reasons they shouldn't. Period. But if you want to read them the riot act, read it to them later.

9. *Showing scary photos.* Cutting open an eye makes people run the other way. So show only happy photos and "before and after" or "after" shots. Forget the "during" photos! They're not "professional"; they're anxiety-producing.

10. *Stiff, no-action photos.* Photos are suppose to illustrate a point, usually that you make people feel good, that you're friendly or that people love you. If you look mummified, uncaring or numb, you're just filling space. If you can't think of anything for a photo, at least have you touching a patient on the shoulder or arm while talking intently and gesturing grandly.

And if it's a facial close-up, make sure you're looking *straight* at the lens and smiling.

11. *Putting your building on the cover.* Who cares if you have a building? Certainly not prospects. They want to buy you, not your assets. Instead, if you're proud of your building, carry a photo in your wallet.

12. *Printing photos in colors besides black and white or on uncoated paper.* Ever see a photo printed in only blue? It makes people look either sick or martian. It's never flattering. So print photos in black ink on white paper (unless full color is so cheap you can afford it, but that's rarely true—or necessary.)

Also print your brochure on coated (shiny) paper. Otherwise photos appear dull.

13. *Low contrast printing.* Always make sure there's much contrast between ink and paper. Sometimes, graphic artists get too artsy and use a screen (soft shade) of a color for the typography which doesn't give

enough contrast for an easy read. So don't use screens for body or headline copy.

14. *Out-of-date colors.* Color combos are associated with different decades. Brown on brown, maroon or blue on grey and all earthtones come from the 1970s. Soft skytones come from the '80s. And if people have only seen your brochure and not you, then the decade of your brochure's colors helps date you.

Colors of the 1990s cover the full spectrum of color, but they tend to be *bold and intense.* That's cutting edge.

15. *Small sized, over-italicized or big blocks of type.* If you make your type size smaller than about ten points or if you set more than a short paragraph in italics, it makes people work too hard to read. So they won't.

Or if your paragraphs are longer than about seven or eight lines (not sentences), the same is true. Break up the copy into small chunks. Also no-no's: justified right type (all lines end at the same length) and not indenting the first sentence of each paragraph.

■ **More Tips.** One contest entry put their appointment card on the front cover so tons of brochures get out and get read. Good idea.

No maps, please. Maps inform; they don't convince. One exception: If your location is *ultra*-convenient, you can use a map to prove the convenience claim. Otherwise, just list *the area* you serve.

Beware thinking that if you've got a good-looking piece, it's a winner. Eye-catching colors and an ingenious layout only help get prospects into a brochure. The copy must then *sell and close.* So the brochure may look great, but it may not motivate. And you need both. Many, many entries failed on this important count.

☐ THE 9 SHREWDEST WAYS TO USE YOUR PRACTICE BROCHURE

There's nothing worse than having great *sales literature* that gathers dust. So to make sure yours gathers prospects instead, use your new magnetic promotion cleverly:

1. *To precondition the first visit.* When a new patient's first visit is more than two days away, drop your practice brochure in the mail with your "Welcome to the Practice" letter. The purpose her ᵉ is to create great expectations and, therefore, cut down on no-shows.

2. *To convert prospects' phone contacts.* When a phone inquiry comes in but doesn't immediately convert, send them your red-hot brochure to get their blood moving.

3. *To keep the sale from unraveling.* Sometimes new patients or clients don't exactly have the best experience during their first visit. (Of course, it's probably the staff's fault!) Your practice brochure handed to them with your Waiting Room Resume can convince them there are

other things about the practice that are exceptionally wonderful and that it's worth coming back. In retail, this phenomenon is known as buyer's remorse. In psychology, it's cognitive dissonance. Call it what you will, your brochure keeps the sale from unraveling.

4. *For your staff's patient recruitment program.* The staff can talk excitedly about you, but they're not professional salespeople. When pros sell, they listen first. Then they probe for the prospect's hot buttons. Only then do they present what they have and they couch it in the prospect's terms. Since your staff can't do this well, the practice brochure does it for them. It covers all the hot buttons, many of which the staff would surely miss.

5. *To help you recruit, too.* When you meet people, don't use your business card alone to convince them to finally call you. Use heavy duty, people-moving equipment—like your brochure.

6. *To help your clientele refer.* Clients and patients also aren't professional salespeople. So to help them recruit for you, give them a copy to pass on to a friend, loved one, or colleague. Your brochure again hits the hot buttons they'd miss. No, don't mail it. Hand it out when you ask them for referrals.

7. *To help new patients or clients refer, too.* When handed to all new patients or clients at the first appointment, your brochure also gets passed along to friends, associates, and loved ones to help recruit them.

8. *As a leave-behind at talks.* You'll surely dazzle prospects who come to hear you talk before a group. But when they leave, life intrudes: The kid's got a cold; the credit card bill this month is enormous; they're spouse picks a fight. You know—*life.* And your great impression fades away. But your practice brochure can reinforce the impression and, in fact, add to it by saying things about you that you couldn't say because it would sound like bragging. Remember: Repetition works.

9. *As a promotional piece to get you talks.* Oftentimes you call an organization to arrange a speaking engagement or even a talk show. The chairman or program director then says, "Send me something on you." That should be your practice brochure, an outline of the topic for the talk or appearance and a list of previous gigs. Your brochure not only sells you, it "shows" how professional you are, especially if it looks slick.

■ **Conclusion.** Every practice needs sales literature. And that's your practice brochure.

☐ **BROCHURE ANALYSIS: SALES LITERATURE**

The terrific brochure shown in Figure 12.2 is what a practice brochure should be. All selling with nothing that merely informs—and doesn't inspire.

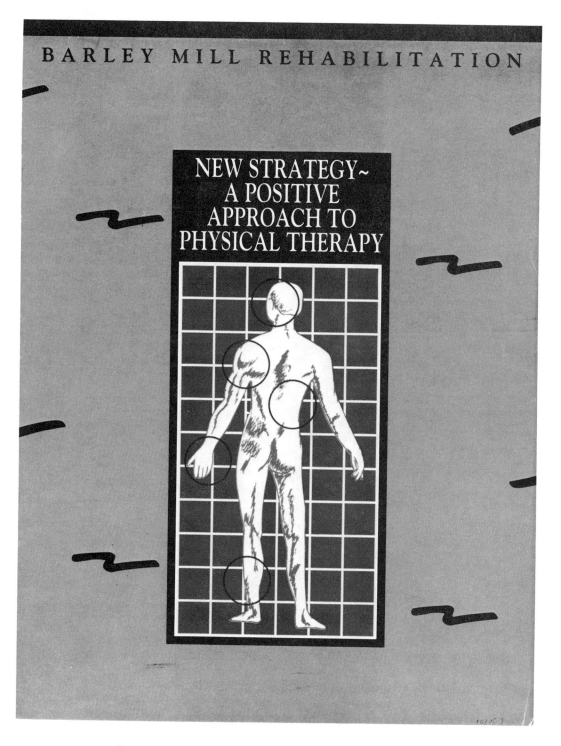

Figure 12.2a Barley Mill Rehabilitation Brochure, Front Cover

For a long time, physical therapy has focused on what physical therapy patients wouldn't be able to do after an accident — the activities they'd have to give up, the time they'd have to take away from work, the possibility of not being able to go back to their jobs at all.

At Barley Mill Rehabilitation, physical therapist Greg Rybicki sees things differently. He believes in a positive approach to physical therapy, and has the experience and the advanced equipment to implement it.

In this brochure, you'll read about some of the innovative approaches that are moving the science of physical therapy forward in the hands of Greg Rybicki and the staff at Barley Mill Rehabilitation.

KEY FUNCTIONAL ASSESSMENT

"Our patients can go back to work without risking reinjury - studies prove it."

How does Key Functional Assessment work?

The assessment begins with an interview for a detailed medical profile. Then, we test our patients' ability to perform functional activities — lifting, pushing/pulling, carrying, sitting, standing, walking, bending, kneeling, crawling, balance, and functions of the hands and feet — patients are evaluated in a total of 22 areas.

When all is said and done, we'll tell our patients what they can do, how long they can do it, how often, when they can begin, and under what other limits they can function. These limits are set not at maximum levels, but at safe levels. So there's much less chance of being injured again.

Key Functional Assessment tells us what we need to know.

Past methods of testing our patients' ability to go back to work have been hit-or-miss at best, but Key Functional Assessment has changed all that. A recent study of patients who went back to work after Key Functional Assessment showed that 100% of those who worked at or below the safe limits were not injured again. 56% of those who worked at levels above the safe limits were injured again.

With the Key Functional Assessment, we'll be able to confidently assess capability, assist in determining disability ratings, objectively measure improvement, and determine whether the patient is a candidate for a work hardening program.

Figure 12.2b Barley Mill Rehabilitation Brochure, Inside Front Cover

PREVENTION PROGRAMS FOR A STRONGER WORK FORCE

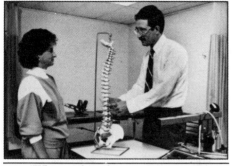

"When you know how to prevent injury, you're working smarter."

You know what they say: "An ounce of prevention is worth a pound of cure." At Barley Mill Rehabilitation, we want our patients to be skilled in preventing injury, so we've devised two programs to educate and alert them to the possibilities for an on-the-job injury.

THE LOW BACK SCHOOL

"Here's the easy way to prevent low back pain."

Surveys tell us that 80% of the population will experience low back pain, and that for 50% of these people, back pain will be a chronic problem.

In the Low Back School, our patients learn how to avoid all that pain. With a combination of education, exercise, class participation, and an ongoing maintenance program, they learn how to manage their own back pain. They're instructed in correct posture, relaxation techniques, stress management, and proper exercise to decrease pain.

Patients can attend the Low Back School separately, or in conjunction with their acute care treatment. Either way, they'll learn how not to be just another statistic with chronic back pain.

EMPLOYEE PREVENTION PROGRAMS

"Everyone should know how they can prevent injury."

It's much easier to avoid injury with a little preventive know-how.

We'll present an individualized, job-specific Employee Prevention Program in the work environment. We'll show employees what steps to take to keep on-the-job accidents from happening. Finally, everyone can work smarter — without accidents. It's a comforting thought.

With our Employee Prevention Programs, everyone can finally have the knowledge it takes to stop injuries *before* they happen.

WE'LL PUT YOUR MIND AT EASE, TOO

"We want you to feel confident about every aspect of our service."

It's important that our patients feel comfortable here at Barley Mill Rehabilitation, so we take the time to answer their questions — on procedures, payment, recovery time. You'll find that the staff is friendly and willing to help.

Our helpfulness extends to insurance, too. We don't think our patients should have to worry about the paperwork, so we'll do it for them. We accept Medicare and insurance assignments. If you have questions, just call us.

We've been a part of the Wilmington community for over a decade in an easy-to-find location. Our personalized morning and evening hours are easy on everyone's schedules.

Figure 12.2c Barley Mill Rehabilitation Brochure, Inside

MORE ABOUT THE MAN BEHIND BARLEY MILL REHABILITATION

"I'm dedicated to making physical therapy better and more accessible."

Greg Rybicki wants physical therapy to be the best it can possibly be — not only for his patients, but for patients all over the state.

He's ensured that his own patients are getting the best possible care by adding the most advanced equipment in the state to his office. . .by taking over 60 hours of continuing education annually to make sure he stays abreast of the latest developments in physical therapy. . .by maintaining a cheerful, caring staff who make patients feel a little bit better the minute they walk in the door.

Greg Rybicki sees the big picture also — that's why he's involved in professional organizations on the national, state, and local levels, working tirelessly for reforms in legislation on physical therapy and instituting new college-level programs to train physical therapy assistants.

With these credentials and professional affiliations, Greg Rybicki is truly taking a positive approach to physical therapy.

Certified as a Key Functional Assessment Specialist
Member, American Physical Therapy Association
President, Delaware Physical Therapy Association
Chairman, Legislative Committee, Delaware Physical Therapy Association
President, Delaware Private Practice Group
Treasurer, Physical Therapy Political Action Committee
Member, Advisory Board, Physical Therapist Assistants Program, Delaware Technical and Community College

Barley Mill Rehabilitation
Barley Mill Plaza
Greg Rybicki, PT
Kirk Mill Building - Suite 100
4305 Lancaster Pike, Wilmington, DE 19805
302-995-6095

Figure 12.2d Barley Mill Rehabilitation Brochure, Inside

THE WORK HARDENING PROGRAM

"Here's how our patients unlearn the behavior that keeps them from returning to work."

Studies have shown us that long-term disability is a learned behavior, reinforcing a physiological weakness that slows down the recovery process. But with the work hardening program, we actually teach our patients not to be disabled.

We'll treat the whole person.

For three to five days a week, between two and four hours a day, patients are part of a comprehensive, job-specific rehabilitation program. During the sessions, they'll undergo physical conditioning to restore their strength. We'll simulate their on-the-job activities to reassure them that they can do their jobs again. . .and, they'll learn what steps they can take to avoid being injured again and still lead an active life. We'll even do a job site analysis to let employers know how our patients can modify potentially harmful job activities.

Patient safety is our first concern.

Of course, our patients may have just sustained serious physical injuries, but the positive attitude they'll learn in the work hardening program keeps physical injuries from becoming emotional ones as well. We teach our patients that there is hope, that their injuries are temporary. And with periodic Key Functional Assessments, we show our patients what they can do and how they're progressing throughout their recovery.

THE MOST ADVANCED PHYSICAL THERAPY EQUIPMENT

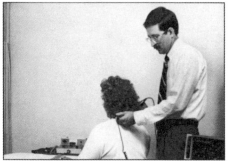

"You won't find more advanced equipment anywhere else in the state."

Two new, more effective ways to relieve pain.

Two of the newest pieces of equipment are the Electro-Acuscope and the Myopulse. These two devices operate on micro-amperage current to dramatically reduce pain, inflammation and muscle spasms. The Electro-Acuscope and the Myopulse treat sinus and tension headaches, sinus congestion, myositis, muscle strain, sprains, and tendonitis with excellent results. We're the only physical therapy practice in Delaware to have them.

We're fully equipped to help our patients get better.

At Barley Mill Rehabilitation, you'll find a full range of equipment and therapies. We're so concerned about providing advanced treatment that we've made an effort to get the newest equipment available.

Equipment like interferential electric stimulation, high voltage galvanic stimulation, and transcutaneous electric nerve stimulation also help us treat pain and swelling.

An isokinetic device called an Orthotron exercises and strengthens quadriceps, hamstrings, ankle plantar-flexors, ankle dorsi-flexors, and shoulder flexion/abduction. Other exercise equipment, including trunk extension and rotation units, free weights, lift dynamometers, exercise cycles, and pulleys are also used in work hardening programs.

And, of course you'll find a whirlpool, ultrasound, paraffin bath, ice, moist heat, parallel bars, mat table, lumbar and cervical traction to aid in pain relief and rehabilitation.

Figure 12.2e Barley Mill Rehabilitation Brochure, Inside Back Cover

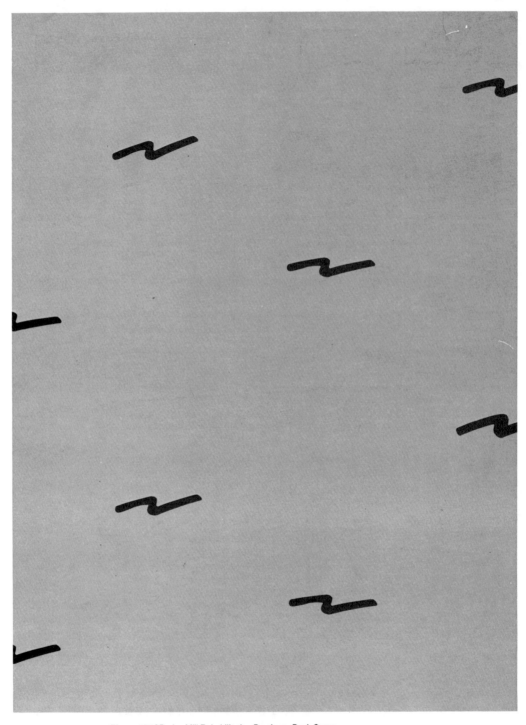

Figure 12.2f Barley Mill Rehabilitation Brochure, Back Cover

The headline on the cover positions the practice as innovative which the copy inside further explains. Then the subheads tell the entire story *without* every word having to be read. The quotes give the piece a personal, non-institutionalized touch, and the back panel adds to the already strong credibility.

The brochure is an 11 × 25" paper, folded twice to an 8½ × 11" finished size. The colors are grey, black, orange, and red on white paper, a very modern combo. The layout and typography are simultaneously both professional and contemporary. That's the image the piece creates.

It's true sales literature the way it ought to be.

☐ THE GREAT PRACTICE BROCHURE: BEING EMPATHETIC

The headline in Figure 12.3a looks to enlarge the market for psychotherapy as well as tease you into the copy. Notice how the graphics on the cover have a feminine feel. That's because most of the market is female.

The subheads then empathize with the reader's feelings. And once that's done, trust is established. The reader is then more ready to consider the answer recommended by the brochure. And in psychotherapy, trust is everything.

Even though the brochure is copy intensive, see how easy it looks to read, thanks to the subheads. Also study how the photos reflect the copy. Very slick and effective.

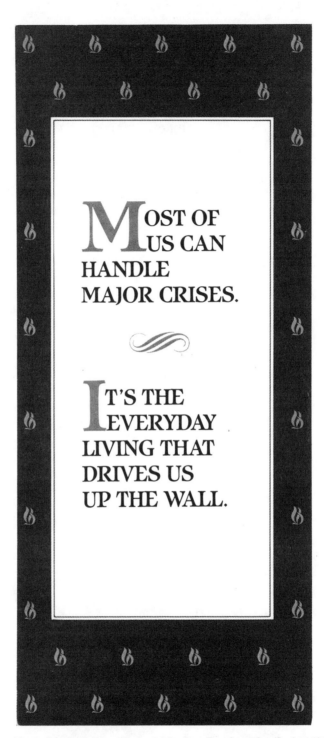

Figure 12.3a Family Counseling Service Brochure, Front Cover (Specifications: 9¼ × 15½", three folds, eight panels, three colors (maroon, gray, and black), 70-pound white coated [shiny] paper. Cost about 20¢ each to print in quantity of 5,000.)

YOU'RE HURTING.

Let's face it. Life is rough. Day-to-day living is the hardest work in the world. Your car needs new tires. Your kids are having problems in school. Your job is boring. You and your spouse aren't communicating. And day by day the pressure is building inside you. *That's* stress.

At **Family Counseling Service** we understand what you're going through. And we can help you deal with it.

YOU'RE MISUNDERSTOOD.

"If I could find just one person who understood!" How many times have you said that? Well, how about three people who understand? We're a small, caring group with a complete range of licensed, professional services to help you solve life, family and personal problems. You don't have to run all over town trying to find the right kind of help. We're nearby, and one phone call is all you have to make.

Figure 12.3b Family Counseling Service Brochure

YOU'RE
STRUGGLING. When your life
just isn't working, we understand. And
we can help, whether you come in alone or
with others. Our goal is to help you have
the life you want. Whatever you're struggling with, at Family Counseling Service
you can get the help you need to grow and
take charge of your life.

And, of course, all services are confidential.

Despite what you may be feeling, your
situation is not hopeless. We're here. And
we'll help.

YOU'RE
HESITANT. Like most people,
you're probably struggling to meet all
your current financial commitments. We
know that money is a problem for almost
everyone these days, so we make sure our
fees are more than reasonable. You and
your therapist will set a fair and affordable
fee *together*—no surprises. We participate in
CHAMPUS and other insurance programs,
and your insurance will usually cover the
cost of your visits.

When you need to talk, don't hesitate to
call: 571-0300. You'll find us warm,
friendly and *personal*—we even do our
own billing, so you'll never be dealing with
a computer.

YOU'RE
BUSY. You work long hours. Your
kids go to school. And there never
seems to be enough hours in the day to do
everything. We understand, so we're here
from 7 a.m. to 9 p.m. And we're on call
24 hours a day for emergencies.

YOU'RE
READY. Now that you know our
services are convenient, comprehensive, confidential and affordable, all you
have to do is call us at 571-0300 and we'll
see you *now*—no waiting six weeks for
an appointment.

Whatever you're struggling with, we'll help
you find ways of dealing with it immediately. We know you can't wait for long,
drawn-out solutions—in fact, you'll probably feel better after your very first visit!

YOU'RE
WELCOME. At Family
Counseling Service you'll find the
special understanding and help you need.

We're no strangers to the problems that
individuals, couples and families face, and
we've been helping them cope with those
problems for over ten years...single persons
battling loneliness...single parents carry-

Figure 12.3c Family Counseling Service Brochure

ing all the responsibility, with no time for themselves…couples caring for elderly parents…housewives too tired to stay awake past 9 p.m.…husbands hating their jobs, and teenagers getting into trouble.

These problems are *real.* And painful. And the stress they cause can make you physically ill. It's simply too high a price to pay.

So please let us help you today. We're ready to take your call right now: 571-0300.

It's the phone call that can make the difference between just "getting along" and "doing great"!

James H. Kleckner, Ed.D.
Clinical Psychologist, PL3499
Individual & Family Therapy

Robert B. Paxton, M.D.
Diplomate, American Board of Psychiatry and Neurology
Adult and Adolescent Psychiatry

Peggy Cossolias, R.N., Ph.D.
Marriage, Family & Child Counselor

FAMILY COUNSELING SERVICE
9420 Farnham, Suite 118
San Diego, CA 92123

571-0300

© PBAA 1986

Figure 12.3d Family Counseling Service Brochure

Figure 12.3e Family Counseling Service Brochure

☐ THE GREAT PRACTICE BROCHURE: SELLING FEELINGS

In Figure 12.4, the teaser on the cover brings you inside. There the copy talks about how the reader will feel: great, confident and comfortable. Each feeling is then supported by facts. So is the claim of saving time. No unsupported claims to diminish credibility here.

Notice how concerned and contemporary the practitioner appears in the copy. Isn't that what sells today in OB/GYN? Isn't that what sells in most professions?

Done in pink and aqua, this piece feels very Miami Nice.

☐ CAN YOU USE YOUR PRACTICE BROCHURE AS DIRECT MAIL?

Plain and simple—no. Multiple failures have proven conclusively that practice brochures as self-mailers to generate direct response just don't work. Yet, the idea persists as *common wisdom* throughout the professions.

This doesn't mean direct mail doesn't work in cold prospect mailings to the world at large. Or to warm prospects already on your database. It just means that a practice brochure *alone* as a direct mail package doesn't work.

These types of mailings do much better with a strong and lengthy, pull-out-all-the-stops letter. Sometimes the addition of a brochure helps response. Often it doesn't.

And because adding a full-blown practice brochure to a direct mail package is prohibitively expensive, a scaled-down, cheaper version is always used (four panel, 3⅔ × 8½" finished size, two- or three-color.) After all, you usually don't want a direct mail package to cost more than 50¢ apiece delivered. And that covers printing, labels, mailing house, and postage.

Instead, use your practice brochure as intended. Not as direct mail.

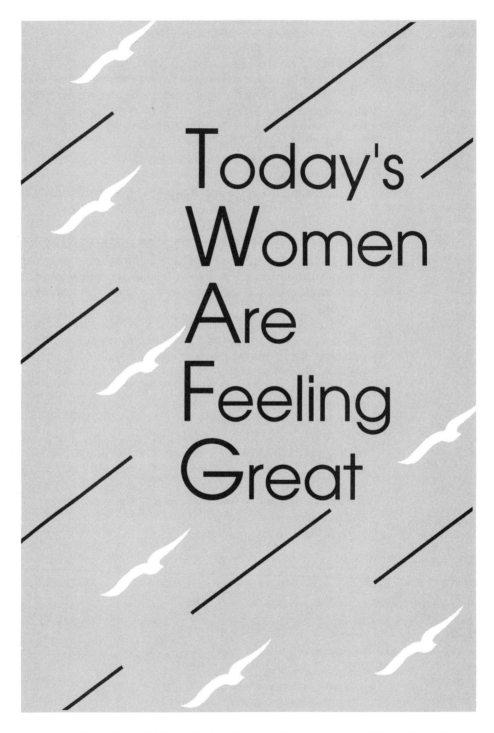

Figure 12.4a David A. Howard Brochure, Front Cover (Specifications: 8¾ × 17¼", two sides, two folds, six panels, three colors (pink, aqua, and black), 70-pound white coated [shiny] paper. Cost about 20¢ each to print in quantity of 5,000.)

You'll Feel Confident.

Discover contemporary women's health care that's **modern and complete**. Even our basic exam is more thorough than most others, because we believe **preventive medicine** is the best kind.

You'll feel so much more confident with the protection of some of the most modern women's health care available.

- **Pelvic Exams**
- **Pap Smears**
- **Chlamydia & Yeast Infection Treatment**
- **Breast cancer screening**
- **Complete lab work:**
  - **urinalysis • anemia testing**
  - **hemoglobin screening**
  - **occult blood test**
  - **venereal disease checks**
- **Patient education in preventive health (Breast self-examination)**
- **Hormone balance maintenance**
- **PMS treatment**
- **Birth control services**
- **AIDS screening**
- **Infertility & reproductive analysis, with endocrinology studies**

Your care is administered by a **qualified, licensed gynecologist** who's a member of the American and Florida Medical Associations. You'll have the most **up-to-date diagnostic and treatment equipment** available.

We're advanced, but we're conservative. If there's a way to avoid costly procedures, you'll be the first to know. And if surgery or advanced medical care is required, we're on-staff at these major Miami facilities:

- **Victoria Hospital** • **Mt. Sinai Medical Center**
  - **Miami Heart Institute**

Figure 12.4b David A. Howard Brochure, Left Panel of Inside Spread

You'll Feel Comfortable.

The most special thing about our care is that **we care.** We've taken your suggestions to heart, and put them in practice. So, when you visit our downtown offices, you'll feel comfortable in spacious surroundings, decorated with you in mind.

All materials and instruments used in our exams and procedures are always at a comfortable temperature, and everything is set up and ready before you arrive. Everything runs smoothly, and quickly. After your check-up, there's ample time to discuss your health with your personal physician. Say what's on your mind in a relaxed, intimate atmosphere.

Then, as you're leaving, we'll set your next appointment, one that's convenient for your schedule.

We've listened to your ideas, and brought them to our program. For your comfort.

You'll Save Time.

You'll find us in downtown Miami -centrally located off I-95. Minimize time away from your home or office, and protect your privacy. We've brought quality women's health care closer to where you are.

Your appointment will be convenient. And *on time.* You'll like our office hours... designed for the contemporary woman who's active and on the go.

Figure 12.4c David A. Howard Brochure, Middle Panel of Inside Spread

You can arrange **same day, morning, afternoon, evening and even lunch hour (1 - 2 pm) appointments.** And, of course, we're *on-call 24 hours a day* for emergencies. When you arrive for an appointment, we'll be ready.

You're busy, but **we make health care convenient** for you.

You'll Have A Personal Confidant.

We're experienced in handling all facets of contemporary women's health care and we're comfortable in discussing it with you. **No question is too intimate, no subject taboo.** Your health is too important to risk by avoiding sensitive issues. **Ask us anything, and get straight answers**. Naturally, all discussions and treatments are confidential - bound by the sacred patient-doctor relationship.

You can talk to us. Even about things you can't tell your closest friend.

It's A Great Feeling...

Knowing that women's health care, designed with your interests in mind, is so close. So convenient. And so considerate. **Call us at 371-7528** to set up a preferred appointment.

371-7528
David A. Howard, MD

Member, American Medical Association
Florida Medical Association
Dade County Medical Association

Ingraham Building 25 SE Second Avenue, #321
(1 block North of the new Centrust Building) Miami

© 1987 PBAA

Figure 12.4d David A. Howard Brochure, Right Panel of Inside Spread

About Our Contemporary Women's Health Care.

And so will you. Because we've taken the way you feel about gynecology seriously...bringing women's health care up to date. To meet your expectations. Your concerns. Your feelings.

You'll discover a new era in modern health care. With modern convenience and modern attitudes. And as a result, you'll feel just great.

Figure 12.4e David A. Howard Brochure, Left Panel of Outside Spread (the next thing seen when the front cover is turned)

Figure 12.4f David A. Howard Brochure, "Back Cover" When Brochure Is Folded

Figures 12.5 and 12.6 show the winners of THE PRACTICE BUILDER'S Practice Brochure Contest.

Proud to serve Orange County

Drs. Kushner and Brown have each been in dedicated practice since 1979. Having known each other since dental school, they've decided to combine their talents and experience into one comprehensive dental practice. Dupont Dental Group is the result of this partnership.

When they decided to open their Southern California practice, they settled on the vibrant Irvine/Newport Beach area. They knew that this was a fast-growing community of hard-working and highly-motivated people who cared about their appearance and their health. But they realized that because of their busy schedules, some people couldn't get the regular dental care they needed to maintain healthy teeth and gums.

That's why Drs. Kushner and Brown decided to do the unconventional. They have opened a practice that provides a complete range of services, the highest quality care, and **flexible hours that meet the needs of the community**. In short, they're providing progressive dental care for a progressive community.

Gerald Kushner, D.D.S.
Charles Brown, D.D.S.
Academy of General Dentistry; American Society of Cosmetic Dentistry; American Dental Association; California Dental Association; Orange County Dental Society; Orange County Implant Society; Irvine Medical-Dental Society; International College of Craniomandibular Orthopedics

Beautiful Smiles...

Figure 12.5a Dupont Dental Group Brochure, "Cover" (Specifications: 14 × 17" unfolded; 3½ × 9¼" folded, three colors (salmon, teal blue and black) on white coated [shiny] stock.)

. . .by Dr. Gerald Kushner and Dr. Charles Brown.

"Our most important job is to give you complete quality care. That's why we've taken hundreds of hours of continuing education and utilize the most state-of-the-art dental equipment available. We want you to benefit from every innovation in dentistry."

Dr. Gerald Kushner

Dr. Charles Brown

G Dupont
Dental
roup

**Advanced Comfort Conscious
Dentistry**

Figure 12.5b Dupont Dental Group Brochure

"Everything you're looking for in advanced, comfort-conscious dentistry is right here in our office. If you want a smile that will last a lifetime, read on."

Call on us when you need to see a dentist now

If you have a dental emergency, we're here for you 24 hours a day. A toothache, chipped or broken teeth can be treated quickly and effectively with the latest, most modern dental techniques and equipment. We're skilled in everything from fillings to oral surgery and extractions. And you can count on us to always treat you with a soft touch and plenty of TLC.

Call on us again when you need skilled care

- All care with a soft touch
- Bonding, veneers & cosmetic dentistry
- Crowns, bridges, caps
- Full & partial dentures
- Periodontics, help for bleeding gums
- Cleaning, polishing
- Full mouth reconstruction
- Dental implants
- Jaw & headache (TMJ) treatments

Figure 12.5c Dupont Dental Group Brochure

Effective help for TMJ

The symptoms of TMJ can be as simple as headache pain or as unrelated as shoulder pain. . .and it can sometimes be tormenting. TMJ can even masquerade as many other problems. Here are some chronic symptoms that could mean you suffer from TMJ:

- Headaches at temples
- Chronic earaches
- Clicking or popping of the jaw
- Stiff neck
- Pain around and behind eyes
- Ear and sinus congestion
- Limited opening of mouth
- Upper back and shoulder pain
- Facial pain
- Dizziness

Help is here:

We use a number of advanced techniques and diagnostic equipment to treat this oftentimes painful condition. With our years of continuing studies in TMJ treatment and diagnosis, and these advanced, computerized systems, we are able to reduce pain and effectively treat the condition. If you or someone close to you is suffering from this disorder, call us, we're ready to help.

Figure 12.5d Dupont Dental Group Brochure

A beautiful

The advanced new science of dentistry

In addition to taking the guesswork out of TMJ diagnosis, we also use this advanced equipment to treat and monitor the progress of many other dental problems, like hard-to-fit dentures. Gone are the days of ill-fitting, uncomfortable dentures. With our specialized equipment, we can obtain a more detailed analysis of your mouth to give you the best fit possible.

You may have endured discolored, chipped or unevenly spaced teeth since childhood. But now, with the latest technology and techniques, you can have a dazzling smile easier than ever. There are numerous options for improving your smile. And each one looks so natural that only you (and your dentist) will know for sure.

Cosmetic bonding and veneers are used to correct color and shape. Crowns and caps are a natural for beautifying damaged teeth. We use all the latest technology and can meet your special needs with beautiful choices. Why not let us make your smile sensational.

Comfort, convenience, and more

You're busy and your time is valuable. That's why we won't keep you waiting. And we'll schedule your appointment when it's convenient for you — that means evening, early morning and weekend appointments.

General dentistry: regular maintenance

Figure 12.5e Dupont Dental Group Brochure

mile is your best investment

High tech means a higher degree of care

You'll also be glad to know that our office uses state-of-the-art heat sterilization techniques, like those you'd find in a hospital. In fact, our office meets federal government guidelines for safety and cleanliness.

Dental Vision is another way we're making dentistry easier through technology. Using a small pointer, we're able to show you exactly what's going on in your mouth, and you see the results on a computer screen situated right next to your chair.

Emergency services: we're here to help

Emergencies don't wait for a convenient time to happen, and neither should you. That's why we're available 24 hours a day, seven days a week.

Don't let gum disease take *your* teeth

It's today's leading cause of tooth loss.

Dental implants are a permanent solution to missing teeth

Dental implants offer a permanent and life-like solution to dentures - they actually replace lost teeth, as well as add support to existing crowns and bridges. We'll coordinate your case, and work in conjunction with a skilled oral surgeon. You'll be free of dentures forever. Although implants aren't for everyone, we'd be happy to discuss them with you.

You have a choice of payment options

You are covered with most major insurance plans, or use one of our flexible payment plans. Visa, MasterCard and American Express are also accepted.

Treat yourself to something special

Of course, you don't choose your dental care from a list. So we'd be happy to talk to you about your own dental needs. Just call and make an appoint-

You'll love our comfort-conscious dentistry. From thorough, regular cleanings to sealants and fluoride treatments, we'll help you and your family keep healthy teeth and prevent future problems.

Figure 12.5f Dupont Dental Group Brochure

If you think you have any of the symptoms of gum disease, we're skilled in all the new ways to keep it under control.

ment. Dr. Gerald Kushner and Dr. Charles Brown are ready to give you the smile you've always wanted.

Call now for an immediate appointment: (714) 833-8020

Gupont
Dental
Group

Advanced Comfort Conscious
Dentistry

Gerald Kushner, D.D.S., P.C.
Charles Brown, D.D.S., P.C.
2646 Dupont, Suite C-200
Irvine, CA 92715

Figure 12.5g Dupont Dental Group Brochure,

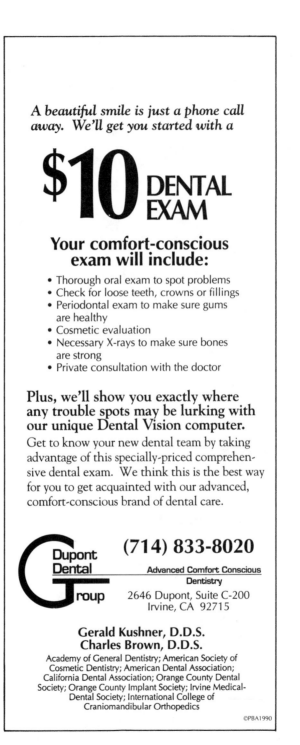

Figure 12.5 Dupont Dental Group Brochure

Figure 12.6a South First Street Veterinary Clinic Brochure, "Cover" (Specifications: 16 × 9¼" folded, three colors (rusty burgundy, soft mustard and black) on white coated [shiny] stock.)

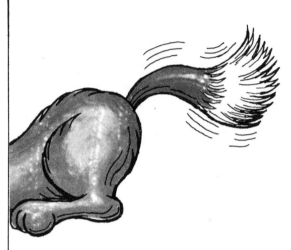

Pet care to go

Have a busy day ahead? Leave your pet with us on your way to work or shop. Our drop-off service is at no extra fee. And we're open at 7:30 every weekday morning. Just stop by on your way home and we'll ha your pet ready and waiting. Our pleasure.

If you'd rather come in with your pet, we'll reserve a time for you. Everyone appreciates our long hours — we're open till 7:30 on Tuesdays, a on Saturdays from 9:00 till noon. And all day o weekdays, of course.

Pet Paks · everything you nee for a healthy p

This is the best idea yet — pet packages! For one low price, you can get everything your pet will need for everyda health. Now, that's convenience! There are pack ages for puppies, kittens, adult dogs and cats, geriatric pets, and more.

Our Puppy-Pak includes first vaccines and exam, a medical record book, training guides, si month checkup, and everything else we could th of to protect your puppy's health.

Our Kitten-Care includes first vaccines and exam, toenail trims and dental checkups, six month check, and many more services and prod ucts that will help your kitten grow up to be healthy and happy.

Call us for more information on these packag and for descriptions of our other packages!

We want to be your pet's second best friends

A visit to the veterinarian shouldn't be an agonizing experience for you or your pet. It should be comfortable, caring and warm. In a healthy environment that puts your pet at ease. And with good results that keep your pet hale and hearty and you happy.

That's why Drs. Michael and Ann Hays have been so successful. They've built the South First Street Veterinary Clinic from a small country clinic, into a home away from home for all the pets of Yakima. A place where small animals can get the help they need, from toenail clipping to immediate emergency care. And where you can rest at ease knowing your pet is being cared for by a full staff of competent, caring professionals.

Your pet will get vitamins after each visit, and we have toys and little gifts for your children while you wait. Every pet gets to take home vitamin samples, and every new pet gets a New Pet Care Kit.

From our friendly receptionist and helpful assistants, to Drs. Michael and Ann Hays themselves, we want to be the best friends your pets have ever had. Next to yourself, of course.

Whatever the need. . .w

Pet Paks	Ge
No-charge drop off	Ac
Advanced diagnostic equipment	Me Fre
Vaccinations	S
Dentistry	Su
Spaying and neutering	En

Figure 12.6b South First Street Veterinary Clinic Brochure, Inside

Deliver your pet into ou capable hand

When your pet gets care at South First Street Veterinary Clinic, he's getting a complete package of attention. From our complimentary early bird drop-off service to our annual vaccination reminders, we're right there with you to care for your pet.

Whether yours is a young or an old pet, a dog or a cat, a bird or even a hamster, we're ready. Our care is convenient, friendly, affordable, and efficient. And it's administered by veterinarians who have dedicated their careers to learning and practicing the most effective treatments in the most attentive fashion.

When you call, we're ready. Please l over the information we're providing fo you here. Then call for gentle and prof sional veterinary care for your pet.

HANDLE WITH CARE

Figure 12.6c   South First Street Veterinary Clinic Brochure, Outside

SPECIAL!
Puppy-Paks, Kitten-Care, and Mature Pet-Paks

Our Special Care Pet-Paks are designed to take care of your pet's needs from infancy to old age. Bring your puppy or kitten in today for our comprehensive first visit package and we'll start him or her out on the right road to a long and healthy life! And, bring your older pet in for our preventive mature pet care and we'll help to increase the quality and longevity of his or her life.

In their Mature Pet-Paks, both dogs and cats receive...

- ❑ internal parasite check
- ❑ thorough exam
- ❑ toenail trim
- ❑ health care report with specific recommendations
- ❑ 6 month dental checkup
- ❑ dog or cat health care guide

Mature Dog-Pak $44.25

Dogs will also receive...
- ❑ distemper & parvo booster
- ❑ corona or bordetella booster

Separately, a $62.00 value.

Mature Cat-Kit $44.25

Cats will also receive...
- ❑ distemper & upper respiratory complex vaccine booster
- ❑ feline leukemia virus vaccine
- ❑ "Favor" cat kit

Separately, a $62.00 value.

Figure 12.6d South First Street Veterinary Clinic Brochure, Loose Insert (Front)

In their Special Care Pet-Paks, both puppies and kittens receive...

- ❑ internal parasite check
- ❑ thorough exam
- ❑ toenail trim
- ❑ new pet kit
- ❑ health care report with specific recommendations
- ❑ medical record book
- ❑ dental checkup at 6 months

Puppy-Pak $44.25

Puppies will also receive...

- ❑ 1st distemper shot (DHLP)*
- ❑ 1st parvo shot*
- ❑ 1st corona or bordetella vaccine*
- ❑ training tips
- ❑ nutritional recommendations
- ❑ rawhide chew to aid in training
- ❑ puppy training guide

Separately, a $62.00 value.

Kitten-Care $62.50

Kittens will also receive...

- ❑ 1st distemper & upper respiratory complex vaccine*
- ❑ 1st feline leukemia vaccine*
- ❑ feline leukemia blood test
- ❑ pet carrier
- ❑ cat health care guide

Separately, a $84.00 value.

* This is the first in a series of vaccines; boosters are not included.

**Call today
for an appointment!**

South First Street
Veterinary Clinic

401 South First Street, Yakima

248-0084

Figure 12.6e South First Street Veterinary Clinic Brochure, Loose Insert (Back)

PROMOTIONS IN MOTION

1. A New York City ophthalmology group faced the same problem all urban practices face—how to promote efficiently given the incredible costs of city media. Their answer was 1,500 hand-distributed flyers within a two-block radius.

The flyer described the practice and offered a free glaucoma screening for one day only. On that one day they saw a 1% response or 15 people and so far have converted two into patients for a 3:1 return on investment. More are certain to convert over time. Suggestion: Repeat quarterly and reach bigger numbers, like 10,000 to 20,000 for a bigger response.

Chapter 13 □

EVERY BIT COUNTS: TURNING YOUR BUSINESS CARDS, LOGO, AND STATIONERY INTO PROMOTION

□ CONVERTING YOUR BUSINESS CARDS INTO PROMOTION

What's the function of your business card? Most would say it's an easy way to give someone your name, address, and phone number. Others, who rarely give them out, can't come up with a good reason—just that they're suppose to have them. And still others use them as patient recruiters.

The first two groups treat them as an expense and leave tons of money sitting on the table. They simply haven't used their business cards as an additional way to convince someone to come to them. However, cards haven't traditionally been potent recruiters because name, address, and phone number fall far short of motivating people.

So to turn your cards from an expense into an income generator, treat it *like an ad*. Use sharp graphics and tell people what you do and why they should come to you.

■ **What You Do.** Few people know what an otorhinolaryngologist does. (Even fewer know how to spell it.) Most don't know that chiropractors treat headaches. And chances are that many aren't familiar with all the major problems you take care of.

So put the biggies on your business card. Then people will know if you're the right type of professional to service them. Without this list you're leaving it up to serendipity.

■ **Short "Why You" Copy.** Now you've got to differentiate yourself from the competition. But limit your promotional copy so it succinctly states why people should come to you in a couple of lines or phrases. No more.

Writing short, potent copy where every word counts is not easy. In fact, in copywriting there's an old adage, "If I had the time, I'd write it shorter." Good advice: Take the time.

Sample one- or two-liners:

■ High in Technology ... Gentle in Care.

■ Back & Neck Pain Relief—Without Surgery.

■ 94% Success Rate.

■ Hospital. Home. Alternative Birth Centers. Deliveries planned to your wishes.

■ Emphasizing short term therapy for individuals and families.

■ Beautiful Dentistry.

Can't fit all this plus graphics on one side of a business card? No problem. Design a foldover card. This gives you three sides to put copy and graphics on. The fourth side provides a place to write in their next three to five appointments. A multiple appointment schedule makes for increased compliance. This also avoids having to print a separate appointment card.

■ **Combine Copy with Graphics.** Here's where most professionals tend to put their efforts. But be careful to use three guidelines to ensure your success:

1. Graphics should get the card noticed and read.
2. They should convey the proper image. And that does not mean a boring one!
3. Graphics should expand on the copy points or provide a secondary benefit to the reader. Marketing-based logos, photos, drawings, or a simple, clean layout with some graphic enhancements can achieve this.

Strive for a *slightly* understated elegance to convey quality. If it's too elegant, you'll look too expensive.

Use a clean, easy-to-read, non-retail typeface. And print in classy color combos: light grey paper with dark blue and maroon inks; white stock with gold and dark green or blue inks; ivory stock with ice blue and creamy burgundy; white stock with black and red; even white stock with purple and teal green. Please, no boring brown ink on boring brown paper to make people believe you're still practicing in the earth tone '70s. Today's colors are sky tones and bright.

Paper should be a shiny, coated stock (especially if there's a photo) *or* have a linen or laid texture. Also acceptable but not a show-stopper: a flat vellum finish. Money saver: When your printer suggests a name-brand paper, ask if he's got a comparable and less expensive brand. They almost always do.

■ **Passing Them Out.** Some professionals only go so far as to create the perfect card, but seldom pass them out. But how?

Simple. Ask everyone you meet for their card. They'll ask you for one in return. For those who obviously don't have a card, just say, "Allow me to give you my card." *The wider the distribution, the bigger the return.*

Do your staff people need their own cards? Yes. But only if you want your them to recruit new patients or clients for you. Then you'll need individual cards, a killer practice brochure, and a Frequent Recruiter Program.

☐ **BUSINESS CARD CONTEST GRAND PRIZE WINNER**

The card in Figure 13.1 carries lots of benefits on its cover. First is comfort. The logo creatively conveys the message in a tiny space. Then the tagline reinforces the claim. And the name indicates an office worthy of respect. Very slick.

On the second panel of this foldover design we discover a list, but not just some lifeless laundry list of what he treats. Look at the way they're expressed to heighten the reader's hormone level.

The third panel provides proof that you can trust this practitioner. Remember: People can't appreciate quality of credential, *only quantity.* So the panel's loaded.

And the fourth contains a list of multiple appointments. For greater compliance, it's better to make a series of appointments at one time and gain their commitment to the package than making them one at a time.

This cleverly designed card contains all sorts of savvy strategies and deserves the designation as the Business Card Contest Grand Prize Winner.

another patient.
the appointment time for
so that we can reschedule
at least 24 hours in advance
appointment, please notify us
If you are unable to keep this

_____
o'clock am/pm
at _____

_____
o'clock am/pm
at _____

_____
o'clock am/pm
at _____

_____
o'clock am/pm
at _____

Dr.Neuman on:
appointment with
I have reserved an

the Foot Care

I N S T I T U T E   O F
NORTHRIDGE
Helping People Walk In Comfort

(818) 885-8400

Using the latest in-office diagnostic & treatment techniques:

- Lasers to vaporize calluses, warts, ingrown & fungus nails, lesions, adhesions and scarring
- Effective treatment for bunions, hammertoes, heel & arch pain
- Custom orthotics to relieve foot problems without surgery

Dr. Thomas Neuman, DPM, FAAFS

Medical Consultant to Dept of Social Services and Social Security Administration
Diplomate, National Board of Podiatry Examiners
Fellow, Academy of Ambulatory Foot Surgery
Member, Academy of Podiatric Sports Medicine
Member, American Podiatric Medical Association
Member, California Podiatric Medical Association
Member, Los Angeles County Podiatric Medical Association
Member, California Podiatry Council

9017 Reseda Boulevard Northridge, CA 91234

(818) 885-8400

Figure 13.1

☐ BUSINESS CARD CONTEST RUNNER-UP WINNER NO. 1

The one thing we want people to remember about this office if they could only remember one thing is that it's cozy. Look at Figure 13.2. Warm and fuzzy. So that's what goes on the cover. The logo states it. And the tagline reinforces it, while it assures the reader of modern services as well.

The second panel inside informs the reader of what the professional does and adds secondary benefits. The third carries name, address, and phone number which is all that most business cards display. And the fourth is a place for the next scheduled appointment. When you add this panel, more promotional business cards get out ... and more are seen. Very smart.

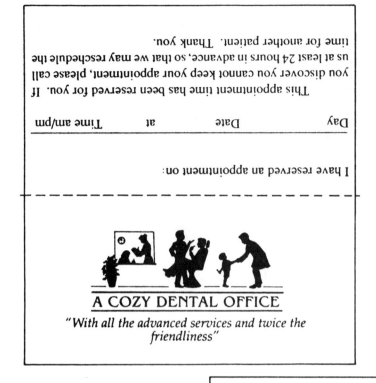

time for another patient. Thank you.
us at least 24 hours in advance, so that we may reschedule the
you discover you cannot keep your appointment, please call
This appointment time has been reserved for you. If

Day   Date   at   Time am/pm

I have reserved an appointment on:

A COZY DENTAL OFFICE
"With all the advanced services and twice the friendliness"

All phases of General Dentistry:
- ☐ Cleaning and periodontics
- ☐ Crowns, bridges, implants
- ☐ Porcelain bonding
- ☐ Evening and Sunday hours
- ☐ We'll file your insurance

Mitchel S. Rosner, D.D.S.

41 A West Merrick Road, Ste 8, Valley Stream
(516) 568-2888

Figure 13.2

☐ BUSINESS CARD CONTEST RUNNER-UP WINNER NO. 2

The terrific card in Figure 13.3 has all the right elements for strong promotion. First, the name repositions this chiropractic office into a back and neck pain specialty practice to gain more of the medically oriented market. The logo then reinforces the effectiveness of the treatment. And the tagline promises modern care.

The inside of the foldover card covers what he treats and how he does it. Plus there's a long list of credentials to answer the question of trust and confidence. The card also answers many of the basic questions a prospect has with a slick, professional image, and that's why it works.

This two-color card on 24-pound Cambric white paper looks great, feels great, and works great.

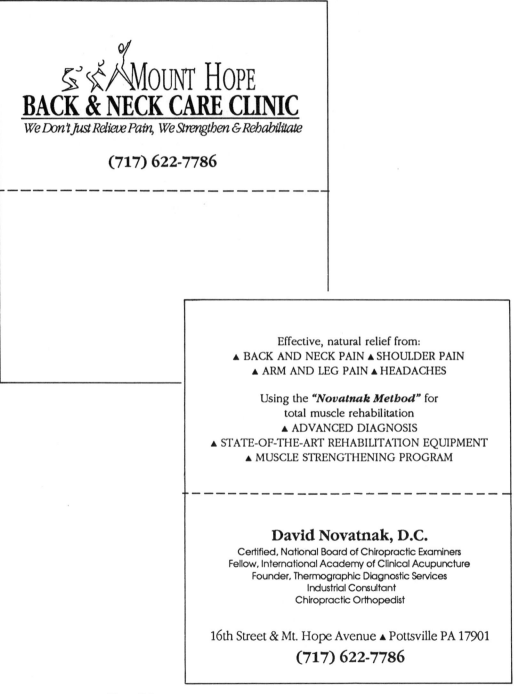

Figure 13.3

☐ BUSINESS CARD ANALYSIS: ALL THE RIGHT INGREDIENTS

In Figure 13.4 the logo on the cover first positions the practice as serving the entire family. Then the grid behind the practice name gives it a high-tech, modern image. The tagline reinforces the family theme while adding another big benefit of pain relief. All this on the cover alone.

On the inside, his photo is compelling because of its size and his smile. Good shot to establish trust. And you know specifically what he treats, so people can say, "He's for me." Notice the quote to help people self-diagnose themselves into the practice. And the back is cleverly designed as the appointment card to assure card circulation.

The card stock has a nice textured feel which says quality. The typefaces are also quite professional to reinforce quality. And the ink colors of forest green and rust are very today. Great card!

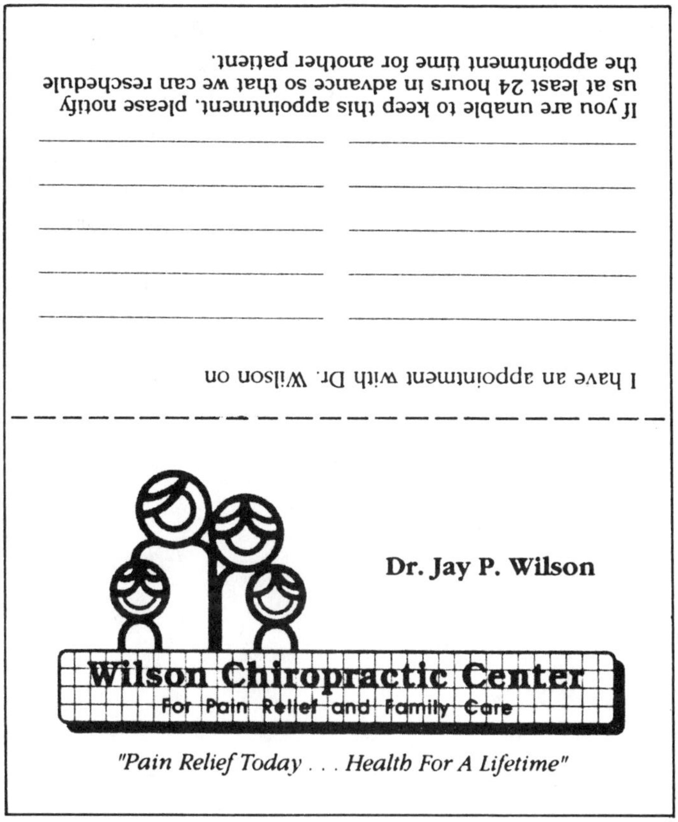

If you are unable to keep this appointment, please notify us at least 24 hours in advance so that we can reschedule the appointment time for another patient.

_____   _____

_____   _____

_____   _____

_____   _____

_____   _____

I have an appointment with Dr. Wilson on

Dr. Jay P. Wilson

Wilson Chiropractic Center
For Pain Relief and Family Care

"Pain Relief Today . . . Health For A Lifetime"

Figure 13.4

☐ BUSINESS CARD ANALYSIS: UNUSUAL LAYOUT HELPS

The six-paneled card with red, blue, and black inks on white stock (Figure 13.5) looks and feels different. Because it's different from the expected, it gets more notice. And the offers for referring and being referred obviously help response.

But think about two changes. First, when you have a difficult name to pronounce, share your nickname with the readers so it isn't a major stumbling block for them. They may remember you then. Second, improve the typography. There's too much capitalization which creates the feeling of too much screaming. Use a graphic artist next time to avoid the retail impression printers often create through ignorance.

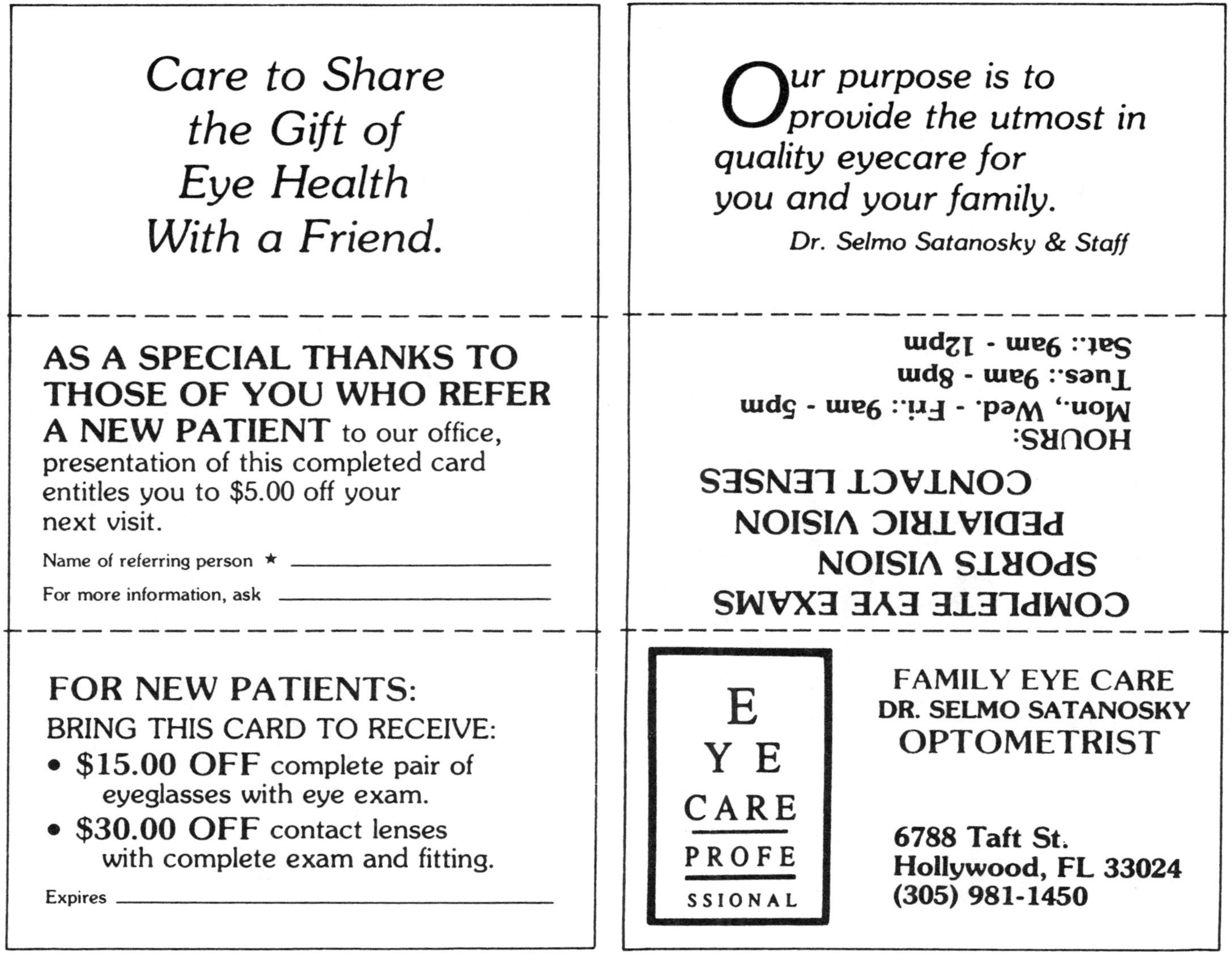

Top panel

Our purpose is to provide the utmost in quality eyecare for you and your family.

Dr. Selmo Satanosky & Staff

HOURS:
Mon., Wed. - Fri.: 9am - 5pm
Tues.: 9am - 8pm
Sat.: 9am - 12pm

COMPLETE EYE EXAMS
SPORTS VISION
PEDIATRIC VISION
CONTACT LENSES

FAMILY EYE CARE
DR. SELMO SATANOSKY
OPTOMETRIST

6788 Taft St.
Hollywood, FL 33024
(305) 981-1450

E
Y E
CARE
PROFE
SSIONAL

Bottom panel

*Care to Share
the Gift of
Eye Health
With a Friend.*

AS A SPECIAL THANKS TO THOSE OF YOU WHO REFER A NEW PATIENT to our office, presentation of this completed card entitles you to $5.00 off your next visit.

Name of referring person ★ _____

For more information, ask _____

FOR NEW PATIENTS:
BRING THIS CARD TO RECEIVE:
• $15.00 OFF complete pair of eyeglasses with eye exam.
• $30.00 OFF contact lenses with complete exam and fitting.

Expires _____

Figure 13.5

☐ WHY YOU DON'T NEED A LOGO—AND WHEN YOU DO

After six years on the job, C.J. had just left a large practice to start his own practice. He took a few patients with him, but not enough to make the practice self-sufficient. Marketing was the answer, but what was the first step?

A trusted colleague advised C.J. to invest in a logo for his business cards and letterhead. After all, image was important and a logo would create one.

C.J. spent $850 with a recommended graphic artist. She gave him three thumbnail sketches from which to choose, but he liked none of them. So she drew three more—for an additional $350. One was acceptable and finalized into camera-ready artwork.

But in the back of his mind, C.J. was wondering if all the meetings, two months of time and a sizable chunk of his teensy-weensy budget were worth it. C.J. was right to wonder, but he should have wondered *before* he paid any money—because the answer was NO.

■ **When Logos Produce Business.** Logos produce actual dollars in the bank only when you give them extensive exposure. Why? Because they work by generating recognition for the practice through recognition of the logo. And to break through the clutter of 5,000 commercial messages each day shoved into the average person's mind takes mega-repetition. But if you expose your logo enough, it then improves the response to your promotions in visual media.

Key: If you plan to promote *consistently or over the long term in a repetitive, visual medium,* a practice logo makes sense. That means newspapers, magazines, direct mail, co-op coupons, or TV. *Yellow Pages* alone doesn't justify a logo because *Yellow Pages* is a one-time exposure for the user.

■ **If You Don't Need A Logo.** With no great plans for repetitive, visual media exposure, you don't need a logo. Still, set the practice or your name in a typestyle that "says" what you want to communicate about your practice. Different type styles create different feelings. For instance:

- ■ Traditional, trust-producing: Use Goudy, Times Roman, Baskerville, Caslon.
- ■ High fashion: It's Avant Garde.
- ■ No frills or business-oriented: Helvetica.
- ■ High tech: Futura (regular and italicized).
- ■ Friendly or caring: Bookman.
- ■ Children-oriented: Cooper Black.

So if you're like C.J. with no exposure plans in the media, set your name in an appropriate typestyle and blow the logo money on a good meal. (Bring lots of friends.) But if you have external media plans for the long term, a logo not only makes sense, it's an investment you'll need to make immediately.

■ **Two Varieties of Logos.** The first variety is simply a design element. The logo looks pretty and, at best, simply catches attention. It communicates nothing.

These *Design-Based Logos* can be expensive when done by an accomplished graphic designer, or inexpensive when done by an art student. The point being that you don't need to spend your inheritance if all you're looking for is something "nice."

But design-based logos require tons of megabuck exposures to be remembered in today's information pollution. (Even most of the Fortune 500 can't achieve that!) So it's better to have your logo work right away—with just a single exposure—by communicating one important point about your practice. This point is the *one thing you want people to remember most about your practice if they can only remember one thing.*

If the logo can "talk" this way, you don't need to take out a bank loan just to get it recognized. This talking variety simply works faster and, therefore, results cost less.

■ **Marketing-Based Logos.** The talking variety is called a marketing-based logo. As in any market planning, the first steps are:

1. To figure out whom exactly you want as patients or clients.
2. Are they present in sufficient numbers in your locale.
3. If so, what do they want to hear most (the one thing you want people to remember most about your practice if they can only remember one thing).
4. If that's already being said by a competitor.
5. And if so, is it being said convincingly? (If not, you can still say it.)

If done correctly, your marketing based logo will communicate the most convincing message to the most desirable prospects in the most convincing way.

And it will do it *instantaneously*. In one quick glance. If it doesn't, it fails. Send it back to the drawing board.

■ **Logo Tips**

1. Place the logo in all promotion, including the *Yellow Pages*, outdoor office sign, even on name tags for the staff.

2. Good logos incorporate the practice name into the design or have the name printed close to it in a complementary typestyle. This helps build recognition of the name.

3. Logos must communicate instantaneously when reduced quite small, such as on business cards or in small-spaced ads.

4. Logos must work in black and white, such as in newspaper and the *Yellow Pages*. You can use colors to help create a feeling, but the logo cannot be dependent on color. Numerous colors also drive up the price of printing stationary and direct mail.

5. Logo development costs vary between $350 and $1,500 depending upon the experience of the designer. Marketing-based logos cost in the upper half of the range because of the additional marketing analysis and planning. Since you only want a marketing-based logo, don't compare the price to a design-based one. They're apples and oranges.

If you're going to have graphic artists design your logo—*beware.* They know nothing about marketing, so you'll need to do the analysis and planning yourself. Then you'll give them very specific directions as to what the logo should communicate. If you have an ad agency design it, they may or may not need this same direction. Ask them first about their process. It'll tell you whether or not they know what they're doing.

☐ **LOGO ANALYSIS: MODERN GRAPHICS**

Figure 13.6

The logo in Figure 13.6 has three very strong components. First is the name which promises the benefit of a cure, but without violating any state laws. Second, it immediately tells you what this practice is all about.

And third is the graphic that has such a modern flavor it makes the practice tasty to new prospects. The progressively thickening lines behind the foot set against the drop shadow are both modern graphic techniques. If it *looks* modern, and it *feels* modern, the practice must *be* modern. That's what people think.

This is another good marketing-based logo.

☐ LOGO ANALYSIS: POSITIONING AS A SPECIALIST

Figure 13.7

Look how the logo in Figure 13.7 communicates an awful lot in one glance. This chiropractic practice has been repositioned with a new name to emphasize its special expertise and appeal to more medically oriented prospects. The typeface is classic and adds a solid feeling to the artwork.

Also notice the tagline. It not only communicates specialization but also modernity. Its typeface is modern to reinforce that idea.

The stylized "B" says "caring." And the logo works both in small and large spaces. Plus, it's not dependent on color. This is a well thought-out logo.

☐ COORDINATING AND STRATEGIZING FOR LOGO, STATIONERY, ENVELOPE, AND BUSINESS CARD

Everyone knows to put their logo on their business card and stationery, but not everyone knows to coordinate the selling messages. That's what this system does so well.

The planning started with the *positioning* question of what's the one thing we want the public to remember about this professional if they could only remember one thing? The answer was that he produces *beautiful skin*. Then, what was his *market*? The answer: middle-upper and upper income.

Consequently, the logo was designed to say beauty and look high-line. The logo's two-tone light blue and grey-blue colors also enhance the elegant, upper-end feeling. Then a tagline was added to reinforce the idea: *The art and science of healthy skin*. And the logo was designed to work as a unit with the professional's name and field. Very nice.

But the logo alone is insufficient to convey all the things this professional does. Therefore it can't do a complete selling job. And the consequence is oftentimes a patient or client won't know all their professional does and go elsewhere for services he could provide.

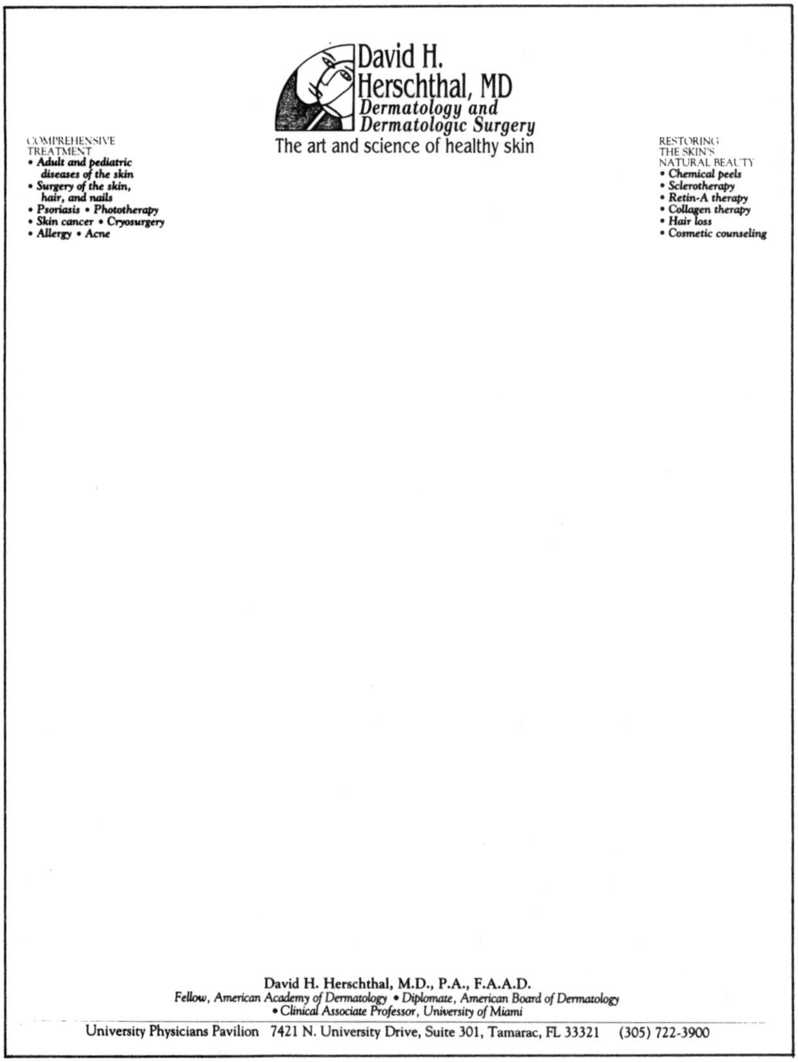

Figure 13.8 Letterhead

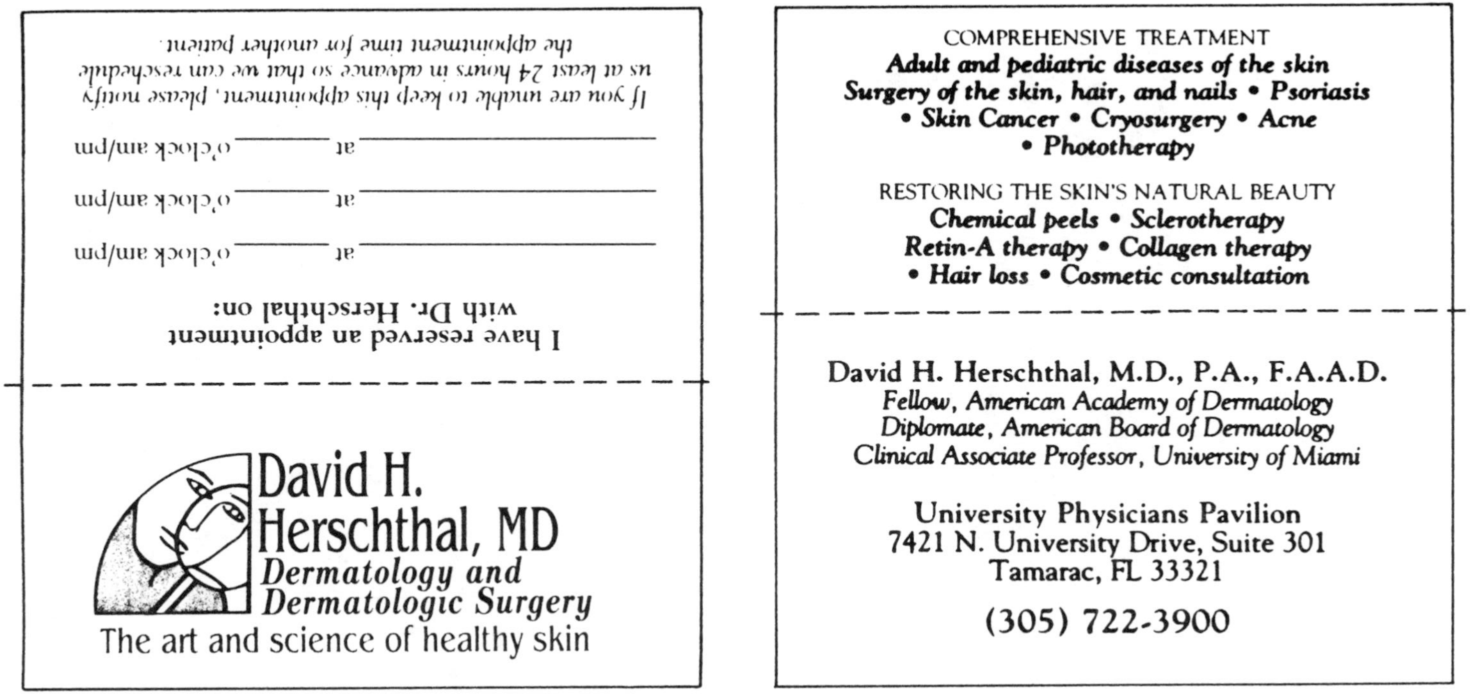

COMPREHENSIVE TREATMENT
Adult and pediatric diseases of the skin
Surgery of the skin, hair, and nails • Psoriasis
• Skin Cancer • Cryosurgery • Acne
• Phototherapy

RESTORING THE SKIN'S NATURAL BEAUTY
Chemical peels • Sclerotherapy
Retin-A therapy • Collagen therapy
• Hair loss • Cosmetic consultation

David H. Herschthal, M.D., P.A., F.A.A.D.
Fellow, American Academy of Dermatology
Diplomate, American Board of Dermatology
Clinical Associate Professor, University of Miami

University Physicians Pavilion
7421 N. University Drive, Suite 301
Tamarac, FL 33321

(305) 722-3900

David H.
Herschthal, MD
Dermatology and
Dermatologic Surgery
The art and science of healthy skin

I have reserved an appointment
with Dr. Herschthal on:

_____ at _____ o'clock am/pm

_____ at _____ o'clock am/pm

_____ at _____ o'clock am/pm

If you are unable to keep this appointment, please notify
us at least 24 hours in advance so that we can reschedule
the appointment time for another patient.

Figure 13.9 Business Card (front and back)

So the designers also placed a service listing on the stationery. (See Figure 13.8.) Since people don't often know if they need certain types of procedures, they also listed symptoms or problems.

Then on top of that, the designers added mega-credentials, including his patient-impressive teaching appointment. These answer the question of why you should choose him rather than someone else. Now you've got a *complete* sales presentation—and you've turned your stationery from a supply expense into a promotion.

The business card is designed with the same strategy, with one enhancement. (See Figure 13.9.) On the fourth side of the foldover, the designers placed the appointment card. This assures a ton of cards will get distributed—and read.

And the system is carried over onto the envelope (Figure 13.10). Same logo, same colors, same elegant typeface.

David H. Herschthal, M.D., P.A., F.A.A.D.
7421 N. University Drive, Suite 301, Tamarac FL 33321

Figure 13.10 Envelope

So when you create your new system or have it created, make sure all your pieces answer the *positioning, target market, what-you-do,* and *why-choose-you* questions.

☐ EXPENSIVE PAPER IS NOT WORTH IT

Expensive stationery does nothing for the marketing of a practice except make the professional feel proud and poor at the same time. Test after test show that investing in expensive paper does nothing to enhance the message you put on it, nor the response you hope to get.

It's particularly bad if you've ever watched your front desk make a typing mistake, take out the paper and crumple a dollar-a-sheet stationery in front of your eyes. Then do it again.

This is not to say you shouldn't have classy stationery. Just get an inexpensive paper with some discernable finish on it, like a laid finish. Inexpensive, off-brand names in paper is fine.

As for direct mail, use 60-pound offset paper for the letter and a 24-pound white wove envelope. You don't need anything more expensive. No matter what your spouse or graphic designer says.

Chapter 14 □

MAKING A MAJOR IMPACT WITH PR AND PUBLICITY

□ GETTING CHARITIES TO PROMOTE YOU FOR FREE WHILE LOOKING LIKE A HERO

The program's called "Donation Dollars" and is already used by big companies everywhere. Here's how it works.

Say the local Boy Scouts are going door-to-door selling $1 raffle tickets to raise money for playground equipment. The grand prize is a bike. With this program they can now add more value and make the sale easier: "Each ticket is $1.00, but with every one you buy, you also get [a free cholesterol check/consultation/$15 off an exam/etc.] from a well-respected ___."

The charity can be any organization like the Campfire Girls, high school band, Optimist Club, and they can sell anything. It doesn't matter. And charities love the program.

But what do you get? A live, five-second commercial from a highly regarded group—with an implied endorsement—in hundreds of homes and businesses. Plus, you get your Donation Dollars distributed free to all who buy. As a result, you not only generate foot traffic, but seemingly contribute thousands to charity. And for you these are cheaper "service dollars," not out-of-pocket dollars.

When you prepare your Donation Dollar Certificates, print the following on the front to encourage more charities to participate: "[Your name or your practice name] supports a wide variety of community projects. S/he may be able to help you with your next fund-raising drive. Contact [professional's name] for further details."

Keep the front generic so it can be used for all charities. On the back, just change the charity's name and the expiration date. Then you can just call your printer to print some up and the charity's chairman can pick them up directly. Your time cost: almost nil.

DESIGN AND INSERT COUPON

Certificate Copy-Front:

Reversed-Out Head: **Donation Dollars for You and Our Community**
Large Subhead: A free cholesterol check and consultation.
Body:

Since you were nice enough to support one of our local charities, you've earned a special free cholesterol check and consultation. Good for the entire family.
Redeemable only at Dr. Simon Benefit, 1721 Roosevelt Ave., Johnsonville. Call 576-8009 for your convenient appointment.

Photo: Close-up of internist
Caption:

Dr. Simon Benefit, M.D.
Diplomate American Board of Internal Medicine
and Cardiology
Member: Rotary Club, Stop Drugs Coalition, PTA
Supporter of Community Charities
Emphasis: Stress and cholesterol management
Dr. Simon Benefit supports a wide variety of community projects. He may be able to help you with your next fund-raising drive. Contact Dr. Benefit for further details.

Certificate Copy-Back:

Reversed-Out Head: **Donation Dollars for You and Our Community**
Large Subhead: Compliments of **Boy Scout Troop #61**
Small Subhead: A Free Cholesterol check and consultation
Large: EXPIRES *February 28, 1992*
Body:

Since you were nice enough to support one of our local charities, you've earned a special free cholesterol check and consultation. Good for the entire family.
Redeemable only at Dr. Simon Benefit, 1721 Roosevelt Ave., Johnsonville. Call 576-8009 for your convenient appointment.

■ **Getting Off the Ground.** Get a list of non-profit organizations, usually available from your local Chamber of Commerce. Then mail everyone a flyer describing your program. Headline the flyer:

> If You Have a Good Cause, Then (Your Name) Has $25,000 Worth of Local Help for (Town/City Name).
>
> And use this explanative copy:
>
> Raising funds for your neighborhood or community projects may have become increasingly difficult in recent months. If so, [your name] would like to help you ... and here's how.
>
> It's called "Donation Dollars" and they're good for [insert offer]. When your group is holding a raffle, dance, candy or bake sale, car wash, bazaar or other event, giving a Donation Dollars Certificate with every purchase seems to remarkably increase the dollars you'll raise.
>
> As our way of making a contribution to our community, we've set aside $25,000 worth of Donation Dollars Certificates for fund-raising projects this year. To find out if your group qualifies, just contact us.

Also promote the availability of your Donation Dollars Program in your reception area. Put a Take One stack of flyers out. And ask your printer to blow up your flyer to $11 \times 17"$ on a PMT, film positive, or velox. Now you've also got a terrific, image-building poster (and promotion) for your waiting room.

■ **Another Idea.** When someone approaches you for a charitable donation, offer to give thousands of your Donation Dollars instead. Contact the charity's person in charge to explain your program.

The bottom line is that everyone wins. The charities win. The people who buy win. And you get charities to promote you for free while looking like a hero.

Jeff Slutsky, *Street Smart Marketing*, John Wiley & Sons, New York, 1989, $14.95 and THE PRACTICE BUILDER.

☐ COMMUNITY INVOLVEMENT PAYS UP TO 28:1 ROI

Two Eastern optometrists know how to combine goodwill and good profits. In order to reactivate patients or clients who seemed to have fallen off the face of the earth, these two practitioners wrote them a letter with a simple proposition: Bring in any non-perishable food to feed the hungry through the local food bank and get an eye exam—which you need anyway—for only $1.

To their surprise, scads did. And when the numbers cleared on all the glasses, contacts, etc. they'd provided, their return-on-investment was a mighty 28 to 1! Obviously this was the best promotional effort they'd ever run. But now their challenge was how to push it.

They decided the next step was to take it to the community at large. They ran a low-cost ad in their local publication, but upped the exam to $10, only to see another gratifying response. One respondent even went out and bought $100 worth of canned food to donate. Everyone had positive comments and good feelings to share with the doctors. Even with those who didn't respond, name recognition of the practitioners soared.

The 26:1 return-on-investment wasn't too bad either. (See Figure 14.1.)

Figure 14.1

What next? Run it more, a lot more until the response dies. By tracking results when people first call for an appointment, you know exactly when the ad's dipping below an acceptable ROI. At that point, pull it. And replace it with a *new ad* promoting the same thing!

A new creative approach to an "old" idea can substantially increase the response rate. The concept will usually continue to work unless something radically changes in the market, like the competition copying it and flooding the market.

■ **Another Approach.** Optometrist M.T. had a new piece of equipment to check the eyes of infants as young as six months. And to get parents to come in, he also tied into the local food bank, but this time with a heart-rendering twist. "Bring in a can or two of baby formula to help feed the hungry babies of our community and get an eye exam for your baby for free." *Wow!* Talk about tugging heartstrings!

M.T. will make money when the parents bring their babies back in a year for their now regular eye exam. So he gets the kids as perhaps lifelong patients—and he then gets many of the parents, too.

Plus everyone who's seen the local ad now knows about this guy. Consequently, his *Yellow Pages* response rate has gone up. Oftentimes, when people don't respond immediately, it still shows up later on the tracking sheet as *Yellow Pages*.

Good vibes. Great profits.

☐ CHARITABLE PUBLICITY THE SMART WAY

E.R. was approached to sponsor a charity's golf tournament. For $750 he'd get his name on a plaque with 19 others. He countered with a better idea.

E.R. said that this was such a special charity that he'd put up $10,000 if anyone got a hole in one on the ninth hole. The golfer would win $5,000 and so would the charity.

Well the charity got excited at the prospect and E.R. got interviewed by every paper, radio and TV station in town. He couldn't buy that exposure anywhere for $750.

But what if someone did get a hole in one? Just in case, E.R. bought Lloyds of London insurance for a premium of $450—$300 less than the no-publicity sponsorship. And then three years later when someone did win the prize, E.R. got even more publicity!

Jeff Slutsky, *Street Smart Marketing*, John Wiley & Sons, New York, 1989, $14.95 and THE PRACTICE BUILDER.

☐ WHY HIRING A PR FIRM IS A BAD MOVE

The two-man Connecticut practice learned this the hard way. With only $1,000 a month in the promotional budget, they dumped it all into public relations. After six months, their carefully selected PR firm had this to show: two articles in small weekly newspapers, none in the business press, and one interview on a virtually unrated radio station.

There was nothing in the list that they couldn't have done themselves, not only cheaper, but faster. In fact, they probably could have developed better PR opportunities without their hired mavens of the press. The reason? Professionals have more credibility with reporters than PR agents.

■ **The PR Mistake.** Essentially, there are two types of public relations firms—the good and the cheap. The good has contacts within the press in which you want entry. So when you hire them, evaluate them for their contacts. Can they pick up a phone and get through—that's the key.

Then there's the cheap. They know how to write a press release and leave a phone message. But theirs is one of the 100 messages a day that a newspaper editor trashes unreturned. They also know how to get you in the unread and unlistened to media, so at least they have something to show you. Besides, they'll always hide behind the untrackability of their efforts, so all they need to show is something, no matter what.

But as one reporter recently said, "Most PR agents have no more idea of how to get into (the media) than the average goat knows how to pilot the Concorde."

So professionals don't really have good choices—or luck—when it comes to PR firms. They can't afford the big guys with prime contacts. (Even if they hire a name firm, they get delegated to the summer intern who has no contacts and can't spell their profession.) And those they can afford, they're better off doing it themselves, because reporters respond more to professionals than to a hired lip.

■ **But PR's Important.** Nothing can match the credibility of being in the major papers or on TV, etc. Even though placement is inconsistent and, therefore, you can't rely on PR alone, it adds increased response to your more consistent efforts, whether seminars, advertising, direct mail or so forth. So it makes sense as a last layer in a layered approach.

What also makes sense is to hire a PR firm or freelancer to create a press kit for use with the media. You may also ask them to recommend media to approach. Then get rid of them.

■ **The Key.** Study the publications, programs or stations yourself. Understand the kind of stories they cover. Look at what they've done over the past year. Then fit yourself into *their* scheme of things. If you take this approach, you'll be in the media 20 times more often than if you send out the same press release to every editor around.

Work the media yourself. There are no great tricks. Think of a good story, write a short letter outlining it and follow up with a call. If you've picked the right story, you're in. If not, you're still out.

If this sounds too hard, skip it. You can't rely on PR alone for your external promotion anyway. Even though most professionals prefer PR to anything else, it's too iffy to bet the whole bottom line on.

THE PRACTICE BUILDER and *INC. Magazine,* p. 137, April, 1988.

☐ PATIENT/CLIENT APPRECIATION DAYS BRING 10:1 ROIS

Chiropractor L.H. knows a good thing when he sees it. And he knows it because he's seen the numbers. As a "Born Again Promotional Tracker," L.H. tracks and analyzes his every effort by return-on-investment (ROI). The numbers tell him his last Community Appreciation Day six months ago brought in $14.37 for every $1 spent on promotion. So he's going to do his second one this year.

■ **The Promotional Equation.** A Patient or Client Appreciation Day is a high profile, special event to generate a horde of new people into the practice and to reactivate a slew of old ones. The basic concept calls for setting aside a day when you do exams or consultations for free for past patients or clients and their family and friends. Anyone they can bring in.

A takeoff on the concept is The Community Appreciation Day where the offer is open to everyone in the community.

Let's look at the twist mentioned earlier to capture the public's imagination. In order to receive the free service, you must bring in a can of food to be donated to the hungry. Not only does this *increase participation,* but it makes the professional look like a million dollars.

And the *big plus* is that local newspapers and radio stations love it and will give you *free pre-publicity and event coverage.* One newspaper recently gave L.H. a free insertion of his freestanding, 8½" × 11" flyer to encourage participation.

■ **How to Spread the Word.** First, the event needs to be talked up in-house. That means by the professional with each patient or client. The front desk also needs to repeat the message and hand out a flyer as people leave.

Then, the event requires its own mailing to the patient or client base. Oftentimes a postcard is enough, but it must explain and encourage, not simply announce.

And crucial to super-success is telemarketing. Temporary hires call from their homes between five and nine p.m. to encourage patients or clients to come, donate food and to recruit others, too. The callers ask to book an appointment.

If it's a Community Appreciation Day, you'll need community media. That means an outside banner, if permitted. L.H.'s read, "Bring a Can of Food for the Hungry and Receive a Free Exam & X-rays. Call 668-9100."

It also means local newspaper, radio and TV. Call first to see if they'll do free insertions of your ads or freestanding inserts as a community service. Pay for it if they won't.

■ **Results.** L.H. shares his numbers, "I've run three of these now and each one has returned over 10 to 1. All three combined average $12.80 income to every $1 of expense. I keep thinking that they've got to start declining as I hold more of them, but that's not the case. The repetition seems to enhance the next effort."

■ **Some Additional Helpful Hints**

- **The atmosphere is FUN for family and friends.** Yes, it's going to be a busy day for the professional and staff, but the patient/client should leave with a warm and happy feeling about your practice, the event and your contribution to the community.

- **Encourage appointments.** Like a RSVP for a party, appointments let you plan your time and resources. They also form a commitment from the individual to attend.

- **You may need some help.** You may want to recruit one or more fellow (non-competitive) professionals to assist in consultations and/or exams with a big turnout. You can either pay for their time or return the favor on the day of their event.

- **Convert screenings to regular appointments.** When your free consultation or exam finds warrant, be prepared to schedule a regular appointment for follow-up. Book these on the day of the event for a date within the next week.

- **Handle overflow.** If you find yourself with many more non-pre-appointed attendees than you anticipated (or can accommodate) on the date of the event, simply offer to honor the free exam or screening during the upcoming week and offer to schedule an appointment time for them so they won't be inconvenienced by having to wait around indefinitely. This strategy also neatly fills any holes you may have in your upcoming appointment schedule.

☐ LEVERAGING MUCH APPRECIATED APPRECIATION DAYS

Podiatrist G.K. ran his first *Patient Appreciation Day* about two years ago. He promoted his free foot exam day to patients and their families and friends by mail, handouts in the office and telemarketing. Return-on-investment was 17.6 to 1. Cowabonga!

So he repeated it six months later. Same results. Holy cow!

Then he got to thinking. He knew he couldn't do one too often because he'd then condition his base to wait for a free exam day and he'd lose income. So he thought he'd target different external segments, each for their own appreciation day.

So his next one was for everyone—*Community Appreciation Day.* That drew nicely due to a combination of newspaper advertising and a banner draped on his building's fascia.

Then G.K. ran a *Women Appreciation Day.* Then a *Hard Workers Appreciation Day* targeted to people who work on their feet all day, like mailmen, factory workers, hair stylists and alike.

Then *Seniors Appreciation Day.* And *Office Workers Appreciation Day.* Also *Weekend Athletes Appreciation Day, Diabetics Appreciation Day* and *Arthritics Appreciation Day.* Holy cow pie!

This gave him a lineup of about an appreciation day a month. But why not? They all produced, thanks to newspaper, banner and some direct mail promotion, coupled with internal marketing to generate referrals.

G.K. leveraged a proven idea into a larger share of the real pie.

☐ SPREADING YOUR "FAME"

People who believe you're famous are more likely to refer to you than those who don't. That's why, for instance, you see products advertised in newspaper ads as "Seen on TV." It's a bandwagon effect.

So when you get in the papers or on radio or TV, it's important to leverage the exposure. And it's simple.

Create a buckslip (8½" × 3⅔") showing the publication's cover and article or photo of you on the air with an explanatory caption. Mail this with all outgoing mail for 60 days. All bills owed you. All checks to vendors. All correspondence, including your Internal Prospecting direct mail to your base. All mail!

Then give a copy of the publication's cover and the article to your framer to mat and frame nicely for your waiting room. If you appeared on radio or TV, frame a photo of you on the air with an explanatory caption.

Now everyone will know that the press or electronic media thinks you're an expert. And they'll refer more.

☐ SURE-FIRE PUBLICITY

Physician S.D. knows how to get publicity. A few years ago when the FDA approved Minoxidil for hair growth, the big city press covered the story, but small local papers rarely reported on this national news. So to get in the papers, S.D. wrote a press release about how this breakthrough would affect local balding men.

He wrote of the benefits of Minoxidil, except when he would normally have written "patient," he substituted "the men of Parkerville." The whole article took on a very local flavor.

Then to give it even more of a local angle, he had a staff member go downtown to do a survey. Out of 500 men, she counted those with a balding problem. Then S.D. was able to compare the incidence of balding in Parkerville to that of the nation as a whole.

The local daily loved it. And the upshot for him was that he got over 60 calls from interested men and women—even though he was a general practitioner, not a dermatologist. This gateway into his practice helped expand his base. He was then able to provide these people with other medical services.

■ Press Release Guidelines. Take any interesting development in your field. The professional literature abounds with them. Ideas are also found aplenty at professional meetings.

Draft a press release that answers the who-what-why-where-when questions in the first paragraph. No hype please. Write it like a newspaper story. Just the facts, Ma'am.

Then talk of how this development or problem will affect the people or businesses in your market. It's crucial to insert the name of your town, city or area *every few lines*. Explain things in detail—without using jargon. Limit the release to two pages.

Put a headline on the release. And absolutely, positively make sure your area's name is *in the headline!* The key here is that local papers want local news. And what we're doing is taking national news and localizing it.

If there's an angle to the story which is particular to your area, also write about it. Think hard on this one. H.P. did and related how the affect on local industry might affect the welfare of the town. S.D. also did and came up with his local survey which showed an incidence of balding greater than the national average.

Or take an *old problem* you're seeing more of in your practice. Try to quantify the increase. Then write a release how this particular problem is on the rise in your area. Make sure you give symptoms to watch out for so people and businesses can diagnose themselves into the problem and the practice. Remember to keep mentioning your area's name every few lines in the release.

One last cardinal rule. Always send an *action photo* of yourself that relates to the story. Even if it's you behind a desk speaking and using your hands to gesture. Photos always grab more attention in print to get your story read. You can take them with your 35mm camera and have the right print blown up to a 5 × 7". If the quality isn't perfect, don't worry. They can reshoot you, but at least your photo gives them the right visual idea.

And when you appear in the papers, you'll be a star. But to be a well known star, you've got to repeat the procedure often. As in all marketing, repetition is the key. Especially in public relations.

■ Example:

NEW CURE STOPS McLEAN RESIDENTS FROM SNORING
"A new oral orthotic, similar to a mouthguard, is now available to McLean residents who have suffered for years from snoring," according to Dr. Arthur Strauss, a McLean dentist. The new device decreases snoring in over 95% of sufferers without the need for traumatic surgery.

"Until now, the only effective means of curing snoring was surgery by an Ear, Nose, and Throat specialist or sleeping in a different room. Neither one of these was a particularly desirable alternative," points out Dr. Strauss. But now a new device called a Snore Guard is available which provides McLean residents with a better choice.

Snoring is caused by improper breathing while sleeping. Often a person's jaw will interfere slightly with the wind passage due to gravity and muscle relaxation while sleeping on his or her back. The Snore Guard simply and safely positions the jaw forward to prevent the air passage from closing.

The Snore Guard was developed by Dr. Thomas Everett Meade, a leading sleep specialist, and Dr. Wolfgang Schmidt-Nowara of the University of New Mexico's Sleep Laboratory. Over the five years of development, the Snore Guard underwent clinical studies to refine it and prove its effectiveness.

Now it's available for the first time in McLean at the office of Dr. Arthur Strauss, who studied directly with Dr. Meade.

Interested people (both snorers and spouses of snorers) should contact Dr. Strauss at 356-0077 for more information.

☐ EASY WAY TO GET LOCAL PUBLICITY

When reading a professional or general publication, you'll see remarks made by colleagues with whom you agree or disagree. Send off a press release to your local papers, radio and TV stations refuting or supporting their remarks—*and tie them into local concerns.*

The media likes controversy so refuting is more powerful. Also, the more important the person you're refuting and the more controversial you appear, the more likely you are to receive coverage.

Since you're not likely to do business with everyone, it's okay to be somewhat controversial. Half the market may not like what you say, but the other half will think you walk on water.

■ **Getting Response.** Publicity won't do you much good unless people can get hold of you. But the press doesn't want to be your ad agency. So always offer to provide free information or a consultation regarding the information in the press release. *Just get your phone and address in there.* It's vital.

And remember: A cold lead is a dead lead. So answer inquiries ASAP.

Howard Shenson, "How to Get Quoted & Talked About by the Press," Howard Shenson, CMC, 20750 Ventura Blvd., Woodland Hills, CA 91364, $6, 1990.

PROMOTIONS IN MOTION

1. Hypnotherapist C.N. gets a great percentage of his practice from speaking engagements. And he gets a great number of speaking engagements. Here's his secret.

   He reads the local newspaper's column of upcoming association and club meetings. Then he evaluates the business-getting potential of each organization. If it fits his niche, C.N.'s on the phone with the program chair.

2. OB/GYN T.N. knows how to get name recognition. When he delivers a newborn, he arranges to have a large wooden stork placed on the new parents' front lawn for 30 days. Of course it has his name on it. The parents think it's absolutely terrific. And the neighborhood remembers who delivered the child.

3. Physician P.T. has held a flu-shot clinic each December for the last three years. Promoted as a community benefit through the local newspaper and on store posters, it finally topped the 500-patient mark this year. The county provides the vaccine for free, the newspaper the publicity and P.T. pays for the store posters and gives the shots. Over the three years, he figures about 100 have become regulars.

Chapter 15

THE HIGH-YIELD DYNAMICS OF DIRECT MAIL

□ ULTRA-PROFESSIONAL, MULTI-PAGE DIRECT MAIL FORMAT GIVES FOUR
BIG BENEFITS PLUS BIG RESULTS

Dentist F.K. has successfully sent direct mail to his surrounding community for years. His tracking mechanism confirms that 52% of his new patients comes directly from his direct response. That's impressive, but it becomes even more so when you discover that collections in his solo practice for last year were $807,000.

Last year his direct response arsenal included:

- 180,000 postcards to the general public, 15,000 each month
- 160,000 co-op coupons to the public, sent four times a year using two coupon companies
- 18,000 direct mail packages to new residents, averaging 1,500 pieces and 25 new patients per month
- 36,000 direct mail packages to existing patients (in addition to re-calls), sent quarterly to stimulate referrals
- 8,000 direct mail packages to reactivate past patients, twice yearly
- 90,000 postcards to his patients announcing his monthly late night radio topics (He buys inexpensive late night spots to create the aura

of a media maven, then drives home the point with patient mail to stimulate referrals)

■ 7,500 birthday cards (but no holiday cards which often go unnoticed in the Christmas clutter)

This man knows direct mail. But even so, this year he made some changes, mostly in format. In addition to his postcards, he selectively sent a more complete (and expensive) format.

■ **The More You Tell, the More You Sell.** His promotional postcards offered a $10 checkup which requires very little explanation. But in an effort to upscale, he decided to promote nonmonetary aspects of the practice, especially cosmetic dentistry and "invisible braces."

This was impossible to do on a postcard's limited space. A writer needs to show beauty in order to sell beauty. Hence, a multi-page letter and a highly visual brochure. Then when F.K. tested different direct mail packages, he discovered that when he put in an separate note in addition to the letter and brochure, his response rate went up even more. So he tested two notes ... and that helped.

■ **Direct Mail Advantage #1.** *Length is unlimited.* Therefore, you can explain benefits over and over, because as the copywriter's axiom puts it, "The more you tell, the more you sell." It's true.

■ **Direct Mail Advantage #2.** *You have more room to create the right image.* Image is most often created by graphics. Not only do you have more room to tell, you have more room to show. The result is a greater percentage response.

■ **Direct Mail Advantage #3.** *You can target exactly whom you want your mail to reach.* The most effective direct mail is written to a specific person with specific concerns and specific needs. Since this is impossible, the next best thing is to mail to a *class* of people with similarities and to reveal your solution to their particular needs. Targeting messages to specific groups is what direct mail offers which no other communication pathway does as well.

F.K. knew the entire population was not prime for his new promotion, so he decided to be more selective about the prospects he mailed to. He targeted females, 21-49, with household incomes over $25,000. The list was easy to get from a local mailing list broker he chose from the *Yellow Pages* under Mailing Lists.

First, he tested 5,000 randomly selected names from the list to give him reliable data about future success without gambling oodles of dollars at the start. Smart mailing. Then he mailed the remaining 20,000 after the test pulled a comfortable .08%, which translated into $29,000 in income on a cost bed of $4,000 (plus $3,000 in a one-time creative cost). This compared to a .02% response from his postcards.

■ **Direct Mail Advantage #4.** *Direct mail is affordable.* Although some will consider it expensive, if the average case size is at least $300 or $400 for a *commonly needed* profession, the numbers wash for stand-alone direct mail. They look even better if you know how to keep costs under control. But beware. Concentrate more on the response rate, rather than costs. *Responses to direct mail can be so dramatic that saving a few bucks that will decrease your response is beyond foolish.* It's megadumb.

■ **Results.** The addition of this new mailer to F.K.'s arsenal is geared to add over $100,000 in production per year. (Because of the lengthy treatments, full cash flow won't be realized until year two.) "Direct mail has built my practice. I use it to maximize referrals from my patients as well as introduce myself to new people ...

"If I could give my colleagues one bit of advice it would be don't quit. You never get a hit 100% of the time. If you hit .600, that's very profitable. But you can't hit .600 if you quit after one time at bat."

☐ DIRECT MAIL SUPER TARGETING

Audiologist E.P. had three offices and a total direct mail budget of $2,000 per month. Quite logically, he shifted the direct mail coverage from office to office monthly. But in reality, that wasn't quite logical.

Upon close scrutiny, E.P. discovered that different ZIP codes pulled differently as did different times of the year. So instead of spending one-twelfth of $24,000 each month, he redistributed the budget to spend more in the more productive ZIPs during the more productive times of year.

And without spending one dime more, he increased his direct mail ROI from 4:1 to 6:1.

☐ NEW RESIDENT DIRECT MAIL—IS IT FOR YOU?

When done correctly, new resident direct mail can capture up to 10% of new people in an area. And when done wrong—0%. So the initial question is *do you have the market* and *the type of practice* that makes this strategy work.

First, you need to be in a market where there's enough turnover in the existing population or an influx of new people. That would mean at least 50 to 100 new residents per month in a ZIP code. Your *main* drawing ZIP codes need to give you these numbers for the program to be viable.

To find out the average number of new residents *per month per ZIP code* in any market, ask New-Resi Data Marketing in Hillsdale, New Jersey (1-800-221-6293). Identify yourself as a PRACTICE BUILDER member and they'll do it for free. Then they'll try to rent you that list. Feel free to say no, but if you want it, their list is better and cheaper than anyone else's.

The second part to the answer is that this type of promotion is only for select professions. These are those professions for which people either have *a predictable yearly need;* they *use them frequently;* or they use them infrequently, but *so many people use the profession* that there are great numbers of prospects at any one moment; or that *the case size is so large* that a small response is profitable. Examples:

■ General dentists

■ Optometrists

■ Physicians—general and family practitioners; ophthalmologists for primary care; OB/GYNs; pediatricians

Other professions tend not to have enough need at any one time within the population to make this specific strategy work. Exceptions occur, but caution is advised.

☐ WHY MOST NEW RESIDENT SCHEMES FAIL:
HOW TO ATTRACT 8% OF ALL NEW RESIDENTS TO YOUR PRACTICE

Chiropractor A.G. rightly figured that in his growing community, there were all sorts of new people in need of all sorts of professionals. And if he targeted them just right, he would have them as patients for years and years. Confidently, he invested in both The Welcome Wagon and a new resident mailing program. Unfortunately, both were duds.

The Welcome Wagon promised to introduce new residents to A.G.'s practice, but the concept of "introducing" was fuzzy. Its promotional material states its reps do not blatantly "sell" the practice to the prospect, but isn't that what you want? Instead, you "sponsor" the welcome program. Essentially, they hand out something from you and may say a few words—or not—depending on how rushed they are and how much they know.

Also, The Welcome Wagon can't reach all new people. The average ZIP code turns over about 15% per year to produce 100 to 200 new resident households per month. And if it's a growing area, the number of new resident households can go to 500 a month—even 1,000 in hotbeds of expansion. One Welcome Wagon rep can't even come close to those numbers.

So it's not surprising that A.G. saw only a trickle of one to two a month from this source. But because of his high case size and the program's relatively low cost, the return-on-investment (ROI) was good. It's just that the total was bad.

■ **List Broker Hustles.** When A.G. went to a list broker to direct mail to new residents, the costs went up and the ROI went down. The reasons were two-fold. First, the list was compiled from new magazine orders. This method doesn't distill out only new residents and the printout is dirty with *existing* residents who order new magazines. (See following article.)

A.G.'s second mistake was that he used the letter provided by the list broker. *Big, big mistake!* Brokers know nothing about marketing and they know even less about what motivates prospects in your area for your type of practice. Their standard letters hardly even talk about the individual professional so they fail to establish trust and convincingly differentiate you. But they still give you the letter for free because without it, they can't sell their lists.

■ **But Direct Mail Is Still THE Answer.** Direct mail is the only way to effectively reach all new residents in an area. In fact, it's a must because this is really just a numbers game. If played right, you can attract about 8% of all new prospects in an area. But to accomplish that, you need to reach 100%. Yes, 92% will say no to you. But you can't get the eight without the 92! So you need large numbers and direct mail delivers them.

The mailing package is where most professionals trip up. They send a nonmotivating letter, written in sleep-inducing prose, usually devoid of meaningful benefits to differentiate them. Yaaaawwwwwnnn!

Now compare that approach to this letter:

Dear New Neighbor:

Unfortunately, among all the headaches of settling into a new home lurks a problem that's crucial to your well-being. Namely, how can you find a new family eye doctor you'll trust as much as you did your last doctor ... perhaps even more so.

This isn't easy considering it's yours and your family's eyesight at stake. And chances are you haven't been in the neighborhood long enough to judge the quality of the referrals made by your new neighbors and acquaintances. Do they have the same standards as you—or are they lower? Only trial and error can answer that, but perhaps you don't want to risk getting a bad referral in the process.

Also risky is pulling a name out of the *Yellow Pages*. Those big ads don't really tell you about the important things in choosing an eye doctor—his or her quality, concern for you, friendliness, affordability, how long it takes to get an appointment, how long you typically have to wait in the waiting room, credentials, experience and special expertise. These are critical items to know.

So you see how difficult it can be in carefully selecting a new doctor. But I hope I can make it a lot easier for you, since I'd like to present to you all the important information about myself for your consideration. Then you can make a smart and informed decision. And then perhaps you can feel as comfortable and trusting as you did with your last eye doctor ... perhaps even more so.

The True Meaning of Quality Eyecare

Quality is an overused word these days and has really lost its meaning. But let me see if I can be very specific in describing what goes into quality eyecare. First, the doctor must not rush. It's possible to miss things if a doctor doesn't take the time to do a thorough exam. And with economic pressures on doctors the way they are these days, the temptation is often there.

But I refuse to cut corners. In fact, when I perform an eye exam, I go to the other end of the spectrum. You'll discover I not only take the time to be exceptionally careful, but I ask a lot of questions most other doctors don't think about. Questions about how you use your eyes at work, hobbies and sports. Do you use a computer? How much do you read? Do you lie down or sit up when watching TV? Because without knowing these and many other details, you'll probably get the wrong contacts or the wrong eyewear with the wrong lenses.

Because I take the time, patients often remark that they feel like they've never really had a thorough eye exam before. That's a comforting feeling.

Second, quality eyecare means keeping up in a field that's changing faster than the nightly news. New contact lenses are coming on the market all the time. And not only that, they're made of new materials with revolutionary new designs.

If a doctor doesn't make a conscious effort to go to professional meetings and take courses frequently, that doctor will be out of date in no time at all. And quite frankly, the temptation is to do the minimum because these night and weekend courses cut into relaxation time.

But my staff and I are extraordinarily active in continuing education. The State Board of Optometry requires only 20 hours of education a year to renew a doctor's license, but I take over twice that much, almost 50 hours. And I require even my most junior staff to take at least three weekends a year of new coursework to keep current.

I don't know how we could stay on top of so many changes and provide you with the newest developments if we didn't study so much.

How a Doctor's Office Can Show Real Concern for You

Concern is also one of those terms used loosely today. But allow me to share with you how our office specifically shows our concern for our patients. First, you'll find we'll always recognize you when you come in. Ours is a small office so we remember all of our patients.

Next, you'll appreciate our *No Waiting Policy.* Personally, I don't like to show up at an office at the appointed time and wait. It's rude. So unlike most offices, we don't schedule patients so tightly that we get backed up all the time. In fact, if you wait more than 10 minutes to be taken care of, we have a nice gift for you as our way of apologizing, because it just shouldn't happen. I know how valuable your time is and we treat it with respect.

Also, when you call, *you'll get an appointment quickly.* Unlike the big commercial type offices, we're not so busy that I can't see you within a day or so ... or the same day for an emergency.

Along the same lines, I've set early morning hours starting at *7:30 am for Tuesdays and Thursdays* to make it convenient for you if you work. Also, you might like my late hours to *7:30 pm on Mondays* which makes it easy if you have kids and work. Plus, *I'm open Saturday mornings* because that's what you do when you're concerned.

What We'll Do for You

[These paragraphs describe what the professional treats and the kinds of eyewear he carries.]

Affordable, Too

Just a word about fees. Everything costs too much these days. So I've decided to hold the line on our exam fee and keep it below what many other eye doctors charge. In fact, I have not raised it in two-and-a-half years. You'll also discover we discount most contacts and frames below the manufacturers' list prices, again unlike many other offices.

You'll be pleasantly surprised that overall *you'll actually spend less* with us for the same exact eyewear than with the big commercial outlets, but you'll enjoy a small office's personal atmosphere and you'll benefit from the most thorough eye exam you'll ever have.

And if you have Medicare coverage, you'll be happy to know that we accept that, too. As with all insurance, we do all the paperwork so everything's easy for you.

We're located at 5697 Thomas Road and you'll see plenty of free parking in the back.

Isn't This What You've Been Looking for in Your Eye Doctor?

Allow me to summarize exactly what you'll find at our office.
1. The most through, unhurried eye exam you'll have ever received.
2. The most up-to-the-minute knowledge in eyecare today.
3. Easy to get appointments.
4. A complete selection of fashion, sports, business and budget eyewear. Plus a huge selection of contact lenses from our Great Wall of Contacts.
5. Very affordable prices with the total less than what the big commercial outlets charge.
6. Acceptance of all insurance and complete filing of all paperwork for you.
7. Office hours to suit your schedule, not ours.
8. Our NO Waiting Policy.
9. And above all, the highest quality and the greatest concern.

Now that you're moved in and the important problem of choosing an eye doctor is upon you, I hope that this information has made your job easier. I also hope that you'll allow me to care for you and any family members you have. I truly believe you'll feel as comfortable and trusting with me as you did with your last eye doctor ... perhaps even more so.

Sincerely,

P.S. As my way of welcoming you to our community, I've enclosed a money-saving "New Neighbor Welcome Certificate." It's good for one of my especially thorough eye exams for you and other adults for just $25 each (normally $42). And for your kids, for just $15 each. Please note the expiration date on the certificate, so take advantage of it soon.

■ **Power Prose.** What a letter! Study its construction. It starts out by identifying a problem which is a sure fire way to get a reader's attention. After discrediting other solutions, it provides a new solution—this letter—thereby ensuring the rest will be read. That's half the battle.

The letter then talks of those things important to most people— quality, concern and money—and provides specifics and proof to help differentiate you from every other competitor. After all, that's what they're interested in.

By providing specifics and injecting personal feelings into the letter, readers get a feel for the professional and conclude they *like and feel comfortable* with him.

Notice how the subheads are used to break up the long copy and make it readable. They also tell the entire story for skimmers.

Other tricks of the trade: short paragraphs, short sentences, no complex words, a summary of benefits at the end of the letter, a P.S. with a low risk way to try the practice, and a separate certificate to make sure the offer gets attention because it's the closer.

■ **Multiple Mailings.** Mailing this letter once is not enough to capture big numbers of new residents. The reason is that most people aren't in the market for professional services the minute or month they move in. It takes awhile and you need to be in front of their eyes when they are.

Therefore, it makes sense to mail it when they first move in because some will be ready. Then to mail again three months later. Also in six months. Nine months. And twelve months. That's four times over the first year. Use the same letter because they won't read it until they're in the market.

Mail third class, bulk rate, using a postage meter mark on the envelope, not a preprinted indicia which says "junk mail." The envelope should be 24-pound, inexpensive paper and the stationary should be 60 lb. offset. Nothing fancy, because direct mail tests show that expensive paper does not add to response.

Have the local quick printer print everything and deliver directly to the mailing house, which will store your excess printing until they use it.

Again, only order a new resident list gleaned from credit card changes of address. Not only are the intra-ZIP movers deleted leaving only truly new people in an area, but the people have been credit checked. So you know they have resources and their credit's good.

When you order your new resident list, get an original and three carbon copies for the repetitive mailings. (The cost goes down for carbons.) Mark on the top of each list when it should be mailed. Then at the appropriate time, give each to a local mailing house to do the whole job for you.

Don't be cheap and try to mail the list in-house!!! The mail won't get out, you won't make money and your staff will stick skewers into a voodoo doll of you. It's penny-wise, dollar-foolish and the skewers really hurt.

■ **Cost Savings.** With low case sizes, the mail can get expensive. So it makes sense to double up with a professional in another profession but in the same area to share the package and the cost. Optometrists and veterinarians, for instance. The results won't go down, but the ROI will double.

■ **Results.** Dentist R.L. is doing quite well, thank you. With killer copy, multiple mailings and the right list, he's capturing 8.2% of the new people in his area. With 12 new patients per month from the mailings and a $684 average case size during their first year with him, he's generating $8,208 additional production per month or $98,496 per year.

Costs run 19.8¢ each for postage, 15¢ each for printing and mailing house costs, and about 15¢ for each label—for a total of 50¢ per package delivered. With four mailings per household per year and 145 new move-ins per month, total yearly costs (once the program is up and fully running) totals $3,271 (145 move-ins per month × 12 months × 4 mailings per household × 47¢ per mailing = $3,271).

R.L.'s return-on-investment is $98,496 ÷ $3,271 = 28.30 to 1. That's over $28 in for every $1 spent and does not take into account referrals. "I used to send a letter to new residents which got me only two to three new patients a month. Obviously, being careful about the letter I now use and the quality of the list paid off because I increased the program's productivity by five times and made about $75,000 more than before."

☐ NOT ALL NEW RESIDENT LISTS ARE ALIKE

Texas dentist N.D. is a true believer, but he wasn't before. Professional lore told him to pursue new move-ins since they were more-than-likely prospects. But his whole mailing strategy was wrong: what he said in his letter; how he presented his information; and how often he sent it. But with his PRACTICE BUILDER Hotline Advisor, that was straightened out by following the strategies described above.

Unfortunately, the list he mailed to was also less than optimal. *And if you don't mail to the right people, it doesn't matter what you mail.*

N.D. got his list from a local list broker. One of the problems was the list was six to twelve months old already, so tons oᶠ competitors had beaten N.D. to those mailboxes. Secondly, the list didn't have apartment numbers, and without numbers, postal carriers often dump them in the bottom "throwaway" bin where guess what happens.

Other glitches that could have befallen N.D.'s list but didn't include: not having apartment dwellers at all if the list was compiled from changes in property registrations at the county recorder; and not having a complete list of those you want.

■ **Self-Compiled Lists.** Many professionals will go to their local utility companies to rent a list of new hookups. These are prime, accurate and avoid the no-apartments problem. Unfortunately, they're not always available.

Oftentimes, there's a local publication called a *commercial recorder*. Subscribed to by banks, attorneys and businesses, it lists law suits, births, deaths, new utility hookups and property ownership changes registered at the county seat. The problem here is that they miss the incredible turnover with renters. And the names are not labels. Therefore, you need to manually input them into your computer or type onto a 33-per-page photocopy grid so you can reproduce them onto self-adhesive labels and mail the number of times you need to.

■ **Computer-Compiled Lists.** There are now literally hundreds of choices of new residents lists. The reason is the power of computers. Monster computers grind mountains of info into little mag tapes in minutes. And it's all done by the big compilers in New York, LA and Chicago. So even when you rent a local list from a local broker, the list comes from one of the big boys. The local broker is just a salesman for them who'll order a list sorted by local ZIP codes. It's *not* locally generated.

This is why the concepts of exclusivity is a farce. A company or broker will promise that they won't rent the same list to a competitor of yours. But a broker down the street will because it often comes from the same compiler. So there's nothing proprietary or exclusive about the names.

All you should really worry about is how the list was compiled and how old the names are. Your list should never be more than three months old. And the most responsive lists according to THE PRACTICE BUILDER's tests are the ones compiled in the following way.

First, names are taken by one of the big, central clearinghouses from credit card changes of address. So the list won't include those people new to your area who can't qualify for a credit card, but they tend not to be the preferred patient anyway.

Then those who have moved within the same ZIP code are removed. The list is then matched against the Master Change of Address List from the US Postal Service. This verifies the addresses to make the list super clean and avoid 5-10% undeliverables.

Key Concept: Don't worry about the cost of the list. Just worry about how current, complete and accurate it is. If it fits these criteria, the increase in business will much more than pay for any higher fee. Make sure you order only this kind, either through your broker or The Practice Builder Agency.

■ **Results.** N.D. finally got the right list and mailed the right package six times during the next 18 months. That means he purchased an original copy of the list plus five "carbons" for later use. He did this each month for each list of new residents.

"I've been tracking very closely and I've found we're getting about 11% of the names on the lists to come into the office. Compare that to less than 1% when we started this newcomer program about three years ago ... This is the only external marketing we do."

☐ HOT DIRECT MAIL: TIPS, LEADS, AND IDEAS

1. Direct mail packages all looks alike these days. But notice how this letter starts—to get you to read the whole thing.

Looking for a doctor you can trust to relieve your back or neck pain?
—a specialist who's cured over 5,000 acute and chronic bad backs and necks,
—without surgery,
—without drugs that make you feel drowsy,
—and without hocus pocus?
Phone me at 786-6788. Let me examine you for free to discover exactly why you hurt. Then I'll tell you exactly how I can help relieve your pain.

Cordially,

Dr. P.W.

P.S. Just in case you're busier than usual, I've given you the letter's final, summarizing paragraph first. When you have the time, here's the rest.

Dear Neighbor, ...

2. Here's another lead guaranteed to wake up even the sleepiest of readers. Written for a CPA, the technique is adaptable to any service that has a prevention aspect.

Dear Neighbor:

[handwritten:] Wham!!

That's the sound of a taxpayer being hit between the eyes with income taxes.

This is the time of year when we dig deep into our pockets to pay taxes. Even as we pay them, we know we'll pay them again next year—and probably pay more. Wham!

But this year's blow can be cushioned, and next year's felt even less, if you put us to work for you.

3. People want to know you're talking specifically to them. That's why the more you can personalize your letter, the better. But because using computers to do this is still pricey, mention specifics in your preprinted letter that make you different from everyone else on the planet. For instance, smart professionals often mention the town or area the reader is in—three, even five times in the copy.

4. Here's a lead-in that's designed to get people to act now. Combine it with a limited time offer and lots of nonmonetary reasons to come to you and you'll see how successful you can be in motivating people to act—now.

Hurry!!!

It may be a slight shock to get mail beginning with "Hurry" from me. "Hurry" is not exactly my middle name. It usually hurts me to even think about rushing someone else. But this time it's a favor ... to you.

5. Here's an excellent lead for a cold prospecting letter to a targeted list:

Quite frankly, _____ is not for everyone. And not everyone who calls for an appointment is accepted as a patient.

However, I discovered your name on a select list of people in our community who I believe will benefit greatly from _____. So I've enclosed a special invitation for you to ...

6. Mailing to new residents or newlyweds is nothing new, but how about newborns?

I trust this is the first letter you've ever received.

The letter goes on to welcome the baby to the world and to the community. Plus it offers the baby a free exam by the writer, a general

MD, within the next 60 days as a congratulatory gift after its recent journey. P.S. Mom can come, too.

7. Another winning lead to get a middle- to upper-income reader to read.

Surely you must see the logic in my belief that sometime soon you and I must cross paths.
If you live in our community, you most likely have discriminating tastes. And I provide discriminating care.

8. Another compelling lead using questions.

Have you ever felt lonely—even with other people around? Or like your whole world seemed to be coming apart? Or asked yourself, "Is this all there is for me?"

9. Here's another effective way to lead with questions and then provide specific solutions to specific problems.

First, three brief questions, if I may:
1. Did your feet hurt you today—your toes, your heels, the balls of your feet or perhaps all over?
2. Has one of your toenails turned a funny color?
3. Do you have low back pain that you can't seem to lick?
Well, if you answered "yes" to any one of these, you're going to discover *good news* in the next two minutes.

10. Another lead that gets people to read.

If you wouldn't give 2¢ to see how masterful cosmetic surgery can make you look more beautiful and younger, would you give 29¢?
Because a postage stamp is all a unique, one-hour videotape about the promise of cosmetic surgery will cost. In it, you'll uncover exactly what cosmetic surgery can and cannot do, what it can do for you, and all about the procedures—all it the privacy of your own home.

11. And still another.

It is late at night. I'm tired and my burning eyes are telling me it's time to quit.
The last of my staff packed up and headed home around 8 p.m. The light over my desk is the only one still burning. But before going home, I wanted to write to you about what's been keeping me so busy lately.
It's a new, miniature hearing aide. In fact, it's startling. Let

me tell you in the next minute or so exactly why so many people have come in to buy one.

12. By putting a message *before* the salutation, you get a chance to highlight an idea or offer that the reader may not get to otherwise. The way to draw attention to it is the Johnson Box. Draw a heavy line around your message, enclose it with *****, or just type it with smaller margins than the letter.

```
******************************
*                            *
* Then you'll see            *
* how things can pop!        *
*                            *
******************************
```

☐ DIRECT MAIL TIPS

1. *Self-mailer vs. envelope—which to choose:* A tough call. The main purpose of any envelope is to get opened. If you don't get opened, you don't get response—so that argues for the self-mailer. But an envelope can carry a persuasive letter, which is almost always more effective than a self-mailer brochure. But the self-mailer at least gets a glance. But so what if it doesn't move the reader to action as well. Trade-offs. Trade-offs.

The answer is to test the two formats. But you need a large universe of at least 20,000 for a rollout to make testing profitable. Otherwise it pays to go with the envelope and lengthy letter.

Make the envelope look serious and formal. Use your office envelope layout. It needs to create the question, *"Could this office be writing to me about something important?"* Remember—if you don't get opened, you don't get response.

2. *Bulk rate vs. first class postage:* Use bulk for anything over 200 pieces (except when mailing to other professionals for referrals. Then use first class). Bulk's cheaper (19.8¢ vs. 29¢) and usually takes only a day or two in additional delivery time.

Only use a postage meter or a precancelled, bulk rate stamp for an envelope mailing. A preprinted indicia costs a hair less but destroys the impression the envelope needs to convey. But indicias are fine on self-mailers.

Get your bulk rate permit from the post office and then find a lettershop, also called a mailing house. For 2¢ to 3¢ apiece, they'll insert, affix labels, sort by ZIP to the required order, postage meter and mail, usually within one day. It's a bargain, so don't be cheap! Your staff will love you and the mail will get out. Besides, the Supreme Court just ruled that making your staff do the mailing constitutes cruel and unusual punishment.

3. *When to mail:* Start mailing for new business at the start of your busy season and continue to just before its end. Don't mail during low seasons. There's a reason people don't buy then and they won't respond to your mail. If you do, you'll feel rejected and poor.

4. *Don't invest in paper:* Tests keep showing that fancy paper doesn't buy you more response. People don't care about paper and you shouldn't either. Cheap 60-pound offset paper and 24-pound white wove envelopes are costly enough for most public mailings.

5. *Long letters sell:* It's a fallacy that people don't have time to read. What they don't have time for is *boring* letters. But doesn't it make sense that the more you tell about the benefits you offer people, the more people will be convinced? That's what the tests show.

6. *Sweat the details:* A direct mail effort has a hundred details—copy, typography, lists, offers, printing, timing, inserting, postage, sorting, how inquiries are handled and so on. If a crucial detail is mishandled and you lose your shirt, don't blame the staff or the gods. Blame yourself. Details are the nature of this beast and if you won't sweat the details, don't play with the beast.

☐ NEW TWIST TO TARGETED DIRECT MAIL SCORES 22:1 ROI

For his three locations, hearing specialist R.W. just mailed 5,000 pieces of direct mail and got 500 calls! That's quite a response rate, but actually meaningless because most purchased nothing. But what is impressive is the $22 in for every $1 out in expense.

What made so many people respond is the fact that the package explained that many people over 50 experience a hearing loss and to discover whether they had or not, a free hearing test had been set up just for them at a specific time and date. *The letter told them the time set aside for their free test.* It further instructed the reader to call to confirm the appointment. Five hundred did.

The package was targeted to seniors in an area close to R.W.'s locations. These were medium to large size cities. A presumptuous strategy like *preappointing* could well backfire in a small town setting where there aren't an abundance of new prospects all the time. But the strategy has done well in *larger* population areas.

■ **Results.** Of the 500 who called to confirm, 300 showed. Lots of people who couldn't come called to explain. Many asked for a different time. Of the 300 who showed, 50 purchased 80 hearing aides. Another nice thing about it, in addition to the 22:1 return-on-investment, was the speed. It all happened in 30 days.

Other professionals who have successfully used the preappointment tactic in direct mail to seniors: ophthalmologists, podiatrists and optometrists.

CUTTING PRINTING COSTS

Cardiologist L.T. publishes a successful patient newsletter called *The Hearty Life: Tips for Everyday Living.* Number of copies printed quarterly: 3,000. Printing cost quarterly: $1,783 for a first-class job.

But L.T. felt—rightly so—that the cost was excessive. However, he didn't want to sacrifice the quality of the printing. Instead of getting a new printer, he simply called and asked if his present small printer would work with him if L.T. bought the paper and had it delivered to the print shop. After protesting that this was not the way his industry worked, the printer agreed. The printing price without paper was negotiated and L.T. had his front desk shop local paper suppliers.

■ **Results.** The same print job with the same paper but without the printer's 20 to 30% markup now costs $1,406 every three months. Annual savings: $1,508. Total cost: One-half hour of L.T.'s time and an hour of staff time.

☐ WHAT TO DO IF YOU'RE CLOSED OUT OF CO-OP COUPON PACKS

Say you want to do a 10,000 or 20,000 mailing in Val-Pak or another coupon deck to generate some fast business, but a competitor has it reserved up. What to do?

Instead, use stand-alone, first-class postcards. The pluses are many. First, you can mail at any time you want. Second, you can mail to any area, not only the one the coupon pack specifies so you get better targeting.

Third, you can use a bigger size than their normal dollar bill layout to convince more. Fourth, you can mail as few as 500 (less doesn't make monetary sense). And most importantly, by mailing alone, you're sure to get noticed, rather than being buried in a mound of 20. So your response rate is always higher.

The downside is that stand-alone postcards cost more, presently 19¢ each. But if you're closed out of the choice packs, you'll do fine—assuming your average case size is over $200.

■ **Creative Strategy.** Use the same copy and graphic ideas you would on a co-op coupon. That's a symptomatic list for a specific problem or gateway into the practice, several reasons to choose you rather than a competitor for the specific solution to this specific problem, and a low-risk offer to try a bite-size piece of service.

■ **Cost-Cutter.** If you don't use glossy photos, then you can cut your cost by buying pre-postaged postcards from the Postal Service. That way you just pay for the postage and the postcard is free. This cuts your printing cost way down because paper is such a large component of the total price.

■ **Results.** Dentist P.N. mails 5,000 postcards per month at a cost of $1,150. The offer is a low cost exam. An average of 27 respond with a typical case size of $589. Total income per mailing averages $15,903. Return-on-investment is 13.83:1.

☐ TEST BEFORE YOU ROLL OUT A MAILING

Chiropractor M.T. was distraught. He had just mailed 30,000 flyers to his surrounding ZIPs but had ZIP to show for it. M.T. had the piece designed by a local agency which had assured him they knew what they were doing. So what went wrong?

No one knows. There are simply too many variables. How do you prevent this from happening to you? You taste the chili pepper to see how hot it is *before* you chomp the whole thing and set your eyeballs aflame.

M.T. should have mailed only 5,000 to start. This number is statistically large enough number to assure him 95% of the time that on the roll out his results will be within 30% of the test. (Make sure your mailing list of 5,000 is composed of a representative sample. Tell your list broker you want an "*n*th select.")

If M.T. had done this and tracked the results, he wouldn't have lost $11,842.

☐ DOUBLE CHECKING YOUR MAILING HOUSE

Mailing houses (also called lettershops) are a must for any sizable mailing. They're relatively inexpensive and usually get your mail out in one day.

But like all kinds of businesses, there are good ones and super duds. So how do you know if they got your mailing out at all—and got it out on time?

Simple. Ask for a Form 3602. This validated post office sheet of bureaucracy states how many pieces were mailed and on what day. Make it a policy for your lettershop: No 3602, no payment. This will keep them on their toes and assure your mail gets out on time, especially if it's got an expiration date.

☐ WHY YOU NEED YOUR OWN MAILING LIST: HOW TO BUILD IT

There are three main marketing assets of any practice: your staff, the drive- and walk-by traffic past the office, and your patients. The staff can make a mediocre practice great if they act like owners rather than workers. Hence the whole concept of staff incentive programs based on individual productivity and practice profitability.

Walk-by and drive-by traffic, if harvested, can produce five to 10 new patients or clients per month. (How many dollars would that represent?) Hence the concept of locating next to heavy traffic flow and using external signage that gives good reasons to come in, instead of merely announcing your existence.

And your patients or clients are a valuable asset because your goal of a word-of-mouth practice depends upon them. To foster referrals and to protect your base against the raids of marauding colleagues, you must mail to your people periodically. The forms it can take are numerous, but the fact remains: *You must mail.*

■ **Building Your List.** If you have a computer, it's simple. Push a button to generate labels for just the kind of patient or client you want, or for the whole enchilada. If you don't have a computer, look around for a service bureau. This is a firm with big hardware that can put your files up on a data base in a matter of days. Then when you want a mailing list sorted to third class specifications, no problem.

But only use a service bureau that's been around awhile. We want no chance they'll go out of business and lose your data.

How many years of data should you put up on your list? Minimum three. Then take a random sample of 25% of the three- to five-year group. Test their responsiveness with a reactivation mailing. If the returns are handsome, load the rest and rollout. In the same way test the six- to 10-year group, also the 11-plus group. Don't just load everything. Test first.

Now you're ready to take advantage of the most profitable—and underutilized—asset of your practice.

PROMOTIONS IN MOTION

1. What's the best way for veterinarians to sell pet insurance? By the numbers! Use direct mail to your clients to show their actual savings in chart form:

	Pet HMO	Non-HMO
Office Visit	$ 3.00	$ 18.45
X-rays	N/C	$128.75
Anesthesia	N/C	$ 22.85
Surgery	N/C	$275.70
Hospital Care	$12.00	$196.20
Total Cost	$15.00	$641.95

Add in the policy cost and the numbers do the selling.

2. Like others, Dentist F.T. includes an enticing certificate to pass on to a friend or loved one with his Quarterly Internal Prospecting letter to his base. But unlike others, F.T. also makes the certificate good for the reader. Super response.

3. More pinpoint marketing. A large veterinary practice used their computer to track breeds of dogs they treat. This showed them where their business was. Then they cranked out direct mail targeted to the breeders of these dogs indicating they have a specific interest in the breed. The multiple mailings have now begun to produce referrals—inexpensively.

4. Hypnotist G.B. knows if he doesn't promote, he doesn't make a comfortable living. But he also knows how important return-on-investment is. So when postage rates recently went up, less costly postcards sent to his mailing list became more attractive. That's how he successfully kept the lid on expenses.

Chapter 16

NO STONE UNTURNED:
EXPLORING PROFITABLE NEW MARKETS

□ HOW TO HAVE EASY PICKINGS AND AVOID THE CONTINUOUS STRUGGLE

There are 1 urologists in one middle-sized market. So when D.K. decided to open his practice in the area, he rightly checked the professional-to-population ratio first. The number wasn't encouraging. It told him the going would be tough.

Too much competition. Too hard to get started. But yet there was family close by to bind him to the area. What to do?

By looking further, the answer emerged. He noticed that the central city drew from a wide area. There was only one urologist office in the hinterlands—and that was only staffed one day every other week. If a person had a problem, most needed to drive up to 45 minutes to see a specialist.

Therefore he decided to "bring medicine to the people." He opened four offices in small towns over a two-county area. No longer did prospects need to drive long distances. He promoted to GPs and FPs the idea that a specialist was now in the area and that meant tip-of-the-arrow care locally. And, more importantly, he promoted directly to the public so they didn't drive 45 minutes anymore.

Also a good move was D.K.'s idea of space sharing. To keep his overhead down, he rented space on an as-needed basis from other practitioners. This usually meant one to one-and-a-half days a week per office. The other doctors were happy to get the income. D.K. was happy not to have to pay full-time staff for each office.

■ **Concept Worked.** Why it worked so well is simple. D.K. located in areas where *there was no competition.* Period.

If he had situated in the city as his 11 other colleagues had, the going would have been slow. The city was already tied up. And there was nothing to distinguish him from the pack. Yes, he was good, but that didn't matter. The city couldn't handle another "good" urologist.

The proof of the concept's power is the fact that the original four offices have *mushroomed to seven* with the addition of a partner. This has made him the second largest practice in a 100-mile radius. Not bad for four years in practice.

■ **Beware.** But D.K. recently consulted with THE PRACTICE BUILDER about his plans to expand into the central city in his marketplace. The advice was *don't!*

What has built this practice to incredible heights was *finding underserved markets, locating there and keeping overhead under control.* Going into the fray of cutthroat competition with still nothing to distinguish D.K. from the pack is an exercise in futility—and bad marketing.

A better growth strategy is to expand into a contiguous marketplace with the same idea: numerous, convenient offices with little competition and low overhead.

What also makes this *easy* is the lack of sophistication in marketing among professionals in the hinterlands. The farther out you go, the less the sophistication. Therefore, anything works. Not so in the big city.

■ **Staffing.** This becomes the big expansion problem. How do you attract a well-qualified practitioner/partner/associate to an area without a health spa and a French restaurant? The biggest point is to recruit a professional with a small town upbringing. They fit in better and feel more comfortable. It's frequently too big an adjustment for big city folk. Of course, make the money attractive. But you can afford it since the market is there for the taking.

If you want to be big, this is a way to go.

■ **Results.** An ophthalmologist, who asked that even his initials be withheld for competitive reasons, practices in one of the true hotbeds of eyecare competition in the country—Denver. This market has too many ophthalmologists, too many optometrists, too many HMOs, too much cataract advertising on TV, plus, now, an optometry-ruled organization to control referrals to surgeons. And with recent reductions in Medicare, the picture has become even gloomier.

When markets like this become saturated with colleagues, all professionals can only get so much. Then there's no more, especially when the competition is smart and well financed.

Recognizing this, he looked around for an area where the pickings were easier. And found them in western Nebraska. Now he has two part-time offices which are rented from local optometrists only on days he's there (to keep overhead down).

Fully one-third of the practice gross now comes from the satellites even though he spends nowhere near one-third of his time there.

"I could never do this in Denver. No matter how good a surgeon I am, the business is just not there ... When you don't have to struggle so hard, everything's more pleasant."

☐ HOT GROWTH SPOTS

What are the liveliest metropolitan growth spots in the U.S.? And where will they need a bumper crop of professionals to serve

There are several ways to analyze the question: straight population growth; job creation rates; the number of new business start-ups; and business growth rates. When you use all those indices together, here are the top 50 hot spots for growth according to *Inc.* magazine given in descending order (the listing includes the metro area surrounding the city):

1. Las Vegas, NV
2. Washington, DC
3. Orlando, FL
4. Tallahassee, FL
5. San Jose, CA
6. Atlanta, GA
7. Charleston, SC
8. Lincoln, NE
9. Raleigh-Durham, NC
10. Orange County, CA
11. Charlotte, NC
12. Hickory, NC
13. Wilmington-Jacksonville, NC
14. Ventura, CA
15. Nashville, TN

16. San Diego, CA
17. Chattanooga, TN
18. Greenville-Spartanburg, SC
19. Fort Meyers, FL
20. Sioux Falls, SD
21. Stockton-Modesto, CA
22. Reno, NV
23. Baltimore, MD
24. Jackson, MS
25. Lancaster, PA
26. Fort Pierce, FL
27. Columbus, OH
28. Jacksonville, FL
29. Lexington, KY
30. Norfolk-Portsmouth, VA
31. Richmond, VA
32. Honolulu, HI
33. Atlantic City, NJ
34. Tampa-St. Petersburg, FL
35. El Paso, TX
36. Huntsville, AL
37. West Palm Beach, FL
38. Melbourne-Titusville, FL
39. Ft. Lauderdale, FL
40. Seattle, WA
41. Portsmouth, NH
42. Panama City-Ft. Walton Beach, FL
43. Reading, PA
44. Grand Rapids, MI
45. Riverside-San Bernadino, CA
46. Madison, WI
47. Columbia, SC
48. Wilmington, DE
49. Houston-Galveston, TX
50. Mobile, AL

A different list highlights other boom towns of the '90s. Here are some downtowns that are bouncing back plus communities located 20 to 40 miles from downtown, beyond the old suburbs and malls. These former sleepy towns are drawing new business and the quality of life is just fine:

Marietta-Rosewell, GA

Richardson (Dallas) TX

Troy-Warren, MI

Scottsdale-Sun City, AZ

Herndon/Manassas, VA

Santa Ana-Costa Mesa-Laguna Niguel, CA

Virginia Beach-Chesapeake, VA;

East Brunswick, NJ;

Orlando-Kissimmee, FL

Melville-Smithtown, NY

Elk Grove Village-Arlington Heights, IL

Bethpage-Farmingdale, NY

West Chester-Wayne, PA

Des Plaines-Northbrook, IL

Livonia-Plymouth, MI

Edison-Woodbridge, NJ

Holmdel-Red Bank-Eatontown, NJ

Pittsburgh Central Business District

St. Louis-Chesterfield, MO

The Woodlands (Houston), TX

These may already seem booming, but this is nothing compared to ten years from now.

But hot growth doesn't mean you should pack you bags just yet. To figure out if you should, see the article on how to site select.

☐ CAPTURING THE HOTEL TRADE

Chiropractor G.T.'s office is surrounded by hotels. Even though people who stay there won't become long-term patients, he still wants the business. Unfortunately he's gone about it the wrong way.

He put an ad in the publications placed in hotel rooms. Zero results. But it's not surprising when you realize what people are thinking when they browse through these. They're looking for enjoyment—dining, dancing—certainly not dealing with one of life's problems. So the result is zero attention, zero recall and zero calls.

Instead, G.T. needed to go to the concierge. A quick introduction, an explanation of what G.T. treats and why he's so good, and an offer to treat the concierge at a reduced rate will do the trick nicely. After all, he's the person guests go to when they don't know where to go.

Then repeat the process with the people who work the front desk. (Make sure you catch all shifts.) Or start with them if there's no concierge. What's key is becoming the *professional of choice for the staff* because they'll then naturally refer to you. This networking approach is much surer and less expensive than catch-as-catch-can ads.

■ **Results.** G.T. has now become "House Chiropractor" to four hotels in his area. But with an average of seven guests-turned-patients a month, G.T. still doesn't make his big money here. He makes it from the hotel staffs. They're physically active people with bad backs and good insurance.

☐ HOW TO GET PATIENTS OR CLIENTS FROM THAT PART OF TOWN

Podiatrist O.L. was located just a mile-and-a-half from a ritzy development of homes, but hardly any of his patients came from there. He even promoted in the local weekly newspaper that covered that area, but still zip to nil.

What O.L. didn't realize was that there was a strong mental market barrier between his office and the target community. Not only was the ritzy, glitzy development more expensive than his office's area, it was *much more* expensive. At least two rungs on the economic ladder.

And people don't shop for services in areas of lower socioeconomic levels than where they live.

So how can he attract the well-to-do to his middle-lower market location (which also happens to be economically declining)? Simple. Open a new office in an area they'll come to because it sure isn't his present one.

A better strategy would be to concentrate on his surrounding area and forget the snooties—unless everything's going down with the neighborhood and then it's time to think about relocating anyway.

☐ BUILDING THE BUSINESS DISTRICT PRACTICE
(WITH 100 NEW PATIENTS/CLIENTS A MONTH)

Dentist B.W. was located in a suburban boom area—but at the wrong time. It had since gone bust. With everything on the wane and competitors closing offices, B.W. decided to move to the downtown business district. His thoughts: Downtown with its range of businesses was less susceptible to the ups and downs of the one-industry suburb; also it has more turnover and, therefore, always a new supply of prospects.

So B.W. opened and waited and waited—until at *THE PRACTICE BUILDER's How to Build a $1,000,000 Practice Workshop*, his Market Planner put him on the right road.

■ **Walking Turf.** The problem with practices in a big city business area is that there's no easy way to reach the people who work there. Major media usually costs too much for a solo professional to afford, even though it nicely reaches all those areas from which people commute.

Direct mail doesn't work either. Company turnover is too great to have accurate mailing lists—but you can toss that idea out the window because companies won't rent their employee lists anyway.

The *Yellow Pages* work well, especially when you promote the convenience of going to a professional near work and not having to take off half-a-day to go near home. But the *Yellow Pages* don't produce enough business to fill the entire practice, especially with the cost of downtown rents.

That leaves a labor-intensive approach which is very powerful and almost always works for *frequently used* services. In this strategy, the professional walks the turf introducing him- or herself. Going building to building, office to office, he greets secretaries and anyone else he can. First, he tells the listener that:

■ There's now a practice devoted solely to the businessperson.

■ That means convenient morning and lunchtime hours.

■ It's only a short distance away so they needn't take several hours off work to get service.

■ Plus expertise in all those services that are so important in a business environment.

Then he hands out his one-page flyer. It *must* look easy to read. Two to three short paragraphs tops, centered on the page with lots of white space above and below, on his practice stationery. The letter reiterates the benefits and gives a low-risk way to try a bite-sized portion of service.

He asks the receptionist to tell everyone about the practice and introductory offer as well as to pass a letter out to each person who works there. Since the front desk is your entry point into the business, you'll most likely get lots of secretaries and administrative assistant types.

That's whom the receptionist will tell and that's great. These are word-of-mouth-generating types with good insurance who are big consumers of most professional services.

Key Points: (1) The professional must present the practice enthusiastically. (2) The pricing of the offer must be right. Testing different prices will dramatically affect results. This must be done in each market because there's no consistency in how different prices work.

■ Sample Letter

Dear Neighbor,

As a way of introducing our new concept of dentistry just for the downtown businessperson, you can take advantage of *a complete examination including four x-rays, head and neck cancer screening, and a thorough dental cleaning for only $44.* This is normally a $76 value. It's our way of introducing you to a brand new idea of a dental practice exclusively designed for the businessperson.

That means convenient hours (7 A.M. - 5 P.M., including lunchtime appointments), a convenient location (2nd & Hill Sts.), a complete range of dental services, and cosmetic dentistry to assure a successful smile. Remember: A businessperson's smile may not land you a job, a client or a promotion. But not having one could cost you any one of them.

So call 766-2900 now to reserve a time for your complete exam and cleaning and your businessperson's smile.

Yours truly,

B.W., DDS

P.S. Please note: This introductory offer expires March 31st.

■ Variations.
For busier practitioners, you can leverage your time and hire a practice representative to do this for you. The rep must dress professionally and exude enthusiasm. *An infectious smile is a must!!!* Remember, you're hiring a salesperson.

The wrong rep can kill a well thought-out program so be careful in your choice. Remember, there are only two types of reps—the good and the fired. Give the rep two weeks to produce. That's enough for most types of practices.

To encourage results, pay the rep a modest base salary with a big commission structure based on the actual number of people who walk in with letter in hand.

■ **Results.** Dentist E.H. walks his turf everyday, totaling 12 hours each week. And every month 4,000 letters are distributed. With a conversion ratio of 25 new patients for every 1,000 letters, he's generating *100 new patients per month.*

E.H. is so good at walking his turf, he's hiring an associate to do much of the work while he continues to build—and walk. Walking turf not only builds leg muscles, it builds muscular business-area practices.

☐ **HOW TO PROMOTE AN URBAN PRACTICE**

Urban practices have special problems when it comes to external promotion. Oftentimes, big city media cost too much for a one location practice. And there are few neighborhood newspapers in which to advertise. What to do?

For inexpensive *external* promotion, test a few ideas from this list. Remember, not all are appropriate for every practice.

1. *Special promotions for neighborhood, block, area or building associations:* Various types of associations exist, complete with a communication avenue to their members. See if you can run an ad in their newsletter or can rent their mailing list. Hand delivery of flyers to members with a special offer can also be viable. Also do a talk or training session for the association members.

2. *Outside office sign:* For practices with street exposure, signage can be a real boon: perpendicular to the street and attached to the building; a removable "sandwich" sign placed on the sidewalk daily; an interior lit sign on the facia of the building; two signs coming out at a 60 angle from the facia and joined together; the side on a building painted to draw attention.

3. *Window signage:* Whether outside signage is available or not, it's always a good idea to use window signage to draw further attention. This type of signage can also be changed quickly for short term promotions.

4. *Hallway signage:* If you're tucked away in a professional building with foot traffic in the hallways, use a movable, metal hallway sign with a changeable cardboard poster like the department stores have at their entryways.

5. *Elevator signage:* See if you can buy signage to place on the elevator walls of yours and surrounding buildings. One very enterprising professional bought space on the inside of toilet stalls in all his surrounding buildings. No one had ever done that before in his area and it was extraordinarily successful. Talk about a captive audience!

6. *Cross-promote with other practices in your building:* Seek out other professionals in your building and offer to place their promotional literature in your waiting room. They need to do likewise.

7. *New resident or business direct mail:* For appropriate practices, new resident or business direct mail can capture up to 10% of this new group in your area. They're prime prospects looking for a new set of professionals. And they're highly targetable.

8. *Handouts to walk-bys:* For some practices looking for high volume, hiring a part-timer to handout flyers to walk-bys can be juicily profitable. This is not for the high-line practice, but for one which targets the middle to middle-lower part of the market.

9. *Walking the surrounding office turf:* Hiring a part-timer to approach local offices with promotional handouts for distribution—or doing it yourself a couple of hours a day—is also very lucrative. Your one-page flyer must be short and talk of how your practice, hours and benefits are designed for business people. Include a direct response, limited-time offer.

10. *Co-op coupons:* These come 20 to an envelope and are put out by ADVO, Val-Pak, Money Mailer and others. Printing and mailing costs are $300 to $450 for 10,000. Some will also print and mail yours *alone* for about $500 to $750 for 10,000. Contact them by looking in your *Yellow Pages* under *Advertising* or *Advertising-Direct Mail* or asking local merchants which coupon companies solicit them.

11. *Local and specialty newspapers and shoppers:* Some do exist which target a section of the city. Test your advertising in these, tracking each for return-on-investment. If you have a predominant minority group in your area, also seek newspapers which specifically cater to them and test your advertising in these.

12. *Specialty Yellow Pages:* Again, if you have a predominant minority group in your area, see if there's a *Yellow Pages* designed for them. Remember: You must be in a geographical center of that group for the directory to pay.

13. *Targeted direct mail:* Stand-alone direct mail is an expensive proposition and the most tricky of all promotions to execute well. So make sure you have your ducks in a row on this one. But if you do, then you're marketing to a tightly targeted geographical area and that's exactly what you want.

14. *Patient or client recruitment program for your staff:* They know and meet lots of prospects. So motivate them for their recruitment efforts

with rewards and give them the practice brochure and business cards they need as tools.

15. *A greater emphasis on internal promotion:* Since external promotion in an urban area is difficult and expensive, place extra emphasis on the internal side. Use direct mail (Internal Prospecting) to your existing base to promote old and new services and products. Use interior signage and handouts, verbal One-Minute Messages, Reactivation efforts, Patient/Client Appreciation Days, Open Houses, a revamped Recall system, a Frequent Referrer Program, a Waiting Room Resume, and, above all, ask for referrals.

☐ AN ALL NEW RESIDENT PROGRAM WITH SECRET AGENTS

Dentist H.S. is thinking all the time. Located in a hotbed of competition, he has to. So when he went after the 150 new residents per month in his area, he figured a new way to outsmart three other docs with similar intentions.

First, H.S. mailed repetitively at the one-, three-, six- and twelve-month marks to the new residents after they moved in. He knew not everyone was ready for a G.P. as soon as they moved. And as important, he prepared his direct mail package according to guidelines described in the chapter on direct mail. The results: Even with three competitors, he still captured 12% of the business on the list. Not bad, but not good enough for him.

As a second layer, H.S. tried The Welcome Wagon, but found its efforts puny, unpersuasive and barely break-even. Even though it didn't do well, H.S. still liked the idea of a personal presentation and endorsement.

So, as the thinking G.P., he went to real estate agents in the area. His reasoning: The new resident has a personal relationship with his or her agent. There's trust there. Why not have the real estate agents recommend him?

After all, he was paying The Welcome Wagon every time they made a presentation for him. Why not pay real estate agents instead? They could work as his secret agents. Unlike The Welcome Wagon, there's less competition because the agents aren't recommending anyone else. And they're much better salespeople.

What do the agents get? He does their and their family's health care for free, except for out-of-pocket expenses like lab fees.

H.S. now has six agents talking him up. And they should because he is their doctor. They not only praise him to the sky as only real estate agents can, they hand out his practice brochure with a direct response, limited time offer. Plus, their recommendations aren't extra work for the agents since it's part of their after-sale service.

He still continues his direct mail program because some people will forget their agent's recommendation. The mail catches them later. Also, the mail hits renters who the agents don't.

■ **Results.** The direct mail response rate has risen to 17% after six months of field agents. And the agents directly generate a total of 11 new patients per month. All at no extra cost to H.S., just his time of doing their care.

"It did take some time contacting them and keeping up the contacts. You can't just see them once, set it up and let it go. No, your manager needs to call them every two weeks to check if they need more brochures and to remind them you exist. But this is a small amount of effort for the payoff."

☐ BECOMING THE PROVIDER OF CHOICE FOR SMALL COMPANIES

Optometrist H.R. was very frustrated. Down the block was a large industrial plant that could feed big numbers into his practice. But when he approached them with the classic discount-for-your-employees ploy, all he got was a firm, but polite "no."

However, they were nice enough to tell H.R. why they couldn't do business:

1. We have to have everything approved by corporate in Cleveland and they only approve benefits that are the same for all employees in all their subsidiaries.

2. Besides, you don't have enough capacity to comfortably service all or even most of our employees.

3. Even if that were the case, you have only one location and couldn't possibly be convenient for all our employees and their families who live all over the county.

■ **A Better Approach.** If you're looking to recruit patients or clients who aren't referred directly by the company, then big, self-insured corporations of over 200 employees are difficult to get into. They're bureaucratic and require networks of professionals like PPOs. H.R. finally wised up to this and changed directions. Instead he went after *small businesses.*

These 10- to 50-employee firms offer fewer fringe benefits. The reasons are that they don't have deep pockets and the cost of benefits is much higher than if they had the buying power of 200+ employees.

Small biz managements would like to give their employees more benefits, but costs right now are shooting through the roof. A 30% price rise for health care was the norm, not the exception. So they're a perfect target.

H.R. told them he had a way to increase employee benefits *without additional costs*. They could in fact add an Eyecare Plan for free. That got their attention. Here was his arrangement.

He would issue employees and their families a yearly Eyecare Benefit Plan Card which would be good for a 20% savings on all eyecare and eyewear. In exchange, the company had to agree to promote availability of the plan in the following ways:

1. Announce the plan as an addition to the company's benefits so it would enjoy the company's endorsement.
2. Enclose a twice-a-year paycheck stuffer that H.R. provided.
3. Post a promotional poster H.R. also provided.
4. Hand out each new year's Eyecare Benefit Plan Cards.

His initial approach to small business owners was through the mail. With a list broker's help, he selected and rented a mailing list of companies with 10 to 50 employees. His letter contained the add-to-your-benefits-package-at-no-cost pitch and told the reader to call or return the enclosed card for more info.

Of the 309 mailed, 27 responded and H.R. closed 16. These 16 averaged 21 employees in size plus 2.2 dependents per each employee. This totaled 67.2 enrollees per company or *1,075 total*. Nice numbers!

And costs were minimal: (1) inexpensive, once-a-year, heavy paper membership cards; (2) twice-a-year paycheck stuffers measuring $2\frac{5}{8} \times 6\frac{1}{4}$"; and (3) a once-a-year poster. H.R. sent all materials by mail for the companies to distribute so his legwork was minimal. This repetitive promotion assured that most enrollees would utilize the plan.

You may want to recruit a noncompeting colleague to cover the areas where employees may live but you can't serve. This will answer the lack-of-coverage objection. In addition, you can share costs.

Don't Have Enough Time? Then hire a practice rep to do the whole program for you.

■ **Results.** H.R. wasn't finished. He kept on enrolling companies by mailing to new ones as well as to those he'd already mailed. And after he finished everyone, he started calling those who didn't respond and got even more response.

"At the one-year mark, I had enrolled over 5,000 card-carrying people, whereas I couldn't get to first base with the bigger companies." H.R. analyzed, "All the new patients who came from the plan were in addition to my regular practice. Since I have my regular patients paying for my overhead anyway, the profit from the plan patients has been pure profit except for the eyewear and lab costs."

One problem that dentist T.O. saw with the above plan was that he feared insurance companies auditing his records to discover he gave a discount and then arguing that all he could charge them was the same and they'd pay 80% of that. His whole profile would be lowered.

So he executed a bit differently but has still discovered an immediate and bountiful response. Instead of offering a discount, T.O. offers several free services which have proven a powerful lure.

T.O.'s plan offers an initial exam one time only and only for new patients. Twice a year plan members can receive a free re-exam and bite-wing x-rays. And once a year they can have a free simple extraction and emergency exam. Lots of neat services—most of which either he can deliver quickly or are rarely used.

Each plan member gets a card to carry for emergencies and which describes the plan. (See Figure 16.1.) The staff notches the right side next to service used.

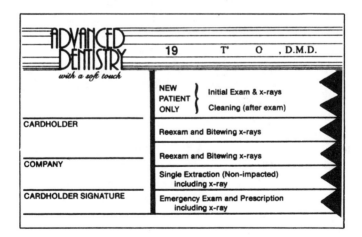

Figure 16.1 Tom Orent's Plan Card

■ **Results.** He's only test mailed to a handful of companies and quickly enrolled 50 employees onto the plan. They in turn quickly booked $1,000 worth of work. Not bad for a quick and dirty. Now he's rolling out aggressively.

PROMOTIONS IN MOTION

1. One chiropractic physician recently opened a Women's Health Center. That's not news, but he opened it in a downtown office high-rise and that is.

He's added an MD for complete service and three marketing reps for complete market penetration. Two part-time reps hand out 11,000 direct response flyers a week to walk-bys. The full-time rep walks the buildings, introducing the practice to receptionists and asks them to hand out direct response flyers to the other women in the office. It's a bonanza and it's smart, targeted marketing.

2. One of the classic promotional strategies for ophthalmologists is to screen seniors out in the community for glaucoma. They discover tons of cataract cases. More and more dermatologists are also getting into the act by screening for skin cancer. And, of course, this is old hat for hearing aid dispensers.

But now, an ophthalmologist, dermatologist and hearing aid dispenser have teamed up to jointly screen. For senior centers and nursing homes the package is more attractive than individual players. Plus the cost of the screenings is now borne jointly. The savings are dramatic.

3. Last year chiropractor H.Y. added massage therapy to his practice and grossed an additional $41,000 at 50% net. But he really didn't discover the power of adding massage until he put it in his advertising.

With massage therapy as a leader in his co-op coupons and *Yellow Pages* and newspaper ads, he pushed the right hot button. It now accounts for over $73,000 in billings.

Another DC put into local stores 50 stand-alone, suggestion-type boxes with a cardboard header and a tear-off pad. Its message: If you want one to three massages per week and you have something wrong with you so it could be paid for by your insurance, fill out a slip and place it in the box. The DC's staff collects the slips weekly and telemarkets to follow-up. The 50 boxes generate plenty of slips and about one qualified patient per month per box.

4. Podiatrist N.B. works downtown in a small, cash-tight practice. With media costing so much, he's gone to targeting the people who literally hobble by his office—through the use of handbills. The return-on-investment is phenomenal because the cost is so low ($3.35 an hour to hand them out and 2¢ each to produce) and the case size so high. With these figures, you don't need many responses to get in the plus column fast. But the reason the responses are many is that people are right in the area already.

5. Dentist W.R. went to his local hospital's Emergency Room, not to get care, but to give it. It took four meetings with the ER staff to gain hospital privileges and referrals, but the outcome was nice. There were relatively few midnight emergencies he actually had to get out of bed for ... and a large number of high-ticket personal injury cases covered by insurance.

6. With few resources, dentist F.P. has been cold calling the mega-offices in his business-oriented area. He introduces himself to the receptionist, chats up the practice and leaves a flyer with an offer for distribution. Successful, but nothing new here. Except that F.P. wears his white doctor's coat on his jaunts. He's more impressive and his productivity for the strategy is well above average.

7. Optometrist T.N. has a high traffic mall location. So he decided to take advantage of it along with his investment in his practice brochure. He spent $5.95 on a Plexiglass "Take One" display and affixed it to the outside of the office. Now, window shoppers can read about why they should come to T.N. without having to walk in first. He needs to replace the rack's brochure supply every third day.

Chapter 17   □

THE SECRETS OF TELEMARKETING

□ NEWEST CONCEPT IN TELEMARKETING

Chiropractor S.A. was running a study. To get enough subjects he had to resort to having his staff call people in the community.

During the call the staff person politely explained that the doctor was conducting a study on the incidence and types of back and neck problems in their community. And that if the person has a back or neck pain problem, would they like to participate. All they need to do is have an exam at no charge. The doctor would explain his findings to them and they would discover the cause of their pain. The overall findings in the community would then be submitted for publication in a professional journal.

A funny thing happened on the way to the article. After the doctor said, "Here are the findings. Now you're free to go," most of the participants said, "Help me! Help me!" So he did. And *Boom!*

"Not only do I get more than enough data for my research," S.A. confides, "I'm averaging nine new patients a month from the study at about $1,500 per case."

Another recent takeoff on this theme: An optometrist has been running a newspaper ad seeking subjects for a hard-to-fit contact lens study. The O.D. provides new contacts for free for 30 days (taking a credit card imprint as security for their return). He counts about 16 takers a month off his little, reversed-out ad. And nine subsequently buy the contacts at $275 per pair plus ancillary products and insurance.

☐ THE DEDICATED PHONE RECALLER

Veterinarian O.F. had almost 20,000 charts. Over the years, the practice had boomed. And because of the growth, he didn't pay much attention to those clients who didn't bring back their pets after he'd sent a recall postcard. Then business went bad. Lots of competition and a stagnant population slowed his growth considerably.

But in talking with his PRACTICE BUILDER Hotline Advisor, he made a bold move and hired an additional staff person just to phone-recall past and present clients. She had no other duties.

Logic dictated that if he brought back in lots of neglectful clients, he'd make a fair return from the inoculations alone. Plus surgeries and ancillary sales of products and boarding would also go up. But what he didn't anticipate was the rise in referrals. With more interaction, past clients were now telling more friends and neighbors about O.F.

And on top of that, he discovered that although some pets had died, many of their former owners had new pets in need of care. And even of those who had deserted to the enemy camp, some were now wanting to come back.

The recaller's message was always the same. She explained the doctor asked that she phone because he was concerned. The script then had her tell the client why it's important to bring their pet in now ... and what *specifically* could happen if they don't. There were different scripts for different types of pets.

■ **Results.** "The results were so spectacular, I couldn't believe it. I was dubious in the beginning because dollars per case aren't very big in veterinary medicine. But my dedicated recaller pays for herself the first week of every month. She keeps me busy."

☐ CONVERTING INQUIRIES INTO PATIENTS OR CLIENTS

Facial surgeon K.R. had a successful ad campaign but a less-than-successful conversion rate. Tons of people responded to his tasteful and titillating ad, but too few were actually signing up for the nose job of their dreams. What to do?

With a pool of over 1,000 inquiries, K.R. had a group who already expressed an interest in his services, but for some reason had not yet made a decision. So his tack should be to get one or more people from his office on the phone to call and counsel.

"But we've already done that with few results." Upon close inspection, however, it became apparent their past efforts were energetic, but unconvincing. There was *no financing* information mentioned, *no offer* given and the *wrong person* called.

■ **Three Keys.** For most high-ticket, out-of-pocket expenses, financing is a critical variable in the decision process. And not just the mention that financing is available, but the advising that payments are *as low as $75 a month* or whatever the specific figure is. (See "New Financing Plans Boost Growth" in Chapter Four.) Otherwise, prospects are wondering if they have to write a check *for the entire amount right away*. Most don't wonder very long. So get it as low as possible.

Second, the caller needs to offer something new to the prospect to get them into the office. In this case, K.R.'s perfect offer is a computer imaging analysis so the prospect can actually see what they'll look like after surgery—all at no cost. The more powerful the offer, the greater the response.

And third is an extraordinarily important variable—who's doing the calling. No, you don't need someone familiar with what you do because you can always train a person in the information. You need someone who can *get the appointment*. It's called sales ability and you can't train that. Few have it. Rarely does someone on staff have it, so you've got to hire it. Part-time, hourly is fine.

To find a good one, run a classified ad for a telemarketer under "Sales." Look for someone with past telemarketing experience. Out-of-work actors are also often great telemarketers. And people with prior *commission* sales experience are usually good. Interview *by phone* since they'll be working by phone. Pay by the hour with an incentive for each appointment booked and kept. Script the approach to standardize it for quality.

You need to remember these three crucial variables. Without them, you'll get few results. With them, you'll nose out all the competition.

□ **"I NOW CONVERT ABOUT 50% OF PHONE SHOPPERS."**

Veterinarian G.H. gets calls from price shoppers all the time. Being in a price-sensitive profession and a penny-pinching locale, G.H. finally got smart, but only after years of experimentation. Here's his tested strategy.

G.H. keeps prices on commonly shopped services competitive. (He does this by calling competitors' offices and price-shops himself.) He never charges the least of the pack. Instead, he opts for the middle. He rightly argues that those shopping for the absolute lowest price—who ignore the differences he points out between his practice and others—won't be loyal anyway. It's one shot and they're gone.

When people call, his front desk never gives the price until last. *Following a script*, they first talk about G.H.'s expertise in the service the caller asked about. G.H. has a different script for each often-shopped service.

Each script talks about how many similar patients he's treated for that problem, how he's taken extra continuing education specifically on that problem, that he only uses the most recently developed technique unlike other DVMs, and that he's proud of his extraordinarily high success rate. And all that only costs $___ .

G.H. has discovered that if you just say the price or you say it in the beginning, they compare you on price alone. Results: "I now convert about 50% of phone shoppers, whereas before it was maybe half of that."

☐ INBOUND TELEMARKETING: HOW TO CONVERT AN INQUIRY INTO AN APPOINTMENT

In a recent telephone survey of 20 practices in which the caller acted as an interested prospect, 19 of them failed to get the appointment! They either didn't ask for it, degraded the practice, implied that the price was high, couldn't answer important questions, didn't describe anything to make the practice seem special, put the caller on hold for over 2½ minutes, and/or asked the caller to call back later! *That means there's a 95% chance this is going on in your practice.*

You work hard to get people to call. Yet most of your staff can't present your most important points, in the most convincing order, expressed in the most convincing terms to get the appointment.

In any case, you don't want to blow the opportunity with a less than optimal presentation—since you only get it once. Therefore, you're smart to carefully *script* the entire spiel.

This is what the pros do. In fact, they not only script everything tightly, but they also *don't let their people deviate* from it. If there's a better way to express something, then consider changing the script, but no one should freelance on the phone.

One of the big reasons for this is that the front desk is usually harried and won't give enough effort to the conversion process. On top of that, they hate inquiries, especially price shoppers, so sometimes their surliness comes through.

■ **What Your Script Should Say.** If someone asks if you provide a certain service, the script should speak of how that's one of your areas of *special expertise,* that you've taken extra coursework in the area, that you've helped hundreds or thousands of people with that service, that other professionals' come to you for that service, and that your results are usually exceptional. Then specifically list your most *potent proof.*

The better the case you make that you're taking care of their *specific* problem, the more convert to appointments.

If someone calls for a *price, don't* give it to them right away. If you do, they'll only compare you to others on the basis of price alone.

First find out *what's their problem*. Then tell them how great you are for their problem. Then give them the price. You may charge more, but now they'll think you're worth it.

At the end of each script, *always* ask for the appointment: *We can see you tomorrow or the day after. Which would be better for you?*

If they balk at the appointment, tell them you'd be happy to send them more complete information in the mail and ask for their name, address and phone number. You'll want to follow-up with a cover letter—easily generated by your computer—along with your practice brochure. If the brochure's done right, it should finish the job.

Remember, you'll need a script for:

1. All the major problems you deal with;

2. Your major services about which people inquire;

3. The major objections people raise.

For easy access you can keep your scripts in clear plastic sheets on an 8½ × 11" flip chart right by the phone. Don't bury them in a book. They'll never be used.

This step-by-step approach is the only way to avoid being in the 95% of practices that don't get all the appointments they should.

☐ KNOCK-'EM-DEAD SCRIPTS FOR OUTBOUND TELEMARKETING

The "why's" are simple. Because it pays big: for hearing aid dispensers; chiropractic physicians; allergists; ophthalmologists; GYNs; podiatrists; dentists; orthodontists; hypnotherapists; and others. Just about any professional with a high case size and low case incidence in the population or a moderate case size and high incidence.

Outbound means you initiate the call—either to your past base to promote more services or to prospects at large.

And while there are lots of variables in this equation, the key is a knock-'em-dead script. Enticing, definitely not hard sell. But how?

■ Three Steps to Opening. Your opening must answer a prospect's three questions in the first ten seconds: Who is this? Why is he calling? What's in it for me?

1. *Identify yourself and your affiliation.* The telemarketing representative (TR) simply says: "Good morning, Mrs. Jones. I'm Alan Parker with the office of Dr. John Simon."

2. *State the reason for the call.* "I'm calling you today because a neighbor of yours, Mrs. Thompson, had a problem with severe back pain that another doctor had wanted to operate on. But using the latest,

non-surgical, high tech treatment, Dr. Simon was able to relieve her pain quickly and get her back to work in just two week's time. I'd like to determine today if anyone in your household has back, neck, shoulder, or leg pain or headaches that Dr. Simon could help in the same way ... ."

3. *Get the prospect involved.* "May I ask what kind of pain do they have and how long have they had it?" Your goal is to get the prospect to talk about his or her needs and then briefly answer them with your practice's benefits. But don't talk too long.

Ask feeling questions. Asking someone how they feel about something usually gets an insightful response. Then keep them revealing by saying "Oh?," "Interesting," and "Tell me more about ... ." The purpose is to get enough information so you can then answer their needs with your practice's services.

Also ask key questions: "If you could change anything about your situation, what would it be?" "Is there anything else I should know before I tell you about how we could help you?"

■ **The Sales Message.** After your fact-finding, bridge into the presentation: "Susan, based on what you've told me, I'm confident we could help you."

Then summarize their needs. "If I understand your situation correctly, you've had debilitating headaches for six months which medication and your family doctor hasn't helped. Your headaches make working difficult and take most of the joy out of life. And you're looking for something that works, but doesn't include medication that makes you feel foggy. Is all that correct?"

This restatement makes the prospect more receptive to your solution—which comes next: "Dr. Simon has a special program just for headaches like yours. His cure rate is over 92% and has helped more than a thousand people with just your problem. His 92% success rate comes from using the latest in special chiropractic techniques which Dr. Simon learned from one of the most respected headache specialists in the country. And you'll be glad to know it's non-surgical and doesn't use medications that make you feel foggy. There aren't any needles or anything like that. So it's painless."

■ **Closing.** Timing is crucial to when you close. Wait for the right time: a positive or enthusiastic statement; frequent questions about your service or product; the prospect becomes at ease; or talks about how they would personally benefit from your service.

Now entice them with a specific offer and *ask for the appointment.* Both are key: "But we've got to make sure that you're the right type of person who could benefit from Dr. Simon's headache program. Now we think that's our responsibility to find out if you are and you shouldn't have to pay for that. So the doctor has authorized me to schedule a free exam for you in which we'll find out for sure. And if we can't help you, we'll refer you to a qualified and respected doctor who can. So either way, you can get better."

Then *assume* they want it: "I have an opening on Wednesday at 3 P.M. or Thursday at 11 A.M. Which is better for you?"

If that close doesn't gain a commitment, try these.

The Elimination Process Close: Present three alternatives—a dog, a middle-of-the-road option, and your best. (Restaurant waiters do this all the time when they describe two dishes plus "their" favorite.) "Well, it seems you have several options. One is to continue to live in pain, not enjoying life as you could, and missing work. Two is to take medication which makes you feel woozy. Or three is to let us examine you for free to see if you can be cured for good so you can feel really good about your life again and live it headache-free. Quite frankly, don't you think your third option is your best?"

The Payback Close: "Susan, as you mentioned, when you get headaches, you can't concentrate at work and must often go home, feeling guilty about leaving. Plus, your headaches have ruined some family get-togethers for you. I'm sure Dr. Simon's headache program could probably solve both problems, so you wouldn't feel bad about work and you'd feel better at family gatherings. Wouldn't you like to find out if Dr. Simon can help you—especially when it doesn't cost anything?"

■ **Answering Objections.** Good questioning helps uncover all the objections. Resistance to closing, or "I'll think it over," should prompt you to ask: "What exactly doesn't fit your needs?"

Then turn the objection into a question to make sure you have the real objection: "You've raised a good question. Would the cost be truly worth the expense? Is that the question?" Then answer the real question with the appropriate benefits.

If the objection is *no money* or *no time*, don't stop. *Everybody has enough money or time* IF they thought your services were worth it. Restate the benefits so the prospect sees the value more clearly.

■ **Scripting.** Now type it so your TR can follow it easily. Use one sheet of paper or several 3 × 5" color-coded cards for different openings, info-gatherings, closings and objections.

Make sure you script in a conversational style, not a stilted one. Call length—five to seven minutes. Use tight scripting where the TR is relatively new to your type of practice or to telemarketing. Use loose "prompt" or "outline" scripts when you have real pros as TRs. Then *you* do a few calls for one hour and improve the script. It always needs it.

Your script's not working? Test different offers. And different TRs. Remember: There are only two types of TRs—the good and the fired. Never accept excuses for low productivity. Fire them.

Complex? Somewhat. Artful? Definitely. Profitable? Extraordinarily.

THE PRACTICE BUILDER and *Encyclopedia of Telemarketing*, edited by Bencin and Jonovic, Prentice Hall, Englewood Cliffs, NJ 07632, 1989.

☐ TELEMARKETING TIPS FOR SUCCESS

1. Get your telemarketing lists from any mailing list broker listed in the *Yellow Pages* under "Mailing Lists."

2. Assure speech privacy for your telephone representatives (TRs.) Use acoustic partitions and carpeting to make sure no more than 20% of speech can be heard 10 feet away.

3. Use headsets (about $150 each) for hands-free operations and to avoid back and neck problems.

4. Have a daily TR reporting sheet by the number of hours worked, numbers dialed, people reached, complete script deliveries, and appointments.

5. TRs who can close are worth a fortune to you. So don't be chintzy. Keep your top performers *very* happy. Pay a moderate base salary. Then step their commissions: $X extra for every appointment made *and* kept over a certain number; $X + $Y for each over a higher number, etc. The more they book, the higher the commissions go.

And don't cap the commissions. You'll demotivate your best people after they've reached the cap. Even add a plum for extra high achievement.

6. Sample TR recruitment ad:

   Telemarketer - APPT SETTER for busy _____ office. Sharp; motivated; energetic phone voice; telemktg, acting or sales experience preferred; top money plus bonus; call _____.

7. Interview TRs over the phone for these characteristics: good listener; believes in your services; cool under fire; extroverted, reliable; intelligent; rapport builder; clear communicator; financially oriented; and a *closer*—ability not to let people off the hook, tactfully putting them in a position where saying "no" is somewhat uncomfortable, asking for the appointment and not accepting "no" the first time.

Who makes the best TRs? Former TRs, out-of-work actors, and salespeople. Can others do the job? Yes, but hire for the above characteristics.

8. Train your TRs thoroughly. Have them observe you for a day or two to viscerally understand your services. Then role play the script over the phone.

9. And remember that this is a numbers game. So you only evaluate results by ROI, nothing else.

☐ HELPLINES EXPANDING QUICKLY

What's the professional service that spends more on advertising than any other? Attorneys—specifically personal injury attorneys. With an average case size of a few thousand dollars, they can afford it.

And which PI attorneys spend the most? No, it used to be Jacoby & Meyers ($6,580,000), but today it's the Injury Helpline ($6,760,000—a 53% increase over last year.) This bears note because the type of marketing they do is applicable to many types of professional practices.

Helplines and hotlines come in all shapes and sizes today. They pull callers with simple newspaper ads and/or radio and TV spots. And the ads and spots have only one purpose—to get prospects to call an 800 number for free information.

See Figure 17.1.

Drunk Driving?
PRE-RECORDED MESSAGE explains the California law.

First Offense Legal Hotline: **1-800 874-3333**
Second Offense Legal Hotline: **1-800 824-9999**

ATTORNEYS SPECIALIZING IN D.U.I. • CALL 1-800 532 3300 FOR AN APPOINTMENT
Drunk Driving Legal Hotline (sm)   © 1990 Mark D. Olson Law Offices

Figure 17.1

At the end of the phone line is a short tape on the latest info about the problem they're advertising. One key to success is that the tape not only explains advances but how members of the helpline solve the problem, not how the profession in general does it.

The offer of free information gets people to call, but the main purpose of the tape is to position them as experts on the subject and establish trust. Because then the tape instructs callers to hold on and someone comes on the line to ask them more about their situation. This screener evaluates each case and either asks for an appointment or refers them out. A free evaluation, consultation or exam is used to get them into the office.

■ **What Can Helplines Be Used for?** Problems with marriages, chemical dependencies, children of alcoholics, depression, eating disorders, allergies, back and neck pain, foot pain, chronic pain, loss of hearing, skin cancers, smoking, and weight loss. Personal and malpractice injuries, cosmetic surgeries, cataracts, obstetrics, orthodontics, and cosmetic dentistry. The main characteristic needed is a large case size to justify the advertising expense—over $150 case size if advertising in inexpensive local papers; more if using pricier media.

■ **Want to Test the Idea Inexpensively?** Run a one-inch × two-column ad (with the top half and headline reversed out to make it pop) about four times in an appropriate medium. Name the helpline after the problem your promoting—*The Chronic Pain Helpline*—and put the problem in your headline. Instruct the reader to call for free for information about the latest news and advances. The more it works, the more times you run it, and the more media you run it in.

Remember to answer the phone with the helpline's name, to play a killer tape, and to ask for the appointment after screening the cases.

PROMOTIONS IN MOTION

Optometrist G.L. is informing all the seniors in his community that Medicare now pays most of his eye exam. Not many knew this before. And he's using telemarketing to do it. College students follow a script and work the phones between five and nine P.M. G.L. pays them an hourly rate plus a commission for every appointment booked and kept. What he's discovered: (1) Running a telemarketing operation takes constant management. (2) It's very cost-effective.

Chapter 18

WINNING BIG IN TOUGH MEDIA: YOUR YELLOW PAGES AND NEWSPAPER ADVERTISING

☐ SCORING BIG AND AVOIDING FAILURE IN THE *YELLOW PAGES*

The *Yellow Pages* don't work. I had a big ad and lost about $5,800."—Chiropractor B.L.

"I had a single column ad about 2½" high that made about five times my cost."—Pediatrician G.F.

"Here are my computer's *Yellow Pages* figures: $7,615 cost; $96,711 revenue. That's a 12.7-to-1 return on investment!"—Podiatrist C.G.

All three accounts came into THE PRACTICE BUILDER's Advisory Hotline the same week. In the first case, chiropractor B.L. should never have made such a large investment in the *Yellow Pages* since his triple-half-column ad was 19th in line. Not only that, but he failed to differentiate himself and simply listed all the things he does—which are all the things everyone else does.

In the second case, pediatrician G.F. ran an ad too small to do anything but announce himself, certainly not large enough to convince anyone to call. But in spite of his cheapness and poor strategy, G.F. still made five times his money. And if done right together with an investment four times the size, he would have made an additional $90,000.

Podiatrist C.G. scored big. His *Yellow Pages* ads alone brought in 28.3% of his total dollars, 32.8% of his new patients. The reasons aren't a mystery. C.G. first identified which economic strata of the market he wanted. Then he studied his competitors and THE PRACTICE BUILDER's strategies. And finally, he balanced ...

■ **The *Yellow Pages* Equation.** Like all other promotion, the *Yellow Pages* is a composite of variables. Forget a variable—or don't execute one correctly—and it spells disaster. Ask B.L. True, all variables aren't equally important, but you can't figure out which is which beforehand, so you've got to treat all with respect.

YELLOW PAGES SUCCESS = Right Directory(ies)
+ Right Section
+ Right Size Ad (vis-a-vis competition)
+ Right Visual
+ Right Headline
+ Right Differentiation
+ Right Image
+ Right Copy
+ Right Typeface
+ Right Layout.

And what is success? *At least ten dollars in for every one dollar invested in the Yellow Pages.* (Income should reflect all dollars generated by patients or clients during his or her first 12 months with you.)

But who uses the *Yellow Pages*? If you just look at the numbers, it's the *middle and middle-lower segments* of the market—exactly those that account for most of the market. That's why the big numbers.

If your target is middle-upper, the *Yellow Pages* is still viable. Don't expect big numbers, but solid profitability is for the taking.

■ **This Year's Top *Yellow Pages* Successes:** Chiropractor D.H.'s practice produced $1.8 million gross with 58% of all new patients coming from the *Yellow Pages*. And dentist F.R. has tracked just over 51% of his new patients coming from his four *Yellow Pages* ads. This is not to say that F.R.'s word-of-mouth is bad, just that his *Yellow Pages* efforts are *great!*

You can't expect these results, but it's nice to know they exist.

☐ HOW TO CONSTRUCT A KILLER *YELLOW PAGES* AD

Yellow Pages readers have *only* three questions, so block out all other thoughts and concentrate on these. The ad that answers them best makes the big killing. Ignore them and you'll be killed.

The first is *"What do you do?"* People need to know that you take care of their *specific* needs or problems. So list them, but don't list only modalities. Prospects don't know if they need a specific way to solve or cure a problem. They only know if their back hurts, their heart hurts, their wallet hurts, and so on. You must list symptoms so they can self-diagnose themselves into your office.

The second is, *"Why should I choose you rather than someone else?"* Think about this. If you received a call from a prospect asking that question, what would you answer? Your response goes in your *headline*.

Need help? Underline the answers that best apply. Do you offer: quick relief; quick service; years of experience; a specialization; great expertise in an area; caring (you must give examples for credibility); friendliness; affordability; an opportunity to improve people's ability to earn (improving one's appearance or reducing stress); convenience (hours, location, we come to you ...); services catering to a particular type of person (e.g., income level); newer technology; aggressiveness; or conservativeness (e.g., surgeon)?

■ **More Ideas.** Beauty-oriented; used by colleagues or other respected people; credentialed; an author; a professor (very impressive); famous; gentle; giving individualized service (must give examples for credibility); fashion-oriented; "one of the guys"; comfortable; specializing in fearful people; modern; offering a family tradition of professional service; in sync with their values; accept emergencies.

Now choose one or two to hang your hat on. *It or they must differentiate you from direct competitors in the book and be important to your market.* Put the one or two distinctions in your headline. Professionals' names as headlines don't impress anyone enough to read the ad. Yet they appear in over 70% of your section's display ads. *A big mistake!* (See Figure 18.1.)

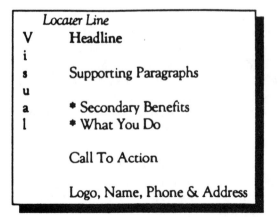

Figure 18.1 Prototypical *Yellow Pages* Layout

Locater Line

V
i
s   Headline
u
a   Supporting Paragraphs
l
           * Secondary Benefits
           * What You Do

           Call To Action

           Logo, Name, Phone & Address

Then add one or two *short* paragraphs explaining the claim made in the headline. *If there's no proof, there's no credibility, and no calls.* If the ad's visual also proves your claim(s), all the better. (More on that in a moment.)

Remember: Your major claims must have *proof* to be believed. If your headline says "I care" and you don't prove it, the reader won't believe the ad. There's too much puffery in advertising and people are too cynical. So play the game right, because the market's very unforgiving.

Now add secondary benefits in a list below those paragraphs. Make sure you also include the symptoms and conditions you treat, solve or help.

Only information that *convinces* the reader to call belongs in your ad. Anything that only *informs* is left to the receptionist or a handout.

That means *no maps!* True, people shop by location. But to save space yet make the point, use a locater line in small type above the headline. It'll be the first thing they read, and it's small size gives you the chance to put a stronger differentiation in your headline. Rule: You only need a locater line if you cover a smaller area than the directory.

To end the ad, tell them to call now. Who knows why people respond to commands like these. But tests show over and over and over that they do. So don't forget this call to action.

■ **Visual Strategies.** The main purpose of a visual is to grab attention to get the headline read. The headline then promises or implies a benefit. A top-notch visual also supports the headline's claim(s) or shows you. If you don't have a strong visual, you probably don't have a strong ad.

Photos almost always outpull drawings, so it makes sense to use a *big, close-up* photo. They're attention-getting and look modern, which makes you look modern.

A photo of the professional lets the reader see whom they'll be seeing. In their minds, it lessens the risk of calling an unknown, so response almost always jumps—assuming you don't look too young, old or (how shall we say this) "unphotogenic." Plus, the right photo can project how *likeable* you are, one of those emotional intangibles by which people choose their professionals.

Interestingly enough, graphics are the answer to your prospects' third question: *"Can I trust you?"* A clean, professional-looking layout says "Yes." So does the right typeface. A cluttered, haphazard layout with six different retail typefaces (like you always get from the *Yellow Pages'* artists-in-training) screams *"No!"*

■ **Do You Need Color?** *No!* Good design and a great headline will always outpull a poorly designed ad with color. And since color ups your monthly cost from 40 to 90%, it's far cheaper to get it designed professionally one time only. Plus you get far more response because now it's a great ad.

Add a hefty border to help solve the attention-getting problem and you've got your killer ad. It'll slay your competition and solve your part of the national debt.

☐ ADVERTORIALS: EFFECTIVE AND EASY

Have you ever created an ad that fell flat on its bottom line? Everyone who runs ads has. And while the reasons are many, probably two of the biggies are: (1) the lack of credibility of most advertising; and (2) the difficulties of good graphic design.

Most people don't read most ads. But if you create an ad that looks like an article, readership zooms. The reason: It looks more credible. (This is not to say that "regular" ads don't work. Only that they're more difficult to craft.)

Also, unless you have a real pro laying out your ads, they tend to look done by a teenager promoting a midnight stereo blowout sale. But the advertorial has little art direction. You just match your typestyles to the newspaper's and make sure the ad looks editorial.

■ **Guidelines.** Even though advertorials tend to be easier to create than other types of advertising, they still have strict guidelines for success:

1. *The advertorial must look newsy.* People read papers for news. A breakthrough. A new service. A goal you've achieved which few others have (or many have but the public isn't aware of that.) A new achievement for one of your patients or clients. A special promotion that no one or few have. New hours ...

2. *The article must talk about you,* not how your profession provides a service. But how YOU do it. If you promote your profession, then anyone in it can provide the service. This is your professional society's job, not your budget's.

This is the main reason canned editorial ads don't work. They're written for anyone in the profession and, therefore, consistently bomb.

3. *It helps to put your area's name in the headline.* People like to read about local news. It's what affects them most. So placing your town's or area's name in the head makes them want to read the advertorial more.

4. *Include an offer.* Direct response always pulls better than name recognition promotion. By promoting a non-monetary aspect of the practice in the copy, the offer becomes a low-risk way to try a bite-size

piece of service. Phone consults, free literature, and free care kits also work, but not as well as a free- or low-cost first meeting or exam.

Lack of direct response is another reason canned editorials don't produce.

So if you're stymied in your newspaper or magazine advertising, try advertorials. You'll probably get better results ... plus they're easier to create. (See Figure 18.2.)

New Local Record of Vision Improvement- from 20/400 to 20/30 Without Surgery or Lenses

Many Windsor residents are seeing more clearly, thanks to computerized vision training

The recent introduction of computerized sight training has given thousands of people dramatically better vision without glasses or surgery.

DRAMATIC RESULTS, PROVEN EFFECTIVENESS
"Hundreds of local residents have now completed the treatment with positive results," says noted area behavioral optometrist, Dr.

One commercial pilot set the record for vision improvement in Hartford. After entering therapy with 20/400 vision, he achieved 20/30 vision, and had his pilot's vision restriction removed.

A 27-year-old female, who had worn thick glasses all her life, began therapy with 20/400 vision. Inside of three months, her vision was 20/50. She now wears glasses of normal thickness.

VISION IMPROVES WITHOUT SURGERY
These dramatic results were obtained by using an advanced computer to strengthen the focusing eye muscle. Over 90% of those who complete treatment reduce their prescriptions. No surgery is involved. Up to 80% of the cost can be covered by insurance.

LOW-COST EVALUATIONS OFFERED
To determine whether a person can benefit from this new technology, Dr.
is offering an evaluation for $19. His offices are located at
For further information, please call 555-1212.

Advertisement

Figure 18.2

☐ HOW TO CREATE WINNING NEWSPAPER ADVERTISING

Weekly or daily, community or area-wide—newspaper advertising is often the best media vehicle for external promotion. But you must be located somewhat central to the area the paper covers. Keep in mind the full run of the paper covers a large area while its local zone section covers a smaller part. Whichever edition you choose, you want to be pretty much in the middle of its area so you don't buy too much wasted coverage from which you can't draw.

Then, of course, different *papers* will pull differently so testing and tracking different ones is a must. And different *sections* and different *days* will do likewise. No one knows for sure which combination works best until you actually test.

But how do you create the winning ad to flood your phones and create standing room only in your reception area? There are specific rules to follow. If you obey them, your risk plummets. Ignore them and the market will teach you a nasty lesson.

Step 1. First decide what to promote. For each type of practice there are natural "gateways," those services or problems that people normally call you for. The other type of gateway is announcing a breakthrough or news. So don't mess with esoteric services since your responses will be fewer and farther between.

Step 2. Then you need a headline and visual to work together. The visual helps grab attention. Think of them as *one unit* to accomplish the task of telling readers *instantaneously what this is all about.*

This is where you should put a major portion of your creative effort. After all, most ads aren't even noticed. Then, of 100 ads whose headlines are read, only 25 are read completely. *Bad numbers.* So to make your numbers look good, work hard right here.

Headlines and visuals can give people information so they can *self-diagnose themselves into your practice.* Or can *choose you* over the competition. Study the examples of the outstanding ads in Figures 18.3, 18.4 and 18.5, and you'll see how the creators crafted their leads.

Are allergies making your life miserable?

If you're tired of sneezing, wheezing, headaches and coughing, now you can breathe a sigh of relief. Allergy Respiratory Medical Group has helped hundreds find lasting relief from allergies and other breathing disorders.

No more puffy eyes and runny nose. No more over the counter medications with more side effects than relief.

Come in for a $40 allergy screening, and find out what's causing the problem, and what can be done. It may be easier than you think.

Don't suffer another day. Call us.

ALLERGY SCREENING - $40

Major Insurance Accepted

James Orlowski, M.D.

Member: American Academy of Allergy and Clinical Immunology, American College of Allergy and Clinical Immunology On staff at St. John's Regional Medical Center

003

For $40, you'll learn what's causing your problem, and the best way to treat it. You'll also learn how to manage your problem on a daily basis.

Allergy Respiratory Medical Group

983-0771   451 W. Gonzales Road, Suite 150, Oxnard

Offer expires

Figure 18.3 Allergy Respiratory Medical Group Ad #1

Is asthma keeping your child from leading a normal life?

A child who suffers from asthma misses out on so much. You may think he'll grow out of it.

But, children don't always "just grow out of it." They may grow up to be adult asthmatics, unable to fully enjoy life.

At Allergy Respiratory Medical Group of Ventura County, pediatric asthma is our specialty. Our aggressive treatment plan allows kids to lead a regular life. Best of all, it helps turn kids into healthy, productive adults.

Call today for a special screening to see if we can put your child on the road to a normal life.

20% OFF INITIAL VISIT

Major Insurance Accepted

James Orlowski, M.D.

Member: American Academy of Allergy and Clinical Immunology, American College of Allergy and Clinical Immunology On staff at St. John's Regional Medical Center

© 1990 PBA

001

You'll learn what's causing your child's problem, and the best way to treat it. You'll also learn how to manage your child's problem on a daily basis.

Allergy Respiratory Medical Group

983-0771   451 W. Gonzales Road, Suite 150, Oxnard

Offer expires _____

Figure 18.4 Allergy Respiratory Medical Group Ad #2

Write 10 to 20 headlines and combine them with an equal number of visuals. The visual must always *work in concert* with the headline. Mix and match 'em. That's the way the best combinations emerge.

Sometimes you can use the headline as your main visual if you print it in large type. You can also reverse-out the headline. (A black area surrounds and outlines the headline so that type looks like its the color of the paper on black.) But don't reverse-out the entire ad. This reduces readership because of perceived eyestrain.

Step 3. Often, people don't know they need your services. They may not know what a podiatrist, CPA, or physical therapist does. Or they don't know what you can do for them. So telling them "if you need a podiatrist, call me," won't cut it.

Instead state a problem you treat. If they suffer from it, that's a good reason to call you. Quite often they don't even know if they have a

Do you or your child have any of these symptoms?

☐ Chronic allergies
☐ Nasal congestion
☐ Sinus trouble
☐ Constant cough

☐ Allergic reactions to food
☐ Frequent headaches
☐ Difficulty breathing

☐ Coughing or difficulty breathing during exercise
☐ Poor performance in school or work due to chronic illness

We can help.

At Allergy Respiratory Medical Group of Ventura County, breathing disorders are our specialty, and we're helping people breathe easier every day.
Whether it's a simple allergy or chronic asthma, we'll find out what's causing the problem, and prescribe the best treatment for it. Then, you can breath a sigh of relief.
Call today for a special allergy screening.

ALLERGY SCREENING - $40

Major Insurance Accepted

James Orlowski, M.D.

Member: American Academy of Allergy and Clinical Immunology, American College of Allergy and Clinical Immunology On staff at St. John's Regional Medical Center

© 1990 PBA   002

For $40, you'll learn what's causing the problem, and the best way to treat it. You'll also learn how to manage the problem on a daily basis.

Allergy Respiratory Medical Group

983-0771   451 W. Gonzales Road, Suite 150, Oxnard

Offer expires _____

Figure 18.5 Allergy Respiratory Medical Group Ad #3

specific problem. They only know if they have certain symptoms. For instance, their back hurts, their feelings hurt, their wallet hurts.

Therefore, provide a checklist so people know you deal with their symptoms. You can do this in the headline or in a box beside the body copy. The allergy checklist ad is a good execution of this concept since people rarely know if they have allergies.

Step 4. Answer the question of why people should choose you for their problem. The veterinarian ads provide three excellent reasons: (1) pickup and delivery service; (2) 24-hour emergency service; and (3) a "we care" claim. Look at Figures 18.6, 18.7 and 18.8.

Support the reasons with proof. On the caring claim, notice how they back it up with the doctors taking a personal interest in your pet, that they're happy to answer questions, and with 24-hour service. A naked "we care" statement would be simply unbelievable.

Figure 18.6 Willowdale Animal Hospital Ad #1

Step 5. Use an offer to get them to call now. Since people procrastinate, the offer gets them off their wallets and onto the phone. And the deadline makes them do it now. (See Figures 18.9, 18.10 and 18.11.)

Highlight the offer in the ad and at the bottom again. Use an "eyebrow" at the top as in the vet ads; put it in the headline and visual as in the eye exam ad; and in the body copy in the allergy ads. Notice how, when handled by a pro, the offer doesn't cheapen the practice's image.

Step 6. The ad's graphics are super important since they: (1) Create your image; and (2) Make it easy to read so people will.

FREE PET EXAM

Experience the advantage of 24 hour pet care.

When your pet is sick or injured, time is important. That's why, at Willowdale Animal Hospital, we're equipped to handle emergencies, 24 hours a day, 7 days a week.

1 There's always someone to answer the phone and answer your questions.

2. When your pet is sick at 3 am, a doctor will see you at 3 am.

3. When an overnight stay is required, your pet's condition is monitored and cared

for, by a doctor, 24 hours a day.

Day or night, we're here for you and your pet. You may not always need us at 3 am, but isn't it nice to know we're here when you do?

Call to schedule a free introductory pet exam for your dog or cat.

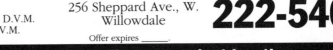

Willowdale
ANIMAL HOSPITAL

Day or night, we're here for your pet

John Catherwood, D.V.M.
Sheldon Jafine, D.V.M.

256 Sheppard Ave., W.
Willowdale

Offer expires _____.

222-5409

© PBA 1990

Call for our three other convenient locations.

Figure 18.7 Willowdale Animal Hospital Ad #2

To avoid looking dated, dowdy, retail, unprofessional, and schlocky, use graphic artists. (The newspaper's artists only know retail. Beware!) Real graphic artists pick professional-looking headline typefaces like the ones in the examples.

Use serif typefaces (ones with tails on the ends of letters) for body copy since they're easier to read in blocks of small type. Also, no more than two or three typefaces per ad—unless you want to run a fire sale.

Write short paragraphs for easy reading.

And don't have competing visual elements. One dominant element should grab your eye and tell you to start here. Two large elements compete and confuse.

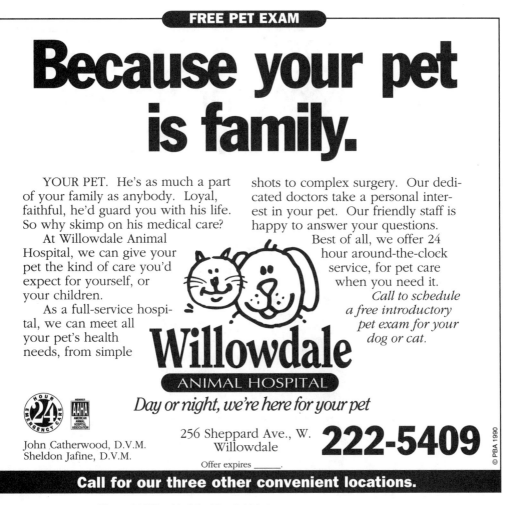

FREE PET EXAM

Because your pet is family.

YOUR PET. He's as much a part of your family as anybody. Loyal, faithful, he'd guard you with his life. So why skimp on his medical care?

At Willowdale Animal Hospital, we can give your pet the kind of care you'd expect for yourself, or your children.

As a full-service hospital, we can meet all your pet's health needs, from simple shots to complex surgery. Our dedicated doctors take a personal interest in your pet. Our friendly staff is happy to answer your questions.

Best of all, we offer 24 hour around-the-clock service, for pet care when you need it.

Call to schedule a free introductory pet exam for your dog or cat.

Willowdale
ANIMAL HOSPITAL
Day or night, we're here for your pet

John Catherwood, D.V.M.
Sheldon Jafine, D.V.M.

256 Sheppard Ave., W.
Willowdale
Offer expires _____.

222-5409

© PBA 1990

Call for our three other convenient locations.

Figure 18.8 Willowdale Animal Hospital Ad #3

All fulfillment information then goes at the bottom. Including your logo for visual continuity. Only convincing copy goes up top.

Watch out for appearing t-o-o-o-o professional. That usually means a *very quiet* ad and in the clutter of any newspaper that's suicide. Your ad's got to be noisy enough to turn heads—or at least eyes. If not, don't bother to play this game.

This doesn't mean gaudy or retail. It means eye-popping, like the examples.

Step 7. How big should your ad be? Good question. As big as it needs to tell your story—and no more. Commonly understood services like dental cleanings take little space while cosmetic dentistry take more.

Figure 18.9 Fashion Optiks Ad #1

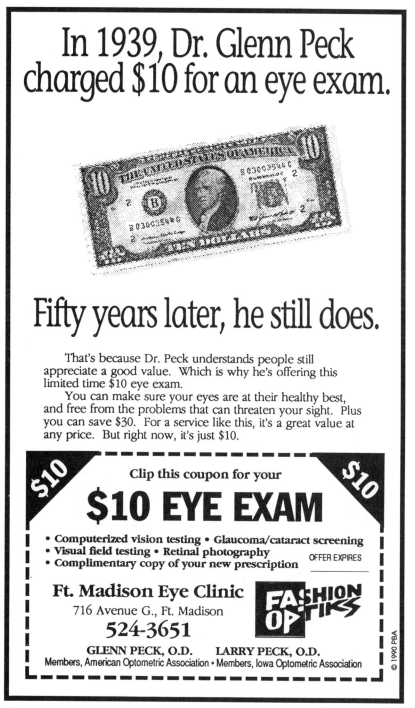

Figure 18.10 Fashion Optiks Ad #2

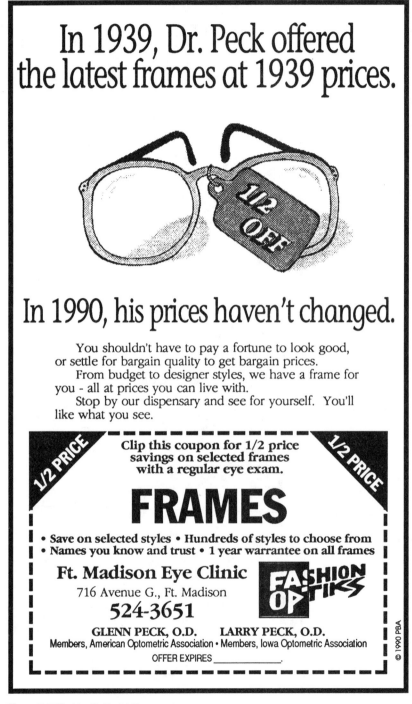

In 1939, Dr. Peck offered the latest frames at 1939 prices.

In 1990, his prices haven't changed.

You shouldn't have to pay a fortune to look good, or settle for bargain quality to get bargain prices.

From budget to designer styles, we have a frame for you - all at prices you can live with.

Stop by our dispensary and see for yourself. You'll like what you see.

1/2 PRICE   **1/2 PRICE**

Clip this coupon for 1/2 price savings on selected frames with a regular eye exam.

FRAMES

- Save on selected styles • Hundreds of styles to choose from
- Names you know and trust • 1 year warrantee on all frames

Ft. Madison Eye Clinic
716 Avenue G., Ft. Madison

524-3651

FASHION OPTIKS

GLENN PECK, O.D.   LARRY PECK, O.D.
Members, American Optometric Association • Members, Iowa Optometric Association

OFFER EXPIRES _____.

© 1990 PBA

Figure 18.11 Fashion Optiks Ad #3

As a guideline, you'll need at least eight to ten column-inches of space just to get noticed in the paper's clutter. (One column-inch is one column wide by one inch high. Four column-inches can be one column by four inches or two columns by two inches.) Fourteen to 15 column-inch ads are common.

More complex problems and services can take 18 to 21 column-inches. Rarely do you need more. Half- and full-page ads are usually a waste.

In an expensive paper, you can run small (two to three column-inch) ads just to generate leads. But these are better run after a larger and more attention-getting big brother appeared earlier.

Given a certain budget, the idea is to run as many times as possible with a large enough ad to convince.

Step 8. Don't create just one ad. Create a series of three or more.

You'll need different ads for different gateways into the practice. And some gateways will do better than others, so don't put all your ads in one basket.

Also, ads will burn out with overexposure. People will see them too often and stop responding. Your astute tracking will tell you when the party's over and you need a new ad. Since ads are easier to create all at once, have one or two in the wings. Otherwise you may take at least several weeks creating another winner and that means lost income.

Notice how a three-ad series has the same graphics and feel throughout, even though each ad promotes a different gateway. This is important in building recognition in your community.

Step 9. Allow yourself 60 days to get your ads together. It just takes that long to create good stuff.

You'll get an idea, write it down and play with it. After a few days you'll come back and redo it. And redo it and redo it again, getting better each time. Then the typesetting and layout takes time and so forth. So 60 days is safe and safe is better than sorry.

Step 10. Copyright all your ads. In this way your competitors will think twice before stealing it. Without C, your name, and year, your ads are not *your* ads ...

That's it. A bit more complex than most think. But if you don't follow the rules, the marketplace is extraordinarily unforgiving. It'll take your money and run.

☐ HOW MANY TIMES TO RUN AN AD BEFORE YOU KNOW IT'S A WINNER—OR LOSER

Psychotherapist R.M. had been running an ad for smoking cessation in the local newspaper twice a week for the last three months. As far as he could tell, not much was coming in. But he kept with it anyway.

The newspaper's saleswoman told him that you've got to repeat the ad for several months before people respond. Readers must feel comfortable with it and only then will the calls start coming. So R.M. waited, waited, and waited as his anxiety rose and cash dipped.

■ **No Long Tests.** If R.M. had included an offer with an expiration date in the ad along with the strong benefits of his service, then he'd have only run the ad about *four times.* This would be enough to give a definitive reading on whether it was a winner or loser.

Without the offer and expiration date, the ad becomes straight *name awareness* which takes deep pockets and a long run to make work. Of course salespeople tell you to keep spending. That's the way they make commissions. But if you run *name awareness* plus an offer, you'll test inexpensively and quickly.

☐ **WHICH *YELLOW PAGES* TO CHOOSE**

Yellow, Silver, Green, White, Better Business Bureau, Donnelly, U.S. West Direct, NYNEX, Bell, GTE, Lusky, United, National ... the only one who isn't competing for your directory business is the Harvard Lampoon. The $5,000 question is "With a limited budget, which one(s) do I choose for the best return?"

■ **Answer.**

1. First, choose the *Big Book,* whatever the big book is in your area. It's the one that people have been using for 70 years. Since old habits die hard, most of the walking fingers walk here.

2. *Community books:* If the Big Book covers a large area, the most often used community book makes a lot of sense. (If you don't know which one that is, survey your patients or clients.) If there's no community book at all, take a flyer on the first one out and track its results for a year.

3. *Copy cat books:* These books look like the Big Book. If they're virtually the same, pass on them—even if they come around to solicit you a month before the Big Book's rep, as they often do. If, however, they're *significantly* different and more advantageous to the consumer (e.g., they cover a smaller area), then you can test them for one year and track closely.

4. *White Pages:* Just your name in plain type. Since no one shops here, don't even spend 10 cents.

5. *Senior citizen books: If* they have large distribution and *if* you're willing to give a discount, test, track, and evaluate for one year. Results have been a mixed bag.

6. *Green pages:* This is a new directory for health care only. It's too new to have a proven track record, so test, track, and evaluate at your own risk. The key: Will the publisher distribute enough copies to make the idea work? Then will people use it?

7. *The talking Yellow Pages:* Also a relatively new concept but one with a beginning track record. The idea: You call to get three referrals in an area as well as information on any specials the referrals are running. The specials can be changed. The key: Will the publishers promote enough to convince people to use it? So far, the answer's been no. Of all the professionals we've surveyed, none report a bonanza. But the publishers' promotions are increasing so there's hope.

8. *All others: Pass.* Including any the Harvard Lampoon may publish.

PROMOTIONS IN MOTION

1. Chiropractor R.O. has been inserting a four-page, two-color, freestanding insert into his local newspaper to attract new patients. It's bold and garish—and it works. The reasons for its success are: (a) The market is low- to middle-income and very blue collar; (b) Few of his competitors are aggressive; (c) And its brash colors command attention. Without these conditions, the piece would fall flat.

   Freestanding inserts (FSI) are preprinted single or multi-page flyers inserted into a newspaper or shopper. They tend to get more response than the same ad printed in the paper. Experts can only guess that the separate sheets have to be handled individually and, therefore, are more visible than their buried cousins.

   They also cost more—2¢ to 4¢ per copy inserted *plus* printing. But the additional cost is usually more than compensated for by a larger response. How much larger? Only testing on a case-by-case basis can tell.

   Testing guide: FSIs are a particularly good test when you have a complex subject and you need room to explain and show it. Also when the case size is large. Make sure to include a direct response offer to track results.

2. Chiropractic physician M.G.'s *Yellow Pages* ad was third in his section. So he put a reversed-out burst atop to highlight this offer: "Cut out and bring us the two previous ads under this heading and get a free exam and free massage." (The massage was a 15-minute head and shoulders

varieties.) So if M.G. couldn't buy first position in the *Yellow Pages*, he got it with readers' help.

3. It wouldn't pay for dentist H.P. to buy a big *Yellow Pages* ad because he couldn't get close enough to the front of the section to make it pay. It's that treacherous. But he's cleverly discovered a way to leapfrog over 20+ pages of big-time *Yellow Pages* ads. He placed an ad in the section called *Dental Hygienists*.

This section immediately precedes Dentists in his *Yellow Pages*. It's true he can't promote *himself*, but he can promote his hygiene department under his hygienist's name, who happens to be in his office. Everything's kosher.

Even though H.P. can't promote himself directly, the ad works. It seems that the concept of forward location is so powerful, that some people will stop at the first ad *for their area* no matter what it says. Of course, if it's the right ad, the results will multiply by a megafactor, up to 20 times.

If you don't see a *Dental Hygienists* section, ask your directory. It's not shown because there aren't any ads in it right now. If they don't have such a section, ask if they'll create one. It's more money for them.

Chapter 19

A SECOND TAKE AT COUPONS—
THEY'RE NOW LEGITIMATE

□ COUPONS GAINING ACCEPTANCE

Veterinarian B.L. would never consider using them for his practice. In fact, his skin crawled at the thought of sending out coupons. They were unprofessional, unethical, *and* when his colleagues found out, their eyes would widen and they'd slowly shake their heads.

Besides, think of whom they'd attract. Nothing but problem people with little money. The headache producers of the world.

But business slowed so much, B.L. got scared. It was then that he re-evaluated his reluctance, which he'd caught from ivory tower profs and already successful practitioners who dominated his professional societies—both of whom weren't volunteering to pay his bills. In fact, business got so bad he figured he didn't have much to lose.

So he tried a Val-Pak Coupon. There were 13 other coupons in the envelope sent to the closest 10,000 residences. Bingo! Thirty-two calls; 21 new patients; $2,484 in immediate revenue; and a 5.5:1 immediate re-turn-on-investment (ROI).

But what about the type of clientele? Normal people. Teachers, secretaries, plumbers ... and, surprisingly, professional people. People with discretionary income. Of course, there were problems, but not any more than from the *Yellow Pages* or in general.

So B.L. did it again. And again. In different areas—and found out he could mail out to about four miles away from his office. And tested different offers—the $1 rabies shot and a free flea dip were both winners.

This was over two years ago and today B.L. mails out almost 250,000 coupons a year. Why? Because they work. In fact, coupons are one of the *fastest growing* external ways for professionals to market—second only to the *Yellow Pages*.

■ **How to's.** Coupons work for practically all professions and in all markets except the very rich. Prime are middle and middle-lower incomes, but middle-upper also works, especially in real-estate-rich, cash-poor communities.

The co-op coupon companies are best for getting coupons printed and delivered inexpensively. These franchises of national companies go under the name of Val-Pak, Money Mailer, and ADVO, but locals also abound. They're usually listed in the *Yellow Pages* under *Advertising-Direct Mail* or you can find them by asking local retailers who have been solicited by them.

These companies give exclusivity by profession and by area so you won't have competitors' coupons in your pack. Prices range from $350 to $550 per 10,000 printed and delivered. And a 4:1 immediate ROI or more is a real winner.

Not all coupon packs are equally read or responded to. So ROI varies. Therefore, you must *test various packs* in your area and use all that produce ROI winners.

Timing's also important. You'll notice that sometimes your coupon pulls well and other times poorly. The culprit may be an on-rushing competitor, but often it's seasonality. So make sure you track your historic seasonality to avoid slow times. (A plotted three-year average by month will graphically show you your high and low seasons.)

To which areas you can mail also varies by community and office. To find out, first mail in close to the office. If it doesn't work there, it won't work. When you have a winning coupon and pack, only then can you test farther out. Sometimes you can mail five miles away ... and sometimes two. It depends. Testing and tracking by area tells you everything.

■ **Killer Creative.** Coupons are a money-driven medium. And if you forget that, you automatically lose this game. No offer, no response. So lead with the offer printed *large* in the headline. (See Figure 19.1.)

Expand upon the offer in the copy. Tell them what it's normally

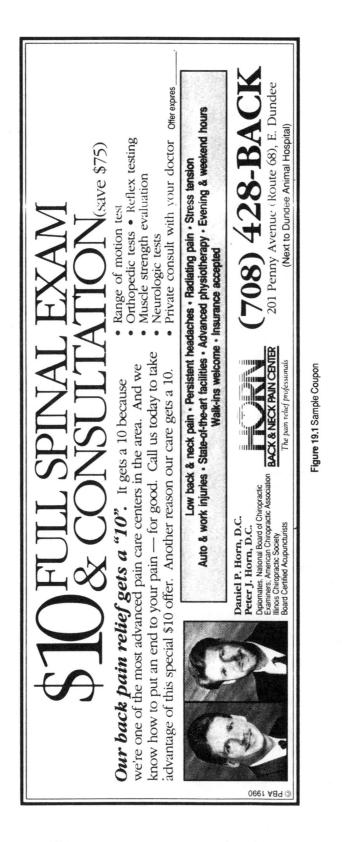

Figure 19.1 Sample Coupon

worth. Tell them all that's involved in the services they'll receive so they can appreciate the value. Tell them how good it is.

Then tell them whom it's for—by symptom so they can self-diagnose themselves into your office. If they already know this, skip this part.

Also tell them how good you are. Use mega-credentials. How many patients or clients you've helped. That famous or respected people use you. That you've been in the papers or on radio or TV. That you're an author or a professor. Or that you're a scholar and study in excess of what's required for relicensure.

And make sure they *like* you. Use a smiling, professionally taken photo. A personal quote. A caring tone. And/or warm graphics.

Add secondary benefits: extended hours; financing options; walk-ins or emergencies welcomed; insurance filled and filed; little or no waiting; and so forth.

Definitely use a deadline. People procrastinate otherwise and your ROI will look sleepy. Thirty days from the mail date is usually perfect.

If you're concerned that your existing patients or clients will take advantage of the offer and you'd lose money, mark *"For new patients only"* on the coupon. If existing patients or clients see this, rarely will someone get bent out of shape. If they do or try to use the coupon, have your front desk say, "Well, we're not suppose to do this, but for you, of course, we'll accept the coupon. But please don't tell anyone we're treating you so specially." No more problem.

■ **Testing to Find a Bigger Winner.** The offer is what initially attracts people's attention. If you've got the wrong offer, then you die (or at least your effort does). So the smart professional usually tests two different offers in successive months in the same pack. This controls enough variables to give you a fair reading.

Then roll out your winner. But every once in awhile, test a new offer. If you don't, you can't discover a bigger winner than you've already got.

You'll also discover that after awhile, your coupon's response rate will nosedive. Usually it's because people have seen the coupon so often they stop reading. Then you need a new coupon. Either a new offer and a new layout ... or a brand new way of expressing your existing offer. Either way can bring the response rate back up. It's not guaranteed, but test to find out.

■ **Results.** B.L. mails between 10,000 and 30,000 coupons per month in three different co-op coupon packs. The yearly ROI is 4.8:1, but the word-of-mouth and repeat business from new clients has helped boost the top line up 183% over two-and-a-half years.

"I was the last guy in the world you would suspect of trying this.

But I guess need is the mother of invention and I was needy. In retrospect, I'm glad things got as bad as they did or I never would have discovered this way of marketing."

☐ WINNING THE COUPON GAME

"While I'm still not crazy about them, it's pretty hard to feel too bad about 36 new patients last month from a $600 expenditure. Coupons work for me." But they won't work as well for everyone as they have for optometrist B.T. Here's what to think about.

1. Coupons work best in middle income to lower-middle income areas. They'll also work to a lesser extent in those upper-middle areas that are real estate rich and cash poor. Forget them in wealthier areas.

2. Coupons come in an envelope with several others from area merchants or as a stand-alone. The stand-alones obviously have less competition for attention, but can cost more. Which company (ADVO, Money Mailer, TriMark, Val-Pak, etc.) and which format work best are total unknowns and you must test each and track results. There's just too much inconsistency in results to generalize about them.

3. At the heart of any coupon is an offer. (If you won't use an offer, don't bother.) Different offers get different response rates so, again, testing's required. But by and large, you don't want to be the cheapest office around. That would require a high volume operation and stringent cost controls to protect thin margins. It's also difficult psychologically.

Instead, be the *best value*. A moderate offer plus strong non-monetary reasons to come to you equals beaucoup value. E.g., you're experienced, credentialled, famous, a teacher, author, better educated, more convenient, more caring, high tech, conservative, beauty-oriented, gentle, etc.

■ **Another danger:** If you just promote an offer, over time you become known as the cheap guy on the block. That doesn't have to happen if you just remember to promote a quality image at the same time.

4. Using coupons is like fishing with a big net. You cast out and haul in lots of fish. Then you've got to sort through them to discover the big fish you're going to keep. You and your staff must be mentally prepared for this process. Spend a little less time than normal in your screenings and don't worry about not converting everyone who comes in. Some are shoppers. That's fine because in order to get the big fish,

you need to see the guppies—the shoppers. No shoppers means no big fish.

Then analyze the effort in only one way—return on investment (ROI). Nothing else matters, not percentage response, not how many people called, not whether the staff likes it. Only $IN/$OUT. If you concentrate on your ROI and forget everything else, you'll avoid all the *emotionally based, profit-minimizing* decisions you'll want to make. *Caveat emotionalis!*

5. Coupons will work one time, then the next time they won't, then they will, etc. The uneven response is due to seasonality, whether a competitor mailed just ahead of you and the market hasn't replenished itself yet, the amount of competition, and 14 other unknown reasons. But don't stop mailing if one mail drop doesn't work. Chances are it will the next time.

Also make sure you change the look of your coupon and the offer every year or so. The public will stop reading it if they've seen it too often. Your ROI statistics will tell you when you need to change.

■ **Results.** Northwest veterinarian L.P. uses Val-Pak coupons four times a year in his blue-collar and low, white-collar, residential market. He includes a total of six separate offers for dogs, cats, horses, and exotics. "This way I have something for everyone. I mail 20,000 coupons each time at a cost of $800. I get about 50 responses and 40 new patients. During the first year with me, the average new client will spend about $100, so return on investment is $5 in for every $1 out."

□ **DO CO-OP COUPONS WORK IN UPSCALE MARKETS?**

Common wisdom says that co-op coupons don't work in middle-upper to upper income markets. They've historically worked in middle to middle-lower markets, but not as well once you crossed into wealthier areas. But things may be changing.

Several tests now show that real estate rich, cash poor communities may respond well. Also some older, middle-upper income areas as well. The upper income places still don't respond. So testing, tracking, and evaluating by your return-on-investment is the only way to find the truth.

If co-op coupons may be viable for your practice, ask local merchants which coupon companies operate in your area. There's usually ADVO, Val-Pak, and Money Mailer, but there may be more. You can also locate them in the *Yellow Pages* of a bigger city under "Advertising-Direct Mail."

☐ JOINT PROMOTION CUTS COSTS & BOOSTS RESPONSE

Podiatrist F.R. couldn't get into the local Val-Pak co-op coupon package. Another podiatrist had already taken its exclusivity. When he went to ADVO, the story was the same. F.R. knew he needed new patients, he knew co-op coupons worked in middle-class markets, but how could he make it happen?

If you can't join 'em, beat 'em. So F.R. decided to start his own co-op coupon group. Quarterly, they'd mail out a "Health Care Savings" envelope to 20,000 area homes. With design costs, printing, postage, labels, and mailing services, it would run about $24,000 for the year.

To share the cost, F.R. wisely called a dentist and a chiropractor who he knew promoted externally. They then recommended a general physician, optometrist, and veterinarian for the group. Everyone committed for a year (complete with promissory notes) so the cost dropped to $4,000 apiece or $1,000 every three months.

■ **Results.** On the first mail drop, F.R. got 37 calls, 26 appointments, several surgeries, and a 9.38:1 return-on-investment—all within 90 days. That's about twice as good as the average ROI for a co-op coupon drop. The rest of the group got mixed results. The DC, OD, and DDS did very well, too. The DVM acceptable. And the MD broke even. In this case, the suspicion rests with what the MD promoted on his coupon and less with the packet.

Then other professionals who received the packet at home called to join. The group added a CPA, a hypnotherapist for smoking cessation and weight control, an obstetrician-gynecologist, and a personal injury attorney.

Their new advertising coordinator then changed the envelope to read "Big Savings on all Professional Services." Plus she added a list of criteria that professionals must meet to join the group and put them right on the envelope so people would have more confidence. Since the packet now appealed to a wider spectrum, it got more readership and response. And with more professionals participating, each was able to cut his or her investment and actually mail to 10,000 more homes.

☐ CO-OP COUPON ANALYSES: MAKING THE PROFESSIONAL LIKEABLE

Figures 19.2 and 19.3 show two similar co-op coupons, but there are significant differences. The first is that one has a headline that explains the savings available in the offers. The other doesn't. In fact, the other uses the name of the practice as the headline, a cardinal sin because it's meaningless to new patrons and doesn't get a prospect to read further.

The second is that the coupon with the real headline makes the

Figure 19.2 McDonald Animal Hospital Coupon

Figure 19.3 South Laguna Village Animal Hospital

professional likeable. The subhead talks of concerned pet care and the photo nicely supports it. The other one gives no reasons to like or trust the practitioner. Therefore, if this "Free-Free-Free" promotion is repeated often, this professional will become known solely as "The Deal Guy."

Lesson: Always imbue offers with strong nonmonetary reasons to come to you.

PROMOTIONS IN MOTION

Podiatrist K.J. is using *free-standing* coupons from ADVO at 5.5¢ each (delivered) to prospect for new patients. These are the ones with the picture of the missing child on the front and a coupon on the back. Tacky? The public apparently doesn't think so since it gave him a 12:1 return.

These separately delivered coupons get more response than those which come 20 to an envelope and can also be mailed anytime. Plus they're a lot less expensive than postcard postage.

Chapter 20 ☐

NOT FOR THE FAINT-HEARTED:
RADIO AND TELEVISION ADVERTISING

☐ **WHERE YOU CAN USE TV AND/OR RADIO**

Even though his office was located on Long Island, a gutsy podiatrist tried to advertise on television in the New York market with just $5,000 a month. His results: a handful of limping patients or clients, but not enough to pay for all the wasted coverage he bought in this most expensive of U.S. TV markets.

On the other hand, for the same investment a smart chiropractic physician dominates the Anchorage TV market.

When can you use *radio or TV?* When the market is ...

- small (therefore affordable)
- stand-alone and not under the media umbrella of a large city market
- one in which your office is *convenient* to most people in that market

Since TV spots are here and gone in 30 seconds and radio spots vanish in 60, a professional must buy a ton to make them work. A small buy—even if it's a test—never works.

Then you must be able to draw from most of the market's area so you aren't buying wasted exposure. If your office is off to one side of the market's area, you can still use radio or TV but you'd better buy a bigger ton of spots to make up for the diminished draw. To counteract this, you can form a consortium of non-competing colleagues to share the cost and buy the lesser amount.

So markets like Midland/Odessa, Texas; Chico, California; North Platte, Maine; Lima, Ohio; Altoona, Pennsylvania; Bangor, Maine; and Dothan, Alabama are prime electronic media places. They meet all the criteria and the competition is usually laid back.

The suburbs of New York, Los Angeles, Washington, D.C., San Francisco, Chicago, Atlanta, Boston, and the like are the *worst* places to use electronic media. Big city media is too expensive, and at the same time it delivers too much wasted coverage. And little local stations in suburbia have few listeners or viewers and only exist because local businesses need an affordable place to advertise. Since advertisers rarely track, these local boys aren't held accountable for their inability to produce.

So be wise ... or be poor.

■ **Radio or TV?** If you're in a market that makes sense for electronic media, then which one? Each case is different, so weigh the advantages and disadvantages. With either remember to have your office open or operators waiting to schedule a large number of calls when the spot runs, because few people will call back if they can't get through right then.

Radio's pros and cons: (1) Can change copy quickly, especially if it's announcer read; (2) usually cheaper per spot than TV—but sometimes not by much; (3) usually there are more radio than TV stations so you must buy more of them to reach the same number of people; (4) can't show visual impact (befores & afters), so copy must paint powerful visual images; (5) can reach working people well with morning drive-time spots.

TV's pros and cons: (1) Nothing can convince as well as TV because of its visual impact.; (2) can generate large number of leads quickly, but also more low quality prospects which must then be weeded out; (3) more costly per spot to run; (4) more costly to produce spots than on radio; (5) high involvement shows like news, sports, talk, and game shows produce fewest responses even though they may have big audiences; lower involvement shows where people can pull themselves away to call are better.

With either medium, buy by the numbers. From the stations request Arbitron (radio) or Nielson (TV) ratings by time of day or show, and their type of audience by age and sex. Then you'll know how many of which type of people are paying attention to that station at that time of day.

Then figure the cost of one spot to reach 1,000 of your *prime market segment* (e.g., females, 24 to 49 years old). With these cost per thousand figures, you can now compare which stations are giving you the best buys. Remember to bargain ferociously because if you don't, they're going to chew you up and spit you out. They expect you to bargain hard.

☐ PUBLIC SERVICE RADIO SPOTS TOO SOFT FOR BIG RESPONSE

Psychologist G.F. bought a canned, public service radio campaign with nifty informational blurbs. "Very professional," he thought. He tried to convince two local radio stations to air them for free. But they're inundated with similar requests so G.F. had to pay for the twice daily, 90 seconds of air time.

His money lasted one month and while he got a few calls and a couple of patients, the costs were too high for the return so he cashed in his remaining chips. ROI was only 1:1.

■ Economics to Blame. While some companies sell prewritten, editorial ads for professionals to run in their local papers, there are now some selling the same format for radio. The problem is that the newspaper ads haven't work and neither do their radio sound-alikes.

The reasons go back to the economics of the *Name Awareness* type of advertising. *Name Awareness* typically requires an inordinate amount of repetition before people respond.

Eventually they will—*if* the advertising is great. (They never will if it isn't.)

This means a big and long outlay of cash to see the crop come in. So you can play this game only if you have *deep pockets.* How deep depends upon how often you run the spots, what stations you choose, how many stations you air them on, how many people are listening, what times of day they air, what the competition is doing, and so forth.

The newspaper versions can take six months and often longer to produce results. The radio versions work faster since radio is more intrusive, but it's also more expensive.

There's another problem. Namely that people seem to take public service information in and forget the sponsor's name. They just don't put any energy into remembering it. And why should they? There's nothing in it for them. Therefore, public service sponsorships require *extra* repetitions of the message to get the sponsor remembered. And that means a bigger budget and a longer payback period.

What makes more sense is the following Direct Response formula. First state a problem complete with symptoms so people can identify with them and self-diagnose.

Second, describe how *you* provide the solution to it. This should be explained in such a way so that people can't or won't want to go anywhere else for the answer. It differentiates you. Never describe the solution in terms of how the profession as a whole does it. This creates the idea that any old body in your field will do.

And finally, to increase response and hasten it, offer people a bite-size piece of service at a low cost to try you. Set an expiration date for the offer. This gets them in now.

This formula obviates the need for a lengthy radio campaign before knowing whether your spots are motivating. There's nothing worse than underwriting a whole *Name Awareness* campaign, only to discover afterwards the ads were rotten and incapable of producing. The *Direct Response* formula gives you immediate feedback.

Name Awareness is a sucker's play. It makes the professional fe-e-e-e-el good. It just doesn't make the public fe-e-e-e-el good enough to respond in big numbers.

☐ HOW TO GET INTERVIEWED ON RADIO

Most radio stations run "public affairs" programming that consists of daily or weekly interviews with personalities on topics of community interest. Professional services rank high on the interest list.

Your first step to becoming an "on air" personality is to create a mailing list of radio stations and their public affairs program directors. Get the address and phone number of each station from the phone book. Call to get the public affairs director's name and the name of the program.

■ **Next Step.** Write a pitch letter to the director about a specific topic that would be informative to the community over a staff member's signature. Five working days after mailing, have the staff member phone each program director and ask if there's interest in scheduling you.

Candice Caruthers, contributing producer of "Good Morning, America!" advises stating in your letter that the writer will telephone. "That makes me stop and think right then about whether we are interested or not." When she gets the call, she's better prepared to say yes, no or maybe and to discuss the maybe.

■ **Sample "Pitch" Letter**

John Smith
KNTN Radio
100 Center Drive
Pleasantville, CA 90001

Dear Mr. Smith:

Work loss, as it relates to both men and women, is a concern among employers who pay for lost time, insurance premiums, and lost productivity. Among female employees, premenstrual syndrome (PMS) is a natural, cyclical function that affects their lives to varying degrees. In many cases, as it is now proven, PMS contributes to loss of productivity and time on the job.

According to a recent article in *The Business Journal*, "PMS is responsible for an estimated 8% of the work loss in the United States. Many women who suffer from moderate to severe PMS find their lives so disrupted by fatigue, memory loss, confusion, mood swings, and irritability that their work is affected—and men affected by their wives' PMS may find that their productivity at work is altered as well."

As a pioneer in the treatment of PMS symptoms, Dr. Joseph Jones, OB/Gyn, provides unique solutions to the problems of PMS. His comprehensive program has a proven 91% success rate.

An interview with Dr. Jones would be both educational and informative for your listening audience. I'll contact you in five days to see if you feel you would like to schedule Dr. Jones.

Best regards,

Ms. Staff Member

Normally, stations appreciate it if you prepare a list of questions. This also gives you a method to practice your interview. Then watch the business roll in.

Suggestion: Ask the radio station for a tape copy of your interview (or have someone tape it for you) so you can use it for future reference. Also to spruce up your presentation.

Laine Medina, Medina & Associates, 15922 Pacific Coast Highway, Suite 213, Huntington Beach, CA 92649, (213) 592-2521

☐ RADIO SPOT ANALYSIS: DECIDING THE PURPOSE

Any ad or spot needs to accomplish one job and one job only. Whatever that sole job is, if it's clear in your mind, then you're more likely to accomplish it.

Most ads or spots want the reader or listener to call. That's it. If the practice gets them on the phone, it can usually get them in. The problem is getting them to call. Therefore the ad's only purpose is to generate a call, not necessarily to sell services.

Note how all this radio spot wants you to do is call for information. And it tells you to call how many times!?!

■ 60-Second Radio Spot

To help an alcoholic, you have to become a better friend than the bottle's been. And that's not as easy as it sounds. Because people who need help with alcohol, or any other drug, tend to resist help—especially from their closest friends and family, especially at the earliest stages.

Dr. Solomon is one of the real pioneers in the research and treatment of alcohol and drug dependency. And Dr. Solomon and his associates can help you.

If someone close to you seems on the edge of alcohol or drug dependency, call Dr. Solomon's office for free, confidential advice. You don't have to mention the person's name, or your name. Just call.

To help an alcoholic, you have to become a better friend than the bottle's been. And the first step is to call.

Dr. Solomon's free, confidential advice number is 466-6000. 466-6000. Call now. 466-6000.

☐ RADIO TIP: GETTING WHAT YOU PAID FOR

Of every 20 radio spots you buy, one will be aired incorrectly. Sometimes they'll play only part of the spot, so the whole thing is wasted. Or they'll air it at 3:15 A.M. instead of P.M. Mistakes are especially true of small stations, but even large ones royally screw up.

So to make sure you get what you paid for, request an accounting of exactly when your spots aired. You'll usually find mistakes. And ask for a tape copy of the actual airing so you can hear if they did you a dirty.

If the station erred in any way, request a "make-good." This is a free replay of your spot. They may initially say no just as a matter of course, but insist and they'll usually do it. They do it everyday.

☐ HOW TO USE CABLE TV

True, cable TV is growing and the networks are shrinking. And true it's cheap. But these don't automatically make cable the right avenue for you.

Cable's a tricky medium. The problem stems from the fact that there are so many channels with more coming on line all the time. Consequently, the cable market is extremely fractionated—few people are watching any one cable station at any one time. Even though the cable company tells you thousands of homes have a channel hooked up, there's no existing measurement of how many people actually watch a specific cable channel.

So how do you avoid paying cheap rates for something that won't work? There are two ways and these are predicated on two concepts. One is that you can reach and convince a great number of people to call in 30- or 60- second commercials. This is the great reach theory where you look for a needle in a haystack but don't spend the money for the time to convince them thoroughly.

The second concept is that you can buy very little reach, but because rates are inexpensive, you can buy big chunks of time. So your 15- or 30-minute "program" can now convince a greater percentage of those few watching.

If you play the *big reach-short commercial* game, then buy the highest rated cable stations around. This usually means a combination buy of CNN, CNN Headline News, ESPN, and USA. With enough frequency, these will give you plenty of market penetration.

If you play the *limited reach-long commercial* game, then you'll buy low-rated, local cable stations. And on these, you'll run a 15- to 30-minute "program." The usual format calls for you to be interviewed by a professional who knows how to bring out the best in you. Oftentimes, there are before-and-after-photos of your work and/or testimonials by ecstatic patients or clients. Sometimes, interspersed within the program are short commercials for the practice. By keeping the editorial and commercials separate, you increase the credibility and the response rate.

You still need some reach with this format so you must repeat your program often. One last word of advice on this format: If you're not a dynamic TV presence, forget it.

Production costs on this format are obviously higher and run between $2,500 and $10,000, depending on quality of talent and length. Production costs on 30- or 60- second spots can be minimal if you can talk the cable company into doing the production for free or at a cut rate. In all cases, for increased response have your spots contain some direct response offer: free information, free or low-cost consultation, free care kit, free booklet, etc.

Both formats can work, but as you see, cable's tricky. What you want to avoid at all costs is the trap most professionals fall into. *Namely, buying 30- or 60- second spots on low-rated, local cable stations.* This is the allure of the super cheap buy. And it's the one that never works.

☐ AD TIP: HOT TV

TV is a tough medium ... and highly productive for many, many professionals. Usually a professional opts for standard 30-second spots on one or more stations without a lot of thought or understanding of how TV works. So here are some guidelines for those interested in TV with guile.

1. Try to buy a few 60-second spots. Sixties give you enough time to do a complete presentation and get people to call, while it's tougher with 30s. So consider buying some 60s to run periodically with your 30s. They'll increase the response rate to your shorter spots.

2. Sixties don't necessarily cost twice as much as 30s. Oftentimes, they cost just 40% more—depending on your negotiating skill. Also while negotiating, get the station to throw in a ton of ten-second spots for free. You can get 20% more total media from these 10s for free if you bargain hard. But remember, the 10s won't work without their bigger brothers.

3. Buy your 60s and 30s in fixed times to hit a specific market watching a specific program. The 10s can be scheduled ROS or Run Of Station. That means anytime as long as it's not late night.

4. Buy a minimum of 125 gross rating points per station per week; 150 is better. This means 125% to 150% of the entire station's weekly audience will see your spots on that station. (This normally equates to 15 to 18 weekly spots scheduled mornings and middays on weekdays, the most likely buying times.) This is enough repetition to make them work. If you don't want to buy this much, reconsider TV. Electronic media is so fleeting that buying tonnage is necessary.

5. To keep production costs down, shoot sixty-second spots and edit them down into 30s and 10s. Don't shoot separate 30s and 10s.

☐ WHEN TO USE JINGLES TO PROMOTE A PRACTICE

"Jingles are the bells and whistles of promotion," says Cynthia Berryman, Creative Director of The Practice Builder Agency. So only once in awhile are they appropriate for a professional practice.

"By their very nature, jingles are light-hearted," she explains. "But we deal in *life's problems*, many of which are quite serious. In certain circumstances, you can make light of them, but this must be done carefully by a pro or else the professional's image would suffer greatly, especially since you're using fast-acting, high-profile electronic media."

Berryman suggests jingles can be used on radio or TV only when: (1) The service isn't considered very serious, but yet it's necessary, such as a dental check-up; or (2) the market is middle-lower or lower income.

And when you use one, it better be *cute* to be remembered and work.

■ **Example:** Written by Cynthia Berryman and sung to the tune of "The Boogie Woogie Bugle Boy of Company B."

Dogs that have long ears
Dogs with waggily tails
Dogs that climb up trees

And run through the dales.
He likes their company
He checks their anatomy
He's the bowzer wowzer doggie doc from Washington, DC.

Spaniels, setters, greyhounds,
poodles, pugs, cockapoos,
labradors and shepherds,
collies and terriers, too.

He likes their company
He checks their anatomy
He's the bowzer wowzer doggie doc from Washington, DC.

ANNOUNCER READ AS BACKGROUND INSTRUMENTAL CONTINUES:
Dr. Herman Shepherd has been taking care of dogs all his life.
From his high school days...
when he volunteered time at the animal shelter...
to now...
treating the medical needs of Washington's top dogs.
Dr. Shepherd has earned his reputation...
a reputation of generous, kind care...
and care that employs the most sophisticated medical knowledge.
Warm blanketed beds, not concrete kennels...
24-hour watch for seriously ill or injured pets...
Playful exercise for pets visiting while the family's away...
Isolation for contagious pets to ensure our other patients' health...
And pampering from a staff that knows how to love pets as much as
they know how to care for them.

[Jingle begins again]
He likes their company
He checks their anatomy
He's the bowzer wowzer doggie doc from Washington, DC.
[Voice over] Call 777-PETS for your appointment.
Dr. Herman Shepherd
Pet care for your top dog...or lap cat.
Call 777-PETS. That's 777-PETS.

■ **Jingle Concepts.** The tune catches attention by being unusual. The words position the professional, repeating that position over and over. Oftentimes, there's a direct response offer with a deadline to respond to now. And the phone number's repeated three times and it being the last thing said.

PROMOTIONS IN MOTION

1. Dentist T.O. knows that to gain referrals, you need to be perceived as an expert. And then to repeat the message again and again. So he became an instant expert by buying a radio show—cheaply. Late at night, during the cheapest time he could find, T.O. bought a 60-second radio spot.

   But instead of a commercial, he put on "Dental Update"—a public information show that sounds like it's being brought to you by the station. So he gets the implied *endorsement* of the station and becomes an instant celebrity. Not among the public because hardly anyone listens late at night to this low-powered station. But among his patients to whom he sends a monthly postcard announcing the "show" and this month's topics.

   The radio endorsement makes him an expert worthy of referrals. The monthly postcard mailing provides the repetition, as does office hand-outs and promotion within his quarterly Internal Prospecting direct mail packages to patients. Very smart, cheap, and easy.

2. Chiropractor K.S. has evening hours during the week. But with three doctors, he usually has empty slots. So to fill them, he went to radio—in an unusual way. He runs 60-second spots just in the late afternoon and early evening—with the spots promoting his evening hours. A super-success because of people's impulse for a convenient quick fix.

3. Physician E.L. lives and works in a small Georgia city in which he advertises on TV to reach his retirement age target. And what's his best time to air spots for the greatest response? At noon weekdays, sponsoring the midday news.

4. Physician H.S. promoted a seminar on Epstein-Barr Syndrome. Forty-five people came and 17 became patients. (Only three actually had the yuppie disease.) What's interesting here is the testing and success of a new seminar topic...and the use of Christian radio to promote it.

   Christian radio has high listener involvement. And because a good portion of the audience is older, health care does well. Actually any professional service does just fine—given the right radio spot—because of the intensity of belief in the station.

5. Audiologist J.L. bought one hour of TV time on a small, Texas, non-cable independent for a call-in talk show that the station produced. Then to make the sale, the TV station also threw in 10,000 door hanger flyers, printed and distributed. His total cost was $2,000 and his return-on-investment over 10:1. The credibility of a talk show format made the whole thing work. And the adding of a second medium for free sweetened the pie.

6. Ophthalmologist B.D. runs TV spots to attract cataract prospects in his small, affordable market. Over the past two years of experimenting, he's discovered that the noon news pulls the most prospects. More discoveries: That he can get free 15-second booster spots if he bargains right. And that split 30-second and 60-second spots work well. (These are two 15- or 30-second spots run within the same commercial time out during a program but have another sponsor's spot run between them. They're bought, however, as a 30- or 60-second unit for economy sake.)

    And more findings: Running the ads on a fixed schedule pulls better than a random one because specific TV programs outperform others. And that a TV spot to attract the ignored diabetic market works very well.

7. Dentist S.J. runs TV ads in his small, stand-alone, Midwest market. But after the first return-on-investment analysis, he was ready to can the whole effort. Lucky for him he also analyzed his *Yellow Pages* ROI at the same time. There S.J. discovered a big jump in production and when he put the TV with it, the two together were highly profitable. One obviously boosted the other.

    So if you run TV, make sure you analyze your *Yellow Pages* with it. And show your logo in both to better make the connection.

Chapter 21

PROPELLING GROWTH WITH EXTRA-SPECIAL PROMOTIONAL TOOLS

□ FREE SEMINARS GENERATE UP TO 250 NEW PATIENTS OR CLIENTS PER YEAR

S.F. looked out over the audience. Tonight's count was 23, an average crowd for his *public service* seminar "The Newest Techniques to Cure Chronic Back and Neck Pain without Pills or Surgery." Before he spoke, he already knew he would convert about ten into patients, either directly or through referrals. At an average case of $1,000, that would be $10,000 gross, less the $75 cost of the room, less the $1,780 cost of seminar promotion, to give an $8,145 clean bottom line. He did this twice a month.

The seminar game is profitable—if you have a modicum of stage presence. But if you don't inspire, your efforts will expire without a handsome return.

Why do they work so well? (1) They let people see what they're getting before they commit. (2) They create the aura of being an expert, so patients or clients refer more. (3) Seminar promotion generates recognition which translates into increased *Yellow Pages* responses.

■ **The Seminar Equation.** Like all promotion, success here depends on an equation of variables. Screw up one variable and you screw up the results. For instance, the topic is the biggest variable. Seminars are prime for *elective services* of any kind, e.g., cosmetic dentistry, RKs, anything financial. Or anything *complex,* e.g., psychological problems. Putting the big benefit of the seminar in the title is also crucial. Adding "New" in the title inevitably boosts response.

Location is obviously important. As local as possible, please. Also, holding your seminar in a library, or a room rented out by a local bank, savings institution, utility company, or local government adds lots of credibility and a pseudo-endorsement.

Making your seminar free is almost a must. Remember, this is a numbers game. We want to turn out big numbers and *then* identify prime prospects—not the other way around.

To help convert attendees into paying patients or clients, handout a strong sales piece at the seminar—your "selling" practice brochure—not a low key, nonmotivating patient pamphlet. It reinforces their impression when they get home and you're no longer in the room. Also helpful: a seminar attendee certificate good for a free consultation in your office.

Since this is like looking for a needle in a haystack, newspaper is the vehicle of choice. Ads within the paper or free-standing, preprinted announcements machine inserted into the paper are best. For a really big turnout, add a burst of radio, but only if affordable. Start promoting two weeks prior to the seminar night. Run twice in the Sunday paper prior to the night, and also the two days prior. If daily papers are not available, use an insert in the weeklies. (See Figure 21.1.)

■ **Results.** Optometrist R.R. promotes a monthly seminar on how to detect if a visually related disability is the real reason your child is doing poorly in school. Average conversion: three spending $2,000 each out of 12 attending. Cosmetic dentist V.F. harvested 63 new patients last year from six local seminars, which she reports were underpromoted.

☐ SEMINAR PROMOTION TIPS

Who uses seminars to generate leads for high-ticket services? Lots of professionals: cosmetic surgeon; radial keratotomy surgeons; cosmetic dentists; CPAs looking for new clients; chiropractors; PI attorneys looking for referrals from DCs, MDs, and DOs; estate planning attorneys; psychotherapists; hypnotherapists; equine and bovine vets; and many more. If seminars are on your game plan, then study these tips to refine your promotion and boost your response.

1. Use direct mail *if* you can find a highly targeted mailing list for your locale through your list broker. That means a list of prospects who have somehow *indicated an interest* in your service: buying a book;

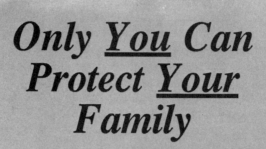

Only *You* Can Protect *Your* Family

JAMES A. HUMPHREYS, JR.
LAW FIRM OF HUMPHREYS & BROWN

GET THE FACTS
Regarding Wills, Trusts and Conservatorships
From A Leading Estate
Planning Specialist

Learn How To
AVOID PROBATE
MINIMIZE TAXES

*Come and
Bring a
Friend*

FREE
Seminars

WEDNESDAY
January 20, 1988
California Federal
Savings & Loan
24264 El Toro Road
Laguna Hills
1:30 p.m. - 3:00 p.m.

THURSDAY
January 21, 1988
Laguna Beach Library
363 Glenneyre
Laguna Beach
10:30 a.m. - Noon

JAMES A. HUMPHREYS JR., ATTY.

TUESDAY
January 26, 1988
Holiday Inn
25205 La Paz Road
Laguna Hills
7:00 p.m. - 8:30 p.m.

THURSDAY
January 28, 1988
California Federal
Savings & Loan
31872 Del Obispo
San Juan Capistrano
1:30 p.m. - 3:00 p.m.

CALL 581-6300 TODAY
Reserve Free Seating & Seminar Materials

Figure 21.1 Humphreys Ad

subscribing to a magazine; attending a health or business fair; purchasing a mail order product to accomplish what your service will; etc.

2. If you test direct mail, mail twice. The second will pull one-third to one-half of the first.

3. Start your first mailing three to four weeks ahead of time. The second mailing then goes out two weeks prior to the event.

4. Hold seminars early in the week: Monday or Tuesday nights get the highest attendance. Late in the week is poor.

5. If you can't find a highly targeted and responsive list—and your market is literate, high income or over 40—run a newspaper ad on the previous two Sundays and the day before the seminar.

6. Also test a freestanding insert instead of an ad. They cost more, but get more.

7. In copywriting, avoid giving many options. Testimonials work. What-you-will-learn benefits are better than an agenda. Include an act-now incentive. A premium is better than any discount.

8. Sell books, tapes, etc. at the back of the room. Those who won't buy your service will buy these instead. Can increase income greatly.

9. Seminars sponsored by colleges, trade organizations, clubs, non-profits, etc. carry credibility. Also, they do the promotion and logistics. Explore the concept, but usually there's too much bureaucracy, long lead times, and they're not repeatable often enough.

10. Watch out for conflicting events: public, religious and local holidays, major sporting events, low season (December).

11. Evaluate by return-on-investment only. That's total dollars in total cost. Include all revenue you'll realize within the first 12 months. In the cost, remember to include the media, room, refreshments, and labor. Four+:1 = Winner. 3:1 = Success. 2:1 = Marginal. 1:1 = Loser.

☐ CONVERTING SEMINAR ATTENDEES

Northeast ophthalmologist M.R. held four free radial keratotomy seminars open to the public. His advertising for these generated an average attendance of 48 pairs of eyes. He congratulated himself until his analysis showed only two attendees per seminar converted into exams to determine if they were good R.K. candidates.

Seeking a much better return on investment, he decided to offer a free screening exam instead of charging his usual $50.

■ **Results.** In the next seminar with 61 attendees, 27 took advantage of his offer. Then 13 eventually converted into surgeries at $2,800 each.

■ **Strategy.** When you lower the risk to the prospect, you increase the response. But you also lower the quality of respondents. So test charging fees where you can, but if response is underwhelming, lower their risk by lowering their cost.

☐ RESTAURANT SEMINARS ATTRACT BIG FISH

Chiropractor N.B. spends $6.95 apiece to attract a steady stream of new patients into the practice. This is what a fish dinner costs him to reach a prospect with his seminar on chiropractic.

When you go into the local fish restaurant near N.B.'s office, you see a poster announcing a *free* fish dinner every Monday night along with a talk by Dr. N.B. on how chiropractic cures back, neck, leg, shoulder, and head pain and decreases daily stress. On each table you also discover a table tent announcement about the program.

The restaurant loves it because Monday night is by far its slowest night and the promotion fills the restaurant with an average of 34 people. In exchange for the volume, they give N.B. $2.00 off each dinner.

N.B. loves it because it gives him a captive audience from which he converts about 8% into patients. Since his average case size is $927, the return-on-investment runs 10.7 to 1. On good weeks it jumps as high as 24 to 1. And the restaurant does all the promotion.

Plus, people love it because in this middle to middle-lower market, everyone enjoys a free meal at a favorite restaurant.

This is only viable if the professional has a good presentation manner. If so, it's a *win-win-win* situation.

☐ INTERNAL MARKETING WITH AN ELECTRONIC MESSAGES CENTER OR EDUCATING AND PROMOTING IN THE RECEPTION AREA

■ **The Problem.** You provide several different services but your patients or clients don't know about them. They came to you for one reason only, and don't know you can help them in other ways. And they certainly can't refer in friends and family for unknown services. All this while you're running around like a chicken with his head cut off without the time to inform every person personally about what you do.

■ **The Solution.** What you can't do personally, do electronically. Today there are electronic message centers or bars that display any information you want as a moving message. They're small and suitable for waiting rooms.

■ **The Concept.** Don't just put promotional messages on your center. Make it into an *educational message center*. Share with patients or clients important reminders, new discoveries, ideas and products, or those under development in your field. People will pay much more attention to the center if they perceive they'll learn something important.

Then, intersperse your promotional messages among the educational ones. They'll be more receptive to them. The correct balance: two educational messages for each promotional one.

Want ideas? Here's your list:

1. *Announcing new services:* Your message center tells everyone about your recently gained expertise and new service—without you taking the time. Examples: dieting guidance; smoking control.

2. *Reminders:* Checkups, prevention, chiropractic treatments for ailments other than back pain.

3. *Breakthrough products:* New contact lenses. TMJ treatments. New orthotics.

4. *Recommended products:* What you stock and why.

5. *Seasonal promotions:* Sunglasses. Back to school checkups.

6. *Special events:* Patient or Community Appreciation Day, or your Open House.

7. *Asking for referrals:* Your silent assistant does the job quietly and effectively: "We very much appreciate your referrals. You can be certain they'll be treated with our best efforts to justify the faith you've placed in us. I assure you you'll feel good about it."

8. *Publicizing yourself:* Announce your latest published article or upcoming speeches, radio or TV talk shows, or those you've just done. These mean you're an expert. Tell people about the conference you just went to and what you learned. This means you're studious and current. Your message center lets everyone know.

9. *Welcoming new patients or clients:* Recognition strengthens the bond between you and your clientele. And people just love to see their name in lights.

10. *Displaying testimonials:* Historically effective, testimonial displays with your patients or clients' words of what you've done for them tell your new clientele they've come to the right place.

11. *New equipment:* If you've got it, flaunt it. But if your electronic message center doesn't tell them, how can they be impressed.

12. *Mall Location.* Use your message center in your mall window. Everyone will see it. And the right messages will bring them in.

■ **Specifications, Availability, Price.** Easily programmable, electronic message centers have lots of room for three to five minutes of messages. Also, the moving message rivets the eye for higher impact, especially with all the special effects built in. They come in several sizes, so pick one that fits your reception room.

Electronic message centers have become very popular in recent years and are available in various outlets. Office stationery stores often have or can order them. Sign companies always carry them. Even discount stores have sold them.

Prices have come down significantly over the last three years. Instead of the $700 to $1,000 price tag they use to carry, they now run in the $350 to $700 range for compact models.

Remember to change your messages often to get constant readership.

■ **Results.** Southwest veterinarian P.T. began promoting kennel and flea services on his electronic message center along with need-to-know information for pet owners like heartworm and parvo alerts. Plus each day he programmed a welcome to new patients by name.

"The results were astounding. One woman just stood there for about 15 minutes and watched her name come up. That's an extreme case but it shows you how much it's read. And whatever service I put up there, if I left it on for awhile, it always helped promote it."

☐ **HOW TO DO MORE SCREENINGS**

Chiropractic physician W.E. knows that the best thing he can do to find prospects for his services is lots of free screenings.

He's done newspaper and co-op coupon promotion for screenings. Community Appreciation Days. Screenings at health fairs and mall shows. Even at swap meets/flea markets. Every one that had a high volume of traffic has produced a high volume of patients. But these were one- or two-shot deals and he wanted consistency.

So he asked his local high-volume mall if he could set up a *permanent kiosk.* For $1,250 per month rent, they agreed. W.E. now staffs the kiosk seven days a week with $5-an-hour screeners who also make an incentive based upon their number of screenings and conversions.

Now he's got a constant high volume flow of patients at a calculated 14-to-1 return-on-investment.

☐ **LAUNCHING A NEW SERVICE OR PRODUCT FOR STEEP GROWTH**

Massachusetts dentist G.S. likes dental implants. They're intricate and challenging—not to mention lucrative. So when he mastered the technique, he was ready to do a ton. The only problem was how to attract all those weighty profits.

This isn't a unique problem, since every practice introducing a new service or product faces the same situation. Each new service or product has its own attractive attributes. They determine whether it will succeed.

It also depends on the professional's *game plan* for spreading the word. So if you're about to introduce something new (or just did one), take heed.

■ **Working the Inside First.** Introducing any new concept is *tough*. People aren't familiar with it. They're slow to change. They're even fearful of the new. Consequently, an introduction takes a lot of repetition of the message, far more than for the familiar.

Therefore, if you promote to the public, be prepared to spend lots of money, time or effort to get the word out. *Launches take more resources!* But practices don't often have big budgets, so the smart tack is to take the line of least resistance and cost. That means promoting in-house first. If you need resources to promote externally, the in-house effort may generate the bucks needed for the external push to a much larger audience. Here's your line-up of internal strategies.

1. *One-minute message:* This is actually a 15- to 30-second description of the new service or product delivered by the professional: "I'm telling all my patients or clients about a new (service/product) we now have available because it solves the problem of _____. (Describe the problem and the benefits of the new solution.) So if you know of someone who has this problem, please let them know there's now a (new/better) solution. Will you do that for them?" Mark it in each chart to avoid redundancy.

2. *Waiting room placards and brochures:* You can't overpromote a new service, but you can easily underpromote it. Go for high repetition and start with the captured audience in your waiting room.

3. *Direct mail:* Have your computer generate mailing labels for your patient base and write to them specifically about your new offering. Heavy on the benefits, please. If the offering applies only to a certain type of person, have your computer sort them out if you can. If not, mail the whole group anyway.

Also promote the new offering in your quarterly, internal prospecting letter to your base. Remember: You need lots of repetition.

■ **Working the Outside Next.**

1. *Outdoor banner:* If you're not located in a professional building, you probably have an opportunity for an outside banner. This is a low-cost ($100-$200) way to capture walk- and drive-by traffic. Remember: Tell them the benefits and your phone number.

2. *Office sign:* If the new offering will be highly profitable, consider adding it to your permanent office sign. If you have Plexiglass faces, the job's cheap. Yes, it's OK to throw away a perfectly good sign if a newer one will make you more money.

3. *Co-op coupons, newspaper ads, radio or TV spots:* External media come last. But if you're looking to reach big numbers of prospects, here's where you'll end up.

The reason is that there's only so much demand in a finite pool of existing patients or clients. But still promote internally first because if demand is very high, you're bound to have a delivery problem. A good problem, but a problem nonetheless. So don't complicate it with external promotion until you know what demand will be. Your actual choice of media will depend upon budget and the exact target market.

■ **Results.** Dentist G.S. had good instincts. He promoted implants internally by talking them up, sending direct mail to all patients and adding waiting room posters and brochures. Then he promoted a free seminar in the newspaper together with a short burst on local radio.

"The internal efforts produced well, but only in limited amounts. The media spread the word nicely, generating about 30 people for each of the two seminars I've held so far."

☐ MAKING THE MOST OF MALL, TRADE, AND HEALTH SHOWS

Anyone who's done a show *right* knows they work. But the trick is doing it *right.* Otherwise, they're boring and a bust So here are the guidelines that should make the trick easier and profitable.

1. Make your booth pop with *very large* graphics. Use *lots of dramatic color.* Have your visuals display the *benefits* of your service, not your modalities. Another way of thinking about this is that people don't care how you get them there. They care about where they're going. So show them the after (and even before) photos.

2. Add lots of signs with intense information so people will want to stop and read.

3. *Highlight* a free offer in your graphics. Nothing beats doing or giving those unfamiliar with you something for nothing. It's what they want, so why not do it? Free literature *won't* do the job. You've got to give them a bite-size piece of service right there to viscerally show them what you can do. This may be a small consultation, a short exam or screening, or an abbreviated analysis.

4. It's best to break up your free consultation or service into two or more stations if possible. Each step should convince them they need you. Why two or more? Because repetition really works.

5. Then offer them a far more extensive work-up in your office. The charge would normally be $X, but if they schedule it right now, they can have it at a show special of half-off. This must be prepaid. Taking money cuts down on no-shows and gets them to commit now. If they walk away without paying something, the vast, vast majority won't ever return. Bring your scheduling book to set the appointment right then.

6. Now give them literature to take away: (a) information on their problem; and (b) your practice brochure and waiting room resume.

7. Don't wait for people to come to you. Have your staff step out into the aisle and ask passersby if they would like a free such-and-such. This will double or triple your success rate.

Some of these steps may feel uncomfortable, but that only lasts until you see them work. In fact, if you don't follow them, it usually doesn't pay to participate. And if you participate, don't follow them and you still make money, you've left 50% to 90% of what you could have made sitting on the table.

☐ STARTING CLUBS TO RECRUIT NEW PATIENTS OR CLIENTS

Internist D.P. had an extraordinary idea. The senior market was his prime prospects, but he was frustrated with the fierce competition at senior residences and centers. So D.P. decided to start his own club for seniors. The purpose: to introduce and emotionally tie a large number of seniors into his practice, so that when illness strikes, they trust him as their doctor above all others.

■ Modus Operandi. D.P. named his club The Silver Streaks. Membership cards were free to those 55 and over. (D.P. was an honorary member.) And membership does have its privileges:

1. Free monthly socials at a local hotel where members can:

   —receive a free blood pressure check;

   —get free health care information on virtually any topic;

   —hear a 30-minute talk by D.P. on health care tips, followed by answers to their questions;

   —hear a short talk from an attorney or financial advisor D.P. brings in;

   —plus hear a report on and participate in a charitable effort for the health care needs of the elder poor in their "sister" city in Mexico (This ties people in even more.);

2. A discount on services from D.P.;

3. A discount on services from the attorneys and financial advisors who speak;

4. Discounts from local merchants, including restaurants, travel agencies, drug stores, gift shops, etc.;

5. *The Silver Streaks Newsletter*, which contains more health tips from D.P. and an up-to-the-minute list of area businesses giving member discounts.

As membership streaked, D.P. added another dimension—political action. A committee was formed (with D.P. as an advisory member) that sent out press releases expressing opinions on senior health care issues. The committee also made predictions which received considerable press. Plus they gave awards to politicians who represented their point of view well.

The socials were promoted by ads in newspapers and senior publications. And members were recruited from the open socials.

Moneywise, D.P. provided only the organizational seed and promotional funds plus one of his assistant's time. A local hotel donated the meeting room. A drug company underwrote the refreshments and membership cards. And a savings and loan sponsored the newsletter. His costs: pretty small.

■ **Results.** "What is beautiful to see are all their smiling faces, like from the charity work they do. Everything about this feels good, especially the trust they express in me." D.P. also reports membership is over 250 seniors in the first six months ... and practice billings are up 68%. Word of mouth is rampant.

What would work for your practice?

☐ DO YOU NEED AN 800 NUMBER?

In most cases, no. People like to shop for professional services by convenience of location. And an 800 number makes practices feel far away.

If you do draw from another area code or toll zone, then use a local number instead and have it automatically forwarded to your office. This keeps that close feeling people like.

But if your drawing zone is incredibly large as in some rural areas, then an 800 number makes sense. People are *already used to travelling far* and the cost savings of an 800 number is an advantage. However, use it in addition to your local number to let close prospects know you're convenient.

☐ RUNNING THE RECORD-BREAKING OPEN HOUSE

When Physical Therapists M.N. and V.J. relocated to a truly spec-tacular new facility, they naturally wanted to hold an open house. Their feeling was, and rightfully so, that all they had to do was get their patients, and existing referrers into their new shop and the facility would sell itself. Also, that if they could just get some potential referrers in the door, they could also bag 'em by their presentation abilities. No sweat.

So an open house seemed the logical choice. But most open houses turn out to be low-key sleep-a-thons that only close friends and mothers attend. That's because the promotion is low-key and sleep-inducing, not to mention the event's *boring* activities. So M.N. and V.J. decided to do it up right.

They kept one thing in mind—that people like to do things that look like fun and make them feel good.

■ **How to's.** First, they invited everyone they could think of: referring physicians; potentially-referring physicians; past and present patients who could refer friends and family in; city officials to add credibility and to cut ribbons; heads of big companies in town in an effort to get them to know and use the practice; and insurance company executives for the same purpose. Very ambitious.

Of course, not everyone came. It wasn't even close. But several hundred people showed up, including the head of one of the largest supermarket chains in the US. Surprise, surprise.

Another smart move: They knew that physicians oftentimes don't make direct referrals. It's the front desk. So they invited all the physicians' front desk people who came in droves because no one ever invites them to anything—even though they wield much of the power.

Another trick: They followed up their invitations with phone calls to see who was coming. This increased the number of attendees for the very reason that someone asked them personally to come, not just invited them through the mail.

Another embellishment: They asked everyone to bring a can of food to donate to the hungry in the community. It wasn't required, but it would help the needy. This positioned the practice as caring.

And another idea: Everyone was promised a gift if they came. This was a coffee mug of the practice filled with candies, covered with tinted cellophane, and tied with a classy ribbon. Inexpensive, yet beautiful.

And the big one: On top of that, everyone who received an invitation was automatically entered in the drawing for two round trip airline tickets to anywhere in the US. Their invitation had their entry stub enclosed. But you had to be present at the drawing to be eligible. Very, very smart and productive for only a $600 cost. (A Saturday night stay at the destination was required so that the tickets could be purchased at a reasonable price.)

■ **At the Affair.** The catered affair went perfectly. When each attendee arrived, they were greeted by M.N., V.J. and the staff, then given their gift along with an escorted tour. The tour pitches were prerehearsed, emphasizing specific services, depending on the visitor.

Of course, they invited the press. They might normally not have shown up for a "regular" old open house, but this one made good copy. First, there was a ribbon cutting ceremony by the mayor; then the charity angle; plus some brand new, high-tech equipment never before seen in the state; and the promise of a large turnout. The press gave them the exposure they wanted. That let them leverage the event beyond those who actually showed up.

Now M.N. and V.J. have turned their open house into an annual event. If it worked once, they figured, why not do it again ... and again ... and .... The second year's event should turn out many of those who didn't come the first time as well as those who enjoyed last time. And this year they're adding more prizes to the drawing.

■ **When to Hold an Open House**

- ■ When you're opening a new practice.
- ■ When you're taking over someone else's practice.
- ■ When you're moving into a new facility.
- ■ When you're expanding your facility.
- ■ When you're opening a second location.
- ■ When you're adding an associate.
- ■ When you're adding new services or products.
- ■ When you're celebrating your practice's anniversary.
- ■ When you're celebrating a milestone.
- ■ When you're celebrating an award or accomplishment.

Remember: Make people feel good and make it look like fun.

PROMOTIONS IN MOTION

1. Ophthalmologist K.R. has tried everything from TV blitzes to glaucoma screenings in nursing homes. Successfully, too. But still he wanted more new patients, especially with competitors copying his every move.

    His new idea? Sponsoring exercise walks for seniors through enclosed malls in early mornings. Both seniors and malls love it. After each walk, his people screen participants for free. Success again.

2. Podiatrist A.G. knows service. Two days a week a retired friend wears a suit, tie, and chauffeur's hat to pick up patients who don't have transportation (many elderly) in his 1990 Cadillac sedan. A.G. used a cab service before finding his "chauffeur," but the cabbies were rude and in a hurry. A.G. also does weekly house calls to shut-ins.

3. Podiatrist W.R. is giving free seminars. That's nothing new, but where and how he's doing it is.

    He's contacted The Foot Locker stores (athletic footwear) in his area with the idea that he'd give monthly talks to the salespeople on foot care. His pitch: The salespeople will sound more knowledgeable and therefore provide better service, a key point of distinction in this type of business. Also that salespeople will have less difficulty in fitting customers because W.R. will teach them about orthotics. W.R. is happy to do this in the early morning before the stores open.

    With four months under his belt, W.R. reports orthotic sales up over 250%. Plus three additional surgeries have hobbled in. He's now planning on educating regular shoe stores in his area.

4. Dentist G.R. is conducting Saturday morning talks on high-ticket dental implants. To promote them, he runs a professionally prepared newspaper ad two Sundays and one Thursday before the event. He's tried radio, but the stations he chose are weak attractors in his area.

    But whatever he's doing, it must be right. At the first seminar, 31 showed up teeth in hand. At the second, 28 gummed up to the bar. And the return-on-investment—a nice 5:1.

5. Optometrist B.N. knows that women now consider glasses to be a fashion accessory. So why not do it up and throw a fashion show.

    B.N. sent out an invitation to his female patients to come to a free cosmetic makeover and eyewear fashion show in his office. Patients and their guests were invited although seating was limited and an RSVP was required.

For the cost of a couple of makeup artists and the mailing, B.N. drew 30 women who bought. ROI equals 4.1 to 1.

6. Plastic surgeon K.B. has placed a computer imaging system in a busy beauty parlor. K.B. rents the floor space for a modest sum. Interior signs promote a free cosmetic surgery analysis in the beauty parlor plus the cosmeticians get a small spiff for each free analysis they schedule. K.B. comes in to do them twice a week.

   Dispensing audiologist S.L. has done likewise in placing a hearing tester right in a busy senior center. These are classic cross promotions.

7. Chiropractor D.S. had participated in many mall shows and always done well. Finally she figured why not be in a big mall all the time. So now she is, not with an office, but with a permanent kiosk to provide free screenings. It's less expensive than a mall office and more productive because it's in the middle of the main traffic area.

Chapter 22

SPECIAL CIRCUMSTANCES: START-UPS
AND OTHER DESPERATE TIMES

□ HOW TO PROMOTE WHEN YOU'VE GOT NO MONEY, HONEY

Dentist K.D. had the blues from all his red ink. Few new patients were trickling in, mainly because no one knew he existed. Word of mouth wasn't strong enough to fill the chairs of an eight-month-old practice and there was little or no money to help the cause. What should he do? Throw in the towel? Hell, no! It was time to fight.

Everyone has weapons, even if they don't have money. Here's what K.D. did.

1. Sitting in a professional building with three MDs, one OD, and a DC, he decided to cross promote. Logically assuming that people liked to go to the same area for all their professional services, he approached all five neighbors with an offer to place their promotional literature in his waiting room if they'd display his.

All agreed, since this was quite "professional." But on his fold-over business card, he told readers *why* he was the one to choose (in this case, his high grades in school), what services he provides, and the *results* he produces ... *and* an introductory $25 offer to try a bite-size piece of service (an exam, necessary x-rays and a cleaning). He refilled the displays weekly. Cost: $125.

2. He then typed a half-page letter on his stationery with this same information. And two to three times a day, he'd stick a copy beneath the windshield wipers of the cars around his building. His dental school professors would probably cringe if they knew what he was doing, but they weren't the one with his back against the wall—with the rent on the wall due. Cost: $25.

3. Then he retyped the letter with an emphasis on services for businesspeople. He highlighted his cosmetic dentistry; he was open at 7 A.M. for them; had lunchtime hours, too; and was conveniently located so they needn't travel far. His academic achievements, a list of business services, and a businessperson's offer completed the short copy.

With the letter in hand, he walked the nearby offices, introducing himself to each receptionist. This was a novelty to them and he was well received. K.D. asked them to distribute a copy to each employee. Some didn't, but many did. Cost: $50.

4. K.D. then took the same information from his business card promotion and fashioned a co-op coupon that was printed and delivered to 10,000 homes by Val-Pak. This was something he swore he'd never do. But he also swore he'd never fail. Cost: $350.

K.D. not only survived, he prospered. For him, it almost took bankruptcy to motivate him enough to actually get out there and try some things. Results: From 5 new patients per month, he jumped to 28 with an average case size of $827. Return on investment was over 42 to 1.

"If I hadn't come so close to crashing, I never would have gotten out there and done things I'd previously considered unbecoming. What I learned was that what *I* considered unbecoming, many people actually liked."

☐ HOW TO MARKET WHEN YOU HAVE NO MONEY AND GET 50 NEW PATIENTS OR CLIENTS A MONTH

Optometrist E.M. was losing market share to the chains, losing patients to ophthalmologists and other ODs, and losing his shirt in the process. Finally he'd had it and was ready to fight back. But by that time, business was down so much that there wasn't enough cash to fight back with.

His mind was willing, but the body was short on fuel. So with no money for external promotion to attract new patients, he decided to do something no other optometrist had ever done.

E.M. read in THE PRACTICE BUILDER about a dentist, who when he'd moved into a business area, had no good way of reaching the 40,000 people who came to work there everyday. Having missed the *Yellow*

Pages deadline for the year, this motivated dentist started to walk his area and introduce himself.

The dentist trotted from office to office and walked himself into 100 new patients a month. Now he doesn't walk anymore. He drives a BMW 735i, but he still introduces himself for an hour each day. It's what built his practice from a cold start with no patients to a top-of-the-line Beamer practice. So he still does it.

■ **No Money, Established Practitioner.** You needn't be new on the block to walk your turf because the underlying reason for the strategy's success is not whether you're new or old. It has to do with the power of different types of communication.

The weakest form of communication is print. More powerful is telephone. (Hence the success of telemarketing.) But the most powerful by far is *face-to-face.* And the differences in power among the three forms is **ENORMOUS.**

Understanding this from THE PRACTICE BUILDER article, E.M. donned shirt and tie, mapped out a route around his office and started approaching single family homes, condos, and apartments on weekdays between 5 and 8 P.M., Saturday afternoons, and Sunday mornings. (The longer daylight hours helped at night.)

When the door was answered, he'd introduce himself and ask if anyone wore eyeglasses or contacts, or were there adults over 40 or kids in the household. Most said yes.

When they did, he'd ask if they knew there were important differences in eye exams. Then he'd actually describe the differences so people could appreciate what true quality meant in optometry. He discovered this was the only way to get people away from the idea that product is everything and service is inconsequential. That's what the chains want you to think. If anyone wore contacts, he'd tell them about disposables and offer free try-ons and a free pair after an exam.

Then he'd give them a *10-line letter* (a very fast read) which summarized his talk on thorough exams and what could happen to them in detail if they got a quickie instead. The letter also offered a reduced rate to introduce his neighbors to this concept of an ultra-thorough eye exam. Plus, it repeated the contacts offer.

In addition to the letter, he handed them his Waiting Room Resume, prepared according to THE PRACTICE BUILDER's recipe. This convinced prospects of his expertise and quality.

E.M. could have used his practice brochure instead, but it wasn't prepared with THE PRACTICE BUILDER's guidelines. (See Chapter 12.) Therefore, it didn't convince people of anything. If it were an effective leave-behind, unlike his present *patient information brochure,* it would have been more powerful than the resume alone and should have been used.

As a parting line, E.M. told them about his offer of a reduced fee for his ultra-thorough exam. And he explained there was a time limit of 10 days, as ink-stamped on the preprinted letter. Without a deadline, many people would put it off until they'd forgotten.

■ **Requirement.** You need an outgoing personality to use this strategy. If you don't like meeting people, you won't like walking your turf and you won't do it more than once.

■ **Results.** From *16* new patients a month, E.M. jumped to *62* with no out-of-pocket cost. "There's no doubt this approach takes dedication. Lots of people are nice, but some aren't. So you have to be ready to deal with that," he said. "What I do is tell myself I'm not going to let these people prevent me from being successful. Then I straighten my tie and go onto the next door .... It works if you work at it."

☐ TELEMARKETING FOR LEAD GENERATION

Chiropractor C.Z. started off four years ago from scratch. Yet today he's got two offices with expansion plans on the books. What made his practice zoom?

It certainly wasn't the way he differentiated himself. He didn't. He looks like every other chiropractor in the area. Instead his trick was to prospect effectively for people in need of his services. To make sure he was in the right place at the right time.

Quickly he realized that if he waited for people to seek him out, he'd wait too long. Instead, he reached out to them and asked if they needed a chiropractor. But he didn't do it in the same forums most other health professionals use—newspaper, magazine, and the mail. Instead C.Z. used a medium no others utilized—the telephone.

Smart guy. C.Z. soon realized that the phone is a far more powerful medium than the printed word. The numbers told him that. True, it's more expensive than mail or print media, but his case size is so large that the expense is small by comparison. So it gave him a jumbo ROI.

■ **How-To's.** First hire a telemarketer (an experienced one is best). This person needs a pleasant voice, not knowledge of the subject. That can be learned. Homemakers looking for flexible hours are good candidates. Run your ad in the local classifieds under "Sales."

The telemarketer's job is to get appointments. Nothing but. Give them three days to produce significant numbers or fire them. Pay the telemarketer a small hourly rate plus a large bonus for each new prospect that turns into a patient. Purchase the phone numbers from a mailing list broker.

Then script the call and practice it until it flows. Testing it out on 10 prospects will point out all the problems and how you need to modify. And you always need to modify.

The first part of the call should quickly screen for a problem you can solve. If one's there, present the rest of the script. If it's not, go quickly to the next call. You must treat this as a cold numbers game. Otherwise you're doomed before you start.

Telemarketing is relatively new to the profession, so it feels uncomfortable. But since few use it, it's easier now than it will be later when everyone's on the bandwagon. Telemarketing has the potential to be like the *Yellow Pages*, although on a smaller scale. First one practice enters. Then next year everyone's there.

☐ WHAT TO DO ABOUT THE SLOW START

What would happen if you gave a party and no one came? Well, optometrist C.H. had it worse. He opened a practice and no one came. At least not enough to make it profitable or interesting. While he tried to figure out if he should stay or fold, he unintentionally fumbled onto an idea that built his practice.

C.H. wondered if he'd made a mistake in choosing his location. Was there enough demand for optometric services with all the competition so he could get a share ... or was the pie cut up too much already? To answer this and decide whether to move, he thought he'd ask the locals.

So C.H. put together a short questionnaire and walked the surrounding neighborhoods interviewing people during mid-mornings, between 5 and 7 P.M. and on Saturdays. Here's what he said:

Hello. My name's Dr. _____ and I'm a Doctor of Optometry in our community. Quite frankly, I have a problem I'm trying to solve and I need some information from the people of our area to do that.

You see, I opened an office a few months ago and it's not doing as well as I would like. My fear is that there are too many doctors here and not enough demand for optometric services. So I'm studying exactly how much demand there is. I'd be grateful if you would give me your opinion and answer about five questions to help me. Would you do that?

Question 1: Do you or anyone in your family wear glasses or contact lenses?

Question 2: Where do you or your family go for your eyecare and eyewear?

Question 3: How often do you or your family go for an eye exam or new contact lenses or glasses?

Question 4: What do you or did you look for in choosing your eye doctor?

Question 5: Do you think this is a good community for a new Doctor of Optometry to practice in?

Well, I want you to know how insightful I find your answers and how helpful they are to me in deciding whether to continue to practice here. And your name is?

Thank you so much Mr./Mrs./Ms. _____. I really appreciate your opinions and your time.

As he walked away, C.H. wrote down the person's name and address and when he got back to the office, he sent them a little note (off his computer). The note reiterated his thanks for their insightful opinions and how important their input is for helping him decide this most important decision in his professional career. He would let them know what he decided.

From all the positive feedback he got, C.H. decided to stay. So a week later, he wrote everyone another note about his decision. He thanked them for their input again because their answers convinced him to stay in the community. He feels very good about the decision, again all because of their information.

And as a way to thank them again, he enclosed a special $35 credit so his thorough eye exam would only cost them $10. It's good for every member of the household. This credit was printed on a separate enclosure in the envelope so they would see it without wading through the letter.

During the week of information gathering, a couple of the people he interviewed actually came in. During the two weeks after the second note, several more showed up, some with multiple kids in tow. His income went up.

■ **The Next Step.** C.H. is a quick learner and figured he better keep doing this. After all, he had the time and it didn't cost a dime, except the follow-up postage.

Not only did C.H. keep on interviewing community residents, he started sending more letters. In the third one in the series mailed 30 days later to the same person, he talked of how the practice was now picking up, that things were much brighter—and that he would have decided to move had it not been for their input and that of their neighbors. For this he's ever thankful. And to show his appreciation, he's enclosing another credit certificate good for $35, so an eye exam is only $10.

This continued to work well—so he sent a fourth 30 days later. And then one every 60 days. All had the same format of how well the practice was doing (thanks to them) plus a credit certificate.

■ **Why It Worked.** From his responses C.H. learned that people responded because they felt they had a vested interest in what happened to him now. By meeting him in person, his success somehow became of interest and they wanted to help.

(Face to face communication is obviously far more response producing than mail, newspaper, or telephone alone. However, if you're a wallflower and don't present yourself well, this strategy will fail. People will think you're failing because of you, not the market.)

Also more women than men became patients, about 60% vs. 40%. He figured women were more empathetic to his plight.

The credit certificate was more powerful than a discount coupon. People seem to feel they have something they can spend as opposed to saving something if they spend money.

The strategy's ROI (return-on-investment) is humongous because there's no money (except postage) out and lots of it in.

■ **Results.** C.H. talked to over 2,300 households in six months time. And the practice finally topped $20,000 a month from a starting point of $7,000.

"Even though I'm busier now, I'm not going to stop. I'm going to those houses and apartments where no one was home my first time through and to some new tracts farther away .... You got to keep doing what's working."

☐ HOW TO PROMOTE A PRICE REDUCTION FOR FAST INCOME

Personal likes and dislikes aside, price reductions generate fast cash—but only if you follow some rules. Following the rules make the difference between success and failure.

First you need to state the big price reduction *in a headline*. Whether it's a co-op coupon, direct mailer to the world, letter to your base, newspaper or shopper ad, outdoor banner, or telemarketing call, the headline concept is the same.

Then your headline must *validate the big reduction* against the standard price. Plus you must add another benefit, bonus, or extended advantage, in addition to the price reduction.

In a successful "sale," your value must be *extraordinarily appealing*.

■ **For Example:**

> $2,500 braces for only $1,500, with terms up to 24 months interest free. And only $95 down.
> FREE $25 flea dip with every $10 checkup until June 30th. And HALF-OFF on all vaccinations.

Now that you've got their interest with a headline, give them a solid, credible *rationale* why you're offering such a preferential price—one that no one else is offering. Then, you must re-establish the credibility of your price as a solid value by educating the prospect about the pricing structure in your profession.

■ **For Example—Patient Base Mailing:**

> Our practice is busy all spring and summer and peaks in the fall. But come winter, our practice drops 50%. Yet my rent and overhead remain constant. I usually lose $1,000 a month unless I layoff some of my staff, all of whom have families.
> This year I've decided to maintain our patient volume by offering foot exams for free and to accept whatever your insurance will pay, as long as you've met your deductible. All this to keep my staff together.
> No other doctor in our area offers a free foot exam nor accepts whatever your insurance will pay. And as of March 1st, I won't either.
> Or:

> I am willing to lose money to prove to you there is a difference among eye doctors ....

Or the raw truth:

> Frankly, my patient load is way down lately. So are all of my colleagues'. But I don't have to worry about their payroll. I have to worry about mine ....

Now that you've got the idea, you're ready to create your own. Remember: This is a "sale" and these are the sale rules for success. So if you're going to go after the quick fix sale, don't follow just the rules you like. Follow them all or don't do it. Here's your checklist:

- ■ First, you must have a headline that conveys quickly, clearly, and compellingly the exciting essence of your offer.
- ■ Second, any reduction must be validated against a standard price.

- Third, you must add another benefit, bonus, or extended advantage, in addition to the price reduction.

- Fourth, there must be a rationale for the price reduction.

- Fifth, you must have a deadline to compel action now.

Abraham, Jay, *10 Short Term "Quick-Fix" Techniques for a Troubled Business*, Euler Enterprises, Inc., 7910 Woodmont Ave. #1200, Bethesda, MD 20814 and THE PRACTICE BUILDER.

☐ HOW TO FILL YOUR SLOW SEASON

Like most cold weather practices, New York dentist W.G. is slow in January. Too slow, he decided, so he thought he'd pump up the old promotion machine to fill his empty schedule.

W.G. spent $2,746 running three weeks of newspaper ads ... and brought in an underwhelming $879.

But be careful where you point the finger of blame. In this case it could have been the ad he ran, its size, tone, visual, offer, headline, benefits, or placement in the paper. The paper itself might not be well read in his area—contrary to what W.G. thinks. There are lots of variables to go wrong.

In this case, it wasn't any of them. He simply ran it at the wrong time of year.

■ **Seasonality.** People had just finished with the holidays, and it takes them at least two weeks to get back to the real world and their problems. Plus, in cold climates, they like to hibernate until March.

Why? Well, why isn't important because small budgets can't change behavior patterns. Only really big ones can. The fact that people don't spend during certain periods is what's key to know.

That means you can't raise the dip in your production curve by promoting during your slow times. If you do, you simply get a poor return-on-investment (ROI) because people don't have a propensity to buy then. And since you have precious few dollars to waste, why blow it? Instead, why not spend it when people do spend so your ROI can go through the roof?

■ **How to Fill Slow Periods.** To fill the slow periods, you really should promote *during the high times.* This is when people buy. It's also when you're already busy.

But think of this. If you bring in more prospects during the high times, some will come back during the slow times—and they'll refer in more prospects, even then. So this *new* word-of-mouth and repeat business raises your slow periods up a notch.

The more you promote during the high times, the more you raise the low times. Usually there are two or three slow times during the year. So if you promote during all the highs, these compound themselves during the lows.

But this is only true IF you have your basic internal strategies all in motion. That's because you need to *encourage* word-of-mouth referrals and repeat business. How? By:

1. Asking for Referrals
2. A Frequent Referrer Program
3. Internal Prospecting
4. Your Waiting Room Resume
5. Recalls the Right Way
6. Reactivation Efforts and
7. One Minute Messages.

■ **Results.** One bad fall and W.G. was gun shy. But his PRACTICE BUILDER Marketing Director got him to take promotional risks again, but this time safe and sane ones. He prescribed a newspaper promotion with the following schedule:

1. **Start in March** and run until June 15th when school ends and parents take kids away for vacation;

2. **Start again July 5th** and go until August 10th when vacations again cut into buying habits;

3. **Start September 15th** and run until December 10th when the holiday season overwhelms everyone.

In the meantime, W.G. got his internal promotional act together and the results were predictable. Within six months gross was up 39%—not only during the good times, but consistently higher during the slow periods, too.

W.G. never did get the practice to operate at the same level all year round. That's because people won't buy that way. Instead he had to suffer in luxury.

☐ WHAT TO DO WHEN A NEW COMPETITOR HAS A GRAND OPENING

Most professionals sit by and watch as new competitors begin eating away at their hard-won market share. The upstarts nibble and nibble until your bottom line looks anemic—and then you wonder what to do.

Wrong time to ask the question! The time for action is when a competitor first opens.

That's when new competitors are weakest. They have only a few months' working capital to make it. And if they don't, they pull up their tent stakes—and your bottom line.

Let's face it. It's not like the old days where there was always room for one more colleague. Today, there's no more room and you've got to protect market share. That means a preemptive strategy to stop new entries cold.

Grand openings usually attract a lot of attention. So that's where you pull out all the stops to make a new competitor's opening a flop. Then you keep him or her flopping until they run out of dough and go home. It's a wise short-term investment.

So if you know about a grand opening, *immediately* pump up your own external promotion two notches higher than ever before. And don't let the competitor out of the starting gate!

Jeff Slutsky, *Street Smart Marketing*, John Wiley & Sons, New York, 1989, $14.95 and THE PRACTICE BUILDER.

☐ ATTRACTING THOSE WHO PARK IN FRONT OF YOUR OFFICE

Veterinarian T.F. was about to launch a new office on a low budget. But he was worried. Not so much about what he should promote to his middle class area. That was simple: *low cost spays, neuters, and vaccinations* (with higher fees for all other services). *"Low cost spays, neuters, and vaccinations"* actually became the headline and tagline for all his promotion.

But his concern was how he was going to get the word out about his new practice without breaking the bank loan. The answer was fairly straight forward:

- *Yellow Pages*
- Co-op Coupons
- Asking for Referrals
- Frequent Referrer Program
- Waiting Room Resume
- Outdoor Office Sign
- Handing out discount exam cards for clients to pass them on to friends
- Free first shots for puppies and kittens with the pet shop giving out his certificate for the service

But these alone fail to take advantage of one of the biggest assets of this embryonic practice—the traffic in front of the practice's door.

Located in a strip mall, this practitioner pays extra for that prime location—which means for the traffic in front of it.

To make his investment in location pay off, he should use two more tactics targeted specifically at his traffic:

1. *"Grand Opening" Banner:* Most landlords and cities allow a temporary cloth or vinyl banner for 30 to 60 days, oftentimes more, sometimes without restriction. (Check your sign regulations and lease for restrictions.) Cost: about $100. The banner copy for this practice:

Grand Opening

Low-cost spays, neuters, and vaccinations

Practice Name

Phone Number

2. *Flyers:* Every couple of hours, place a flyer beneath the windshield wipers of cars in the strip mall's parking lot. Include an introductory offer for this price-sensitive, middle-class market. Across the street is a major shopping area. Leaflet those cars, too.

At times, there are restrictions on leafletting, so you may want to check with the mall first. But if the mall owners don't have a policy, they'll make one up on the spot just for you—which says forget it. So some may want to assume you can do it until told you can't.

■ **Results.** "Successful" isn't the term. "Wonderful" is more appropriate. "It was definitely the right message for this area. And because I was on a limited budget, the banner and flyers helped enormously, not only from a cost perspective, but also from an effectiveness one. Now that I look back upon it, it makes utter sense ... that the people most likely to come to me are those who already come to shop here."

□ SPECIAL CASES: EXPANDING PRACTICES

■ **Expansion by Buying Records with Nothing Down.** Dentist R.G. is one smart fellow ... and richer for it. When a local competitor decided to cash it in, R.G. approached him, not to buy the practice, but to buy his charts. The deal didn't go through right away. But when the practice didn't sell quickly, the seller called back.

R.G.'s problem then was how to value charts up to 20 or 30 years old? There was no good information on recall percentage or retention.

And the dentist didn't cultivate or protect his base from competitors, which would have made the records more valuable.

R.G.'s solution was ingenious—don't place a value on them now. Instead, pay 25% of their collection over the next two years. In essence, R.G. figured he'd get 75% of his normal fee. And given that his overhead was already covered by his existing practice, the cost of treating the new patients would only be his variable costs, mostly materials and lab work. That made the profit margins on these patients *very big*, even at the reduced fee.

And then after two years, they were all his. And he didn't spend a dime for the records up front. Plus the seller was happy. And another big plus—R.G. eliminated a competitor. A perfect deal.

■ **Converting Records into People.** If you're just going to send an announcement that their former practitioner is gone and now you have their records, forget it. That's using a BB gun when the buffalo you're after are stampeding away. Instead, you need big guns. It's OK to overpromote to your new base, but you can't afford to underpromote. So if you err, err high. Here are your steps:

1. Put your new patients or clients up on a mailing list (in-house computer, computer service, or typed on a photocopiable grid for self-adhesive label reproduction). Then, you write a letter to be signed by the selling professional. The seller signing it must be part of the deal.

In it, the seller announces the retirement or move and how lengthy the search has been for a new professional to entrust their care to. The search has not been easy, for the standards set by the professional were unusually high. He or she could not entrust their records simply to any qualified practitioner—only a very special one. Even though many were available, the right one with the right training, credentials, schooling, experience, and manner was extremely difficult to find.

But now the search is over. The selling professional then lauds the buyer's background and how much he or she can be trusted. A photo of the two shaking hands and smiling is printed on the letter to visually drive home the transference of kudos from the old to the new.

2. A week later, the new professional sends a two-page follow-up. It praises the seller and explains how difficult it is to fill his or her shoes. The letter then adds how fortunate the buyer feels to have been selected and entrusted with the patient's care. That you, the new professional, consider this to be a sacred trust and that they can rest assured they'll receive the kind of service they had in the past.

In fact, the letter explains you're going to give the best service available today because you have new ideas, new services, new techniques and/or new equipment. Then spell out what the new benefits are to the reader. Restate the benefits in a different way because repetition works!

This letter has a different photo of seller and buyer shaking hands and smiling. Also include telephone stickers with your name and the seller's for their phones, rolodexes, and personal phone books.

3. Answer the seller's phone line in your office. That way you won't lose any people who don't read their mail or who have forgotten the seller is gone. This is critical.

4. Then cultivate and protect this base quarterly with THE PRACTICE BUILDER's Internal Prospecting Strategy (see Chapter 6). Also reactivate them with THE PRACTICE BUILDER's Reactivation Strategy (see Chapter 7).

■ **Results.** "Basically I bought several hundred patients with no down for a percentage of what I collected. The deal was so good that I could even buy his old equipment, donate it, and write it off. And the reason it all worked was because I closely followed the strategy to convert those charts into in-the-chair activity."

☐ HOW TO MAKE REAL MONEY FROM AN ASSOCIATE

Dentist B.R. is doing quite well, thank you. Actually, at $1,000,000 a year in production as a *solo practitioner*, he's doing exceptionally well. But his personal goal is higher. And there's no free time in his schedule.

He can't trade up to doing more expensive cases, because he's already there. (How do you think a solo does a million in dentistry?) So he's thinking about adding an associate, but he's heard you can't make money from one. In fact, it's difficult in most cases. Because most *associates are asked to do things they can't.*

■ **How to Make Real Money from an Associate.** If you analyze why B.R. has been so successful, it's not because he does great dentistry (although he does that, too). It's because he presents proposed work so well to patients.

They love him. They respect him. And they want to buy from him.

If associates could present information like B.R., they'd be $1,000,000 dentists themselves. But they can't and they shouldn't be asked to.

So the smart tactic is to have B.R. see all new patients, establish rapport, analyze their needs and "sell the case." Once that's done, he should introduce his associate who has expertise in that type of work to actually do the job.

Are people willing to let someone else do the work once B.R. has sold the case? Yes, *if:* 1) B.R. endorses the associate wholeheartedly; and 2) the associate has a likeable personality. If B.R. doesn't hire a troll or someone who should be in a Stephen King movie, things will work out just fine.

Remember: Figure out what got you to the point of success. Keep doing exactly that. And leverage yourself by delegating everything else.

PROMOTIONS IN MOTION

1. A brand-new dentist opening a brand-new, 24-hour emergi-dent office missed his *Yellow Pages* deadline. Uh-oh! So he went into the newspaper with a bold-looking *attention* notice. His public-service-type ad pulled well.

   He can continue to do this but eventually must convert the emergency business into long-term relationships. It's too tough to build a practice on one-shot, non-repeatable patients. A better positioning than an emergi-center that also provides continuing care is that of a general practice with heavily promoted emergency services.

INDEX

A

Advertisement construction, *Yellow Pages*, 301-4
  color, 303-4
  layout, 302-3
  visual strategies, 303
Advertising:
  Direct Response game, 147
  Hybrid game, 148
  lessons, 146
  Name Recognition game, 147
  vs. marketing, 144-46
  winning the advertising game, 146-48
Advertising Direct Mail, 320
Advertorials, 304-5
  example of, 305
  guidelines, 304-5
ADVO, 33, 97, 320, 323, 324, 325
Affinity marketing, 90-93
  how to start, 91-92
  index carding, 92-93
  notes, types of, 91
  success story, 90
Alerts, obtaining referrals through, 124-25

Analyses:
  brochures, 186-93
  business cards, 230-33
  co-op coupon packs, 325-28
Associates:
  making real money from, 368-69
  and referrals, 140-42
Assumptive close, 65, 94
Authoring, as form of promotion, 41-42

B

Backward planning, 13-14
Balloons, 93
Banners, 93, 161-64
  flyers, 366
  "grand opening" banner, 366
  guidelines, 163-64
  See also Outdoor office signs
Ben Franklin close, 94
Brochures, 170-221
  analysis, 186-93
  colors in, 180
  contents of, 171-72
  examples of, 173-79, 187-92, 194-98, 200-220

Brochures *(continued):*
  final panel, 181
  guidelines for, 172
  headlines, 193
  line drawings, 181
  logo, 181
  mistakes to avoid, 182-85
  need for, 170-71
  patient information brochure, 182
  questions answered by, 180
  size of, 182, 193
  subheads, 181, 193
  underlying principles, 180
  uses of, 185-86
  using as direct mail, 199
Buckslip, 250
Bus bench advertisements, avoiding, 74
Business cards, 222-33
  analysis, 230-33
  Business Card Contest, 224-29
  coordinating with logo/envelope/stationery, 237-40
  copy, 223
  distributing, 224
  examples, 225, 227, 229, 231, 233, 239
  graphics, 223-24
  layout, 232
  purpose of, 222-23
  strategizing for, 237
Business district practice, building, 279-82
  practice representative, 281
  sample letter, 281
  walking turf, 280-81

C

Cable television, 334-35
Calendars, 93
Certificate code, tracking results of promotion
      through, 33
Charity event sponsorship, avoiding, 75
Church bulletin advertising, avoiding, 75
Claims, making, 40-51
Closes for presentations, 94-95
Clubs, starting, 349-50
Cold prospecting direct mail, payback, 7
College newspaper advertising, avoiding, 75
College yearbook advertising, avoiding, 74

Color:
  in brochures, 180
  outdoor office signs, 155
  in *Yellow Pages* advertisements, 303-4
Commitment, as marketing plan secret, 1
Community Appreciation Days, 248-49, 346
Community telephone books, 316
Competitors, 364-65
  and outdoor office signs, 155
Computer-compiled mailing lists, 264-65
Consistency, as marketing plan secret, 1
Conversion rate, referrals, 132-33
Co-op coupon packs, 270-78, 283, 319-28, 365
  acceptance of, 319-20
  analyses, 325-28
  design, 320-22
  how to's, 320
  payback, 7
  pitfalls of, 323-24
  response, 325
  samples, 321, 326, 327
  testing, 322
  and up-scale markets, 324
  See also ADVO; Val-Pak; Money Mailer
Co-operative mailings to new homes, avoiding, 74
Copy cat telephone books, 316
Counter cards, 93
Coupon code, tracking results of promotion
      through, 33
Coupons, *See* Co-op coupon packs
Courting referrers, 128-29
Credentials, 41
Credit cards:
  financing through, 63-64
  guidelines, 63

D

Decor, prioritizing, 77
Dedicated phone lines, tracking results of pro-
      motion through, 33
Design, co-op coupon packs, 320-22
Design-based logos, 235
Direct mail, 254-73
  co-op coupon packs, 270-78
  cost of, 256
  cost savings, 263

Direct mail *(continued):*
  guidelines for, 268-69
  letter:
    samples of, 265-68
    writing of, 262
  mailing house, double checking, 271-72
  mailing list:
    building, 272
    computer-compiled mailing lists, 264-65
    self-compiled mailing lists, 264
  multi-page format, 254-56
  multiple mailings, 262-63
  new resident direct mail, 256-65
  return on investment (ROI), 269-70
  success of, 258
  super targeting, 256
  test mailings, 271
Direct mail package:
  example of, 258-61
  internal prospecting, 83
Direct Response Game, 147
Double positive close, 94
Dual alternative close, 94

E

800 number, 350
Electronic message centers, 93, 344-46
Elevator signs, 282
  availability, 346
  ideas for, 345
  price, 346
  specifications, 345-46
Elimination process close, 296
Employee Referral Contest, 137-39
  rules/prizes, 138-39
Enhanced reactivation effort, 101-4
Envelope:
  example of, 240
  strategizing for, 237
Expansion, *See* Growth
Expected return on investment (ROI), 3
Expenses, prioritizing, 77
Extension numbers, tracking results of promotion through, 32-33
External promotion, *See* Promotion

F

Fee objections, handling, 65-66
Fee raising, 57-59
  guidelines, 58-59
Fee surveys, 66
Final panel, brochures, 181
Financing:
  advertising, 62
  attracting new prospects with, 61
  credit cards, acceptance of, 63-64
  Medcash, 61
  nonrecourse loan programs, 61-62
  obtaining plan information, 62
  PICO financing plan, 61
  prepaid financing, 64
  as pricing strategy, 60-64
  procedure, 62
Flyers, 366
Foldover piece, as reactivation effort, 107, 108
Follow-up, internal prospecting, 84-85, 89
Free exams/consultations, 66-68
Free magazine distribution, avoiding, 73-74
Free screenings, 346
Frequent recruiter program, 135-37
Frequent referrer program, 2, 80, 91, 113-14
  behavior shaping, 113-14
  gift-giving to referrers, 114
    gift quality, 114
    sample gifts, 114-15
  guideline, 115
  results, 115
Friend-Help-a-Friend program, 84, 87

G

Gateways, 146, 306
Gimmicks, avoiding, 73-76
Good/better/best strategy, 68-69
"Grand opening" banner, 366
Graphics, business cards, 223-24
Green pages, 317
Group practice, putting personal touch in, 47-49
Growth, 366-68
  business district practice, building, 279-82
  checklist for, 76
  hotel trade, capturing, 278-79
  hot growth spots, 276-78
  incremental growth goal, 4-5

Growth *(continued)*:
  new markets, exploring, 274-89
  new resident program, with secret agents, 284-85
  pitfalls of, 275
  and staff, 275
  through referrals, 110-31
  urban practice, 282-84
Guarantees, as pricing strategy, 59-60

H

Hallway signs, 282
Handouts to walk-bys, 283
Headlines:
  brochures, 193
  newspaper advertising, 306-7
Helplines, telemarketing, 298-99
High-school yearbook advertising, avoiding, 74
High-volume practice:
  analysis, 65
  external promotion, 64-65
  in-office presentation, 65
Hotel trade, capturing, 278-79
Hot growth spots, 276-78
Hybrid game, 148

I

Impending event close, 95
Inbound telemarketing, 293-94
Incentive programs, 138-39
Incremental growth goal, 4-5
Index carding, affinity marketing, 92-93
Internal promotion, 79-97, 284
  affinity marketing, 90-93
  closes for presentations, 94-95
  frequent referrer program, 2, 80, 91, 113-14
  internal prospecting, 2, 9, 79, 82-87
  internal signs, 93
  one-minute messages, 2, 80, 87-88
  reactivation efforts, 2, 7, 80
  recalls, 7, 80, 98-101
  referrals, 2, 7, 32, 80, 82, 91, 110-31, 365
  waiting room surveys, 96-97
    welcome-to-the-practice letter, 80-82
Internal prospecting, 2, 9, 32, 79, 82-87
  certificate sample, 87
  definition of, 82

Internal prospecting *(continued)*:
  direct mail package, 83
  follow-up, 84-85, 89
  letter construction, 83-84
  postscript, 84
  sample, 85-87
Internal prospecting direct mail, payback, 7
Interviews, radio, 332-33
Investment, as marketing plan secret, 1

J

Jingles:
  concepts, 338
  and television advertising, 336-38

L

Launching new service/product, 346-48
  co-op coupons, 348
  direct mail, 347
  newspaper advertisements, 348
  office signs, 348
  one-minute message, 347
  outdoor banner, 347
  radio/television spots, 348
  waiting-room placards/brochures, 347
Layaway plans, 64
Layout:
  business cards, 232
  Yellow Pages advertising, 302-3
Letterhead, stationery, 238
Lettershops, *See* Mailing house
Line drawings, brochures, 181
Local publicity, 252-53
Logos, 234-40
  analysis, 236-37
  brochures, 181
  business produced by, 234
  coordinating with envelope/business card/
    stationery, 237-40
  design-based logos, 235
  examples, 236, 237
  guidelines for, 236
  marketing-based logos, 235
  need for, 234
  outdoor office signs, 155
  strategizing for, 237
  typestyles, 234-35
  varieties of, 235

Long-Form Game Planner, 22-28
Lost patients/clients, reasons for loss, 45
Lunch-a-week method, of obtaining referrals, 122-23

M

Magazine cover advertisements, avoiding, 75
Mailing houses, double checking, 271-72
Mailing label key code, tracking results of promotion through, 33
Mailing list:
  building, 272
  computer-compiled mailing lists, 264-65
  self-compiled mailing lists, 264
Marketing:
  budget, figuring, 4-5
  cost of, 3-6
  expenditures, 72-78
    gimmicks to avoid, 73-76
    pitfalls, 72-73
  loans, 5
  prioritizing, 2-3
  problems and solutions, 30-31
  secrets of, 1
  strategies, 5
  See also Promotion budget
Marketing-based logos, 235
Marketing director:
  motivating, 139-40
  office manager as, 139
Marketing plan, 9-10, 13-37, 127
  backward planning, 13-14
  Long-Form Game Planner, 22-28
  midyear evaluation, 29-30
  sample plans, 10-11
  Short-Form Game Planner, 14-19
    form, 16-17
    sample completed short form, 18-19
  Strategies and Budget Form, 19-22
    completed form, 20
Medcash, 61
Midyear evaluation, marketing plan, 29-30
Money Mailer, 323, 324
Multiple mailings, direct mail, 262-63

N

Name Recognition game, 147
Negative option close, 95

Networking, 113-14, 119
  See also Frequent referrer program
New markets, exploring, 274-89
New neighbor welcoming services, avoiding, 73
New-Resi Data Marketing, 257
New resident direct mail, 256-65
New resident program, with secret agents, 284-85
Newsletters, 9, 82, 270
Newspaper advertising, 283, 305-16
  claims, 308
  examples of, 306, 307, 308, 309, 310, 311, 312-14
  gateways, 306
  graphics, 309-10
  headlines, 306-7
  offers, 309
  payback, 7
  rules of, 306-15
  series of ads, creating, 315
  size of, 311-15
  stating problem you treat, 307-8
  testing ads, 315-16
  typestyles, 310
  visual effects, 310-11
Nonessential equipment, prioritizing, 77
Nonprofits, obtaining referrals from, 118
Nonrecourse loan programs, 61-62
Notes, affinity marketing, types of, 91

O

Objection handling, 96, 296
One-minute messages, 2, 80, 87-88
  guidelines, 88
  results, 88
On-line Yellow Pages, avoiding, 74
Open house, 351-52
  how to's, 351-52
  when to hold, 352
Outbound telemarketing, 294-97
  closing, 295-96
  objection handling, 296
  opening, 294-95
  sales message, 295
  scripting, 296-97
  See also Telemarketing
Outdoor office signs, 2, 3, 152-69, 282, 365
  color/shape, 155
  and competitors, 155
  construction, 155

Outdoor office signs *(continued)*:
  copy, 155
  examples of, 157-60
  exposure rate, 154
  factors to consider, 153
  harvesting traffic, 156
  location of, 153-54
  logos, 155
  payback, 7
  return on investment, 152-53
  rules for, 161
  size, 155
  See also Banners

P

Paper quality, stationery, 240-41
Patient/client appreciation days, 248-49
Patient information brochure, 182
Payback, promotion, 7-8
Payback close, 296
PICO financing plan, 61
Positioning, 47, 122
Postage-meter imprint advertising, avoiding, 76
Potential referrers, 120-21
Practice brochure, payback, 7
  See also Brochures
PRACTICE BUILDER, address/phone, 115
PRACTICE BUILDER's Office Sign Contest, 164-68
PRACTICE BUILDER Tracking Sheet, 34-36
Practice representatives, 149
Prepaid financing, 64
Press releases, 251-52
  example, 252
  guidelines, 251-52
Price drop close, 95
Price reduction, promoting, 361-63
Pricing strategies, 57-71
  fee objections, handling, 65-66
  fee raising, 57-59
    guidelines, 58-59
  fee surveys, 66
  financing, 60-64
  and guarantees, 59-60
  price competing, 60
  raising gross, 66
Probability close, 95
Productivity, prioritizing marketing by, 2-3
Professional service letters, 125
Professional society, relying on, 75-76

Promotion, 38-56, 144-51
  advertising:
    lessons, 146
    vs. marketing, 144-46
  authoring, 41-42
  business cards, 222-33
  by committee, 77-78
  caring attitude, 44-47
  claims, making, 40-41
  credentials, 41
  differentiating yourself, 39-40, 49
  essential messages, 38-39
  free exams/consultations, 66-68
  gateways, 146
  good/better/best strategy, 68-69
  modesty as hindrance of, 9
  payback, 7-8
  positioning, 47
  practice representatives, 149
  public relations, 148-49
  service, guaranteeing, 42-44
  testing timing of, 34
  tracking results of, 32-36
    by coupon/certificate code, 33
    by dedicated phone lines, 33
    by extension numbers, 32-33
    by front desk, 33-34
    by mailing label key code, 33
    PRACTICE BUILDER Tracking Sheet, 34-36
    tracking the right source, 35
  waiting room resume, 49-54
  See also Group practice; Internal promotion;
    Promotions in motion
Promotional checklist, 9-10
Promotion budget, allocating by seasonality, 6-7
Promotion by committee, 77-78
Promotions in Motion, 12, 37, 54-56, 69-71, 97,
    109, 129-31, 143, 152, 169, 253, 273, 289,
    299, 317-18, 328, 338-39, 353-54, 369
Public relations, 148-49, 242-53
  charitable publicity, 242-44, 246-48
  community involvement and ROI, 244-46
  design and insert coupon, 243
  local publicity, 252-53
  patient/client appreciation days, 248-49, 346
    leveraging, 250
  press releases, 251-52
    example, 252
    guidelines, 251-52

Public relations *(continued)*:
  PR firms, 247-48
  radio/television exposure, 250
Public service radio spots, 331-32
Puppy dog close, 94

Q

Quarterly internal prospecting direct mail, payback, 7, 32

R

Radio advertising, 33, 329-39
  guidelines, 334
  interviews, 332-33
  payback, 7
  pros/cons, 330
  public service radio spots, 331-32
  radio spot analysis, 333-34
  sixty-second spot, sample script, 334
  versus television advertising, 330-31
  where to use, 329-31
  See also Advertising; Promotion; Television advertising
Reactivation efforts, 2, 7, 80
  analysis, 107
  enhanced reactivation effort, 101-4
  strategies, 105-6
  telemarketing script, sample, 104
  value of, 106
  when reactivations won't work, 107
Recalls, 7, 80, 98-101
  contacting right person in, 100-101
  payback, 7
  repetition, 99-100
  specificity, 98-99
Reception area, educating/promoting in, 344-46
Referrals, 2, 32, 80, 91, 110-31, 365
  asking for, 112
  club memberships, cultivating, 119-20
  conversion rate, 132-33
  courting referrers, 128-29
  implementation, 111
  lunch-a-week method, 122-23
  from nonprofits, 118
  old boys' referral club, breaking into, 115-18
  payback, 7
  potential referrers, 120-21

Referrals *(continued)*:
  referral area, enlarging, 118
  referring professionals:
    alerts, 124-25
    boosting referrals from, 126-27
    calling, 125-26
    gaining, 122-26
    generating through leverage, 123-24
    giving gifts to, 121
    professional service letters, 125
    straight introduction, 124
  rules, 110-11
  and spouses, 127-28
  thanking the right people for, 128
  third-party endorsements, 111-12
  and waiting room resume, 121-22
  See also Frequent referrer program
Restaurant seminars, 344
Return on investment (ROI), 3, 7-8
  direct mail, 269-70
  factors affecting, 8

S

Sampling postcard advertisements, avoiding, 75
School event sponsorship, avoiding, 75
Screenings, 346
Scripts:
  inbound telemarketing, 293-94
  outbound telemarketing, 294-97
Seasonality, allocating promotion budget by, 6-7
Second appointment close, 95
Seminars, 340-44
  attendees, converting, 343-44
  promotion tips, 341-43
  restaurant seminars, 344
  success with, 340-41
Senior citizen telephone books, 316
Service:
  defining, 43
  guaranteeing, 42-44
Shopper ads, payback, 7
Short-Form Game Planner, 14-19
  form, 16-17
  sample completed short form, 18-19
Slow season, filling, 363-64
Small companies, becoming provider of choice for, 285-87

Staff, 132-43
  and conversion rate, 132-33
  Employee Referral Contest, 137-39
    rules/prizes, 138-39
  incentive programs, 138-39
  leader, promoting, 142-43
  marketing director:
    motivating, 139-40
    office manager as, 139
  obtaining marketing support from, 133-34
  partners/associates, and referrals, 140-42
  recruitment of new patients through, 135-37
Staff badges, 93
Start-ups, 355-68
  slow starts, 359-61
Stationery:
  coordinating with logo/envelope/business
    card, 237-40
  letterhead, example of, 238
  paper, quality of, 240-41
  strategizing for, 237
Strategies and Budget Form, 19-22
  completed form, 20
Subheads, brochures, 181, 193
Supermarket register tape ads, avoiding, 73
Supermarket shopping cart ads, avoiding, 74

T

Table tents, 93
"Take one" displays, 93
Talking Yellow Pages, 317
  avoiding, 74
Targeted direct mail, 2, 283
Telemarketing, 290-99
  helplines, 298-99
  inbound telemarketing, 293-94
    script for, 293-94
  inquiries, converting into patients/clients, 291-93
  for lead generation, 358-59
  outbound telemarketing, 294-97
  phone recalls, 291
  tips for success, 297-98
Television advertising, 33, 329-39
  cable television, 334-35
  jingles, use of, 336-38
  payback, 7
  pros/cons, 330
  versus radio advertising, 330-31

Television advertising (continued):
  where to use, 329-31
  See also Advertising; Promotion; Radio adver-
    tising
Testing, co-op coupon packs, 322
Test mailings, direct mail, 271
Third-party endorsements, 111-12
Trade and health shows, 348-49
TriMark, 323
Typestyles:
  logos, 234-35
  newspaper advertising, 310

U

Up-scale markets, and co-op coupon packs, 324
Urban practice, promoting, 282-84

V

Val-Pak, 97, 319, 320, 323, 324

W

Waiting room resume, 49-54, 121, 365
  analysis, 51-54
  and referrals, 121-22
  samples, 50-53
Waiting room surveys, 96-97
Welcome-to-the-practice letter, 80-82
White pages, telephone books, 316
Window signs, 282

Y

Yellow Pages, 2, 3, 7, 14, 33, 39, 41, 47, 49, 74, 75,
    115, 132, 234, 283, 300-304, 319, 320, 365
  ad construction, 301-4
    color, 303-4
    layout, 302-3
    visual strategies, 303
  community books, 316
  copy cat books, 316
  cost versus ROI, 2
  green pages, 317
  payback, 7
  senior citizen books, 316
  success using, 300-301
  talking Yellow Pages, 74, 317
  white pages, 316